BIBLIOGRAPHY OF IRISH HISTORY
1912-1921

NATIONAL LIBRARY OF IRELAND

BIBLIOGRAPHY

OF

IRISH HISTORY

1912-1921

BY

JAMES CARTY, M.A.

Assistant Librarian

DUBLIN:
PUBLISHED FOR THE DEPARTMENT OF EDUCATION
BY THE STATIONERY OFFICE

To be purchased directly from the
GOVERNMENT PUBLICATIONS SALE OFFICE,
5 NASSAU STREET, DUBLIN;
or through any Bookseller.

1936

Price : Six Shillings

PREFACE

THE present Catalogue is the first volume of a general Bibliography of Irish history which it is proposed to publish in sections. It has been thought best to begin with recent history, the period immediately preceding the establishment of the Free State, as being that upon which attention is at present largely directed, and for which consequently the need of accurate and detailed information is most felt. This will be followed by the period 1870-1911, covering the Home Rule and other movements.

Mr. Carty's *Introduction* is to be regarded as an explanatory guide to this literature rather than an historical relation of the events recorded. Likewise the notes appended to the various entries are not intended as critical judgments, but rather as indications of the point of view and authority of the writer, and in the case of periodical publications, the circumstances under which they were produced and circulated.

The Bibliography is confined to publications in the National Library collection. Many of these—rare pamphlets, journals and other papers of the period—have been acquired by the Library through the generosity of donors, whose gifts have been acknowledged in the annual reports of the Trustees.

Thanks are due to Mr. P. S. O'Hegarty, Mr. Bulmer Hobson, Mr. Pádraig Ó Caoimh, and Mr. Frank Gallagher for kindly perusing the proof-sheets and for making many helpful suggestions.

R. I. BEST,
Director.

INTRODUCTION

BETWEEN the introduction of the Third Home Rule Bill and the Articles of Agreement for a Treaty between Great Britain and Ireland (1921) there was an interval of about ten years. The problems connected with Irish government and the various phases of the Irish national movement during this period have been discussed from a great variety of aspects in books, pamphlets, bulletins, reports, reviews and political journals, as well as in daily and weekly newspapers. Many of the publications which the student of the period will find it necessary to consult were issued in times of civil disturbance and national insurrection, and must be read with close reference to the position and purpose of the writers and the political conditions at the moment of publication. It must be borne in mind also that Ireland was subjected from 1914 to 1921 to a rigorous censorship of the press, established under the Defence of the Realm Act and continued after the Great War.

Political literature abounds in what Dean Swift described as "temporary occasional things, that dye naturally with the Change of times." No principles of selection have been applied in the following pages, however, except those enforced by restrictions of space. Articles in monthly and quarterly journals have been included, but not those in the daily and weekly press, which are far too numerous. As a rule, leaflets, pamphlets and review articles of less than eight pages have been excluded for the same reason (except in Section 3: THE INSURRECTION OF 1916, which has been treated in greater detail than the other sections). Many of the broadsides, printed forms and leaflets, songs and ballads, etc., of the period are preserved and may be consulted in the National Library of Ireland. Some of these are of no small historical interest, but they issued from the press in such numbers that it would be impossible to catalogue them in detail. The Bibliography is restricted to constitutional and political questions during the period 1912-1921. For the literary, economic and general history of modern Ireland reference may be made to special works of bibliography such as the following:

"A Bibliography of Irish philology and printed literature" by R. I. Best (National Library of Ireland, 1913); "A Catalogue of the Bradshaw collection of Irish books in the University Library, Cambridge," 3 vols. (Cambridge, 1916); "The history of Irish periodical literature from the end of the seventeenth to the middle of the nineteenth century" by Richard Robert Madden, M.D. (London, 1867); "List of books, tracts and broadsides printed in Ireland since 1601" by

E. R. McClintock Dix (Dublin, 1898-1905), and the various papers by Mr. Dix on the history of Irish printing; " The Irish Book Lover " (Dublin, 1909 —), which, in addition to many papers of Irish bibliographical interest, has for several years published a quarterly bibliography of new books relating to Ireland; " Ireland's literary renaissance " by Ernest A. Boyd (Second edition. New York, 1922), and " Ireland in fiction " by the Rev. S. J. Brown, S.J. (Dublin, 1923). [For the literary works of the 1916 leaders, see " Studies, a quarterly review," V. June-December, 1916 (Thomas MacDonagh, Patrick H. Pearse, Joseph Plunkett), and " The Dublin Magazine," VI-VII, July, 1931—March, 1932 (P. H. Pearse, by P. S. O'Hegarty, Thomas MacDonagh, by F. R. Higgins, and Joseph Mary Plunkett)]. " A select bibliography of Irish economic history " by P. L. Prendeville (London, 1932), and " History of the commercial relations between England and Ireland from the time of the Restoration " by Alice E. Murray (London, 1903) should be consulted for economic history, " Labour and nationality " by J. Dunsmore Clarkson (New York, 1924) for the Irish Labour movement, and " The struggle for the land in Ireland " by J. E. Pomfret (Princeton, 1930) for a bibliography of the Irish land question from 1800 to 1923. Publications relating to Irish literature, politics and economics during the period of the Great War and the Peace Treaties are included by M. Maurice Bourgeois in his Catalogue méthodique des fonds britannique et Nord américain de la bibliothèque, III. L'Empire britannique, la grande Bretagne et la guerre (Catalogues des " Bibliothèque et Musée de la Guerre," Paris, 1931). The annual and decennial consolidated lists of British official publications—" General Alphabetical Index to the Bills, Reports, Estimates, Accounts and Papers, printed by order of the House of Commons, and to the Papers Presented by Command " (London, H.M.S.O.) give the titles of the numerous official printed papers relating to the British administration of Ireland in 1912-1921 and previous decades. For material in periodicals, Poole and Fletcher's Index, with supplements (London and New York); Wilson's " Reader's Guide to periodical literature " (New York) and the " Subject Index to periodicals " (London, Library Association, 1915 —), should be consulted.*

---

* Publications which relate to the military, political and economic history of the Great War of 1914-1918 and the Peace Conference are not included except when they refer also to events in Ireland. For war literature some of the following works may be consulted : " A select analytical list of books concerning the Great War " by Sir George Protheroe (London, H.M.S.O., 1920), " War books, a critical guide " by Cyril Falls (London, Davies, 1920) [This work includes Irish regimental histories for the period], " Bibliographical survey of contemporary sources for the economic and social history of the war " by M. E. Bulkley (Carnegie Endowment for International Peace. Economic and Social History of the World War, British series, 1922). *Irische Blätter* (January, 1917–October, 1918), the journal of the German-Irish Society, published surveys of articles relating to Ireland in the German, Irish, English and American press. The annotated index to British war propaganda [Wellington House literature] comprises over a thousand books and pamphlets. Many of these and other publications emphasising the idealist war aims

The entries in the Bibliography have been divided into sections according to periods, each section arranged in alphabetical order. The GENERAL AND INTRODUCTORY section includes: (a) General historical and bibliographical works, annual reports in series, studies of Irish administration and finance, and other publications which treat of the entire period, 1912-1921; (b) Publications relating to the earlier careers and political writings of Irishmen who took a prominent part in the events of the time; (c) Publications issued immediately before 1912 by the more important political organisations, such as the Irish Parliamentary Party, Sinn Féin, and the Irish Unionist Alliance. Thus, among the entries in this section will be found the "Historical and political addresses of John Redmond" (178), "The resurrection of Hungary" by Arthur Griffith (68), "The life of Lord Carson," Vol. I., by Edward Marjoribanks (133), and "Glimpses of an Irish felon's prison life," the autobiography of Thomas J. Clarke (18), who was the first signatory to the proclamation of Easter week, 1916. The second section, 1912-1916, comprises the Home Rule period. When this period began, the principal subject of political controversy in Great Britain and Ireland was the forthcoming Home Rule Bill. It ended (April, 1916) in the second year of the European war, with Home Rule enacted but indefinitely suspended. The third section, 1916, is devoted to the Rising of Easter Week and the weeks immediately preceding and following it. The events of this brief period had so much influence on the subsequent course of events that an exception has been made by including a selection from the narratives of the Rising scattered during the past twenty years through the Irish daily and weekly press. The fourth section, 1916-1918, extends from May, 1916, to the end of 1918. The most important political development during this period was the reorganisation of Sinn Féin after the Rising and its triumph at the General Election of December, 1918. The fifth section, 1919-1921, begins with the establishment of Dáil Eireann in January, 1919, and ends with the ratification of the Anglo-Irish Treaty of December, 1921. Publications which refer to events subsequent to 1921 are included only if they also treat of some part of the period, 1912-1921.

Much of the Irish political literature issued for a generation before 1921 was inspired, either by what M. Paul-Dubois called "ces grandes ligues d'agitation populaire dont il est remarquable que ce soit elle qui ait donné le modèle à l'Angleterre moderne" or by the

---

of the Allied and Associated Powers, especially the principles of self-determination, government by consent of the governed, and the rights of small nations, were extensively circulated in Ireland at the public charge during the war years. For the chronology of the War period the following works may be consulted : " History of the Great War . . . . Principal events, 1914-1918 " compiled by the historical section of the Committee of Imperial Defence (London, H.M.S.O., 1922), and "An economic chronicle of the Great War for Britain and Ireland " by N. B. Dearle (Carnegie Endowment for International Peace, 1929).

wealthy and powerful associations striving to maintain the legislative union between Great Britain and Ireland. Systematic Irish political " propaganda " in the modern sense may, perhaps, be said to date from the end of 1885, when the Irish Parliamentary Party, led by Parnell, won 85 of the 105 Irish seats—" an electoral demonstration," wrote John Morley, " never surpassed in any country "—and Gladstone was converted to the policy of Home Rule. English political students, tourists and special correspondents visiting and writing about Ireland were more numerous than ever before, and the " Irish problem " was regularly examined and often solved in the monthly and quarterly reviews. Irish nationalist organisations now increased their efforts to convince public opinion in England, by the distribution of literature, that the demands for agrarian reform and self-government were reasonable and just. The Irish Press Agency (95), established in London in 1885 by the Irish Parliamentary Party, issued large numbers of leaflets and pamphlets for the next thirty years, showing special activity when the prospects of Home Rule were most favourable (in 1886, 1892-1893, and 1908-1914). A counter-propaganda on a still more voluminous scale was conducted by the Irish Loyal and Patriotic Union, which afterwards changed its name to the Irish Unionist Alliance (98), and continued to diffuse Unionist books, pamphlets and journals, until 1921. The Irish Unionist Alliance worked in close touch with the Union Defence League, formed in 1907 under the chairmanship of Mr. Walter Long, afterwards Viscount Long (Chief Secretary for Ireland, 1905-1906), and the Ulster Unionist Council (568), formed in 1905. The associated Unionist organisations, commanding large financial resources and having the support of great newspapers, showed remarkable propagandist activity in 1910-1914. Lord Long in his " Memories " (117) tells how they distributed immense quantities of literature, and engaged throughout Britain in " missionary work " for the maintenance of the legislative Union. Motor vans were sent through the country with photographs, moving pictures and lantern slides illustrating the arguments of the speakers, who were accompanied by Unionist farmers from Ireland to corroborate the narratives.

In Ireland the Parnell " split " and the rejection of the second Home Rule Bill by the House of Lords diminished the output of controversial political literature for some years. The last decade of the nineteenth century was, nevertheless, one of much interest in Irish history. The Irish Literary Society, London, was established in 1892, the Gaelic League in 1893, the Oireachtas (Literary Festival) in 1897, the Irish Literary Theatre in 1897. Closely associated with these were the Gaelic Athletic Association (1884), the Feis Ceoil (Musical Festival) (1897) and the societies for the preservation and development of Irish industries. In spite of the failure of the latest phase of the nationalist movement there was a hopeful spirit among the younger generation, who were attracted by the new literary societies and especially by the Gaelic League. " For in Ireland just now," wrote Mr. W. B. Yeats, " one has only to discover an idea that seems of service to the country, for friends and helpers to start up on every side " (" Samhain," 1901). Although these new societies had no political aims, they helped to produce a new political movement, which differed essentially from that of the Irish Parliamentary Party. Mr. Edward Martyn (69), an ardent supporter of the Feis Ceoil, who with Mr. Yeats and Lady Gregory, founded the Irish Literary Theatre, became the first President of Sinn Féin in 1905. Professor Eoin MacNeill, Vice-President of the Gaelic League and first editor of its official journal, " An Claidheamh Soluis " (17), was afterwards Chairman of the Provisional Committee of the Irish Volunteers at their foundation in November, 1913, and a member of the Ministry set up by Dáil Éireann in 1919-1921. Pádraic Pearse, President of the Provisional Government in the 1916 Rising, had been secretary to the publications committee of the Gaelic League and editor of " An Claidheamh Soluis," 1903-1908.

The beginning of a new political movement, arising in part from these associated movements and in part from the embers of Fenianism, might be seen in the celebrations held in 1898 to commemorate the centenary of the 'ninety-eight insurrection. The Ninety-eight and Wolfe Tone clubs (the latter usually centres of the I.R.B. or Irish Republican Brotherhood), formed in that year, provided the organisation required for the success of a new weekly journal—" The United Irishman " (209), edited by Arthur Griffith, 1899-1906. This was the first of a series of newspapers which Griffith edited (except— in 1916-1921—during the intervals which he spent in prisons and internment camps), writing the leading articles for over twenty years. " From 1899 to 1911," writes Mr. P. S. O'Hegarty (157), " the ' United Irishman ' and its successor, ' Sinn Féin ' (225) were the chief inspiration of all extreme propaganda and extreme discussion in Ireland, and although from 1911 until 1914 ' Irish Freedom ' more properly represented the Fenian element yet the influence of Griffith has gone heavily in the same direction." The " Hungarian policy," outlined by Griffith at the third annual convention of Cumann na nGaedheal (1902) was fully developed in a series of articles in " The United Irishman " during the early months of 1904. " Sixty years ago," he wrote, " Hungary realised that the political centre of the nation must be within the nation. When Ireland realises this obvious truth and turns her back on London the parallel will be complete." Many well-known Irish writers and scholars contributed to " The United Irishman " and its successor, " Sinn Féin." Of the former Professor Henry (82) says: " The paper was remarkable for the ability with which it was edited, the literary excellence of its articles, both editorial and contributed, the range of its topics and the freedom which it allowed to the discussion of different views in its columns " (p. 54).

The policy of the original Sinn Féin movement was expounded from 1904 to 1916 in a limited number of publications—almost all written or edited by Arthur Griffith: the journals already mentioned, " The resurrection of Hungary " (63), " Leabhar na hEireann " or " The Irish Year Book " (109-111), and a few pamphlets, published on behalf of the National Council, " The Peasant " (94), edited by Mr. W. P. Ryan, and three or four provincial weekly newspapers also supported Sinn Féin. The Dungannon clubs which published some pamphlets in Dublin and Belfast in the early years of the century and during 1907, a weekly journal " The Republic " (191), edited by Mr. Bulmer Hobson represented a movement on kindred lines which became merged with Sinn Féin. With a very few exceptions, the nationalist daily and weekly newspapers adhered to the policy of the Irish Parliamentary Party, and, when, in 1910, the prospects of Home Rule became brighter, the publication of Sinn Féin literature almost ceased until the outbreak of the European War. The spirit of Sinn Féin during its first decade must be sought, however, not only in political propaganda, but in the publications of the Irish literary movement, the Gaelic League and the Industrial Development Association, and in the productions of the Irish Theatre. Unionist criticism before 1914 was directed mainly against the predominant Irish nationalist group, the Irish Parliamentary Party, and its powerful agrarian organisation, the United Irish League, but the appearance of a joint " Irish Ireland " movement of a different character had attracted attention as early as 1906 in " Notes from Ireland " (98).

The general expectancy of changes in Irish government at the outset of the new Home Rule period encouraged the publication of earnest enquiries into the administration, finance, and social problems of the country as they were and as they might be affected by the restoration of an Irish legislature. Among these were the three volumes of Leabhar na hEireann (1908-1910), issued by the Sinn Féin National Council. The object of this Irish Year Book, Griffith explained in his foreword to the original edition, 1908, was " to place before All Ireland a book in which All Ireland expresses itself, and when this book was projected, we accordingly communicated with men and women of all parties, classes, and creeds in Ireland, inviting them to deal in The Irish Year Book with those subjects in which they were skilled." General works which may profitably be consulted as introductory studies to the period include " L'Irlande contemporaine " by M. Paul-Dubois (170), whose survey led him to conclude that, in spite of maladministration, the neglect of her economic well-being, and " the melancholy dilapidation of her towns," Ireland was being transformed by the new spirit of self-reliance; the Report of the

Committee on Irish finance (90); the reprint of "The Times" Irish number (219); the examination of Dominion Home Rule made by Mr. Erskine Childers (15); the Home Rule studies edited by Mr. Basil Williams (233); the elaborate apologia for the Union to which several Irish and English Unionist leaders contributed (529); R. Barry O'Brien's "Dublin Castle and the Irish people" (148); and the collection of essays edited for the Eighty Club by Professor J. H. Morgan (142). In the last-named work Lord (Sir Antony) MacDonnell, Under-Secretary for Ireland, 1902-1908, gives an account of the forty-seven departments which carried on the administration of Ireland, some of them controlled by "Dublin Castle," the headquarters of Irish government, others partly controlled in Dublin and partly in London, some wholly controlled in London, and others "uncontrolled by the Irish government, while the supervision exercised over them by the British government is of the most shadowy character." The published material for the study of the actual workings of the British administration in Ireland in 1912-1921 are not extensive. The student may obtain some guidance as to the frequent changes of policy, the efforts to stem the rising tide of Irish nationality, and the growing militarisation of the régime in the biographies and reminiscences of Cabinet ministers, officials, judges, and soldiers, the proceedings of the Committee of Inquiry into the pay and allowances of the Irish police (197), and the proceedings of the Royal Commission on the Howth gun-running (537) and the Royal Commission on the rebellion (715).

Irish studies by recognised authorities on questions of administration, trade, finance and constitutional law, and elaborate arguments for and against Home Rule which received so much attention about the year 1912 began to be replaced in 1913 by a briefer and sharper style of writing and speaking. The slow but apparently assured progress of Home Rule through Parliament to the statute book was now imperilled by a new Unionist policy—the organisation of an Ulster Volunteer Force and Ulster Provisional Government, under the chairmanship of Sir Edward Carson, to prevent the Bill in the form already approved by the House of Commons from coming into operation. The British public were made familiar with the claim that some portion of Ireland should be withheld from the jurisdiction of the Irish Parliament—at first, as suggested in 1912, the four counties of Ulster in which there were Unionist majorities, then, as proposed by Sir Edward Carson in 1913, the whole province of nine counties, and finally the six counties which were ultimately selected for exclusion in the Government of Ireland Act, 1920 (1159). The propaganda of the Ulster Unionist Council in 1912-1914 attained large dimensions (568-575). It dwelt mainly on the superiority of Belfast and Eastern Ulster to the rest of Ireland in wealth, trade and industrial enterprise, on the alleged lack of appreciation among Irish

Nationalists of Ulster's economic and social interests, and especially on Protestant fears of "a Roman Catholic ascendancy."

The essence of Ulster Unionist literature may be found in the "Solemn League and Covenant" against Home Rule, stated to have been signed by 471,414 Ulster men and women over the age of sixteen, each of whom was presented with a copy of the covenant printed on parchment. Lord Cushendun (Mr. Ronald MacNeill) has given an account (37, p. 104) of the composition and revision of this document in September, 1912. In its approved form it was read out to the members of the Ulster Unionist Council from the arcade at Craigavon House by Sir Edward Carson, who was the first to sign it. The publications of the Irish Press Agency and the Home Rule Council in 1913-1914 consist largely of replies to Ulster Unionist literature. Mr. John Redmond, Professor T. M. Kettle, Mr. Jeremiah MacVeagh, Mr. Stephen Gwynn and other members of the Irish Parliamentary Party took much care to allay the apprehensions of religious persecution and discrimination against Ulster's economic interests in an Irish Parliament. The inferences unfavourable to Irish national unity drawn in the Ulster Unionist Council propaganda were challenged by Nationalist writers, who quoted in support of their arguments from the Irish Census (1911) Reports, the polls at local government and parliamentary elections, and other statistical returns. (See 146, 1188 and 1238).

By the summer of 1913 the Irish situation had begun to assume a military character. The arming of the Ulster Volunteers was now well advanced. Less interest was shown in the details of Home Rule than in the preparations to resist it by force of arms, and English newspapers printed long despatches from special correspondents describing the military parades, manoeuvres and gun-runnings in Ulster. A Unionist member of parliament declared that "as an argument, ten thousand pounds spent on rifles would be a thousand times stronger than the same amount spent on meetings, speeches and pamphlets" (9, p. 14). A very extensive controversy (see the list of references under "Curragh army incident" in Section 1912-1916) followed the intervention of the British army in the Home Rule crisis. The virtual exercise of a veto on legislation by military officers was regarded in the parliamentary debates and periodical press at the time of its occurrence as a decisive event for Ireland and, perhaps, for Britain. In conjunction with the illegal importation of 35,000 rifles by the Ulster Volunteers ("the Larne gun-running") in the following month, it induced Mr. John Redmond for the first time to give public support to the Irish Volunteers.

The enrolment of Irish Volunteers began at a public meeting in the Rotunda, Dublin, on Tuesday, November 25, 1913. Issues of "The Irish Review" (367), "Sinn Féin" (209), "An Claidheamh Soluis" (17), "The Irish Worker" (374), and "Irish Freedom" (92) in the later months of 1913 may be consulted for comment on the new departure, which was largely modelled on the great Irish Volunteer movement of 1782. The Irish Volunteer Fund appeal and other Volunteer manifestoes published in 1913-1914 emphasise the non-political character of the Volunteers. "The movement is not aggressive but defensive; it is directed, not towards the coercing of any section of Irishmen, but towards uniting Irishmen of all sections in the cause of Irish nationality." Some of the nationalist newspapers greeted the movement with enthusiasm; many, including those supporting the Irish Parliamentary Party, regarded it as premature, if not unwise. The influence of the Dublin labour troubles led "The Irish Worker" to treat the Volunteer movement in a critical spirit.

The founders of the Irish Volunteers were mainly young little-known men: teachers, writers and lecturers. Several of the most energetic and determined were members of the Irish Republican Brotherhood ("I.R.B."). This organisation had been moribund for some years until the centenary celebrations of 1898, when it was revived. Among its leading members a few years later was Thomas J. Clarke. "On his return to Ireland in 1907," according to John Devoy (44, p. 392), "the I.R.B., inspired by his resoluteness and singleness of purpose, began to assume new life and vigour and became an active force." The I.R.B. school of nationalist thought found expression for its views in "Irish Freedom." The policy of this paper, although similar in many respects to that of "Sinn Féin," favoured a republic rather than an Irish or dual monarchy, laid more stress on armed than on passive resistance to English rule, and showed greater sympathy with the tendencies represented by the formation of the Irish Labour Party in 1911 and the organisation of the Transport and General Workers' Union by Mr. James Larkin. Both "Irish Freedom" and "Sinn Féin" comment with something like satisfaction on the progress of the Ulster Volunteer Force. "We do not care, fellow-countrymen, what you arm for. We only care that you arm," says "Irish Freedom" in December, 1913. "We regard their proceedings with no unfriendly eye," says "Sinn Féin," May 2nd, 1914, referring to the Larne gun-running. General Sir C. F. N. Macready, who was sent to Ulster on a special military mission after the Curragh army incident, writes: "When going about the country outside Belfast in 1914 it would seem from the reports of police and soldiers that the state of feeling between Protestants and Catholics was improving" (415a, p. 196).

"The Irish Volunteer" (371), a weekly newspaper authorised by the Provisional Committee, made its appearance in February, 1914, from the offices of the Enniscorthy "Echo." "The Irish Volunteer," "Sinn Fein," "Irish Freedom," and "The Irish Worker," although in general agreement on national questions, were controlled by different groups. "The Irish Worker" was the organ of the Transport Union and of a small armed force, the Irish Citizen Army, which had come into existence some months before the Irish National Volunteers. In Mr. W. P. Ryan's "Irish Labour movement" (202a) and Mr. J. Dunsmore Clarkson's "Labour and nationalism in Ireland" (19) will be found some account of the earlier literature of the Irish Labour movement, in which James Connolly took a part analogous to that of Arthur Griffith in the literary history of Sinn Féin. Connolly, while advocating insurrection as early as the year 1900, confesses himself more concerned with Irish housing problems and working-class mortality than with "political oratory, or the almost ephemeral pamphleteering of our more brilliant revolutionists" (33).

The journals mentioned represented the movements which helped to bring about the Rising of 1916 and the subsequent union of national forces under Sinn Féin. The Irish nationalist daily and weekly newspaper press, however, with few exceptions, supported the Irish Parliamentary Party, of which Mr. John Redmond claimed that 95 per cent. of the Volunteers were political adherents. (Correspondence with Mr. Eoin MacNeill, Chairman of the Irish Volunteer Provisional Committee, June 12, 1914). In July, 1914, when the proclamation of an Ulster Provisional Government was believed to be imminent, some English newspapers, according to "The Daily Chronicle," seem to have transferred an important section of their editorial staffs to Belfast. Those Irish newspapers which had hitherto been unfriendly or indifferent to the Volunteers now reported their progress with enthusiasm on the ground that the Larne gun-running and the undisguised hostility of the British army to the Home Rule Bill had placed the whole Irish national movement in a position of extreme insecurity. Estimates of the strength of the Irish Volunteers in 1914 range from 135,000 to 160,000, of whom 38,000, it was claimed, were ex-soldiers or members of the General or Special Reserve of the British Army. The Irish and Irish-American newspapers in June and July contain many reports of meetings and conferences in the United States to discuss the provision of funds and military equipment for the Irish Volunteers on a scale commensurate with the assistance given by Unionist sympathisers to the Ulster Volunteer Force.

The political situation was transformed by the outbreak of the War. The Irish nationalist press divided into two well-defined groups in August, 1914—the daily and weekly newspapers, with few exceptions, endorsing Mr. Redmond's attitude towards the war, the small journals of the advanced groups holding, as Griffith wrote in "Sinn Féin," that "Ireland is not at war." On Wednesday, August 5, the Standing Committee of the Irish Volunteers expressed their "complete readiness to take joint action with the Ulster Volunteer

until February 14th, 1915. "The Spark" appeared on February 7th, "The Workers' Republic" on May 30th, and "Nationality" (440) on June 19th. The circulation of these journals, although not large, showed a tendency to increase during 1915 and the early months of 1916. Along with them may be consulted the series of pamphlets by leaders of Sinn Féin and the Irish Volunteers in the "Bodenstown series" and "Tracts for the Times." These journals and pamphlets were afterwards given considerable attention in the Proceedings of the Royal Commission on the Rebellion (714-715). A list of "Seditious weekly papers circulating in Ireland," produced before the Commission by Sir Mathew Nathan, Under-Secretary for Ireland, is printed in the Appendix to the Minutes of Evidence (p. 118). The list gives particulars (the accuracy of which has been challenged in some instances) of proprietors and editors and of estimated circulations in November, 1915, and February, 1916.

The issues of "The Irish Volunteer" from December, 1914, to April, 1916, are of special interest in the light of later events. The contributors include the chief officer (Professor E. MacNeill), J. J. O'Connell, Eimar O'Duffy, Bulmer Hobson, The O'Rahilly, Pádraic Pearse and Thomas MacDonagh, and a "Headquarters Bulletin" gives particulars of training and appointments. The last number (April 22nd, 1916) contains an announcement by the Director of Organisation, P. H. Pearse: "Arrangements are now nearing completion in all the more important Brigade areas for the holding of a very interesting series of manœuvres at Easter." The approach of a crisis is also plainly indicated in the last numbers of "The Workers' Republic." A leading article [by James Connolly] in this paper on April 8th states that the Council of the Irish Citizen Army had decided to hoist "the green flag of Ireland" over Liberty Hall. This ceremony, which took place in the presence of a large crowd, is described in the last issue (April 22nd). The immunity of "The Workers' Republic" from D.O.R.A. proceedings during the final weeks was due to the fact that Liberty Hall had become a fortress, garrisoned by the Irish Citizen Army.

Publications relating to the Rising will be found in the section 1916, with the exception of a few general works which are included in the earlier sections. It should be noted that the Dublin daily papers, "The Freeman's Journal" and "The Daily Express," ceased publication after Monday, April 24th, "The Irish Independent" after Tuesday. "The Irish Times" continued, though in a much reduced form, until Thursday, and resumed publication on Monday, May 1st. "The Daily Express" resumed on May 3rd, "The Irish Independent" on May 4th, and "The Freeman's Journal" on May 5th. Martial law continued in operation for several months after the Rising, and the censorship exercised over newspapers and other publications became much stricter than previously. (More than two

Force for the defence of Ireland," and " Sinn Féin " held that " if the Irish Volunteers are to defend Ireland they must defend it for Ireland, under Ireland's flag and under Irish officers." Two articles in the " United Services Magazine " (460-461) illustrate what was widely believed to be the War Office attitude with regard to plans of defence which implied any recognition of Irish nationality. " The Irish Volunteer " opposed Mr. Redmond's war policy and supported the original members of the Provisional Committee in repudiating his leadership (September 28th, 1914), but did not come directly under the control of the Volunteer Executive until the following December. " The National Volunteer " (439), a weekly journal supporting Mr. Redmond, began to appear from the offices of " The Freeman's Journal " on October 17th, 1914.

The Defence of the Realm news censorship came into operation on August 15th ,1914.* At first the press restrictions in Ireland applied only to naval and military matters, but those weekly journals which opposed recruiting and maintained that the first duty of Irishmen was to secure the freedom of their own country soon began to attract attention in England. (See a leading article in " The Times " on the latitude allowed to the Irish press, November 3rd, 1914, a reply in " Sinn Féin," November 7th, an article in " The Times," giving extracts from seditious Irish newspapers, November 24th, House of Lords Debates, November 24th, 1914, and January 8th, 1915, and House of Commons Debates, November 25th, 26th, 1914.) Mr. Augustine Birrell stated in the House of Commons that the matter of these journals was receiving attention from the Government. According to the Official Memorandum on the censorship published in 1915 (503a), the Press Bureau had no power to initiate or veto proceedings under the Defence of the Realm Act, that power being vested in the Naval or Military authorities. The latter acted in conjunction with the police on December 2nd-3rd, 1914, when the current issues of " Sinn Fein," " Irish Freedom," " Ireland," and " The Irish Worker " were seized, the printers warned, and, in some instances, type and removable parts of machinery taken away.

The suppressed journals reappeared, some in other forms or under other names. " The Irish Volunteer " continued without interruption under the editorship of Professor Eoin Mac Neill. The publication of " Scissors and Paste " (545) began on December 14th, and continued

---

* The Defence of the Realm Act had been prepared by the Committee of Imperial Defence before August, 1914, to be put into operation in the event of war. Sir Stanley Buckmaster (afterwards Lord Buckmaster), Solicitor-General, who succeeded Mr. F. E. Smith (afterwards Lord Birkenhead) as Director of the Press Bureau, stated in the House of Commons (November 11, 1914) that the Bureau was a safeguard for the press against " the untempered severity of martial law." (See " D.O.R.A. and restrictions on liberty " in " The consequences of the War to Great Britain " by F. W. Hirst, Carnegie Endowment for International Peace, 1934.) The press enjoyed much greater latitude in England than in Ireland, especially after April, 1916.

years later, the Irish Press Censor still found it necessary to warn the editors of all Irish daily and weekly newspapers that speeches and statements justifying the Rebellion of 1916 must not be published). The contemporary English and Irish newspapers contain numerous descriptions of the events of Easter week by onlookers or members of the British forces, but very few narratives by insurgents could be published in Ireland until some years had elapsed. The events leading up to the Rising have been recorded from various points of view by Irish, English, German and American writers, but little authentic information has appeared concerning the plans of the Volunteer Executive or of the Military Council, which is said to have organised the Rising.

The literature printed and circulated by the insurgents during Easter Week included the proclamation of the Republic, which was read out by Pádraic Pearse from the General Post Office on Easter Monday, one or two hand-bills, and one number of "The Irish War News" (646b). The Proclamation is the chief document of the Rising. It is believed to have been mainly the work of Pearse, with emendations by Connolly and, possibly, also by Thomas MacDonagh. It was set up and printed under the protection of the Irish Citizen Army at Liberty Hall on Sunday, April 23rd, from type supplied by Mr. W. H. West, on paper from the stock of "The Workers' Republic" (582a). The copy was handed to the two compositors (Messrs. M. Molloy and C. O'Brien) and the printer (Mr. C. Brady) by James Connolly. It appears that 2,500 copies were printed (for distribution over all Ireland), but that, as the Rising was not general, the greater part of these were destroyed. Only a few hundred seem to have been distributed for public display. A detailed account of the production and typography of the Proclamation, mainly gathered from the recollections of the printers and others concerned, has been given by Mr. J. J. Bouch of the National Library of Ireland in a paper read before the Bibliographical Society of Ireland and printed in the Proceedings of the Society for 1936. "The Irish War News" (646a), the small four-page sheet, dated Tuesday, April 26, is similar in type and paper to "Honesty," and like that journal was printed at the Gaelic Press (Mr. J. Stanley). Reproductions of the Proclamation, "The Irish War News," and several of the printed and typewritten orders issued by the Irish Volunteer forces will be found in various newspapers and illustrated records published in 1916 (e.g., 643a, 646) and afterwards.

Notwithstanding the severe press restrictions and the continuation of Martial law, "rebel" songs, ballads and broadsides were being printed and sold in large numbers very soon after the Rising, and much interest began to be shown in the literary works of the executed leaders—Pádraic Pearse, Joseph Mary Plunkett, James Connolly and Thomas MacDonagh. General Sir John Maxwell, Commander-in-

Chief of the British forces, in a letter to the Prime Minister (585) alludes to the changes in Irish public opinion during the months of May and June, 1916. He mentions the " Skeffington case " and Mr. John Dillon's condemnation of military severity (" Mr. Dillon's speech in the House of Commons did enormous mischief ") as tending to increase dissatisfaction with the British administration of Ireland. By the middle of June, Sir John Maxwell reported, " a revulsion of feeling set in—one of sympathy for the rebels . . . the executed leaders have become martyrs and the rank and file ' patriots.' "

Propaganda on behalf of the Sinn Féin and Irish Volunteer organisations was virtually suspended in May, 1916, owing to the numerous arrests. Notwithstanding the censorship, however, the unpopularity of the military régime was reflected in many Irish newspapers. When the prisoners were released from Frongoch internment camp in December, 1916, the " revulsion of feeling " had become noticeable throughout Ireland and the situation was more favourable to the dissemination of Sinn Féin ideas than ever before. On February 17th, 1917, Mr. Arthur Griffith resumed the publication of " Nationality." During 1917 and 1918 several new weekly journals advocating a similar national policy appeared, and many already in existence gave their support to the new Sinn Féin movement. The Irish nationalist press, while still generally supporting the Parliamentary party, showed increasing impatience at the postponement of self-government, and Irish Unionism as a practical policy was gradually abandoned outside the eastern counties of Ulster. The rise of a new Irish nationalist movement, resolute, well-organised, and largely recruited from the youth of the country, began to be generally recognised by commentators on Irish affairs after the Sinn Féin election successes in 1917. The Home Rule proposals made by Mr. D. Lloyd George in June, 1916 (840) were the first of several plans of Irish settlement put forward by the British Government in 1916-1918 as a matter of war policy. (See the biographies and reminiscences of Mr. John Redmond, Mr. William O'Brien, Mr. T. M. Healy, Lord Cushendun, Mr. D. Lloyd George, Mr. Asquith, Dr. C. Addison, Lord Long and others). For the most important of these settlement plans, reference should be made to " Irish Convention " in the section 1916-1918. For the progress of Sinn Féin, " Nationality " is the chief source of information. The published documents of the tenth Sinn Féin Árd-Fheis (972-977) are also of considerable interest. This Convention, held in October, 1917, decided the form and policy of the reorganised movement and governed the programme adopted at the General Election a year later.

The restrictions on publication under the Defence of the Realm Act in 1916-1919 were set forth in numerous telegrams and circular letters addressed by the Press Censor, Ireland, to the editors of all Irish newspapers and marked " Confidential, Not for publication."

Many of these communications were intended to guide editors in the exclusion from their columns of naval and military information considered likely to be of service to the Central Powers in the European war, but after April, 1916, an increasing proportion refer to purely Irish affairs. "The Press are requested to bear in mind that resolutions or speeches passed or made at the meetings of Corporations; County, Urban or Rural District Councils and Boards of Guardians should be most carefully considered before publication. Criticism of the Government or its administration which is likely to cause disaffection is not permitted" (17th August, 1916). "Editors are again reminded that reports of proceedings before a Court of Justice (including Courts of first instance) are not immune from the operation of those of the Defence of the Realm regulations which govern publication" (3rd March, 1917). "Speeches or articles which suggest that any particular political action by the Government will result in affecting the loyalty or discipline of His Majesty's Forces are in contravention of this [Defence of the Realm Act] Regulation" (13th April, 1917); "The Press are again most urgently reminded that the publication of reports of seditious speeches, articles or other matter which is intended or likely to cause disaffection is forbidden by the Defence of the Realm Act regulations" (19th July, 1917); "It shall not be lawful for any person in any newspaper, periodical, circular or other printed publication, or in any public speech, to publish any report or statement of, or to purport to describe or refer to, any proceedings of the Convention assembled on the invitation of His Majesty's Government for the purpose of preparing a constitution for the future government of Ireland, or of any Committee of that Convention, except such report or statement thereof as may be officially authorised by the Chairman of the Commission" (Defence of the Realm Regulation published in the *London Gazette*, 20th July, 1917). If a prisoner is charged in court proceedings with using seditious words, the words in question may be reported. "This does not apply to speeches or statements made by the accused containing fresh seditious matter" (29th August, 1917).

The warning concerning the Irish Convention is recalled more than once. "Allusions have been made to schemes before the Convention, and to the activities of certain political parties within it; rumours (frequently quite inaccurate) have been reproduced, and various meetings of the Convention and its Committees have been most improperly described as 'critical'" (3rd December, 1917). "The Press are informed that the publication of all reports of parades, drillings and route marches, of Sinn Féin Volunteers should not be published" (5th December, 1917). "The attention of the Press is again called to Defence of the Realm Regulation 27aa, and they are reminded that no reference whatever can be made in the Press to the Proceedings of the Irish Convention. It is therefore necessary in view of the very delicate nature of the Convention's deliberations to issue this reminder, with strict injunctions to comply exactly with terms of [the] Regulation " (20th March, 1918). " In the event of your being asked to publish memorial, anniversary, or other notices in your advertisement columns, which refer to the Rebellion of Easter, 1916, you are requested to submit them to this Office before insertion " (29th March, 1918.) The Report of the Convention was laid on the table of the House of Commons on April 9, 1918, the same day on which the Prime Minister announced the decision of the British Government to include Ireland in their new Military Service [Conscription] Bill. Little public interest was now shown in the Report of the Convention, but the Conscription proposal was regarded by every section of nationalist opinion as an infringement of fundamental Irish rights. It led to an extraordinary demonstration of national solidarity, and the press reported determined preparations all over the country to resist the British law. " In connection with the recently published reports of organisation of resistance to the Military Service Act the attention of the Press is again called to Regulation 27 of the Defence of the Realm Regulation which provides that no person shall by word of mouth or in writing in any newspaper, periodical, book, circular or other printed publication . . . spread reports or make statements intended or likely to prejudice the recruiting of persons to serve in any of His Majesty's forces " (20th April, 1918).

Many of the leading members of Sinn Féin and the Irish Volunteers were arrested and sent to English prisons in May, 1918, and these and other national organisations were proclaimed in the following month. " The Press are advised that letters from the Irish Deportees interned in Great Britain under Regulation 14B of the Defence of the Realm regulations, should be submitted to this Office before publication " (31st May, 1918). " In view of enquiries from many papers, Editors are informed that the proclamation under section six of the Criminal Law and Procedure (Ireland) Act of the Sinn Féin and kindred organisations as dangerous does not of itself prohibit or suppress these organisations but confers upon the Lord Lieutenant in Council the power to do so by Order to be published in the prescribed manner, and is in the nature of a preliminary warning upon which action will only be taken in any district if subsequent misconduct makes it necessary. In the absence of such an order there continues full liberty to publish reports of any meetings or proceedings of the Sinn Féin organisation, the Sinn Féin clubs or the Gaelic League, subject to these reports containing no matter which is likely to cause disaffection or otherwise offends against the Defence of the Realm Regulations. In the case of the Irish Volunteers and Cumann na mBan, the existing rule of censorship that no report of military activities of these bodies may be published (viz., Serial No. 70. 5th

December, 1917) remains in force but subject to that rule and to the general provisions of the Defence of the Realm Regulations the publication of Press matter referring to them is also permissible " (5th July, 1918). " In connection with the General Election campaign the Press is reminded that any person publishing any pamphlets, leaflets, election addresses, or other literature which contain matter offending against the Defence of the Realm Regulations will do so on their own responsibility " (5th December, 1918).

The Sinn Féin Members of Parliament then at liberty (thirty-two of the seventy-three elected were in prison) met in the Mansion House, Dublin, on January 21st, 1919, and constituted Dáil Éireann. The official publications containing the Declaration of Independence, the Democratic Programme, parliamentary reports, proclamations, decrees and other proceedings of the Dáil and its departments are included in the section 1919-1921 (1078-1088, 1187-1188). Some of the early meetings of the Dáil were held in public, and descriptions of the sessions appeared in the Sinn Féin weekly journals as well as in the Irish and English daily press. These descriptions were limited in scope by the warning of the Press Censor to the Editors of all Irish newspapers: " The Press are informed with reference to the Dáil Éireann assembly, which was held at the Mansion House, Dublin, January 21st, that the following are not for publication: (1) The Democratic Programme; (2) Declaration of Independence; (3) Speeches proposing and seconding the Declaration of Independence." In September, 1919, Dáil Éireann was proclaimed as a " dangerous association," and no account of its proceedings then appeared in the public press until August, 1921.

The censorship set up at the beginning of the Great War was continued in Ireland after the Armistice. " The Irish Government has decided to retain the Office of the Press Censor for the present. In the interests of the peace of the country, it is impossible for the Government to permit any section of the Irish Press to be used as an instrument of incitement to organised or other defiance of the law, or for the purpose of inflaming public opinion to a pitch in which acts of lawlessness become possible. There is sufficient reason to fear that [if] there were no effective legal restrictions upon publication, attempts might be made to secure publicity for matter of this description " (28th April, 1919). Four months later, " the Press are reminded that the provisions of the Defence of the Realm Regulations continue to be in force, and that newspapers which publish statements contravening those Regulations will still be liable to such penalties as the Regulations direct " (28th August, 1919). The Censor's office at the same time came to an end. " The Government have decided that the time has now arrived when the Press Censorship in Ireland may be abolished. It will therefore cease to exist from midnight of August 31st, 1919." Major Bryan Cooper (195a), who held the office from April, 1919, in a valedictory letter to Irish editors, writes: "My time of service at the ' galleys ' is at an end."

The abolition of the Censor's office implied no relaxation of the restrictions on publication; on the contrary, the regulations were interpreted with increasing rigour and in a more irregular fashion during the next two years. (The Press Censor's function had been purely advisory; publishers and editors submitted printers' proofs to him of their own volition.) Several weekly papers in Dublin and the provincial towns were suppressed in September and October, 1919, as a penalty for publishing the prospectus of the Dáil Internal Loan. " Young Ireland " (1004) and one or two other journals displaying Sinn Féin sympathies carried on a precarious existence in 1919-1921, but the publication through normal channels of books, pamphlets or journals upholding the authority of Dáil Eireann or commenting on the news of the day in a spirit openly favourable to Sinn Féin became almost impossible.

Two governments—Dáil Eireann and the British—now attempted to exercise absolute jurisdiction in Ireland. By the summer of 1920 a state of active warfare had developed between the forces of the former (Óglaigh na hÉireann, the Irish Volunteers, popularly known as the I.R.A.) and those of the latter, which were now augmented by the " Black and Tans " and Auxiliary Police. The Irish press henceforth became extremely guarded in its news and comments. The Defence of the Realm Regulations were incorporated in the Restoration of Order Act, 1920 (1324), and British military and police officers in many Irish towns, especially in the martial law areas, assumed control of the local press, not only censoring proofs, but compelling the editors to insert matter unfavourable to Sinn Féin and Óglaigh na hÉireann. " The Irish Bulletin " (1188), the official journal of Dáil Eireann, gives particulars from time to time of interference with the press, and states that several newspaper offices were bombed or set on fire by the forces of the Crown, and that some owners and editors were arrested or threatened with personal violence and the destruction of their property.

The circulation of Irish news and literature abroad had been part of the early Sinn Féin programme, but it was not until Sinn Féin had been able to secure the substantial support of the people, confirmed by electoral returns, and the authority derived from a national government and legislature, that its propaganda abroad obtained a sympathetic and attentive hearing. Irish delegations or press bureaux were established during 1919-1921 in France, Italy, the United States, Germany, Spain, and Switzerland. From these was distributed literature relating to the history, culture, economic resources and national claims of Ireland, along with regular bulletins of Irish news to counteract the misleading reports circulated by certain foreign agencies. (See the report on the Department of Foreign Affairs presented to

Dáil Éireann by Count Plunkett, 17th August, 1921, Dáil Reports, 1921-1922, pp. 16-21). Contact with the Irish delegations in foreign capitals and with the numerous Irish societies and sympathisers in Great Britain, the United States of America, Canada, South Africa, Australia, Chile and the Argentine Republic, was maintained by the Dáil Department of Foreign Affairs, which early in 1921 had two " hidden " offices in Dublin—the firm of " Lewis and Lewis, Insurance Brokers " in Harcourt Place and " Iresol Products " in Kildare Street.

" The Irish Bulletin " (1188), produced and circulated by the Dáil Department of Publicity from November, 1919, to December, 1921, was an official gazette and newspaper. It contained summaries of the public and secret sessions of Dáil Éireann, decrees of the Ministry, reports from the Departments of Industry, Trade, Local Government, Justice, Labour, Fisheries, Agriculture, and, when the conflict became intense, regular reports from the Irish Volunteer commandants on active service. The history of " The Irish Bulletin " resembled that of the Polish journal which Marshal Pilsúdski helped to write and print at Lodz under the Russian Empire and that of " La Libre Belge," which appeared in Brussels 1914-1918 during the German occupation. Unlike its predecessors, however, " The Irish Bulletin " was not printed but typewritten, and it circulated mainly outside Ireland. (It was regularly received in 1921, according to the Report of the Department of Publicity presented to Dáil Éireann, by nine hundred newspapers.) The Publicity Department was one of several offices in which the work of Dáil Éireann was carried on during the difficult period, 1919-1921, when the task of the Irish Ministry was described as " setting a tent in face of a gale." Communication between the offices was maintained by cyclist messengers, most of whom were members of the Irish boy scout organisation, Fianna na hÉireann. The offices of " The Irish Bulletin " in Molesworth Street, Dublin, were accidentally discovered by Auxiliary Police on March 26th, 1921, but the publication was continued without interruption from a private house in Rathgar Road, a Dublin suburb. The sheets were rolled off on a Gestetner machine and made up every day into numerous packets and parcels to be dispatched to various addresses at home and abroad. They left the house in various disguises—some in laundry and grocery baskets, some in a child's perambulator; many were taken away by cyclist messengers and distributed at the city post offices; some of the larger parcels contained stamped addressed packets which, in turn, were posted by the recipients.

The Irish national struggle had been regarded with sympathetic interest in the United States since the American Declaration of Independence, and this interest was, perhaps, never more widely expressed than in 1919-1921, not only by Americans of Irish birth and descent but among the citizens generally. Numerous Irish books and pamphlets appeared in the United States, the publication of which would not have been permitted by the British authorities in Ireland. Newspapers devoted mainly to Irish affairs were published in the chief American cities—the majority of these supporting the more advanced type of Irish nationalism. During the period 1912-1921 the two most influential Irish-American newspapers were " The Gaelic American " (56a) and " The Irish World " (103). Among other journals which represented large sections of opinion were " The Hibernian," the official journal of the American branch, Ancient Order of Hibernians, " The Irish Press " (Philadelphia), founded by Mr. Joseph McGarrity in 1918 and edited for a time by Dr. P. McCartan, T.D.; " The Irish Republic " (Chicago), the newspaper of the American Association for the Recognition of the Irish Republic. " The Irish World " represented the American branch of the United Irish League and supported the Irish Parliamentary Party until 1914, when it went over to Sinn Féin in consequence of Mr. Redmond's war policy. One of the principal agencies for the diffusion of Irish books and political pamphlets in America during 1916-1921 was the Friends of Irish Freedom organisation (1137). Dr. P. McCartan in his account of the Irish-American organisations and newspapers at this period states (876) that the " F.O.I.F." distributed no less than half a million copies of Dr. Maloney's pamphlet, " The Irish issue in its American aspect " (1253). The interest of the American people generally in the Irish cause was frequently displayed, not only in books, newspapers, and journals of opinion, but in the Congressional Record and other published papers of the Senate and House of Representatives and in the records of several State legislatures. The Report of the American Commission on conditions in Ireland, 1921 (1011) was extensively circulated in America, England and the Dominions and (in French and Italian translations) on the Continent.

For the Anglo-Irish hostilities of 1920-1921 and the negotiations leading to the Truce and the Treaty, the principal contemporary sources of information, in addition to the newspapers, are " The Irish Bulletin " and other publications of the Dáil Publicity Department, " An t-Óglách," the proceedings of Dáil Éireann, the Parliament of Northern Ireland and the British Parliament, and the official reports published in London and Dublin of the correspondence between Dáil Éireann and the British Government. The Peace with Ireland Council (1303), a society founded by a group of well-known English writers, churchmen and members of parliament of all parties, devoted great energy in 1920-1921 to the rousing of British public opinion against the continuation of the war in Ireland, and with this object circulated many leaflets and pamphlets. A large collection of extracts from the Irish and English newspapers relating to the Anglo-Irish question in 1920-1921 was presented by the Council to the National Library of Ireland.

J. C.

CHRONOLOGY

1912

JANUARY 3—Annual meeting of the Ulster Unionist Council resolves not to submit to the authority of an Irish Parliament should one be established. 26—Mr. A. Bonar Law, at his first public appearance as leader of the Unionist Party pledges unqualified support to the Ulster Unionists.

FEBRUARY 1—A Convention of the Presbyterian Church in Ireland, held at Belfast, protests against Home Rule. 14—A Convention of Irish Methodists, held at Belfast, protests against Home Rule.

MARCH 16—Resolution of the Sinn Féin Executive, published in "Sinn Féin," expresses the hope that the promised Home Rule Bill will be one which may be accepted by the Irish people; if it is not, the organisation is ready to lead the country to self-government by other methods. 31—Home Rule demonstration in O'Connell Street, Dublin, addressed by Mr. John Redmond, Mr. John Dillon, Mr. Joseph Devlin and many other speakers, including Mr. P. H. Pearse.

APRIL 9—Anti-Home Rule demonstration at Belfast addressed by Mr. Bonar Law, Sir Edward Carson and others. 11—Mr. H. H. Asquith, Prime Minister, introduces in the House of Commons a Bill "to amend the provisions for the government of Ireland." 16—First reading of the Home Rule Bill passed. 23—A Nationalist Convention in Dublin approves of the Bill and expresses confidence in the Irish Parliamentary Party. ["A representative Convention of the Irish race in these islands . . . . authorised me to say that I spoke for Ireland."—Mr. John Redmond (70, p. 204)].

MAY 9—Second reading of the Bill passed in the House of Commons. 25—A Convention of the All-for-Ireland League (Mr. William O'Brien, M.P., presiding), decides to support the Home Rule Bill, while disliking its financial provisions.

JUNE 11—Committee stage of the Bill in the House of Commons. 18—Hon. T. Agar-Robartes (L.) moves an amendment (negatived) to exclude from the jurisdiction of the Irish Parliament the four Ulster counties in which Unionists are in a majority.

JULY 19—Mr. Asquith speaks in the Theatre Royal, Dublin. A Sinn Féin meeting in College Green demands for the Irish Parliament the power to collect all Irish taxes.

SEPTEMBER 18—Sir Edward Carson at Enniskillen opens a campaign against Home Rule; parades of the Ulster Volunteers reviewed by the leaders of Unionist party. 28—" Ulster Day "; the Ulster Covenant against Home Rule opened for signature; Sir Edward Carson signs first.

1913

JANUARY 1—Report stage of the Home Rule Bill resumed in the House of Commons. Sir Edward Carson moves an amendment (which is rejected) to exclude "the province of Ulster"; Mr. Bonar Law says that the Ulster Unionists would prefer "the government of a foreign country rather than submit to be governed by honourable gentlemen below the gangway." 16—Third reading of the Bill passed by the House of Commons. 30—Second reading of the Bill in the House of Lords negatived. 31—Annual meeting of the Ulster Unionist Council approves of the draft and articles of an Ulster Provisional Government.

FEBRUARY 14—Sir Edward Carson issues an appeal for funds.

MAY 8—Convention of the Ancient Order of Hibernians in Dublin (Mr. Joseph Devlin, M.P., presiding). 10—Convention of the United Irish League of Great Britain (Mr. T. P. O'Connor, M.P., presiding).

JUNE 9—Home Rule Bill again in the House of Commons; second reading passed.

JULY 12—Sir Edward Carson, addressing a meeting at Craigavon, advises his hearers not to pay taxes to a Home Rule Government, assures them that the Unionist party will support them, and that the British Government would not be able to rely upon the army "to shoot down the people of Ulster." 15—Second reading of the Bill again negatived in the House of Lords. 24—General Sir George Richardson, on arriving in Ireland to take command of the Ulster Volunteer Force, is stated to have "found his command from fifty to sixty thousand strong, with recruits joining every day" (37, p. 162).

AUGUST 31—Labour troubles in Dublin culminate in the arrest of Mr. James Larkin.

SEPTEMBER 11—A letter in "The Times" from Lord Loreburn, suggesting a conference on Home Rule between leaders of the Liberal and Unionist parties "to consider proposals for accommodation," is interpreted by Irish Nationalists as a sign that the Government is weakening on the Home Rule question. 17—Beginning of a series of reviews, lasting a fortnight, of Ulster Volunteers by Sir Edward Carson and Sir George Richardson. 25—Arrangements announced for the constitution of the Ulster Provisional Government with a Central Authority of seventy-six members, a Military Council, and a guarantee fund of £1,000,000.

OCTOBER 1—Sir Edward Carson at Dungannon says that he has given up making political speeches: "I want to speak only to those who are prepared to fight." 12—Mr. John Redmond at Limerick describes the theory recently put forward that there are two nations in Ireland as "an abomination." 14—The first of a series of secret conferences between the Prime Minister and Mr. Bonar Law to seek a compromise on Home Rule. 24—A meeting of Protestant Home Rulers, including Sir Roger Casement, held at Ballymoney, Co. Antrim, to protest against "the lawless policy of Carsonism."

NOVEMBER 9—Major-General Sir Henry Wilson, Director of Military Operations at the War Office, discusses the Irish political situation with Mr. Bonar Law. 11—Captain James Craig estimates the Ulster Volunteer Force at 88,000 men. 25—The Irish Volunteers established at a public meeting in the Rotunda, Dublin.

DECEMBER 5—A proclamation prohibiting the importation of arms and ammunition into Ireland published in the *London Gazette*. 12—Enrolment of Irish Volunteers in Galway begins. 18—Private conference on the Home Rule Bill between the Prime Minister and Sir Edward Carson. 23—First Branch of the Irish Volunteers in Cork City established.

1914

JANUARY 22—End of the secret conferences between the Prime Minister and the Unionist leaders; they reject his offers of a compromise. 25—Mr. John Redmond at Waterford expresses confidence that the Prime Minister will see the Home Rule Bill through. 28—Mr. P. H. Pearse at Limerick says that the Volunteer movement is a weapon to help Mr. Redmond to enforce the demand for Home Rule.

FEBRUARY 7—First number of "The Irish Volunteer" (weekly). 10—The King's speech at the opening of Parliament refers to the failure of efforts "to arrive at a solution by agreement of the problems connected with the government of Ireland."

MARCH 9—Mr. Asquith makes public the terms of his offer to Sir Edward Carson: exclusion of Ulster counties from Home Rule on the basis of county option for a period of **six** years; Sir Edward Carson rejects the scheme but says that "**the principle of exclusion has been** recognised." 19—Orders stated to have been given for the movement of British troops into Ulster. 20—General Sir A. Paget, Commander-in-Chief of the British Forces in Ireland, asks officers either to promise that they will serve in Ulster if required or else to resign; officers of the 3rd (Curragh) Cavalry Brigade refuse to give the undertaking required and resign. 21—The officers, having received "a satisfactory guarantee" from the Government, withdraw their resignations. 22—The Prime Minister authorises "The Times" to state that the recent movements of troops in Ulster were "purely precautionary." 25, 30—Army debates in the House of Commons. 26—Sir Henry Wilson states in his Diary: "All the Commanders-in-Chief and Divisional Commanders informed French that the army was unanimous in its determination not to fight Ulster" (262, p. 143). 27—"The Morning Post" claims that "the army has killed Home Rule." 29—Resignation of Col. Seely, Secretary of State for War, and Field-Marshal Sir John French, Chief of the Imperial General Staff.

APRIL 17—The Ulster Unionist Council issues a statement purporting to reveal the military measures planned by the Government against the Ulster Volunteers in March. 18—Sinn Féin " Proposals to Unionist Ulster " published. 22—Second Parliamentary White Paper on the army crisis published. 24—The Larne gun-running; 35,000 rifles stated to have been brought in for the Ulster Volunteers. 26—Professor MacNeill and Sir Roger Casement on behalf of the Irish Volunteers interview Mr. John Redmond and Mr. John Dillon in London.

MAY 4—The Irish Parliamentary Party decides to give public support to the Irish Volunteers. 16—Mr. Redmond begins a correspondence with Professor MacNeill on the control of the Volunteers. 25—Third reading of the Home Rule Bill passed in the House of Commons. 31—A census of the Irish Volunteers shows the strength of the Force to be 129,000, of whom 41,000 are in Ulster.

JUNE 1—Appeal for funds in support of the Irish Volunteers issued in New York. 9—Defence of Ireland appeal for funds issued at home. A statement published from Mr. John Redmond explaining why he has insisted on having a controlling interest in the Volunteers. 17—A majority of the original committee of the Volunteers agree to the demands made by Mr. Redmond. 23—Government of Ireland Amending Bill introduced in the House of Lords [County option for six years in Ulster].

JULY 7—A statement published by the Irish Volunteers claims that the Force has 891 drill centres and 153,500 men drilling. 8—The House of Lords amends the Amending Bill so as to exclude the whole province of Ulster without limitation of time. 9—Mr. Augustine Birrell in the House of Commons estimates from reports by the police that the Irish Volunteers number 132,000 and the Ulster Volunteers 85,000. 10—First meeting of the Ulster Provisional Government held in Belfast. 14—First meeting of the augmented committee of the Irish Volunteers held; Professor E. MacNeill presides. 15—Validity of the arms proclamation (December, 1913) upheld in the Court of King's Bench, Dublin. 17—" The greatest activity prevails all over Ireland in connection with the Irish Volunteers " (" The Freeman's Journal "). 20—Sir Roger Casement arrives in New York to collect funds for the Irish Volunteers. 21-24—The Irish conference at Buckingham Palace fails to agree " either in principle or in detail " (Prime Minister). 25—A parade in Belfast of Ulster Volunteers stated to be armed with " Larne rifles." 26—Rifles landed at Howth and taken away by the Irish Volunteers; troops, called out to intercept the Volunteers, fire on the crowd in the streets. 31—Home Rule Amending Bill in the House of Commons postponed in view of the European crisis.

AUGUST 3—Mr. John Redmond pledges Irish support to England in the event of war, and promises that if British troops are withdrawn the Irish Volunteers would unite with the Ulster Volunteers to defend Ireland. 4—England declares war on Germany. 5—The Standing Committee of the Irish Volunteers state their " desire on behalf of the Irish National Volunteers to take joint action with the Ulster Volunteer Force for the defence of Ireland." 6—The proclamation prohibiting the import of arms into Ireland revoked. 15—The Defence of the Realm Act news censorship comes into operation.

SEPTEMBER 15—Manifesto published from Sir Edward Carson criticising the Government's decision to allow the Home Rule Bill to reach the statute book. 18—The Home Rule Bill receives the royal assent along with a Bill suspending its operation for an indefinite period. 20—A speech by Mr. John Redmond to Irish Volunteers at Woodenbridge, Co. Wicklow, advising them to join the British army for service abroad, causes a division on the Volunteer Executive. 25—A statement published from twenty of the original members of the Executive repudiating the leadership of Mr. Redmond [The organisation now divided into two groups, one known as the "National Volunteers," under the chairmanship of Mr. Redmond, and the other, the "Irish Volunteers," under Professor MacNeill. It was estimated that over ninety per cent. of the ranks belonged to the former group]. Mr. Asquith, in the Mansion House, Dublin, appeals for Irish recruits and support of England in the war. 28—Sir Edward Carson, in a speech criticising the Government, says: "We will repeal the Home Rule Bill as far as it concerns us in ten minutes."

OCTOBER 4—Mr. Redmond, at a meeting in Wexford attended by a large number of National Volunteers, advises them to go to "the battlefields of Europe." 10—"The Irish World" (New York), hitherto supporting the Irish Parliamentary Party, announces that it will discontinue receiving subscriptions for the Irish National Volunteers until it is clearly decided that they shall not be sent to serve outside Ireland. 12—James Connolly presides at a meeting of the "Irish Neutrality League" in Dublin. 20—Sir Mathew Nathan becomes Under-Secretary for Ireland. 25—First Annual Convention of the Irish Volunteers (Professor MacNeill presiding). 31—A leading article in "The Times" draws attention to the circulation of seditious journals in Ireland. Sir Roger Casement arrives in Berlin.

NOVEMBER 24—An article in "The Times" gives extracts from the Irish "seditious newspapers." 26—Mr. Augustine Birrell, Chief Secretary for Ireland, questioned in the House of Commons on the circulation of these journals in Ireland, says: "The matter has engaged the serious attention of the Irish Government."

DECEMBER 2-3—Suppression of the current issues of "Sinn Féin," "Irish Freedom," "Ireland" and "The Irish Worker" under the D.O.R.A.; the circulation in Ireland of "The Gaelic American" and "The Irish World" prohibited. 5—"The Irish Volunteer" published "under new ownership and editorship." 12—First number of "Scissors and Paste" (545) edited by Arthur Griffith. 26—A supplement to "The Irish Volunteer" explains the new scheme of military organisation approved by the Director of Organisation, Commandant P. H. Pearse.

1915

JANUARY 8—Extracts from the suppressed journals read in the House of Lords in the course of a debate on "seditious" and anti-recruiting activities in Ireland.

FEBRUARY 7—First number of "The Spark" (555b) published.

MARCH 2—"Scissors and Paste" suppressed. 16—Defence of the Realm Act No. 2 in force (allowing British subjects prosecuted under the Defence of the Realm Regulations to claim trial by jury). 25—Review of National Volunteers in the Phoenix Park, Dublin, addressed by Mr. John Redmond. Referring to his offers of military co-operation he asks: "What fatal infatuation prevents the War Office from accepting the offer?"

MAY 16—Mr. Seán MacDermott, formerly manager of "Irish Freedom," arrested for making a seditious speech at Tuam. 19—Formation of a Coalition Government announced in England. 23—Irish Volunteer parades at Cork, Limerick, Killarney and other towns. 30—First number of "The Worker's Republic" (582a); Irish Volunteer Executive decide "to offer the most strenuous resistance to any attempt to force any form of conscription on the people of Ireland" ("Irish Volunteer," 12th June, 1915).

JUNE 26—First number of "Nationality" (440) published.

JULY 12—Orders made for the deportation of Messrs. O'Rahilly, E. Blythe, H. M. Pim, and D. McCullough, officers of the Irish Volunteers. 14—Resolution passed by the Dublin Corporation demanding that the Home Rule Bill be put into operation on September 17th. 20—A public meeting in the City Hall, Dublin, adopts the resolution, "We will not have conscription." 20—Mr. Redmond deprecates "any attempt to bring pressure to bear on the Government" on the Home Rule question. "The war for the moment dominates all other issues." 24—Mr. John Dillon at Limerick declares the opposition of the Irish Party to conscription.

AUGUST 1—Funeral of O'Donovan Rossa in Dublin organised by Irish Volunteers; oration at the graveside by P. H. Pearse (451). 23—Mr. John Redmond at Waterford speaks on Home Rule and the war.

OCTOBER 31—Second Annual Convention of the Irish Volunteers.

NOVEMBER 29—Police inspectors estimate the Irish Volunteers at 10,000 strong in the provinces and 1,500 in Dublin and "rapidly now on the increase."

DECEMBER 2—Sir M. Nathan, Under-Secretary for Ireland, privately expresses the opinion that the Sinn Féin movement is gaining ground at the expense of the Irish Parliamentary Party (714, p. 29). 14—Anti-Conscription meeting in the Mansion House, Dublin. 18—Sir M. Nathan informs the Chief Secretary that the situation in Ireland is "most serious and threatening," that an outbreak is "certain" if any attempt is made to enforce conscription (714).

1916

JANUARY 17—Committee stage of the Compulsory Service Bill in the House of Commons; an amendment including Ireland is negatived without a division; Mr. Bonar Law, Chancellor of the Exchequer, says that it would not be possible to extend the Bill to Ireland without a considerable amount of force.

FEBRUARY 14—Annual meeting of the Irish Parliamentary Party held in Dublin. 18—Message from Count Bernstorff, German Ambassador at Washington, to the German Government: "The Irish leader, John Devoy, informs me that the rising is to begin on Easter Saturday. To put it off longer is impossible. Let me know if help may be expected from Germany." 19—Statement issued "to the people of Ireland" by Mr. John Redmond in favour of recruiting.

MARCH 4-5—Irish Race Convention held in New York; Friends of Irish Freedom organisation formed. 4—The Foreign Office, Berlin, to the German Embassy, Washington: "Between 20th and 23rd April, in the evening, two or three steam-trawlers could land 20,000 rifles . . . at Fenit Pier in Tralee Bay . . ." 12—Message from Washington to Berlin: "Irish agree to proposition." 17—Irish Volunteers hold parades, concluding with a march past the Chief of Staff (Professor E. MacNeill) in College Green, Dublin. 24—"The Spark," "The Gael" and "Honesty" suppressed.

APRIL 9—The ship "Libau" [or "Aud"] leaves Germany with arms for Ireland. 10—Report presented by the Director of Military Intelligence, Irish Command, states: "The general state of Ireland, apart from recruiting, and apart from the activities of the pro-German Sinn Féin minority, is thoroughly satisfactory . . . and very free from ordinary crime" (714, p. 57). 12—Sir Roger Casement leaves Germany for Ireland in a submarine. 15—The number of Irish N.C.O.s and men at this date serving "with the military forces of the Crown" estimated at 150,183 (714, p. 124). 16—Ceremonial hoisting of "the green flag of Ireland" over Liberty Hall, Dublin. [17-18]—British naval authorities aware that a German arms ship is on its way to Ireland [?]. 18—Raid by U.S. Federal agents in New York on the apartments of Herr Wolf Von Igel; U.S. State Department becomes aware of the plans for an Irish rising; British Government warned [?]. 20—The "Aud" anchors near Fenit Pier. 21—Sir R. Casement and two others come ashore from the German U boat 22; the U 22 misses the "Aud" in the darkness and returns to Germany; motor-car accident at Ballykissane pier, Co. Kerry, and three Irish Volunteer officers drowned; the "Aud" weighs anchor. 22—Arrest of Casement; the failure to land the arms becomes known in Dublin; Mr. MacNeill issues orders, published next day in "The Sunday Independent," that "in view of the very critical situation . . . no parades, marches or other movements of the Irish Volunteers will take place on Sunday." The "Aud" blown up by her commander outside Cobh harbour. 23—Conferences of officials held at the Viceregal lodge; the arrest of the Volunteer leaders and other measures already decided examined in connection with the countermanding order and the new situation. Conferences of the Volunteer Executive and of the Military Council held; the latter body decides to proceed with the insurrection. The Proclamation of the Provisional Government printed at Liberty Hall. APRIL (The Rising). 24—The four battalions of the Dublin Brigade, Irish Volunteers, parade at 10 a.m. on an order signed by Commandant T. MacDonagh and Commandant P. H. Pearse. The insurrection begins at 12 noon; positions in the city occupied by the insurgents before 12.30 p.m. and the Provisional Government proclaimed in the General Post Office; all available British troops in Dublin ordered out for service. 25—Brigadier-General W. H. M. Lowe, arriving from the Curragh at 3.45 a.m., takes command of the British forces in Dublin. "The Irish War News" publishes a statement by Commandant-General Pearse, giving the position of the Republican forces at the time of writing, 9.30 a.m.; Martial law proclaimed in the city and county of Dublin. British reinforcements reach Dublin from Belfast, Athlone and Templemore and Dun Laoghaire from England. 26—Owing to the resistance met with from the insurgents, the attempt to bring fresh troops into the city from Dun Laoghaire is abandoned for the night. All insurgent posts held. 27—Insurgents take possession of Enniscorthy, Co. Wexford. "The Irish Times" published up to this date. British cordon closing in on O'Connell Street and the insurgent headquarters. 28—General Sir John Maxwell arrives in Dublin at 2 a.m. to take up his post as Commander-in-Chief of the British forces in Ireland. Manifesto by Commandant-General Pearse states: "We are busy completing arrangements for the final defence of headquarters." Engagement between insurgents and armed police at Ashbourne, Co. Meath. 29—A Council held in the General Post Office. At 3.45 p.m. P. H. Pearse signs the order for a surrender upon which the members of the Provisional Government present at headquarters have agreed "in order to prevent the further slaughter of unarmed people, and in the hope of saving the lives of our followers, now surrounded and hopelessly outnumbered." 30—Last of the insurgent Commandants in Dublin surrender. The General Officer Commanding-in-Chief, Irish Command, "hopes that the back of the rebellion is broken."

MAY 1—"All the rebels in Dublin have surrendered and the city is reported to be quiet" (F.-M. Lord French). 2—"Rebels considered suitable for trial are being tried by Field Courts-martial under the Defence of the Realm Act in Dublin" (Official Press Office, Irish Command). 3.—Pádraic Pearse, Thomas J. Clarke and Thomas MacDonagh executed. "The situation in Ireland is reported as quiet. The collection of arms and the arrests of fugitive rebels is proceeding satisfactorily" (F.-M. Lord French). 4th—Joseph Mary Plunkett, Edward Daly, Michael O'Hanrahan, and William Pearse executed. 5—John MacBride executed. Passes no longer required in the Dublin streets (police notice in newspapers). General resumption of work in Dublin. 6—Further list of court-martial sentences published. 8—Con Colbert, Eamonn Ceannt, Michael Mallin and Seán Heuston executed. End of the period (beginning April 24th) not to be reckoned in computing legal proceedings in Dublin. 9—Thomas Kent executed. Official list of casualties during the insurrection published. 10—Motion in the House of Commons to include Ireland in the Military Service Act is negatived without a division. Statement on the insurrection published from the Irish Parliamentary Party. 11—Speech by Mr. John Dillon in the House of Commons condemning British military severity and praising the heroism of the insurgents. 12—James Connolly and Seán MacDermott executed. 13—A list of Irish prisoners sent to England published. Order issued by General Sir John Maxwell prohibiting parades, processions, political and athletic meetings unless with a military permit. 18—Royal Commission on the rebellion begins its sessions. 25—The Prime Minister (Mr. Asquith) states that the system of government in Ireland has hopelessly broken down and that the Minister for Munitions (Mr. Lloyd George) has been entrusted with the task of bringing about an Irish settlement. 27—Orders issued by the Lords Justices in Ireland that "as disaffection and unrest still prevail in certain parts of Ireland . . . martial law shall continue to exist throughout Ireland until further order."

JUNE 6—Sir Edward Carson explains Mr. Lloyd George's proposals for an Irish settlement at a meeting of the Ulster Unionist Council. 9—Statement issued from the Irish Unionist Alliance on the proposals. 10—Mr. John Redmond explains the proposals at a conference of the Irish Parliamentary Party in Dublin. 17—A conference of Nationalists in six Ulster counties accepts the offer understood to have been made by Mr. Lloyd George—Home Rule, excluding these counties for a period of six years—by 475 votes to 265. 29—Sir Roger Casement sentenced to death at the Old Bailey.

JULY 3—Report of the Royal Commission on the Rebellion published. 11—Statement from Lord Lansdowne on the Irish settlement proposals published. 12—Mr. John Redmond describes Lord Lansdowne's statement as "a declaration of war on the Irish people." 20—Mr. Redmond is informed that the settlement proposals of which he approved have been discarded by the Government and a new Bill substituted, providing for the permanent exclusion of the six Ulster counties; he rejects the latter. 24—Irish debate in the House of Commons; the Government abandons its efforts for a Home Rule settlement.

AUGUST 1—The Irish Press censorship discussed in the House of Commons. 3—Sir Roger Casement executed. 4—Irish Nation League (for repeal of the Act of Union) formed. 23—First session of the Royal Commission on the shooting of Mr. F. Sheehy-Skeffington and others.

OCTOBER 6—Mr. Redmond, in the course of a speech at Waterford, warns the Government that the imposition of conscription would be resisted in every Irish village. 16—Report of the Sheehy-Skeffington Commission published. 18—Mr. Redmond moves a resolution in the House of Commons "That the system of Government at present maintained in Ireland is inconsistent with the principles for which the Allies are fighting in Europe."

DECEMBER 22—600 Irish prisoners released from Frongoch internment camp.

1917

FEBRUARY 3—Count Plunkett elected Member of Parliament for North Roscommon, defeating the candidate of the Irish Parliamentary Party. 17—"Nationality" (edited by Mr. Arthur Griffith) resumes publication.

MARCH 7—The Prime Minister (Mr. Lloyd George) declares in the House of Commons that "she [Ireland] is no more reconciled to British rule than in the days of Cromwell," but expresses the opinion (which is put forward for the first time by a British Minister) that the people of Ireland constitute not one nation but two nations. 22—Mr. Bonar Law announces that the Government is about to make another effort to achieve an Irish settlement.

APRIL 4—The United States of America declare war on Germany.

MAY 9—Mr. Joseph Maguinness (Sinn Féin) is elected Member of Parliament for Longford, defeating the candidate of the Irish Parliamentary Party. 8—A statement published from the Catholic bishops and three Protestant bishops of Ireland declares that "to Irishmen of every creed and class and party the very thought of our country partitioned and torn, as a new Poland, must be one of heart-rending sorrow." 16—The setting-up of a Convention to discuss Irish settlement announced by the British Government. 22—The National Executive of Sinn Féin declines to take part in the proposed Convention unless the members are elected by adult suffrage and the Government pledges itself to "ratify the decision of majority of the Convention."

JUNE 11—Composition of the Irish Convention announced. 16—Release of all Irish prisoners undergoing sentences of penal servitude for participation in the Rising of 1916.

JULY 10—Mr. E. E. de Valera elected M.P. for Clare. 25—First meeting of the Irish Convention.

AUGUST 10—Mr. W. T. Cosgrave elected M.P. for Kilkenny City.

SEPTEMBER 26—Thomas Ashe, Sinn Féin prisoner, dies during a hunger strike in Mountjoy Prison, Dublin.

OCTOBER 25-27—Tenth Annual Convention of Sinn Féin; Sinn Féin reorganised on a popular basis with a new constitution; Mr. E. de Valera elected President of the organisation, Mr. A. Griffith and the Rev. M. O'Flanagan Vice-Presidents, Mr. W. T. Cosgrave and Mr. L. Ginnell, Hon. Treasurers. [27]—Convention of the Irish Volunteers; the Volunteers reorganised with Mr. E. de Valera as President and Mr. C. Brugha, Chief of Staff.

1918

JANUARY 14—Sir A. Geddes states in the House of Commons that it is not the intention of the Government to extend the Military Service [Conscription] Act to Ireland.

FEBRUARY 2—The Irish Parliamentary Party defeats Sinn Féin in the South Armagh bye-election.

MARCH 4—A division of opinion arises in the Irish Unionist Alliance; Lord Midleton and others form the Anti-Partition League. 6—Death of Mr. John Redmond. 12—Mr. John Dillon elected Chairman of the Irish Parliamentary Party. "The Irish Press" established in Philadelphia by Mr. Joseph McGarrity.

APRIL 5—The Irish Convention adjourns *sine die.* 9—Report of the Convention laid on the table of the House of Commons. Mr. Lloyd George, in announcing the terms of the new Military Service [Conscription] Bill, states that the Bill will extend to Ireland. 15—The British Government is advised by the Marquis of Reading, Ambassador at Washington, of a "dangerous reaction" against England in the United States on the Irish question (750). 16—The Conscription Bill, with the clause applying it to Ireland, passed by the House of Commons. 17—The Irish Nationalist members leave the House of Commons and return to Ireland. 18—The Conscription Bill becomes law. 19—A conference of Nationalist, Sinn Féin and Labour leaders meets in the Mansion House, Dublin, and issues a call to the nation to resist the English conscription law "by the most effective means at their disposal." The Irish Catholic bishops meet at Maynooth and describe it as "an unjust and oppressive law" which the Irish people are entitled to resist "by all means consonant with the laws of God." 18-21—The foreign circulation of many Irish newspapers prohibited.

MAY 11—Lord French, Lord Lieutenant, and Mr. E. Shortt, Chief Secretary, arrive in Dublin to take up their duties. 17—The discovery of a "German plot" in Ireland announced by the British authorities; many well-known leaders and members of Sinn Féin arrested. 18-19—Irish Race Convention held in New York.

JUNE 11—Manifesto to President Wilson issued by the Dublin Mansion House Conference. 20—Mr. A. Griffith elected M.P. for E. Cavan.

JULY 3—Sinn Féin, the Irish Volunteers, the Gaelic League and other Irish organisations proclaimed as "dangerous associations" under the Defence of the Realm Act. 4—Public meetings, fairs and sports in Ireland prohibited except under permit.

AUGUST 15—A series of public meetings held in every county in Ireland without permits. 31—First issue of "An t-Óglách" (1287) published.

SEPTEMBER 20—Official announcement that the period within which Ireland must provide 50,000 recruits for the British army as an alternative to conscription has been extended from September 15th to October 15th.

OCTOBER 15—Movements of troops in Dublin are interpreted as indicating that the Government had decided to attempt to enforce conscription and then again abandoned the intention. 29-30—Eleventh Ard-Fheis of Sinn Féin. Substitutes appointed to act during the imprisonment of certain officials, directors, and members of Sinn Féin.

NOVEMBER 11—The Armistice. Cessation of hostilities in the Great War.

DECEMBER 8-15—Irish "Self-determination" week organised by the Irish societies in the United States. 14—General Election. 28—Results of the General Election announced: 73 Sinn Féin, 26 Unionist, and 6 Nationalist candidates returned in Ireland.

1919

JANUARY 21—Sinn Féin members of Parliament then at liberty meet in the Mansion House, Dublin, declare the independence of Ireland and constitute Dáil Eireann.

FEBRUARY 3—Mr. E. de Valera escapes from Lincoln jail. 22-23—Irish Race Convention at Philadelphia; delegates appointed to proceed to Paris and seek a hearing for Ireland at the Peace Conference.

MARCH 4—The United States Congress expresses the hope that the Peace Conference "will favourably consider the claims of Ireland to self-determination." 6—Sinn Féin prisoners in English jails, including thirty-one members of Dáil Eireann, released.

APRIL 1-3—Dáil Eireann in session; Mr. E. de Valera elected Priomh-Aire and Ministers selected to take charge of Departments of State. 8-9—Sinn Féin Ard-Fheis pledges allegiance to the "duly elected Government." 10-11—Dáil Eireann (private session). 28—Irish newspapers notified that the British Government "has decided to retain the office of Press Censor for the present."

MAY 3-12—Delegates of the Irish Race Convention in Ireland. 9—Dáil Eireann (private session). 17—The Irish-American delegates interview President Wilson in Paris.

JUNE 6—The United States Senate requests the U.S. delegates at the Peace Conference to obtain a hearing for the Irish representatives, Messrs. de Valera, Griffith and Plunkett, and expresses its sympathy with the claim of Ireland for self-government. 11—President de Valera arrives in New York. 17-19—Dáil Eireann (private session). 22—A statement on behalf of the Irish Government presented to M. Clemenceau by Messrs. S. T. O Ceallaigh and G. Gavan Duffy.

JULY 12—Sir Edward Carson at Ballymenoch demands repeal of the Home Rule Act and declares his intention of calling out the Ulster Volunteers and summoning the Ulster Provisional Government if the status of "Ulster" is threatened.

AUGUST 19-20—Dáil Eireann (private session). 23—The prospectus of the Dáil External Loan (for $5,000,000) published in American newspapers. 30—Statements of the Irish case heard before the Foreign Relations Committee of the U.S. Senate. Irish Press Censor's office abolished [but the censorship of the Press continues].

SEPTEMBER 7—Houses and business premises attacked in Fermoy by troops [the beginning of "reprisals"]. 10—Dáil Eireann proclaimed a "dangerous association." 17—7 OCT.—Many Irish newspapers, including nearly all those holding Sinn Féin views, suppressed for publishing advertisements of the Dáil Internal Loan.

OCTOBER 11—Order made under the Defence of the Realm Act that "the competent military authority" in every area in Ireland may impose curfew restrictions. 16—Sinn Féin Ard-Fheis suppressed. 27—Dáil Eireann (private session).

NOVEMBER 11—First number of "The Irish Bulletin." 12-13—Hearing of the Mason Bill in U.S. Congress.

1920

JANUARY 3-8—Public offices of Sinn Féin and Dáil Eireann in Dublin closed and boarded up by police and Royal Engineers. 15—Irish Urban Council elections. Sinn Féin majorities returned in the great majority of the city corporations and town councils. [These bodies subsequently declared their allegiance to Dáil Eireann and placed themselves under the control of the Ministry of Local Government.] 17—Dáil Eireann Victory Bond Drive opened in U.S.A.

FEBRUARY 2—Many members of Dáil Eireann arrested. 23—"Curfew" order in Dublin. 25—A Bill "for the better government of Ireland" [providing for partition by the separation of six Ulster counties] introduced in the House of Commons.

MARCH 4—Sir Horace Plunkett, President of the Irish Dominion League, denounces the new Government of Ireland Bill. 10—The Ulster Unionist Council decides to accept the Bill. 18—The U.S. Senate adds a reservation to its ratification of the Treaty of Peace with Germany, expressing "sympathy with the aspiration of the Irish people for a Government of their own choice." 19—Murder of Tomás MacCurtain, T.D., Lord Mayor of Cork. 31—Second reading of the Government of Ireland [Partition] Bill passes the House of Commons.

APRIL 2—Sir Hamar Greenwood appointed Chief Secretary for Ireland. 14—Release of hunger-strikers from Mountjoy Prison, Dublin. General Sir C. F. N. Macready assumes command of the British forces in Ireland.

MAY 24—Sir John Anderson appointed Joint Under-Secretary for Ireland. 28—Mr. A. W. Cope, Assistant Under-Secretary for Ireland. U.S. Congress (both houses) views the conditions prevailing in Ireland "with concern and solicitude" and again expresses sympathy with the aspirations of the Irish people.

JUNE 3, 17, 25—"The Irish Bulletin" gives particulars of the work of district and land courts and republican police of the Dáil Ministry of Justice in maintaining public order. 8—County Council, Rural District and Poor Law Guardians elections in Ireland: 29 of the 33 Irish County Councils and the great majority of the local councils and boards return Sinn Féin majorities. [These bodies subsequently placed themselves under the control of the Dáil Ministry of Local Government]. 29—Dáil Eireann (private session); decrees passed authorising the establishment of Courts of Justice and Equity and Courts of Criminal Jurisdiction; the Minister of Finance announces that the Dáil Loan floated in Ireland has been oversubscribed.

AUGUST 2—Restoration of Order (Ireland) Bill introduced in the House of Commons. 6—Dáil Eireann (private session). 6—Statement by Professor Eoin MacNeill on the Belfast rioting published in "The Irish Bulletin." 9—Restoration of Order Bill becomes law. 12—Terence MacSwiney, T.D., Lord Mayor of Cork, arrested; with other prisoners in Cork jail he goes on hunger strike. 13—"Principal Order" under the Restoration of Order Act issued. First number of "The Weekly Summary" (1385a) published at Dublin Castle. 30-31—Belfast experiences the "worst rioting in its history."

SEPTEMBER 17—Dáil Eireann (private session). 19—Total strength of the Royal Irish Constabulary with the Auxiliary Division stated in the House of Commons to be 9,856.

OCTOBER 24—Irish Dominion League "Peace Conference" held in Dublin. 25—Death of Terence MacSwiney. A motion by the Labour Party in the House of Commons for an inquiry into the official reprisals in Ireland rejected. 27—Ireland's request to the American Government asking for recognition as an independent State transmitted to President Wilson by President de Valera.

NOVEMBER 6—Mahon's printing works (see 1004) closed and the machinery dismantled by troops. 16—American Association for the recognition of the Irish republic founded at Washington. 21—Officers alleged to have been engaged in military intelligence work, players and spectators at a Gaelic football match, and (22) three Irish Republican prisoners, shot dead. 22—Debate in the House of Commons on the occurrences in Ireland on the previous day. Royal Irish Constabulary stated to number 11,766 (including 969 Auxiliary Police). 26—Editor and directors of "The Freeman's Journal" court-martialled. 27—Mr. Arthur Griffith, acting President of the Irish Government, Professor Eoin MacNeill and Mr. E. J. Duggan arrested. 30—A Commission appointed by the British Labour Party to investigate the situation in Ireland arrives in Dublin.

DECEMBER 1—Most Rev. Dr. Clune, Archbishop of Perth (Australia) is authorised by Mr. Lloyd George to come to Ireland as an intermediary to arrange a truce. 8—Having interviewed Mr. Michael Collins and other members of the Irish Ministry, Archbishop Clune returns to London. 10—Mr. Lloyd George in the House of Commons refers to the recent suggestions for an Irish truce, announces the resolution of the Government to go on with the Government of Ireland Bill and to introduce martial law. Martial law proclaimed in the counties of Cork, Kerry, Limerick and Tipperary. 12—Some of the principal streets and buildings in Cork city, including the City Hall, destroyed in reprisal for an ambush of Auxiliary Police outside the city. The damage estimated at £3,000,000. 16—A formula for a truce suggested by the British Executive in Ireland. 22—Archbishop Clune, having returned to Ireland at the desire of Mr. Lloyd George and interviewed Mr. Griffith and other Irish Ministers, again sees the Prime Minister. 23—The Government of Ireland [Partition] Bill becomes law. 31—Archbishop Clune informed that the British Government has decided not to go on with the negotiations for an Irish truce. 25—President de Valera arrives in Ireland from the United States.

1921

JANUARY 1—" The policy of authorised reprisals came into force " [1061, p. 288]. 3—Regulations to be observed by householders and others in the martial law areas published. 4—Martial law proclaimed in Clare, Kilkenny, Waterford and Wexford. 21-25—Dáil Eireann (private sessions).

FEBRUARY 4—Speeches by Sir Edward Carson and Sir James Craig on the partition of Ireland proposals. 11—General Sir C. F. N. Macready, in the Court of King's Bench, Dublin, exhibits an affidavit claiming that a state of war exists in certain Irish districts. 12—A letter sent from President de Valera to British Members of Parliament. 15—Mr. Lloyd George in the House of Commons refers to the Irish truce negotiations of December, 1920.

MARCH 7—Murder of Mr. G. Clancy, Mayor of Limerick, and Mr. M. O'Callaghan, T.D., ex-Mayor. 11—Dáil Eireann (private session); a boycott of Belfast goods, sanctioned by the Dáil in 1920, stated to have " made great progress." 26—Offices of " The Irish Bulletin " in Dublin discovered by Auxiliary Police and documents, records, duplicating machines, etc., removed. [The issue of the " Bulletin " was continued without interruption from other premises]. 31—Report of the American Commission on conditions in Ireland published in Washington and London.

APRIL 4—An interview given to Press representatives, " President de Valera states the national position " published in " The Irish Bulletin." 25—Statement from Sir James Craig to the Unionists of the six counties published.

MAY 2—Viscount FitzAlan sworn in as Lord Lieutenant of Ireland. 4—President de Valera meets Sir James Craig. 10—Dáil Eireann (private session) : " On the motion of the President it was decided that the Parliamentary Elections which are taking place be regarded as elections to Dáil Eireann." 13—Nominations for the two Parliaments in the areas established by the Government of Ireland Act—" Northern Ireland " and " Southern Ireland." All the Sinn Féin candidates returned without opposition in " Southern Ireland." 24—Elections in " Northern Ireland " (Candidates returned : Unionists 40, Sinn Féin 6, Nationalists 6). 24—A statement, " President de Valera on Ireland's demands " published in " The Irish Bulletin." 25, 30—Mr. Lloyd George states that new military offensive measures, including the extension of martial law, are to be taken in Ireland.

JUNE 4—Statement by Sir James Craig published. 7—Preliminary meeting of the Parliament of Northern Ireland; the Hon. Hugh O'Neill elected Speaker of the House of Commons and Sir James Craig Prime Minister. 10—Rioting on a large scale again begins in Belfast and is accompanied during the next few months by great loss of life, damage to property, and the expulsion of many people from their homes. 21—Viscount Birkenhead, Lord Chancellor, announces that " large bodies of troops " are to be sent to Ireland. 22—President de Valera arrested in Dublin and released on the following day. 23—Speech by H.M. King George V to the Parliament of Northern Ireland is interpreted as foreshadowing a more conciliatory Irish policy. 24—Mr. Lloyd George invites President de Valera and Sir James Craig to attend a conference in London. 30—Mr. A. Griffith and other members of Dáil Eireann released from prison.

JULY 4—President de Valera discusses the situation with representatives of the "political minority" (the Southern Unionists). 5—President de Valera meets General Smuts. 9—Order from the Chief-of-Staff Óglaigh na hEireann to the officers commanding all units to suspend hostilities from the 11th. 11—The Truce agreed to by the Irish and British military representatives comes into operation. 14-21—A series of meetings between President de Valera and Mr. Lloyd George held in London at the end of which the announcement is made: "A basis for a formal conference has not yet been found." 18—Sir James Craig states that "it now merely remains for Mr. de Valera and the British people to come to terms regarding that area outside that of which I am Prime Minister." 20—"Proposals of the British Government for an Irish settlement" forwarded to President de Valera. 26—Decision of the Master of the Rolls that the British military courts in Ireland have "no legal status whatever in British law."

AUGUST 1—Irish Labour Party and Trade Union Congress assures the Dáil Ministry of unqualified support. 4—A letter from General Smuts to President de Valera published. 15—The correspondence between President de Valera and Mr. Lloyd George published. 15-16—First session of the Second Dáil (elected in May, 1921). Professor E. MacNeill elected Speaker; the terms of settlement offered by the British Government rejected. 18-31—Dáil Eireann in session. 26—Mr. E. de Valera re-elected President and a new Ministry selected. 31—Memorials on behalf of the Nationalist majorities of Tyrone and Fermanagh presented to the Dáil by a deputation, which protests against the inclusion of these counties within the jurisdiction of the Belfast Parliament.

SEPTEMBER 6—Five plenipotentiaries selected by Dáil Eireann "in view of a possible conference." 7-19—Further correspondence follows Mr. Lloyd George's invitation to Irish representatives to attend a conference at Inverness; the invitation is cancelled. 20—Parliament of Northern Ireland meets. 29—Mr. Lloyd George issues "a fresh invitation to a conference." 30—President de Valera accepts on behalf of Dáil Eireann.

OCTOBER 11—First meeting of the Anglo-Irish Conference held in London. 27-28—Thirteenth Ard-Fheis of Sinn Féin. 31—Debate in the House of Commons on the Irish negotiations.

NOVEMBER 11—Cabinet of Northern Ireland meets in London to consider the British Government's Irish proposals. 17—Unionist Party Conference held at Liverpool decides to support the British Government in continuing the negotiations. 25—Dáil Eireann in session. 29—Statement on the negotiations by Sir James Craig in the Parliament of Northern Ireland.

DECEMBER 6—"Articles of agreement for a Treaty between Great Britain and Ireland" signed in London. 19—Both Houses of Parliament "confirm and ratify" the Treaty. JANUARY 7, 1922—The Treaty approved by Dáil Eireann.

CONTENTS

	PAGE
INTRODUCTION	VII
CHRONOLOGY	XXVII
BIBLIOGRAPHY OF IRISH HISTORY :	
1. GENERAL AND INTRODUCTORY	1
2. FROM THE HOME RULE BILL (1912) TO 1916	35
3. THE INSURRECTION OF 1916	74
4. FROM 1916 TO THE GENERAL ELECTION (1919)	91
5. DÁIL ÉIREANN (1919–1921)	117
INDEX	165

BIBLIOGRAPHY OF IRISH HISTORY,
1912-1921

1. (GENERAL AND INTRODUCTORY.)

1. ABERDEEN (John Campbell GORDON and Ishbel Maria) 1st *Marquess and Marchioness of Aberdeen and Temair:* "We twa," reminiscences of Lord and Lady Aberdeen. 354 pp. illustr. 8vo. London, Collins, 1925.
   Lord Aberdeen was Lord-Lieutenant of Ireland in 1886 and 1906–1915.

Agriculture, *see* 40–43 (Department . . .).

All for Ireland League, 1910–1918, *see* 81 (Healy, T. M.); 150 (O'Brien, W.); 206 (O'Sheehan, D.).

1a. ANDERSON (Robert A.): With Horace Plunkett in Ireland. 293 pp. portrs. 8vo. London, Macmillan, 1935.

Ancient Order of Hibernians, *see* 10c (Bergin, J. J.) and Irish Parliamentary Party.

2. ANNUAL REGISTER, The, 1912–1921: A review of public events at home and abroad. London, Longmans, [10 vols. 1912–1921].
   Summaries of Irish events as they affect British politics are included.

3. ARMOUR (*Rev.* James Brown): Contemporary Ireland and the religious question. (II) . . . A Presbyterian view. In *The new Irish Constitution,* ed. by J. H. MORGAN, pp. 462–471. London, 1912.

3a. ARMOUR (W. S.): Armour of Ballymoney . . . with a foreword by Robert Lynd . . . 396 pp. pls. 8vo. London, Duckworth, 1934.
   The Rev. J. B. Armour, of Ballymoney, Co. Antrim, was for many years a leading figure in the Presbyterian Church. He opposed the policy of Sir Edward Carson and held that the Presbyterian Church in Ireland as a body should not identify itself with the Unionist or any other party.

Army (British), *see* Curragh Army Incident (1914); Recruiting (1914–1918); Connaught Rangers Mutiny (1920); 262 (Wilson, *F. M, Sir* H.); 415, 416 (Macready, *Gen. Sir* C. F. N.); 585 (Maxwell, *Gen. Sir* J.); 890 (Mahon, *Gen Sir* B.); 1136 (French, *F.M. Earl*). *See also* Sects. **1916**; **1916-1918**; **1919-1921**.

Asquith (Herbert Henry), *see* 168 (Oxford and Asquith, 1st *Earl of*).

4. ASTON (E. A.) : Irish national finance, past, present and future. Illustrated by ten coloured diagram tables. 36 pp. 8vo. Dublin, Sealy, Bryers and Walker. Sept., 1911.

5. AUSTRALIA, COMMONWEALTH OF, 1912–1921 : Parliamentary debates.
Occasional references to the Irish political situation.

6. BARKER (Ernest) : Ireland in the last fifty years (1866–1916). 108 pp. 8vo. Oxford, Clarendon Press, 1917.

7. —— Ireland in the last fifty years, 1866–1918 . . . Second and enlarged edition. 148 pp. Oxford, Clarendon Press, 1919.

8. BARR BUADH, An, 1912. 16 Márta, 1912 ; 25 Bealtaine, 1912.
" Do sheinn Fionn an Barr Buadh
Is do ghairm fó luas a throm-shlogh."
Ar n-a chlóbhualadh do P. Cúirtéis.
Edited by Pádraic MacPiarais, who wrote many of the articles. Éamonn Ceannt, Peadar Ó Maicín and Cathal Ua Seanain also were frequent contributors. A preliminary notice in *Irish Freedom* (March, 1912) announces : " *An Barr Buadh* will advocate the political independence of Ireland and will preach the elementary political truth that the liberty of a people can be guaranteed only by its readiness and ability to vindicate it in arms. *An Barr Buadh* will not be identified with any existing organisation. It will be friendly and tolerant, though candid, in its criticism of Irish leaders and parties, and will aim at uniting all Irish forces in a progressive national movement, whether under Home Rule or in its absence."

9. BARTON (*Sir* Dunbar) *1st Bart.* : Timothy Healy, memories and anecdotes. 128 pp. frontisp. 8vo. Dublin, Talbot Press, 1933.
Judge of the Chancery Division, Ireland, 1904–1918.

9a. BATES (Jean Victor) : Sir Edward Carson, Ulster leader . . . Introduction by the Rt. Hon. A. J. Balfour, and foreword by Lt.-Col. Sir James Craig, Bart., M.P. 26 + 50 pp. portr. 8vo. London, Murray, 1921.

10. BÉASLAÍ (Piaras) : Michael Collins and the making of a new Ireland. Vol. I. 15 + 458 pp. Vol. II. 484 pp. illustr. 8vo. Dublin, Phoenix Publishing Co., 1926.
The author, a friend and colleague of Michael Collins, was prominent for many years in the Gaelic League, took part in the 1916 rising, held high rank in Óglaigh na hÉireann and was a member of Dáil Éireann. He was editor of *An t-Óglách* (*see* 1287). Quotes from unpublished documents.
This work is especially valuable for its account of the reorganisation of Óglaigh na hÉireann (the Irish Volunteers, later also known as the Irish Republican Army) after 1916, the establishment of Dáil Éireann (1919), the raising of the Dáil Internal Loan (directed by Michael Collins as Minister of Finance) and the organisation of the departments of national government, 1919–1921.
See also 242.

10a. BEGBIE (Harold) : The lady next door. 330 pp. pls. 8vo. London, Hodder and Stoughton, [1912].
A tour of Ireland. Shows sympathy with the national aspirations.

10b. BELFAST INDUSTRIAL DEVELOPMENT ASSOCIATION, 1909–1914 : [Annual reports. Belfast, 1909–1914].
Mr. Alec G. Wilson acted as honorary secretary to the association, the object of which was " to promote the sale of Irish manufactures and to encourage local industries." The last meeting was held on August 5th, 1914.

10c. BERGIN (James J.) : History of Ancient Order of Hibernians. 9 + 88 pp. illustr. 8vo. Dublin, Ancient Order of Hibernians, [1910].

> With an introduction by the National President of the organisation (Mr. Joseph Devlin).

11. BIRKENHEAD (Frederick Edwin SMITH) *1st Earl of :* Contemporary personalities. 326 pp. 8vo. illustr. London, Cassell, 1924.

> Includes studies of Lord Carson and T. M. Healy.

Bishops of Ireland, *see* 116 (Logue, Michael, *Cardinal Archbp.*) ; 228 (Walsh, William, *Archbp.*) ; 801 (O'Dwyer, Edward *Bp.*) ; 815 (Finlay *Rev.* P.) ;' 900 (Marlowe N.) ; 1027.

11a. BLUNT (Wilfrid Scawen) : My diaries : being a personal narrative of events, 1888-1914. With a foreword by Lady Gregory. 906 pp. portr. 8vo. London, 1932.

> Many references to Ireland : Home Rule, the Curragh (1914), etc. Says : " I have always been a Fenian in my sympathies." Records conversations with John Dillon, and prints four letters from Sir Roger Casement on the Irish Volunteers (May, 1914).

11b. BONN (Moritz Julius) : Irland und die irische Frage. 8 + 268 pp. 8vo. München und Leipzig, 1918.

11c. BROOKS (Sydney) : The new Ireland. 113 pp. 8vo. Dublin, Maunsel, 1907.

> Chapters on Sinn Féin, the Gaelic League, the industrial revival, etc.

Brugha (Cathal), *see* 10 (Béaslaí, P.) ; 160 [O'Kelly, J. J.] ; 594.

> Took part in the 1916 rising ; member of the Executive Com. of Sinn Féin 1917 ; Chief of Staff of the Irish Volunteers 1917-1919 ; appointed " President of the Ministry *pro. tem.*" at the first session of Dáil Éireann, January, 1919. Secretary (Minister) for Defence, April, 1919-January, 1922.

✓**12.** BURNS (Elinor) : British Imperialism in Ireland. 66 pp. 8vo. Dublin, Workers' Books, 1931.

> A survey of modern Irish history from an advanced Labour viewpoint.

12a. BUTLER (Mathew) : Eamon de Valera, a biographical sketch. . . . With preface by Alan Downey. 40 pp. 8vo. Waterford, *Waterford News*, 1932.

> Repr., with some additions, from the *Waterford News*.

Canada (Irish cause in), *see* 1214 (Keane, Patrick) ; 1250 (Magennis, *Rev.* P. E.). *See also* 457 (*Orange lodges*).

Carson (*Sir* Edward Henry) *Baron, of Duncairn, see* 9a (Bates, J. V.) ; 11 (Birkenhead, *1st Earl of*) ; 25 (Colvin, J.) ; 37 (Cushendun, *1st Baron*) ; 112 (Leech, H. B.) ; 133 (Marjoribanks, E.) ; 223 (Ulster Unionist Council).

> M.P., Dublin University, 1892-1918, Duncairn division, Belfast, 1918-1921 ; Chairman of the Irish Unionist Party in the House of Commons, 1910-1915 ; President of the Ulster Provisional Government, 1914 ; Attorney-General for England 1915 ; First Lord of the Admiralty, 1917 ; Member of the War Cabinet without portfolio 1917-1918.

See also Ulster and Sects. **1912-1916** ; **1916-1918** ; **1919-1921**.

Casement (*Sir* Roger David), *see* 73 and Sects. **1914-1916   1916**.

13. Census of Ireland, 1911: General Report, with tables and index. 604 pp. 4to. H.M.S.O. 1913.

14. —— Area, houses, and population: also the ages, civil and conjugal condition, occupations, birthplaces, religion and education of the people. 4to. H.M.S.O.

For criticism and analysis *see* 57 (Gannon, *Rev.* P. J., *S.J.*); 209 (*Sinn Féin*, 1913–1914); 217–218 (Thompson, *Sir* W., *Registrar-General of Ireland*).

15. Childers (Erskine): The framework of Home Rule. 18 + 354 pp. 8vo. London, Arnold, 1911.

Notable for its examination of Anglo-Irish finance and historical survey of the relations of Ireland with each of the British Dominions. Advocates "a definite scheme of government for Ireland" on Dominion lines.

16. ——: The Home Rule Bills of 1886 and 1893 compared and explained. 8 pp. 8vo. London, Irish Press Agency, [1911].

Acting-Director of Publicity to the Dáil Ministry, 1921; Secretary to the Irish delegation in London, 1921; T.D., Wicklow, 1921–1922. *See also* 278–82, 1056–60.

17. Claiḋeaṁ Soluis, An. Márta 18, 1899—Eanair 5, 1918. Pr. for the Gaelic League at An Cló-Ċumainn; from 1907–1913 by "Clóḃuailteann Muinntir Ḋollard"; from 1913–1918 by Muinntir Caṫail. Published at 24 Upper O'Connell Street (later at 25 Parnell Square).

Official journal of the Gaelic League. Edited by Eoin MacNeill. The title was changed in 1903 to An Claiḋeaṁ Soluis agus Fáinne an Lae. In 1903 "it was decided to launch An Claiḋeaṁ Soluis on a new career" with Pádraic MacPiarais as editor and Seágan T. Ó Ceallaiġ as manager. P. Mac P. was editor to July, 1908.

Clan-na-Gael, *see* Irish Republican Brotherhood *and* U.S.A. (Irish organisations).

18. Clarke (Thomas J.): Glimpses of an Irish felon's prison life. With an introduction by P. S. O'Hegarty. 20 + 103 pp. 8vo. Dublin, Maunsel and Roberts, 1922.

First signatory to the Proclamation of Easter Week, 1916. Executed May 3rd, 1916. Recollections of penal servitude 1883–1898, "written mostly at slack intervals in his shop at Great Britain Street." Reprinted from *Irish Freedom*, 1912–1913.

See also 44 (Devoy, John); 92 (*Irish Freedom*); 159 (O'Hegarty, P. S.); *and* Sect. **1916.**

19. Clarkson (J. Dunsmore): Labour and nationalism in Ireland . . . 502 pp. 8vo. New York, Columbia University, 1925 (Studies in History, Economics and Public Law . . . Vol. cxx. Whole number 266).

The author was assisted by Irish political and Labour leaders, Labour officials (who placed at his disposal collections of papers, minute books, etc.) and by relatives of James Connolly. The development of the Labour movement in Ireland, its relations with the political parties and English Trade Unionism, its attitude in the Great War, the rising of 1916 and the Anglo-Irish hostilities up to 1921 are fully considered.

19a. Cleary (*Rev.* H. W.): The Orange Society. 459 pp. 8vo. London, Catholic Truth Society 1899.

Repr. from the tenth Australian edition 1897.

19b. CLEARY (Patrick Scott) : Australia's debt to Irish nation-builders. By P. S. Cleary, Editor of the *Catholic Press*, Sydney . . . . 280 pp. 8vo. Sydney, Angus and Robertson, 1933.

20. [Clery (Arthur Edward)] : The idea of a nation. By Chanel (*pseud.*, i.e., Professor Arthur E. Clery). 76 pp. 8vo. Dublin, Duffy, 1907.

> Was professor of the law of Property and Contracts, University College, Dublin, and a judge of the Supreme Court, Dáil Éireann. Essays expressing the philosophy of Sinn Féin, repr. from the *Leader* (Dublin).

21. —— Dublin essays. 148 pp. 8vo. Dublin, Maunsel, 1919.

22. —— The Gaelic League, 1893–1919. *Studies*. Vol. VII. pp. 398–408. Dublin, Sept., 1919.

> With the text of the proclamation of Field-Marshal Lord French, Lord Lieutenant, suppressing the Gaelic League, along with other national associations.

23. COFFEY (*Rev. Dr.* Peter): James Connolly's campaign against capitalism in the light of Catholic teaching. *Catholic Bulletin*, X. Dublin, March–July, 1920.

> Professor of Logic and Metaphysics, St. Patrick's College, Maynooth

24. COLLINS (Michael) : The path to freedom. 154 pp. portr. 8vo. Dublin, Talbot Press, 1922.

> Took part in the 1916 rising. On the general staff Óglaigh na hÉireann ; Secretary for Home Affairs in the Dáil Ministry, January–April, 1919 ; Minister for Finance, 1919–1922 ; Acting President, November–December, 1920.
> Repr. of a series of articles published in the press in 1922, with introductory notes. Some of the articles review the course of the national struggle, *e.g.*, " Four historic years, the story of 1914–1918," " Collapse of the terror," " Partition Act's failure," " Why Britain sought Irish peace."

—— see 10 (Béaslaí P.) ; 151 (O'Connor, B.) ; 987a (Talbot, H.) ; 68 ; 162 (O'Kelly, J. J.).

See also Sects. **1916–1918** ; **1919–1921.**

24a. COLUM (Pádraic) : The career of Roger Casement. *Dublin Mag.* VI (New Series). pp. 20–25. Oct.–Nov., 1931.

> Personal recollections, with a criticism of Mr. Denis Gwynn's *Life of Casement*.

25. COLVIN (Ian) : The life of Lord Carson. Vol. II. 446 pp. pls. 8vo. London, Gollancz, 1934.

> From 1910 to August, 1914. In continuation of Vol. I by Edward Marjoribanks (*see* 103). The biographer thanks Lord Carson " for patience under examination," Lady Carson for help " in the search for papers," and Lady Oxford and Asquith, Lord Lansdowne, Mr. Richard Law and Mr. Eric Long " for information and for leave to quote from correspondence."
> This work is of special interest for the light which it throws on the secret negotiations of H. H. Asquith with Bonar Law, Lord Carson, and other Unionist leaders in 1913–1914. See *also* 133 (Marjoribanks, E.).

Congested Districts Board, *see* 135 (Micks, W. L.) ; 207 (Sheridan, F. S.).

26. [CONNOLLY (James)] : '98 readings . . . Being a series of reprints of the most important literature, current in Ireland 100 years ago . . . Edited by James Connolly. 80 pp. 8vo. Dublin, 1898.

Published in five fortnightly parts.

27. —— The Irish revolution. 16 pp. 8vo. Dublin, James Connolly Publishing Co., [1923 ?].

28. —— The new evangel. 12 pp. 8vo. Dublin, Socialist Party of Ireland. [1917].

29. —— Erin's hope : the end and the means. 18 pp. 8vo. Dublin, Irish Socialist Republican Party, [1897].

Repr. of five articles, one from the *Shan Van Vocht* (November, 1896) and four from the *Labour Leader* (Glasgow). They were also reprinted soon afterwards in the United States.

29a. —— Erin's hope, the end and the means. 16 pp. 8vo. Rutherglen, P. Walsh, *n.d.*

30. —— The American writings of James Connolly. *An Phoblacht.* N.S. Vol. VI. July 4th–25th, Aug. 8th, Sept. 19th–26th, Oct. 17th, 1931. VII. July 23rd, 1932.

Extracts from the *Irish Harp* (New York), of which James Connolly was founder and editor, edited by his son, R. J. Connolly. They include his criticism of the original Sinn Féin movement (April, 1908), his views on the Irish language, and part of an address to the Irish in America at the time of the Presidential election, 1908.

31. [——] Labour in Irish history. 14 + 216 pp. 8vo. Dublin, Maunsel, 1910.

Published soon after the author's return to Ireland from America. The early chapters first appeared in the *Workers' Republic* (Dublin) in 1898.

32. [——] Labour in Irish history. Cheaper edition. 14 + 216 pp. Dublin, Maunsel, 1914.

33. [——] Labour in Ireland, Labour in Irish history, the re-conquest of Ireland. . . . with an introduction by Robert Lynd. 346 pp. 8vo. Dublin, Maunsel, 1917.

Labour in Ireland had been published in the weekly journal, the *Irish Harp* (New York, 1907-1908). *The reconquest of Ireland*, published in 1915, was his last book.

34.—— Labour, nationality and religion : being a discussion of the Lenten Discourses against Socialism delivered by Father Kane, S.J. in Gardiner Street Church, Dublin, 1910. 66 pp. 8vo. *n.p.*, [1910 ?].

35.—— Connolly souvenir, 1919. James Connolly birthday celebration. Mansion House, Dublin, June 5th, 1919. 20 + 4 pp. 8vo. Dublin, Cumannact na hÉmeann [Socialist Party of Ireland], [1919].

Extracts from his songs and other writings.

—— *see* 19 (Clarkson, J. D.) ; 23 (Coffey, *Rev.* P.) ; 46b (Dublin Trades Union) ; 127 (MacKenna, *Rev.* L. J.) ; 152 (O'Connor, G.) ; 199 (Ryan, D.) ; 203 (Ryan, W. P.).

See also Sects. **1912-1916** ; **1916**.

Acting-General Secretary to the Irish Transport and General Workers' Union ; Commandant-General of the Irish Citizen Army ; signatory to the Proclamation of Easter week, 1916. Executed, May 12th, 1916.

Many of Connolly's writings in the *Irish Harp*, the *Shan Van Vocht*, the *Irish Worker*, etc., were reprinted after 1921 in the official weekly journals of the Irish Transport and General Workers' Union ; the *Voice of Labour* and later the *Irishman*. The following brief biographical notices have also been published in weekly papers : " Some personal memories of Connolly " by Cathal O'Shannon (*Voice of Labour*, May 10, 1924); " James Connolly as I knew him " by Constance Markievicz (The *Nation*, N.S., No. 1, Dublin, 1927) ; " James Connolly, the story of the commencement of his life in Dublin " by William O'Brien (*The Irishman*, N.S. Vol. II. No. 19. May 12, 1928).

Cooper (Bryan Ricco), *see* 195a (Robinson, L.).

36. CORK INCORPORATED CHAMBER OF COMMERCE AND SHIPPING, 1913-1921 : [Annual reports of the Council] : Proceedings of the annual general meeting, statement of accounts, list of members . . . Cork, 1914-1922.

The annual reports review the progress of Irish industry and commerce with special reference to the city of Cork. Reference is made to the Irish Convention (Report for 1917) and the finance of the Government of Ireland Act (Report for 1920). Correspondence with Mr. Lloyd George, Sir Hamar Greenwood and General Strickland on the burning of the city by British forces is given in the reports for 1920 and 1921.

36a. CORK INDUSTRIAL DEVELOPMENT ASSOCIATION, 1909-1916 : [Annual reports. Cork, 1909-1916].

Craigavon (*Sir* James CRAIG) *1st Viscount*, see 9a ; *and* Ulster.

Member of the Ulster Unionist Council and of the Ulster Provisional Government, 1914. Prime Minister of Northern Ireland since June 7, 1921.

36b. CREEL (George) : Ireland's fight for freedom, setting forth the high lights of Irish history. 199 pp. illustr. 8vo. New York, Harper, 1919.

37. CUSHENDUN (Ronald John McNEILL) *1st Baron* : Ulster's stand for the Union. 310 pp. illustr. 8vo. London, Murray, 1922.

An authoritative account of the Unionist movement in Ulster from 1910 to 1921. The author says : " Having been myself, during the most important part of the period reviewed, a member of the Standing Committee of the Ulster Unionist Council, and closely associated with the leaders of the movement, I have had personal knowledge of practically everything I have had to record." He has consulted the minute books and verbatim reports of the Council, letters and papers placed at his disposal by the Marquess of Londonderry and **Lord** Carson, and shorthand notes made by Mr. T Moles, M.P., of the proceedings of the Irish Convention (1917).

38. D'ALTON (*Rt. Rev. Mgr.* Edward A.) : History of Ireland . . . Half-volumes VII and VIII. Ireland since 1906. 454 pp. 8vo. illustr. London, Gresham Publishing Co., 1925.

39. DENNIS (Alfred) : A memory of Patrick Pearse. *Capuchin Annual*, 1934. pp. 181-185. Dublin, Father Mathew Record Office, Nov., 1933.

40. DEPARTMENT OF AGRICULTURE AND TECHNICAL INSTRUCTION FOR IRELAND, 1902-1921. Agricultural statistics, Ireland. Return of prices of crops, live stock and other agricultural products. 8vo. H.M.S.O. 1902-1921.

41. ——, 1912-1921 : Report on the trade in imports and exports at the Irish ports during the year ended 31st December . . . 8vo. H.M.S.O. [The Report for the year ended 31st December, 1921 was published by the Stationery Office, Dublin, 1923].

> The Reports were based upon a system of voluntary returns, the inadequacy of which is explained in the introductory remarks by the compiler. The chief sources were the shippers' consignment notes, " which contain only sufficient information to ensure correct freight and harbour charges and correct delivery of the goods."
> The Irish Returns Order (1918) and the Irish Returns Order (1921) required ship-owners engaged in the cross-channel trade to furnish compulsory returns of the quantities of certain specified articles shipped or unshipped at Irish ports to or from Great Britain. Returns were often refused or imperfectly rendered in the early years, but as the value of the Reports began to be realised, better returns were furnished and the figures for earlier years checked.

42.—— Agricultural statistics with detailed report for the year . . . H.M.S.O. 8vo. 1901-1921.

> Published yearly. These statistics elaborate and give final precision to figures of which preliminary summaries had already been published in general abstracts, showing the acreage under crops and the number of livestock in each county and province. They also furnish particulars of the number, size and distribution of agricultural holdings.

43. —— Annual General Report for the year . . . 8vo. H.M.S.O., [ ].

43a. —— Banking, railway and Shipping statistics, Ireland, 1912-1917. 8vo. H.M.S.O. 1913-1918.

> The Irish banking statistics for each year, 1909–1921, will be found in the Statistical Abstract, 1933 (Stationery Office, Dublin).

De Valera (Eamon), *see* 27a (Butler, M.) ; 51 (Dwane, D.) ; 71 (Gwynn, D.) ; 154 (Ó Faoláin, S.).

> Took part in the 1916 rising. President of Sinn Féin and President of the Irish Volunteers, October, 1917. Príomh-Aire (President) from April, 1919 to January, 1922 (Elected by Dáil Éireann and re-elected in August, 1921).

See also Sects. **1916** ; **1916-1918** ; **1919-1921**.

Devlin (Joseph), *see* 10c (Bergin, J. J.), 224 (United Irish League), and Irish Parliamentary Party.

> M.P. Kilkenny, 1902–1906; W. Belfast 1906–1929; Fermanagh and Tyrone, 1929–1935; M.P. W. Belfast in Parliament of Northern Ireland 1921–1929; Central 1929–1935; General Secretary, United Irish League; National President, Ancient Order of Hibernians.

44. DEVOY (John): Recollections of an Irish rebel: The Fenian movement: its origin and progress: methods of work in Ireland and in the British army: why it failed to achieve its main object, but exercised great influence on Ireland's future. Personalities of the organisation. The Clan-na-Gael and the rising of Easter Week, 1916. 492 pp. 8vo. illustr. 8vo. [New York, Charles P. Young Co., 1929].

> John Devoy (1842–1928) took a prominent part in the Fenian movement and for his work in 1865 was described by William O'Brien (*Recollections*) as " perhaps the most dangerous enemy of England in the entire Fenian body." He was one of the chief influences in the councils of " reorganised Fenianism," 1871–1916. The later chapters are of great importance for the Irish-American side of the 1916 rising.
> Details given of the Irish Volunteer Fund, of interviews with Count Bernstorff (German Ambassador to the U.S.), Sir R. Casement's mission, the Irish Race Convention (March, 1916) and the plans of the " Revolutionary Council " (the seven men who signed the Proclamation in April, 1916).

Dillon (John), *see* 793 and Irish Parliamentary Party.

> M.P. Tipperary, 1880–1883; E. Mayo, 1885–1918; Chairman of the Irish Parliamentary Party, 1918.

44a. [DONNELLY (Mary)]: The last post: Glasnevin cemetery. Being a record of Ireland's heroic dead in Dublin city and county . . . [Compiled by Mary Donnelly]. illustr. 94 pp. 8vo. Dublin, National Graves Association, [1932].

> Biographical notes on men who died in the national struggle since 1916 and in earlier periods.

45. DONOVAN (T. M.): A popular history of East Kerry. 230 pp. p!s. 8vo. Dublin, Talbot Press, 1931.

> Contains a brief account of Sinn Féin and the Irish Volunteers in East Kerry.

46. DUBLIN CHAMBER OF COMMERCE, 1912-1921: Report of the Council of the Dublin Chamber of Commerce (incorporated) for the year 1912 to the members of the Association. 58 pp. 8vo. Dublin, 1913.

> Published each year. The reports refer to many matters of general Irish interest—trade, banking, transport, legal reforms, industry, the effects of the European war, etc. They contain political comments with particular reference to disturbances in the city of Dublin.

46a. DUBLIN INDUSTRIAL DEVELOPMENT ASSOCIATION, 1906-1918: [Annual reports].

> The Association " was inaugurated for the purpose of promoting the sale of Irish-made goods, and advancing the interests of Irish manufacturers in every possible way, acting in sympathy with the kindred other bodies which have been established throughout the country" (First Annual Report).

46b. DUBLIN TRADES UNION AND LABOUR COUNCIL : May-day celebration, May 12th, 1929. James Connolly commemoration souvenir. 32 pp. illustr. 8vo. Dublin, McParland and Hall, [1929].

47. DUNGANNON CLUB, The : To the whole people of Ireland, the manifesto of the Dungannon Club, Belfast. [By Bulmer Hobson]. 8 pp. 8vo. Belfast, 1905.
With the constitution of the Club.

47a. DUNGANNON CLUBS, 1906 : Manifesto to the whole students of Ireland, issued by the Dublin students' Dungannon club. 8 pp. 8vo. Dublin, 1906.

48. DUNRAVEN (Windham Thomas WYNDHAM-QUIN) 4*th Earl of* : The crisis in Ireland, an account of the present condition of Ireland and suggestions towards reform. By the Earl of Dunraven, President of the Irish Reform Association. 64 pp. 8vo. Dublin, Hodges, Figgis, 1905.
With the Irish Reform Association's devolution programme.

49. —— The finances of Ireland, before the Union and after. An historical study, by the Earl of Dunraven, K.P. 10 + 156 pp. 8vo. London, Murray, 1912.

✓ **50.** —— Past times and pastimes. Vol. 2. 244 pp. illustr. 8vo. London, Hodder and Stoughton, [1922].
Includes chapters on Irish politics to 1922, with extracts from the author's speeches in the House of Lords.

51. DWANE (David T.) : Early life of Eamonn de Valera. 236 pp. illustr. 8vo. Dublin, Talbot Press, 1922.

Fianna na hÉireann [*also* " na Fianna Éireann "] *see* 135 (Mellows, L.) and 314.

52. FIELD (William) : Irish industry and Treasury tactics. 72 pp. 8vo. Fourth edition. Dublin, Duffy, [1909].
M.P. (Nat.) 1892-1918.

Finance (Irish), *see* 4 (Aston, E. A.) ; 15 (Childers, E.) ; 43a (Banking statistics) ; 46 (Dublin Chamber of Commerce) ; 49 (Dunraven, 4*th Earl of*) ; 88 (Imperial revenue) ; 90–91 (Irish finance) ; 107 (Kettle, T. M.) ; 109 (Leabhar na hÉireann) ; 124a (MacDonnell, *Sir* A.) ; 164 (Oldham, C. H.) ; 179, 181 (Redmond, John) ; 192 (Revenue and Expenditure) ; 205 (Shaw, T. J.) ; 209 (*Sinn Féin*) ; 230 (Welby, R., 1*st Baron*).
See also Sects. **1912–1916** ; **1916–1918** ; **1919–1921**.

54. FINLAY (*Rev.* Thomas A.) *S.J.* : The significance of some recent Irish statistics. By Rev. T. A. Finlay, M.A., President. *Journal of the Statistical and Social Inquiry Society of Ireland*. Part XCIII. Vol. XIII. pp. 17–25.
A paper read on Dec. 20th, 1912.
Professor of Political Economy, University College, Dublin, 1908-1930 ; Vice-President Irish Agricultural Organisation Society.

—— *see also* 1087 (Commission of inquiry into Irish resources).

Fitzgerald (William J.), *see* 226 (VOICE OF IRELAND, The).

55. FITZMAURICE (*Lord* Edmund) 1*st Baron* : Ireland, 1782 and 1912. In *The new Irish constitution*. ed. by J. H. MORGAN. pp. 268–289. London, 1912.

Friends (Society of Friends), *see* 219 (*Times*, The).

56. FYFE (Hamilton) : T. P. O'Connor. 352 pp. illustr. 8vo. London, Allen and Unwin, 1934.

56a. GAELIC AMERICAN, The [1904–   ] : a journal devoted to the cause of Irish independence, Irish literature and the interests of the Irish race. New York.

> Edited by John Devoy. Organ of Clan-na-Gael, the Irish Republican Brotherhood and the Friends of Irish Freedom. An important source of information for the Irish-American side of the republican movement and for the events leading to the 1916 rising.

57. GANNON (*Rev.* Patrick Joseph) *S.J.* : A study of religious statistics in Ireland. *Irish Ecclesiastical Record*. XVII (5th Series). pp. 141–157. Feb., 1921.

> With special reference to Ulster.

58. GOBLET (Yann Morvran) : La frontière de l'Ulster, par Y. M. Goblet. Extrait des *Annales de Géographie*, tome XXXI, 1922 (No. 173 du 15 septembre 1922). [16 pp.]. Paris, Librarie Armand Colin, [1922].

59. GOOD (James Winder) : Irish Unionism. 240 pp. 8vo. Dublin, Talbot Press, 1920. (*Modern Ireland in the making*).

> A survey of Irish Unionism from 1801 to 1920 by an Ulster Protestant, who contends that the Act of Union operated in a manner injurious to Ireland and that the Unionist *régime* during the period " was not only brutal, it was almost incredibly inefficient."

59a. —— Ulster and Ireland. 12 + 294 pp. 8vo. Dublin, Maunsel, 1919. *See also* 825.

60. GORDON (Edith) *Lady* : The winds of time. 280 pp. illustr. London, Murray, 1934.

> Impressions of events in Co. Kerry, 1912–1923.

61. GREEN (Alice Stopford) : Irish nationality. Revised edition. 8vo. 252 pp. London, Butterworth, 1929.

62. —— Irish nationality. By Mrs. J. R. Green. In *The new Irish constitution* ed. by J. H. MORGAN. pp. 217–250. London, 1912.

See also 337a, 828, 1164.

63. [Griffith (Arthur)] : The resurrection of Hungary, a parallel for Ireland. 100 pp. 8vo. Dublin, Duffy ; Gill ; Sealy, Bryers and Walker, 1904.

> Author's note : ' To the reader : The series of articles on the " Resurrection of Hungary" originally appeared in *The United Irishman* during the first six months of the present year. The object of the writer was to point out to his compatriots that the alternative of armed resistance to the foreign government of this country is not acquiescence in usurpation, tyranny and fraud.' Outlines the Sinn Féin programme of abstention from the British Parliament and the summoning of a National Council in Dublin. The first two editions were published anonymously.

64. —— The resurrection of Hungary. 100 pp. 8vo. Dublin : Duffy ; Gill ; Sealy, Bryers and Walker, 1904. [Second edition].

With an appendix, addressed " to the readers of the second edition," in which the author claims that ' no book published in Ireland, within living memory, has been read so widely as " The Resurrection of Hungary." '

65. —— The resurrection of Hungary, a parallel for Ireland, with appendix on Pitt's policy and Sinn Fein. Third edition. 170 pp. illustr. 8vo. Dublin, Whelan, 1918.

With a new preface by the author, dated January 20, 1918 ; his address, outlining the Sinn Féin programme at the first Convention of the National Council on November 28th, 1905, and a series of articles, repr. from *Sinn Féin*, 1911.

65a. —— How Ireland is taxed. [An address delivered before the Central Branch of the National Council, Dublin, September 16, 1907 by Mr. Arthur Griffith]. 16 pp. 8vo. [Dublin, National Council Pamphlets—No. 6, 1907].

65b. —— Jail Journal . . . By John Mitchel, prisoner in the hands of the English . . . [Edited, with a preface, by Arthur Griffith]. 48 + 460 pp. Dublin, Gill, 1913.

66. —— Sinn Féin at work. 12 pp. 8vo. [Dublin, " Nationality," 1917].

An account of the Leitrim election, 1908, with the election address of C. J. Dolan, Sinn Féin candidate, and " letters to the men of Leitrim, 1908 " by Arthur Griffith.

67. —— Thomas Davis, the thinker and teacher, the essence of his writings in prose and poetry, selected, arranged and edited by Arthur Griffith. 288 pp. 8vo. illustr. Dublin, Gill, 1914.

68. —— Arthur Griffith, Michael Collins. 62 pp. illustr. 4to. Dublin, Lester, [1922].

A memorial album, containing appreciations and biographical details.

—— *see* 106 (Kenny, H. E.) ; 109–111 (Leabhar na hÉireann) ; 120 (Lyons, G. A.) ; 161 (O'Kelly, J. J.) ; 209 (*Sinn Féin*) ; 214 (Stephens, J.) ; 225 (*United Irishman.*)
See also Sects. **1912–1916** ; **1916–1918** ; **1919–1921.**

Founder of Sinn Féin ; President, S.F., and, from 1917 to 1922, Vice-President. Appointed Secretary (Minister) for Home Affairs by Dáil Éireann (April, 1919-June, 1920) and Deputy-President June, 1919-December, 1920 ; Minister for Foreign Affairs, 1921–1922 ; President, January, 1922.

69. GWYNN (Denis) : Edward Martyn and the Irish revival. 350 pp. pls. 8vo. London, Cape, 1930.

Patron of Irish literature, music and drama. First President of Sinn Féin (1904–1908).

70. —— The life of John Redmond. 612 pp. illustr. 8vo. London, Harrap, 1932.

" This biography is based chiefly upon the large accumulation of John Redmond's political papers, methodically preserved by him and providing a unique contemporary record of the events and negotiations with which the Irish Parliamentary Party was concerned, from the time of his election as leader of the reunited party in 1900 until his death early in 1918." (Author's Preface).

71. —— De Valera. 286 pp. 8vo. illustr. London, Jarrolds, 1933.

72. —— Patrick Pearse. *Dublin Rev.* pp. 92–105. Vol. 172. London, Jan., 1923.
> Personal recollections by a pupil of Pearse's at St. Enda's, with a critical estimate of Pearse's political work and aims.

73. —— The life and death of Roger Casement. 447 + [7] pp. illustr. and facs. of a copy in Casement's handwriting of the 'treaty' signed between Casement and the German Foreign Office concerning the formation of the Irish Brigade in Germany. London, Cape, 1930.
> For criticism *see* 24a (Colum, P.), and 673 (Monteith, R.).

74. GWYNN (Stephen) *M.P.* : The case for Home Rule, stated by Stephen Gwynn, with an introduction by John E. Redmond. 12 + 160 pp. 8vo. Dublin, Maunsel [1911].
> "This book has been compiled at my request to put together the main arguments against continuance of the present system under which Ireland is governed, and in support of the demand for Home Rule" (John Redmond).

75. HACKETT (Francis) : The story of the Irish nation . . . Drawings by Harald Toksvig. 402 pp. 8vo. Dublin, Talbot Press, 1924.

76. —— Ireland, a study in nationalism. 410 pp. 8vo. Third edition. New York, Huebsch, 1919.
> Written in 1916–1918. Devotes much attention to economics. Sympathetic to the policy of Sinn Féin and Dáil Éireann.

76a. HAGAN (J.) [*Rev.* John] : Home Rule ; l'antonomia irlandese. 91 pp. 8vo. Roma, Bretschneider, 1913.

77. HAMILTON (*Lord* Ernest) : The soul of Ulster. 200 pp. 8vo. London, Hurst and Blackett, 1917.
> A son of the first Duke of Abercorn. Regards the Unionists of Ulster as a distinct colony, superior in civilisation to other Irish people.

78. HAMMOND (John Lawrence) : C. P. Scott of the *Manchester Guardian.* 366 pp. portrs. 8vo. London, Bell, 1934.
> Chapters on Home Rule, 1912–1916, and "Ireland—the last phase," 1919–1921.

78a. HANNAY (*Rev.* James Owen) : Sinn Fein. Albany Review, II. pp. 610–623. London, March, 1908.
> The author, the well-known Irish novelist, "George A. Birmingham" (whose novel, "Spanish Gold," first appeared as a serial in *Sinn Féin*), writes in a sympathetic though critical spirit of the early Sinn Féin movement.

79. HARMSWORTH (Cecil) *M.P.* : The Imperial Parliament. (I) The state of parliamentary business. In *The New Irish Constitution*, ed. by J. H. MORGAN. pp. 373-387. London, 1912.

80. HAYDEN (Mary Teresa) and MOONAN (George A.) : A short history of the Irish people. New and revised edition. 10 + 586 + 26 pp. Dublin, Talbot Press, 1926.

81. HEALY (Timothy Michael) : Letters and leaders of my day. 2 vols. 678 pp. illustr. 8vo. London, Butterworth, 1928.
>The author, first Governor-General of the Irish Free State, writes with intimate knowledge of Irish political events and leaders for fifty years. The letters were written to his brother, Maurice. About half of Vol. 2 is devoted to the period between the third Home Rule Bill (1912) and his appointment as Governor-General. (1922).

>See also 9 (Barton, *Sir* Dunbar) ; 11 (Birkenhead, 1*st Earl of*) ; 150 (O'Brien, Wm.) ; 156 (O'Flaherty, L.) ; 185 (Redmond, John) ; and Sects. **1912-1916** ; **1916-1918**.

82. HENRY (Robert Mitchell) : The evolution of Sinn Fein. 284 pp. 8vo. Dublin, Talbot Press, 1920. (Modern Ireland in the making).
>" A dispassionate and comprehensive account of the developmen tof Irish nationalism since the death of Parnell " (Publisher). The author is Professor of Latin at Queen's University, Belfast.

83. HIGGINS (Patrick) and CONNOLLY (F. V.) : The Irish in America. 96 pp. 8vo. London, Ouseley, 1909. (*The Irish Library*, Vol. 4).

84. HOBHOUSE (Leonard Trelawney) : Irish nationalism and Liberal principle. In *The new Irish constitution*, ed. by J. H. MORGAN. pp. 361-372. London, 1912.
>Prof. of Sociology, London University.

85. HOBSON (Bulmer) : The creed of the Republic. 42 pp. 8vo. Belfast, The Republican Press, 1907.
>I. R. B. (Irish Republican Brotherhood) point of view.

—— see also 44 (Devoy, John) ; 47 (Dungannon Club) ; 92 (*Irish Freedom*) ; 191 (*Republic, The*) ; 211 (" Defensive warfare "), and Sect. **1912–1916**.

86. HOBSON (Bulmer) and O'NEILL (J. J.) : Ireland or Westminster ! Sinn Fein v. Parliamentarianism. Debate in Glasgow between Mr. Bulmer Hobson, Belfast and Mr. J. J. O'Neill, Glasgow. 24 pp. 8vo. Dublin, Irish-Ireland Printing Works, [1908].

87. HULL (Eleanor) : A history of Ireland and her people. Volume II. From the Stuart period to modern times. 488 pp. illustr. 8vo. London, Harrap, 1931.

88. IMPERIAL REVENUE (COLLECTION AND EXPENDITURE) (GREAT BRITAIN AND IRELAND, 1912-1921. Return " relating to Imperial Revenue (Collection and Expenditure) (Great Britain and Ireland) for the year ending the 31st day of March . . ." Ordered by the House of Commons to be printed . . . 22 pp. H.M.S.O.
>This Return was published each year as a parliamentary paper. The statistics for earlier years—since the amalgamation of the Irish and British Exchequers and the financial union of 1819—are reproduced for convenience in each Return. The tables given include : Revenue as collected in Ireland under principal heads ; Details of Tax Revenue in Ireland ; Revenue as collected in Great Britain under principal heads ; Details of Tax Revenue as collected in Great Britain ; Estimated True Revenue, Ireland ; Details of Revenue collected in Great Britain but attributable to Imperial sources ; Estimate of True Revenue, Great Britain ; Expenditure of Ireland ; Expenditure of Great Britain ; Contributions to Imperial services, Ireland and Great Britain (separately).

Industry (Irish), *see* 10b (Belfast Industrial Development Association); 36 (Cork Chamber of Commerce); 36a (Cork Industrial Development Association); 40-43a (Dept. of Agriculture and Technical Instruction); 46 (Dublin Chamber of Commerce); 46a (Dublin Industrial Development Association); 92b (Irish Industrial Development Association); 109-111 (Leabhar na hÉireann); 193 (Riordan, E. J.); 209 (*Sinn Féin*); 558 (Stanuel, C.).
See also Sects. **1912-1916**; **1916-1918**; **1919-1921**.

Ireland, Government of [British administration; reminiscences of former officials, judges, etc.], *see* 1 (Aberdeen, 1*st Marq. of*); Army; 40-43 (Dept. of Agriculture . . .); 93 (Irish Land Commission); 117 (Long, W., 1*st Viscount*); 142-144 (Morgan, J. H.); 148 (O'Brien, R. B.); 153 (O'Connor, *Sir* J.); 195 (Robinson, *Sir* H.); 196 (Ross, *Sir* J.); 197-198 (Royal Irish Constabulary); 219, 1370a (*Times*, The); 418-419 (Magistrates, Ireland); 537 (Royal Commission into . . . the landing of arms at Howth); 714-715 (Royal Commission on the rebellion in Ireland); 1304 (*Dublin Castle*); *See also* Sects. **1912**; **1916**; **1916-1918**; **1919-1921** (Government of Ireland Acts, Royal Commissions, Martial Law, Restoration of Order Act, etc.). For the government of Ireland in 1919-1921 see 1078-1088 (Dáil Éireann).

Ireland to-day, 1913, *see* 219 (*Times*, The).

89. IRISH CITIZEN, The, 1912-1921. For men and women equally the rights of citizenship; from men and women equally the duties of citizenship.
Published weekly from April 12, 1912—January 8, 1916 (Vol. 4. No. 34), afterwards monthly and at irregular intervals. Advocated woman suffrage. Some general political comment. Founded by James H. Cousins; taken over by Francis Sheehy-Skeffington in 1913 (Sheehy-Skeffington memorial number, July, 1916).

90. IRISH FINANCE. Report of the Committee on Irish Finance. Presented to Parliament . . . 34 pp. H.M.S.O., 1912. [Cd. 6153.]

91. —— Committee on Irish Finance. Minutes of evidence taken by the Committee . . . with appendices. Presented to Parliament. 4 + 248 pp. H.M.S.O., 1913. [Cd. 6799].
Under the chairmanship of Sir Henry Primrose. Reviews the whole field of Anglo-Irish finance, including the early Home Rule Bills and the Irish Councils Bill of 1907. Terms of reference:
(1.) To ascertain and consider the financial relations between Ireland and the other component parts of the United Kingdom as they exist to-day, paying special regard to the changes that have taken place both in Revenue and Expenditure since 1896, the date of the Report of the Royal Commission.
(2.) To distinguish as far as possible between Irish Local Expenditure and Imperial Expenditure in Ireland.
(3.) To consider, in the event of Irish local affairs being entrusted to an Irish Assembly, how the revenue required to meet the necessary expenditure should be provided.
The evidence published includes that of leading officials of the British Treasury and of the Government in Ireland. Much attention was devoted to the nature and extent of Irish investments in Great Britain. The Report recommended that the power of levying all taxes in Ireland should rest with the future Irish Government, subject to the reservations of the Tariff Act. This and other suggestions were rejected by the Government. Mr. Asquith, when introducing the Home Rule Bill (April 11, 1912) said: " We have not been able to adopt the Scheme recommended by the Committee, but we have derived the greatest advantage from their conclusions and suggestions."

92. IRISH FREEDOM. Saoirseact na hÉireann. November, 1910—December, 1914. [Monthly]. Pr. by Sealy, Bryers and Walker, Middle Abbey street, Dublin for the Central Publication Committee of the Wolfe Tone Clubs [*pseud.*, *i.e.*, the Irish Republican Brotherhood], and published by the Committee at their office, 7 Synnott Place (5 Findlater Place from Feb., 1911, and 12 D'Olier street from May, 1914). Printed by P. Mahon, Aug.-Oct., 1911 ; by Devereux, Newth and Co. to Feb., 1912, and again by Mahon from March, 1912.

> Published on the 15th of the month until April 1912, then and afterwards on the 1st. Expresses the views of the Irish Republican Brotherhood (I. R. B.). Mr. P. Beaslaí, a member of the editorial committee, says : ' The new blood in the organisation was responsible for the production of " Irish Freedom," the first for many years to preach the principles of separation ' (*Life of Michael Collins*, I, p. 28). The leading article in No, 1 announces a policy of " complete and total separation of Ireland from England."
>
> [Dr. P. McCartan and Mr. P. S. O'Hegarty were the nominal editors in 1910-1911. Dr. McCartan retired in 1911 and his place was taken by Mr. Bulmer Hobson, who had actually been mainly responsible for the editing of the paper from the beginning and who continued to edit it until the summer of 1914. Seán MacDermott and Thomas J. Clarke supervised the last few numbers. All the editorial and unsigned articles (with the exception of one by Dr. McCartan) and many of the signed articles were written either by Mr. Hobson or by Mr. P. S. O'Hegarty. Other contributors included John Devoy, J. W. Good, E. Blythe, T. MacSwiney, P. H. Pearse.
>
> *Irish Freedom* was suppressed under the D. O. R. A. on Dec. 3rd, 1914.

92a. —— The voice of freedom : a selection from *Irish Freedom*, 1910-13. 154 pp. 8vo. Dublin, Freedom Office, 1913.

92b. IRISH INDUSTRIAL DEVELOPMENT ASSOCIATION, 1907-1917 : [Annual reports]. Dublin, 1907-1917.

> " To promote Irish trade and Irish commerce."

93. IRISH LAND COMMISSION, 1881-1920. Accounts of the Irish Land Commission for the year ended 31st March, 1920 and from 22 August, 1881 to 31 March, 1920 ; together with the Report of the Comptroller and Auditor General thereon . . . 18 pp. H.M.S.O., 1920 [H.C. 203].

94. IRISH NATION AND THE PEASANT, The. 1909-10. Weekly. Vol. I. No. 1. (January 2nd, 1909) [Number of *Peasant* 100] to Vol. II. No. 100 (Dec. 3rd, 1910).

> Edited by W. P. Ryan. A continuation of the *Peasant* (1907-1908), and of the *Irish Peasant*, 1905-1906.

Irish Parliamentary Party, *see* 56 (O'Connor, T. P.) ; 81 (Healy, T. M.) ; 95-96 (Irish Press Agency) ; 98-101 (Irish Unionist Alliance) ; 122 (MacDonagh, M.) ; 132 (MacVeagh, J.) ; 150 (O'Brien, W.) ; 166 (O'Malley W.) ; 224 (United Irish League) ; Redmond, John ; Ulster.

See also Sects. **1912-1916** ; **1916** ; **1916-1918**.

95. IRISH PRESS AGENCY. The : What Home Rule means, and other leaflets issued by the Irish Press Agency. 92 pp. 8vo. Dublin, Maunsel, *n.d.*

> Repr. of 12 leaflets and of a speech by John Redmond in Feb., 1909. Among the subjects considered are Local Government, Finance, Land crime in Ireland and in Great Britain.

GENERAL AND INTRODUCTORY

96. —— Leaflets. London, 1908-1911.
> Arguments for Home Rule by members of the Irish Parliamentary Party, addressed mainly to English readers, *e.g.*, Why Home Rule is necessary for England and for Ireland, by Stephen Gwynn, M.P. (No. 16); The Colonies and Home Rule, by Jeremiah MacVeagh, M.P. (No. 23); The "Ulster" bogey, by Jeremiah MacVeagh, M.P. (No. 24).

Irish Republican Brotherhood (I.R..B.), The, *see* 10, 242 (Béaslai, P.); 18 (Clarke, T. J.); 44, 85 (Hobson, B.); 92 (*Irish Freedom*); 113-114 (Le Roux, L.); 159 (O'Hegarty, P. S.); 190 (Reidy, J.); 658 (Lynch, D.); 963 (*Saoghal Gaedhealach, An*).
> For the origin and aims of this organisation *see* the lives and writings of the Fenian leaders—C. J. Kickham, John O'Leary, T. C. Luby, John Devoy, J. O'Donovan Rossa, James Stephens, etc. *See also* in Sect. 1916.

97. IRISH TRANSPORT AND GENERAL WORKERS' UNION, 1918 : Annual report for 1918. 32 pp. 8vo. Dublin, issued by authority of Executive Council, [1918].
> Gives a brief outline of the history of the Union from its foundation in 1909. *See also* Labour movement (Irish).

98. IRISH UNIONIST ALLIANCE, 1886-1918 : Notes from Ireland. Monthly. Dublin, Irish Unionist Alliance. (From 1886 to 1891 publ. by the Irish Loyal and Patriotic Union).
> Published for the use of Unionist speakers and writers. Gives extracts from speeches, statements, pamphlets, newspapers, etc., and lists of cattle-drivings, shootings and other "seditious" activities. collected as arguments to prove the unwisdom of allowing the Irish people to have self-government. Useful indexes and diurnals of Irish events. Valuable for the details of nationalist activities given under such headings as "Footsteps of Sinn Féin."

99. —— The new Home Rule, and its contemporary associations and considerations. 233 pp. 8vo. Dublin, Irish Unionist Alliance, 1906-1907.
> Selections from the publications of the Alliance.

100. —— Pamphlets and leaflets, 1906-1911.
> Typical of the contents are : The new Home Rule Bill and the old objections (No. 62); Lawlessness in Ireland (No. 108); A Fenian glorification in Ireland (No. 127); Redmond's Imperial-Fenian Home Rule Hippodrome (No. 132); Footprints of Ford (No. 152). The propaganda dwells much on the alleged crimes and shortcomings of the Irish people—fearfully increased by the election in England of a Liberal Government—and on the dire consequences which would follow Home Rule.

101. —— Facts of radical misgovernment ; and the Home Rule question down to date. Presented in grouped selections from current publications of the Irish Unionist Alliance. 228 pp. 8vo. Dublin, Irish Unionist Alliance, 1909.

102. —— Ireland and the Union, a short sketch of the political history of Ireland and of her economic and social condition under the Union. 128 + 9 pp. Dublin, Irish Unionist Alliance, [1914].

103. IRISH WORLD, The, and American Industrial Liberator, New York, 1870—.
> One of the principal Irish-American weekly journals. Supported the Irish Parliamentary Party, but withdrew support in October, 1914, and henceforth favoured the more advanced parties. Opposed the Friends of Irish Freedom organisation in the differences which arose in 1920-1921. See 56a, 1137.

Irish Year Book, *see* 109-111 (Leabhar na hÉireann).

104. IRISHMAN, An : Is Ulster right ? A statement of the question at issue between Ulster and the Nationalist party, and of the reasons—historical, political and financial—Why Ulster is justified in opposing Home Rule. 268 pp. 8vo. London, Murray, 1913.
   Mainly historical. The later chapters deal with the 1912 Home Rule Bill.

105. [KENNY (Henry Egan)]: Arthur Griffith. By "Sean Ghall" [*pseud.*, *i.e.*, H. E. Kenny] In The VOICE OF IRELAND (*see* 226, pp. 100-104). Manchester, 1924.

106. KEATING, Joseph : The Tyneside Irish Brigade. In " Great Irishmen in war and politics," pp. 93–146. 8vo. London.

107. KETTLE (Thomas Michael) : Home Rule finance, an experiment in justice. By T. M. Kettle, Professor at University College, Dublin. 96 pp. 8vo. Dublin, Maunsel, 1911.

107a. —— Would the " Hungarian policy " work ? *New Ireland*, XXII. pp. 321–328. February, 1905.

107b. —— A note on Sinn Fein in Ireland. *North American Rev.*, CLXXXVII. pp. 46–59. January, 1908.

Labour movement (Irish) The, *see* 19 (Clarkson, J. D.) ; 27-35 (Connolly, James) ; 97 (I.T.G.W.U.) ; 203 (Ryan, W. P.).
   See also Sects. **1912-1916** ; **1916** ; **1916-1918** ; **1919-1921**.

108. LAW (Hugh Alexander) : Ireland. By the Rev. R. H. Murray and Hugh Law. 286 pp. 2 maps. 8vo. London, Hodder and Stoughton, 1924. (*The Nations of To-day*).
   Chapters XIV-XX (1885-1922) by Hugh Law, M.P. (Nat.) 1902-1918.

109. Leaḃar na hÉireann, The Irish Year Book, 1908. Issued by An Comairle Náisiúnta, The National Council. 348 pp. 8vo. Dublin : Duffy ; Gill ; Sealy, Bryers and Walker, 1908.
   Year-Book of Sinn Féin. " Sé ruo an leaḃar seo-ċeasḃainṫ do ṁuinntir na hÉireann cionnus an fios agus an t-eolas is riaċtanaċ dá réiṁ-imṫeaċt agus dá ġcosainṫ a ṫarraingṫ as imṫeaċtaiḃ na tíre fá láṫair . . .
   " The object of this book is to render available to the whole people of Ireland that information on the affairs of their country which is necessary for their defence and essential for their progress." (Foreword [by Arthur Griffith]). Articles on Irish agriculture, industry, trade, literature, language, history, etc., by writers, who responded to the editor's invitation to " men and women of all parties, classes, and creeds in Ireland, inviting them to deal in the Irish Year Book with those subjects in which they were skilled."

110. Leaḃar na hÉireann, The Irish Year Book, 1909. Issued by An Comairle Náisiúnta. 478 pp. 8vo. Dublin, Duffy; Gill ; Sealy, Bryers and Walker, 1909.
   Arthur Griffith, Chairman, Publication Committee, An Comairle Náisiúnta, explains in the foreword that " the second Year Book had to be written, edited and printed within six months from the issue of the first, in order that it might appear . . . on the eve of a New Year . . . The majority of the articles in the present issue have either not appeared in the first issue or have been re-written " (December, 1908).

111. Leaḃaʀ na hÉiʀeann. The Irish Year Book, 1910. Compiled by An Comairle Náisiúnta, The National Council. 319 pp. 8vo. Dublin, Kevin J. Kenny, 1909.

111a. LEADER, The, a review of current affairs, politics, literature, art and industry. Weekly. September 1, 1900 ——. Pr. by Cahill, Dublin.

> Edited by Mr. D. P. Moran. An " independent weekly review, written from first to last from exclusively Irish viewpoints " (first number).

112. LEECH (H. Brougham) : The continuity of the Irish revolutionary movement : 1848 and 1912. By H. Brougham Leech, LL.D., ex-Regius Professor of Laws, Trinity College, Dublin. 234 pp. 8vo. London, Simpkin, Marshall, Hamilton, Kent, 1912.

> The first edition was published in 1887. Intended to prove the separatist and revolutionary character of all Irish nationalist movements. Used as a text-book by Unionist speakers. Dedicated to the " unswerving and uncompromising leader of the Irish Unionists, the Rt. Hon. Sir Edward Carson," who contributes a commendatory foreword.

113. LE ROUX (Louis N.) : L'Irlande militante. La vie de Patrice Pearse, avec une introduction historique et 15 photographies. 336 pp. 8vo. Rennes, Imprimerie commerciale de Bretagne, 1932.

114. —— Patrick H. Pearse. Adapted from the French of Louis N. Le Roux. Translated into English by Desmond Ryan. 440 pp. 8vo. Dublin, Talbot Press, 1932.

> An account of the preparations for the 1916 rising, the Irish Volunteers, the Irish Republican Brotherhood, the Irish Citizen Army and the differences of opinion between those organisations.

114a. LOCAL GOVERNMENT BOARD FOR IRELAND, 1872–1920. Annual Reports. Dublin, H.M.S.O.

115. LOGAN (James) : Ulster in the X-Rays : a short account of the real Ulster, its people, pursuits, principles, poetry, dialect and humour . . . with an introduction by Lord Ernest Hamilton. 188 pp. London, Blackwell, [1923].

✓116. LOGUE (Michael, *Cardinal*) *Archbp. of Armagh* : Cardinal Logue, Primate of all Ireland : story of a life spent in the service of God and country. 32 pp. 8vo. Dublin, Nugent, [1925 ?].

> Archbishop of Armagh 1887–1924.

117. LONG (Walter) *1st Viscount* : Memories. pls. 380 pp. 8vo. London, Hutchinson, 1923.

> Chief Secretary for Ireland, 1905–1906 ; M.P. (U.) South Co. Dublin' 1906–10. Had charge of the Government of Ireland Bill (1920) in the House of Commons. Chapters on " Ireland," " The fight against Home Rule," and " Ireland again."

118. LYNCH (Arthur) : Ireland : vital hour. 388 pp. 8vo. Portrait and maps. London, Stanley Paul, 1915.

> Chapters on social and economic conditions, Parliament, Ulster, etc. The author, Colonel of the Irish Brigade on the Boer side in the South African war, was M.P. for West Clare, 1909-1918.

119. LYND (Robert): Ireland a nation. 246 pp. 8vo. London, Richards, 1919.
   Chapters on Sinn Féin, the insurrection of 1916, Ulster, Ireland in the Great War, the first meeting of Dáil Éireann, etc. See also 221, 562, 872.

120. LYONS (George A.): Some recollections of Griffith and his times. portr. 76 pp. 8vo.
   From Griffith's return from South Africa (1899) to the Home Rule Bill (1912).

120a. LYSAGHT (Edward E.): Sir Horace Plunkett and his place in the Irish nation. 160 pp. 8vo. Dublin, Maunsell, 1916. (Irishmen of To-day).

121. Macaoṁ Ań: Edited by P. H. Pearse and written by the masters and pupils of St. Enda's school. Imleaḃ. I. Uiṁ. I. Vol. I. No. 1. Meaḋon Saṁṗaiḋ, 1909. Midsummer, 1909. Imleaḃ II. Uiṁ. 2. Vol. II. No. 2. Bealtaine, 1913. May, 1913. illustr. 8vo. Dublin, Kevin J. Kenny, 1909-1913.

MacDermott (Frank), *see* 233 (Williams, B.).

122. MACDONAGH (Michael): The Home Rule movement. 292 pp. 8vo. Dublin, Talbot Press, 1920. (*Modern Ireland in the making*).
   A survey of the movement from Isaac Butt to the death of John Redmond (1918).

123. —— The life of William O'Brien, the Irish Nationalist. A biographical study of Irish nationalism, constitutional and revolutionary. 282 pp. 8vo. illustr. London, Benn, 1928.

124. MACDONNELL (*Sir* Antony) *1st Baron, of Swinford* : Some suggestions concerning the future welfare of Ireland : An address delivered before the Literary and Scientific Society of the Queen's University, Belfast, on February 23rd, 1911 . . . 30 pp. 8vo. Dublin, Independent Newspapers, 1911.

124a.—— The finance of Irish government, a retrospect and a prospect. *Nineteenth Century*, LXXI. pp. 1-23. Jan., 1912.
   Under-Secretary for Ireland, 1902-1908.

124b. —— Irish administration under Home Rule. In *The new Irish constitution*, ed. by J. H. Morgan, pp. 50–81. London, 1912.

125. MACDONNELL (*Sir* John): Constitutional limitations upon the Irish legislature and the protection of minorities. In *The new Irish constitution*, ed. by J. H. MORGAN (See 142, pp. 90–111),
   Professor of Comparative Law in the University of London.

126. MACGARRY (Milo): The splendid years. In the *Nation* (Dublin) January 29-April 23, 1925.
   " A serial history of the principal events which led to the capitulation of the British Parliament in Ireland "—from the opening of Pearse's school, Sgoil Eanna (1908), in which the author was a pupil, to the 1916 rising.

126a.—— Memories of Sgoil Eanna. *The Capuchin Annual*, 1930. pp. 35-41. illustr. Dublin, Father Mathew Record Office, 1930.

127. McKenna (Rev. Lambert) *S.J.* : The teachings of James Connolly. *Irish Monthly*, Vol. 47. pp. 431-440, 479-490, 532-542. Aug.-Oct., 1919.

128. MacManus (Lily) : White light and flame, memories of the Irish literary revival and the Anglo-Irish war. 228 pp. 8vo. Dublin, Talbot Press, 1929.

129. MacManus (Seumas) : The story of the Irish race, a popular history of Ireland. By Seumas MacManus, assisted by several Irish scholars. 720 pp. 8vo. New York, Irish Publishing Co., 1921.

130. MacNeill (Eoin) : Shall Ireland be divided ? 24 pp. 8vo. Dublin. Irish Volunteer Headquarters, [1915]. (Tracts for the Times, No. 2).

A comment, " written ten years ago," on " The Outlanders of Ulster " by Arthur Synan in the *New Ireland Review*, Oct., 1905 (Author's preface, April 2, 1915).
Formerly editor of *An Claidheamh Soluis*. Professor of Early and Medieval History, University College, Dublin since 1909. Chairman of the Prov. Com. of the Irish Volunteers, 1913. Member of the Dáil Ministry 1919-1921 ; Ceann Comhairle (Speaker) 1921-1922.

See also Sects. **1912-1916 ; 1916 ; 1916-1918 ; 1919-1921.**

McNeill (Ronald), *see* 37 (Cushendun, 1*st Baron*).

131. MacSwiney (Terence James) : Rossa. Born 1831, died 1915 ; buried Glasnevin cemetery, Dublin, Sunday, August 1st, 1915 . . . Second edition. 16 pp. 8vo. Dublin, O'Donovan Rossa Funeral Committee, [1915].

131a. —— Principles of freedom. 244 pp. 8vo. New York, Dutton, 1921.
First published in *Irish Freedom*, 1911-12.

132. MacVeagh (Jeremiah), *M.P.* : Home Rule in a nutshell. A pocket book for speakers and electors. With an introduction by the Rt. Hon. Winston S. Churchill. Third edition, revised and enlarged. 92 pp. Sm. 8vo. London, *The Daily Chronicle*, [1911].

132a.—— Religious intolerance under Home Rule. Some opinions of leading Irish Protestants, written for publication in June and July, 1911. (*Second edition*, revised and enlarged). Together with : Where is the intolerance ? being some notes on the record of public bodies in Ireland. London, [1911 ?].

132b. Maloney (William J. M.) : The forged Casement diaries. By William J. Maloney, M.D., LL.D. 269 pp. illustr. 8vo. Dublin, Talbot Press, 1936.

133. Marjoribanks (Edward) : The life of Lord Carson . . . With a preface by the Rt. Hon. Viscount Hailsham. Vol. I. 456 pp. illustr. London, Gollancz, 1932.

See also 25.

134. MARKIEVICZ (Constance Gore-Booth) Madame de : Prison letters of Countess Markievicz (Constance Gore-Booth). Also poems and articles relating to Easter week by Eva Gore-Booth and a biographical sketch by Esther Roper. With a preface by President de Valera. With illustrations. 316 pp. pls. 8vo. London, 1934.
>See also Connolly, J.; Irish Citizen Army; Labour movement; 150 (Ó Faoláin, S.); 314 (Fianna Handbook); 670 and 898.
>
>Took part in the 1916 rising. Secretary for Labour in the Dáil Ministry, 1919-1922.
>Brief biographical notes published in weekly papers include: "Constance Markievicz, a personal sketch" by Hanna Sheehy Skeffington (*An Phoblacht*, June 5th, 1928) and "Memories of Constance de Markievicz," by John Brennan (*An Phoblacht*, July 21st, 1928).

135. MAXWELL (*Sir* Henry): Ulster was right. 328 pp. 8vo. London, Hutchinson, [1934].
>Unionist. The author uses "Northern Ireland" and "the province of Ulster" as interchangeable terms.

135a. MELCHETT (*Sir* Alfred MOND) 1*st Baron* : Colonial forms of Home Rule. In *The new Irish constitution*, ed. by J. H. MORGAN, pp. 412-426. London, 1912.

135b. [MELLOWS (Liam)] : The Irish boy scouts. By an Irish Volunteer officer [*i.e.*, Liam Mellows]. *Gaelic American*. April 14–May 12, June 2-16, Aug. 4, 1917.
>A history of na Fianna Éireann to 1916, with extracts from the writer's diary. See also 434, 671a.

135c. MICKS (William Lawson): An account of the constitution, administration and dissolution of the Congested Districts Board for Ireland, from 1891 to 1923. By William L. Micks, at first secretary and afterwards member of the Board. 276 pp. pls. 8vo. Dublin, Eason, 1925.

136. MIDLETON (St. John BRODRICK) 9*th Viscount*, 1*st Earl of* : Ireland—dupe or heroine 176 pp. 8vo. illustr. London, Heinemann, 1932.
>Reflections on the Irish Convention (1917), Ireland and America, Ireland and Rome, etc. Lord Midleton, a member of the British Government (1900–1905), was one of the chief spokesmen of Irish Unionism at the time of the Treaty.

137. MOLONY (J. Chartres): The riddle of the Irish. By J. C. Molony, Indian Civil Service (retired). 248 pp. 8vo. London, Methuen, 1927.

138. MOLONY (*Sir* Thomas Francis), 1*st Bart. K.C.* : Judiciary, police, and the maintenance of order. In *The new Irish constitution*, ed. by J. H. MORGAN. pp. 157-165. London, 1912.
>Solicitor-General of Ireland in 1912; Lord Chief Justice of Ireland, 1918–1924.

139. MONYPENNY (William Flavelle): The two Irish nations, an essay on Home Rule. 134 pp. 8vo. London, Murray, 1913.
>Correspondent of the *Times* (London). The argument is suggested in the title.

140. MOORE (*Canon* Courtenay): Contemporary Ireland and the religious question. (II) A Church of Ireland view. In *The new Irish constitution*, edited by J. H. MORGAN. pp. 449-461. London, 1912.

141. MORAN (David P.): The philosophy of Irish Ireland. By D. P. Moran. 114 pp. 8vo. Dublin, Duffy, [1905].

> Founder and editor of the *Leader* (Dublin), *which see*. " The articles contain the reflections, the arguments and register the convictions which led up to the starting of the *Leader* " (author's preface). See also 111a.

142. MORGAN (John Hartman): The new Irish Constitution, an exposition and some arguments. Edited on behalf of the Eighty Club by J. H. Morgan, M.A., Professor of Constitutional Law at University College, London . . . 14 + 490 pp. 8vo. London, Hodder and Stoughton, 1912.

143. —— The constitution : a commentary. In above work. pp. 3-49. London, 1912.

144. —— How Ireland is governed. *Nineteenth Century*, LXXII. pp. 568-579. Sept., 1912.

> A survey of the Irish departments of government and their functions.

145. MORRISON (Hugh Smith), *M.D.*: Modern Ulster, its character, customs, politics and industries. 224 pp. 8vo. illustr. London, H. R. Morrison, [1920 ?].

> Unionist and Presbyterian. Chapters on the Orange Institution, the Ulster Volunteer force and the Covenant, Irish Presbyterianism, etc. Details of Orange lodges and Ulster Volunteers in the author's native county (Derry).

145a. NATIONAL ORGANISATIONS IN IRELAND, their origin, development and aims. [Reprinted from " The Outlook "] . . . 64 pp. 8vo. London, " The Outlook," [1907].

> Unionist.

145b. NIVEN (Richard): Orangeism as it was and is . . . 164 pp. 8vo. Belfast, Band, 1899.

146. NORTH-EASTERN BOUNDARY BUREAU, 1922-1923 : Handbook of the Ulster question. 164 pp. maps. 8vo. Dublin, Stationery Office, 1923.

> Contains a large number of statistical tables with maps and diagrams, showing the distribution of population and religious differences in the province of Ulster from the 1911 census, and the " wishes of the inhabitants " in each electoral district, as demonstrated in the Parliamentary elections, 1918-1921.

146b. " O " : Ireland and the British army. By " O " 32 pp. 8vo. National Council Pamphlets—No. 7 [Dublin, 1909 ?]

O'Brien (George), *see* 193 (Riordan, E. J.).

148. O'BRIEN (Richard Barry): Dublin Castle and the Irish people. 444 pp. 8vo. Dublin, Gill, 1909.

> An attempt to answer the question, " Who (or what) rules in Ireland ? " with a survey of the functions of the Chief Secretary for Ireland in the British Cabinet and his relations with his subordinates. Investigates the work and methods of the forty seven boards, offices and departments connected with the administration of Ireland.

149. O'BRIEN (William) *M.P.*: An olive branch in Ireland and its history. 40 + 480 pp. portrs. 8vo. London, Macmillan, 1910.

150. —— The Irish revolution and how it came about. 462 pp. 8vo. Dublin, Maunsel and Roberts, 1923.

> M.P., 1883–1918. A survey of Irish politics from the foundation of the All-for-Ireland League, March 31, 1910, to the truce of July 11, 1921. Especially well-informed on the various proposals and negotiations for Home Rule, 1910–1918. Criticises the Irish Parliamentary Party with much asperity. Sympathetic to the Sinn Féin movement, but disagrees with Sinn Féin as a political programme.

151. O'CONNOR (Bartholomew): With Michael Collins in the fight for Irish freedom. By Batt O'Connor, T.D. 196 pp. 8vo. London, Davies, 1929.

152. O'CONNOR (Gerald): James Connolly, a study of his life and work. 24 pp. 8vo. Dublin, Curtis, [1917 ?].

153. O'CONNOR (*Sir* James): History of Ireland, 1798–1924. Vol. II [1848–1924]. 396 pp. 8vo. London, Arnold, 1925.

> Solicitor-General for Ireland, 1914–1916; Attorney-General, 1916–1918, and Lord Justice of Appeal, 1918–1924. Takes an unfavourable view of the Sinn Féin movement in all its phases.

153a. O'CONNOR (Thomas Power): The Irish in Great Britain. In " Great Irishmen in war and politics," ed. by Felix Lavery. pp. 15–33. 8vo. London, Melrose, 1920.

153b. —— John E. Redmond. *In same work.* pp. 60–80.

> M.P., Galway, 1880–1885; Scotland Division, Liverpool (as Irish Nationalist), 1885–1918. See also 56 (Fyfe, H.).

154. Ó FAOLÁIN (Seán): The life story of Eamon de Valera. 110 pp. 8vo. Dublin, Talbot Press, 1933.

155. —— Constance Markievicz, or the average revolutionary: a biography. 318 pp. pls. 8vo. London, Cape, 1934.

156. O'FLAHERTY (Liam): The life of Tim Healy. 320 pp. 8vo. frontisp. London, Cope, 1927.

> A study of the first Governor-General of the Irish Free State. Chapters XXII–XXVI deal with the events after 1910. The author says in his preface, " I had to approach my subject with a certain childish abandonment."

157. O'HEGARTY (Patrick Sarsfield) : Sinn Féin, an illumination. 56 pp. 8vo. Dublin, Maunsel, 1919. [*As passed by Censor*].

The author was a member of the " National Council " (1902), and of ' the Executives of " Cumann na nGaedheal," the " Dungannon Clubs," and the " Sinn Féin League," by the fusion of which the old " Sinn Féin " organisation was formed,' and a member of the Sinn Féin Executive until 1911. His object is to give an account of the " historical evolution " of Sinn Féin, " to place it in relation to the antecedent history of Ireland." Seven of the eight chapters were written in October, 1917, and passed for publication in November, 1918.

158. —— A short memoir of Terence MacSwiney. By P. S. O'Hegarty, with a chapter by Daniel Corkery. 98 pp. portr. 8vo. Dublin, Talbot Press, 1922.

Written in Dec., 1920. " The memoir is based partly on materials supplied by Mrs. MacSwiney, by Mary and Annie MacSwiney, and by many of Terry's friends in Cork, but largely on my personal recollections of him " (Author's note).

159. —— The victory of Sinn Féin, how it won it, and how it used it. 220 pp. 8vo. Dublin, Talbot Press, 1924. (Modern Ireland in the making).

Reviews the history of the Sinn Féin and Volunteer movements, the 1916 rising, the establishment of Dáil Éireann, the Treaty negotiations of 1921, and carries on the narrative through the subsequent civil war. Stresses the part taken by the Irish Republican Brotherhood in organising the insurrection. The author says : " This book is not a history. The true history of a passionate period such as that dealt with cannot be written by any contemporary."

See also 18, 92, 963, 1288.

160. [O'KELLY (John Joseph)] : Cathal Brugha—as I knew him. By Sceilg [*pseud.*, *i.e.*, J. J. O'Kelly]. *Catholic Bulletin*, XII. pp. 485–496. illustr. Aug., 1922.

161. —— Arthur Griffith : some reminiscences. *Catholic Bulletin*, XII. pp. 560–565. Sept., 1922.

162. —— Michael Collins, an effort to appreciate his complex personality. By Sceilg. *Catholic Bulletin*, XII. pp. 626–634. Oct., 1922.

163. —— Austin Stack, some recollections and associations. By Sceilg. *Catholic Bulletin*, XXIX. pp. 533-549. June, 1929.

The author was Leas Cheann Comhairle (Deputy Speaker) Dáil Éireann, 1919-1921 ; Minister for Irish, 1920-1921 ; Minister for Education, 1921-1922.

164. OLDHAM (Charles Hubert) : The public finances of Ireland. By Professor C. H. Oldham . . . being a paper read in section F of the British Association meeting at Portsmouth . . . 4th Sept., 1911. 16 pp. 8vo. Dublin, *pr.* Dollard, [1911 ?].

165. —— Changes in Irish exports during twelve years. *Journal of the Statistical and Social Inquiry Society of Ireland*. Part XCVII. pp. 541–553, 629–637.

A paper read on April 26th, 1918 ; a second paper read on February 14th, 1919.

See also 453, 1289.

✓ **166.** O'MALLEY (William) : Glancing back, 70 years experiences and reminiscences of press man, sportsman and member of parliament. 294 pp. illustr. London, Wright and Brown.

166a. O'NEILL (Eamonn) : Patrick Pearse : some other memories. *Capuchin Annual*, 1935. pp. 217-222. Dublin, 1934.

166b. ORANGE INSTITUTION, The : Laws and ordinances of the Orange Institution of Ireland, revised and adopted by the Grand Orange Lodge of Ireland. 48 pp. 8vo. Belfast, 1869.

—— *See also* 19a (Cleary, Rev. H. W.) ; 145 (Morrison, H. S.) ; 145 (Niven, R.) ; 208 (Sibbett, R. M.) ; 221 (Ua Fhloinn, R.) ; 434a (Moore, F. F.) ; 572 (Ulster Unionist Council) ; and Ulster.

167. O'RIORDAN (*Rt. Rev.* Michael) : Contemporary Ireland and the religious question. (1) A Catholic view. In *The new Irish constitution*, ed. by J. H. MORGAN. pp. 427-448. London, 1912.

167a. Ó Siotċáin (Seaġán) : Constitutionalism and Sinn Féin. 16 pp. 8vo. [Dublin, *n.d.*]. (Sinn Fein Pamphlets—No. 5).

168. OXFORD AND ASQUITH (Henry Herbert ASQUITH) *1st Earl of* : Speeches ... 320 pp. frontisp. 8vo. London, Hutchinson, [1927].

"Home Rule for Ireland, 1912 " ; " Ireland, 1920 " ; " Ireland, murders and reprisals, 1920-1921."
See also 352, 465-67, 557.

169. PARLIAMENTARY DEBATES, The (Official Report) 1912-1921 : Fifth series. House of Commons, Vols. XXXIV.—149. House of Lords, Vols. XI—XLVIII. H.M.S.O. 1912-1921.

From Feb. 14th, 1912, when the King's speech informed the Lords and Commons that " a measure for the better government of Ireland will be submitted to you " (the third Home Rule Bill) to Dec. 19th, 1921, when both Houses of Parliament signified that " we are ready to confirm and ratify these articles " (*i.e.*, Articles of agreement for a Treaty between Great Britain and Ireland).
The questions, proceedings and debates relating to Irish affairs were also published in a separate form, up to and including the session ending September 18th, 1914.

169a. PARMITER (Geoffrey De C.) : Roger Casement. portr. map. 14 + 376 pp. 8vo. London, Barker, 1936.

170. PAUL-DUBOIS (Louis) : L'Irlande contemporaine et la question irlandaise. 516 pp. 8vo. Paris, Perrin, 1907.

171. —— Contemporary Ireland. With an introduction by T. M. Kettle, M.P. 536 pp. 8vo. Dublin, Maunsel, 1908.
An English translation of above, with notes.
See also 468-470.

172. PHILLIPS (Walter Alison) : The revolution in Ireland, 1906-1923. 16 + 328 pp. 8vo. London, Longmans, Green, 1923.

173. —— The revolution in Ireland, 1906–1923. Second edition. 20 + 348 pp. 8vo. London, Longmans, Green, 1923.

> Unionist. The greater part of the book appeared in the *Encyclopaedia Britannica* (12th edition) "before the Free State had been heard of. When the concluding chapters were written the new government had only just been established."
> The author was allowed, in 1921, to have access "without conditions or censorship of any kind" to British confidential official documents, including police reports, a great mass of which, he states, were destroyed by the British authorities before they handed over Dublin Castle to the Provisional Government in January, 1922. His narrative is based largely on these documents and on the Unionist propaganda published in *Notes from Ireland* (which see). Regards the Treaty of 1921 as "the great surrender."

173a. PEARSE (Mary B.) : The home life of Patrick Pearse. 167 pp. pls. 8vo. Dublin, Gill, 1935.

173b. PEARSE (Pádraic) : The story of a success : being a record of St. Enda's College, September, 1908, to Easter 1916. Edited by Desmond Ryan, B.A. 128 pp. pls. 8vo. Dublin, Maunsel, 1917.

> "This book was edited and completed in compliance with a last wish of Padraic Pearse, that his notes on St. Enda's should be added to and brought up to Easter 1916 by his friend and pupil, Desmond Ryan" (Publisher).

—— *See also* 8 (*Barr Buadh, An*) ; 17 (Claṙḋeaṁ Soluis An) ; 39 (Dennis, A.) ; 72 (Gwynn, D.) ; 113 (Le Roux, L. N.) ; 121 (Macaoṁ, An) ; 126 (McGarry, M.) ; (O Neill, E.) ; 200–202 (Ryan, D.) ; *and see* Sects. **1912–1916** ; **1916**, and, for a Bibliography of Pearse (by P. S. O'Hegarty) the *Dublin Magazine*, July–Sept., 1931, pp. 44-49.

174. PLUNKETT (*Hon. Sir* Horace) : Noblesse oblige, an Irish rendering. 38 pp. 8vo. Dublin, Maunsel, 1908.

> Addressed "more especially to the resident gentry . . . at a time when many of their class are considering whether they will throw in their lot with the country to which they belong, or with some other country where they think they see a brighter prospect for themselves and their families." The author sets forth the reasons "which have led me to the conclusion that there is no better country for an Irishman to live in, or work for, than his own."

See also 1a, 120a, 256, 494, 940, 1308.

175. POLLARD (*Professor* Albert Frederick) : Ireland as a dependency. In *The new Irish Constitution* edited by J. H. MORGAN. pp. 251–267. London, 1912.

176. POLLARD (*Major* Hugh B. C.) : The secret societies of Ireland, their rise and progress. By Captain H. B. C. Pollard, late of the staff of the chief of police, Ireland. 324 pp. 8vo. London, Allan, 1923.

> Credulous and sensational. The author, who was associated with the Dublin Castle *régime* during the Anglo-Irish war, claims to derive some of his information from "papers which came into possession of the authorities after raids, etc., or from confidential official sources."

177. POLLOCK (*Sir* Frederick) : The Judicial Committee and the interpretation of the new constitution. In *The new Irish Constitution*, edited by J. H. Morgan. pp. 81–89. London, 1912.

Primrose (*Sir* Henry), *see* 90–91.

177a. PROPORTIONAL REPRESENTATION: A short account of the movement in favour of Proportional Representation in Ireland during the year 1911, and of the all-Ireland model election held in December, 1911. 24 pp. 8vo. Dublin, Proportional Representation Society of Ireland, 1912. (P.R.I. Pamphlet A).

—— *see also* 431 (Meredith, J. C.); 1016 (Aston, E. A.).

178. REDMOND (John Edward) *M.P.*: Historical and political addresses, 1883–1897. 390 pp. 8vo. Dublin, Sealy, Bryers and Walker, 1898.

179. —— Home Rule, speeches of John Redmond, M.P. Edited, with an introduction, by R. Barry O'Brien. 348 pp. portr. 8vo. London, Fisher Unwin, 1910.

> From the Home Rule Bill, 8th April, 1886, to "Crime in England and Ireland," 23rd February, 1909.

180. —— Irish Protestants and Home Rule. By John E. Redmond, M.P. 16 pp. 8vo. Westminster, Irish Press Agency, [1912?] (Leaflet No. 19).

> A lecture delivered in the Rotunda, Dublin, 29th November, 1886.

181. —— Ireland's financial relations with England: the case stated: impeachment of reckless and extravagant administration.... Address delivered before the Young Ireland branch of the United Irish League... on January 26th 1905. 12 pp. 8vo. [Belfast, *Irish News*, 1905].

182. —— John Redmond accuses England. 8 pp. 8vo. [Dublin, Sinn Féin], 1919.

> Report of a speech in Dublin, August 9th, 1902. Published by *Sinn Féin*.

183. —— What Ireland wants. 16 pp. 8vo. Westminster, Irish Press Agency, [1912]. (Leaflet No. 17).

> Repr. from *McClure's Magazine*, Oct., 1910.

184. —— "Where Parnell stood." What we mean by Home Rule. 14 pp. 8vo. Westminster, Irish Press Agency, [1911?]. (Leaflet No. 20).

> Repr. from "T. P.'s Magazine," Feb., 1911.

185. —— The industrial and commercial aspects of Home Rule: a speech delivered by Mr. John Redmond, M.P., at the City Liberal Club, in London, on November 2nd, 1911. 8 pp. 8vo. London, Irish Press Agency, [1911?] (Leaflet No. 26).

See 70 (Gwynn, D.); 74 (Gwynn, S.); 81 (Healy, T. M.); 150 (O'Brien, W.); 231 (Wells, W. B.); IRISH PARLIAMENTARY PARTY.

See also Sects. **1912–1916**; **1916–1918**.

> M.P., New Ross, 1881–1885; N. Wexford, 1885–1891; Waterford, 1891–1898; Chairman of the Irish Parliamentary Party, 1900–1918

187. REDMOND (William Hoey Kearney), *M.P.* : In memoriam, Major Willie Redmond . . . Souvenir booklet. [94] pp. illustr. 8vo. Dublin.

    M.P., Wexford, 1883–1885 ; Fermanagh, 1885–1892 ; E. Clare, 1892–1917. Killed in action in Flanders with the 16th Irish Division, 1917.

    See also 948. .

188. REDMOND-HOWARD (Louis George) : John Redmond, the man and the demand, a biographical study in Irish politics. By L. G. Redmond-Howard. 352 pp. 8vo. illustr. London, Hurst and Blackett, 1910.

189. —— Sir Roger Casement : a character sketch without prejudice. 64 pp. 8vo. Dublin, Hodges, Figgis, 1916.

190. REIDY (James) : The Irish Republican Brotherhood. In *The Irish Rebellion of* 1916, ed. by M. JOY.

    A brief historical account. See 649.

191. REPUBLIC, The : Vol. I. Nos. 1–23. Dec. 13, 1906—May 16, 1907. Pr. for the " Republican Press," Belfast.

    Edited by Bulmer Hobson.

192. REVENUE AND EXPENDITURE (ENGLAND, SCOTLAND AND IRELAND) Return " showing for the year ended the 31st day of March, [   ]: (1) the Amount contributed by England, Scotland, and Ireland respectively, to the Revenue collected by the Imperial officers ; (2) the EXPENDITURE on English, Scottish and Irish Services met out of such REVENUE ; and (3) the Balances of REVENUE contributed by *England, Scotland*, and *Ireland* respectively, which are available for Imperial Expenditure . . .

    This Return was published each year as a Parliamentary Paper. *See also* FINANCE.

193. RIORDAN (E. J.) : Modern Irish Trade and Industry. By E. J. Riordan, Secretary the Irish Industrial Development Association. With a historical introduction by George O'Brien, Litt.D., M.R.I.A. 336 pp. 8vo. London, Methuen, 1920.

    See also 954.

194. ROBERTS (Edward F.) : Ireland in America. Foreword by Claude G. Bowers. 218 pp. 8vo. New York, G. P. Putnam's Sons, 1931.

    Contains a brief survey of Irish influence in American foreign policy.

195. ROBINSON (*Sir* Henry) : Memories : wise and otherwise. 348 pp. 8vo. illustr. London, Cassell, 1923.

    Vice-President, Local Government Board for Ireland, 1898–1922. Chapters on " the Sinn Féin resurrection," the Black and Tars, etc. The author writes as an advocate of the Dublin Castle *régime*, and condemns " the Treaty surrender."

195a. ROBINSON (Lennox): Bryan Cooper. 188 pp. portr. 8vo. London, Constable, 1931.

> The subject of this biography, an Irish landowner, was Hon. Secretary, Irish Unionist Alliance, 1912-1914; Press Censor, Ireland in 1919. Showed sympathy with Irish nationalism in 1919 and later. Extracts given from an unpublished book which he wrote in 1919: *Ireland under Sinn Féin.*

196. Ross (*Sir* John): The years of my pilgrimage, random reminiscences. By the Rt. Hon. Sir John Ross, Bart., last Lord Chancellor of Ireland. 304 pp. 8vo. frontisp. London, Arnold, 1924.

> " The great office of Irish Lord Chancellor, which had existed since the twelfth century, came to an end on the 6th December, 1922, by the passing of the Statute at that date " (Author).

197. ROYAL IRISH CONSTABULARY AND DUBLIN METROPOLITAN POLICE. Report of the Committee of Inquiry, 1914. Presented to Parliament by command of his Majesty. 36 pp. H.M.S.O., 1914 [Cd. 7421].

198. —— Appendix to the report of the Committee of Inquiry, 1914, containing minutes of evidence with appendices . . . presented to both Houses of Parliament . . . 6 + 386 pp. H.M.S.O., 1914. [Cd. 7637].

> The Committee was set up to inquire into the pay and allowances of the two forces. The evidence and report contain a large mass of important information regarding the constitution, training and duties of the R.I.C., illustrating its civil and military character. Appendices include figures showing the strength and classification of the police force in each county in Dec., 1913, and statistics of promotions, retirements, length of service, pension charges, etc.

See also Sects. **1916** and **1919–1921.**

199. RYAN (Desmond): James Connolly, his life, work and writings . . . with a preface by H. W. Nevinson. 142 pp. 8vo. Dublin, Talbot Press, 1924.

> For a criticism, adverse to Connolly's social philosophy, see the *Irish Rosary*, XXVIII, June, 1924, pp. 432–436, and a reply by Desmond Ryan in the *Voice of Labour* (Dublin), August 16, 1924.

200. —— The man called Pearse. 8 + 130 pp. 8vo. Dublin, Maunsel, 1919.

201. —— Remembering Sion, a chronicle of storm and stress. 308 pp. 8vo. London, Barker, 1934.

> Reminiscences of St. Enda's School, the brothers Pearse, the Irish Volunteers, the Easter Week rising and the later hostilities in Dublin. The author, the pupil and secretary of Pádraic Pearse, took part in the rising.

—— *See also* 114 (Le Roux, L. N.) and 173 (Pearse, P. H.).

202. RYAN (William Patrick): The Pope's green island. 326 pp. 8vo. London, Nisbet, 1912.

202a. —— The Irish labour movement: from the twenties to our own day. 266 pp. 8vo. Dublin, Talbot Press, [1920]. (*Modern Ireland in the making*).

202b. RYNNE (Michael): Die Volkerrechtliche Stellung Irlands. 12 + 435 pp. 8vo. Munchen und Leipzig, Duncker & Humblot, 1930.

> With an introductory sketch of Irish history to 1921.

203. SHAW (George Bernard) : John Bull's other island . . . 60 + 116 pp. 8vo. London, Constable, 1907.
With a preface for politicians.

204. —— John Bull's other island (*The works of Bernard Shaw.* Vol. 11). pp. 182. 8vo. London, Constable, 1930.
With the preface to the Home Rule edition of 1912, the preface for politicians (to the first edition in 1906), and a postscript " twenty-four years later." The author in a new prefatory note says that readers will not lose much by skipping the 1912 preface, as it was " based upon two confident political assumptions that have been not merely disproved but catastrophically shattered." The first was that a British Act of Parliament could not be " dropped into the waste-paper basket " because " the army officers' messes blustered mutinously against it. The second assumption was that Ireland was politically one and indivisible . . . "
He says : " I guessed ahead and guessed wrongly, whilst stupider and more ignorant fellow-pilgrims guessed rightly." Nevertheless, in the postscript, he foresees " a Federal Government of the whole island."

205. [SHAW (Thomas J.)] : The financial relations of Ireland with the Imperial Exchequer. By an Irishman (*i.e.*, Thomas J. Shaw). 48 pp. 8vo. Dublin, Gill, 1911.

206. SHEEHAN (*Captain* Daniel Desmond) : Ireland since Parnell. 328 pp. 8vo. London, Daniel O'Connor, 1921.
M.P. for Mid-Cork, 1901-1906, 1907-1918.

207. SHERIDAN (Francis S.) : The " congested districts " of Ireland and the work of the Congested Districts Board. By Francis S. Sheridan, Barrister-at-Law, Chief Clerk to the Congested Districts Board. Repr. from the Monthly Bulletin of Economic and Social Intelligence. Year VI, No. 2, February, 1915. 28 pp. 8vo. Rome, International Institute of Agriculture, 1915.

208. SIBBETT (R. M.) : Orangeism in Ireland and throughout the Empire. Vol. I. 272 pp. Vol. 2. 352 pp. 8vo. Belfast, Henderson, " Belfast Weekly News," [1914].
An historical survey, 1689-1829.

209. SINN FÉIN : May 5th, 1906—Nov. 28th, 1914 (No. 240. Vol. 5. N.S.). Sinn Féin Printing and Publishing Co., Middle Abbey Street, Dublin [later at 5 Little Green and afterwards 17 Fownes Street].
Succeeded the " United Irishman, a national weekly review," edited by Arthur Griffith. Published summaries each week of the work done by the National Council, the Gaelic League, the Gaelic Athletic Association, the Irish Industrial Development Association, and " all other bodies the object of which is the recreation of an Irish Ireland." The editor contributed largely to the paper, giving special attention to national finance and economics. Poetry, literary criticism and other contributions bearing on Irish history, literature and economic resources frequently appeared, many of them by scholars and writers not identified with the political policy of Sinn Féin.
A daily edition, published in the afternoons at ½d., ran from August, 1909, to January, 1910. (" As a journalistic experiment," the Sinn Féin daily " was a brilliant triumph ; as a business enterprise it was a dismal failure "—C. A. Lyons : *Reminiscences of Griffith*, p. 70). The directors of the weekly and daily editions were Arthur Griffith, Séumas MacManus, Alderman T. Kelly, W. L. Cole, H. Dixon. *Sinn Féin* was suppressed under the Defence of the Realm Act on December 2nd, 1914.

210. SINN FÉIN POLICY, The. *Fortieth thousand.* 36 pp. 8vo. Dublin, Sinn Féin National Council, [1907]. (*National Council Pamphlets*—B).

With the introduction by Arthur Griffith, dated March, 1906, and additional remarks, December, 1907; the speech of Arthur Griffith setting forth the scheme of " national self-development," proposed as the policy of the National Council at its first Annual Convention, held in the Rotunda, Dublin, November 28th, 1905, and the Constitution of the National Council.

211. SINN FEIN (West Belfast branch) 1909: Defensive warfare, a handbook for Irish nationalists. [By Bulmer Hobson]. 64 pp. 16mo. Belfast: The West Belfast Branch of Sinn Féin, 1909.

—— *See also* 20–22 (Clery, A. E.); 57, 58 (O'Hegarty, P. S.); 63–68 (Griffith, A.); 82 (Henry, R. M.); 109–111 (Leabhar na hÉireann); 141 (Moran, D. P.); 216–217 (Sweetman, J.); 225 (*United Irishman, The*); *and see* Sects. **1912–1916**; **1916–1918**; **1919–1921**.

211a. SMITH-GORDAN (Lionel) and Laurence C. STAPLES: Rural reconstruction in Ireland; a record of co-operative organisation. With preface by George W. Russell (A.E.). 14 + 279 pp. London, 1917.

212. SPLAIN (John J.): The Irish movement in the United States since 1911. By John J. Splain, of New Haven, Conn. (*National Vice-President of the Friends of Irish Freedom*). In *The Voice of Ireland,* pp. 225-235. Manchester, 1924.

The work of Clan-na-Gael, the financing of the 1916 rising, the Irish Race Conventions of 1916 and 1918, and the history of the Friends of Irish Freedom. See 226.

213. STACK (Austin): Austin Stack, 1880–1929. 32 pp. portr. 8vo. [Dublin, Fodhla Printing Co., 1930 ?].

Commandant Kerry Brigade, Irish Volunteers, 1915-1916; Minister for Home Affairs, 1920–1922. Short articles on his career.

214. STEPHENS (James): Arthur Griffith, journalist and statesman. 28 pp. 8vo. Dublin, Wilson, Hartnell [1922].

215. SULLIVAN (Alexander Michael): Old Ireland, reminiscences of an Irish K.C. By A. M. Sullivan, last of the King's Serjeants and one of his Majesty's Counsel. 302 pp. portrs. illustr. 8vo. London, Butterworth, 1927.

216. SWEETMAN (John): Nationality, a paper read by Mr. John Sweetman at the Central Branch of the National Council [Sinn Féin], Nov. 18th, 1907. 22 pp. 8vo. Dublin, Gill [1907 ?].

216a. —— Liberty, a paper read by Mr. John Sweetman at the Central Branch of Sinn Féin on January 18th, 1909. 20 pp. Dublin, Gill, [1909 ?].

President of Sinn Féin in 1909.

217. THOMPSON (*Sir* William) : " The Census of Ireland 1911." By Sir William Thompson, Registrar-General. *Journal of the Statistical and Social Inquiry Society of Ireland.* Vol. XIII. pp. 46–59.
   Read on March 26th, 1913.

218. —— Presidential address. Fifty years vital statistics in Ireland. *Journal of the Statistical and Social Inquiry Society of Ireland.* Part XCVII. pp. 572–605.
   A paper read on December 6th, 1918.

219. TIMES, The : Ireland of to-day. Reprinted, with some additions, from *The Times.* 420 pp. 8vo. London, Murray, 1913.
   Articles from the *Times* Irish number, March 17th, 1913, on religion, literature, agriculture, trade, industry, sport, and other aspects of Irish life. The *Times* published another Irish number on November 4th, 1919.

Trade (Irish), *see* Industry.

220. TURNER (Edward Raymond) : Ireland and England, in the past and at present. 504 pp. 8vo. New York, Century Co., 1919.
   Professor of European history in the University of Michigan. A survey of Anglo-Irish relations, mainly in the modern period. Adverse to the Sinn Féin movement, praises the British Government's Irish policy at the time (1918), and censures the Irish people for their supposed " heartless aloofness " from the Great War.

221. UA FHLOINN (Riobard) : The Orangemen and the nation. [40] pp. 8vo. Belfast, Republican Press, [1907 ?].
   Repr. from the *Republic* (Belfast), 1906–1907. A reply by " an Orangeman " appeared in the same journal, January 24th—February 7th, 1907. See also 119 (Lynd, R.).

222. ULSTER LIBERAL UNIONIST ASSOCIATION, The : a sketch of its history, 1885–1914 : how it has opposed Home Rule, and what it has done for remedial legislation in Ireland. Introduction by Mr. J. R. Fisher. 124 pp. 8vo. Belfast, Ulster Liberal Unionist Association, 1913.

223. ULSTER UNIONIST COUNCIL, 1911 : The voice of Ulster : " We will not have Home Rule " . . . Demonstration of welcome to the Rt. Hon. Sir Edward Carson, K.C., M.P., Chairman, Irish Unionist Parliamentary Party, at Craigavon, Co. Down . . . 23rd September, 1911. 60 pp. 8vo. Belfast, Ulster Unionist Council. (Series U. C. 30).

Ulster [*mainly with reference to the Unionist movement*], *see* 3–3a (Armour, Rev. J. B.) ; Carson (*Baron*) ; 37 (Cushendun, *Baron* [Ronald McNeill]) ; 57 (Gannon, Rev. P. J.) ; 58 (Goblet, Y. M.) ; 59a (Good, J. W.) ; 77 (Hamilton, *Lord* E.) ; 115 (Logan, J.) ; 130 (MacNeill, Eoin) ; 135 (Maxwell, *Sir* H.) ; 145 (Morrison, H. S.) ; 146 (North-Eastern B. Bureau) ; 166a (Orange Institution, The).

See also Sects. **1912–1916** ; **1916–1918** ; **1919–1921**.

223a. UNITED IRISH LEAGUE OF GREAT BRITAIN : Constitution and rules adopted by Convention, 1902. sm. 8vo. 14 pp. [1902].

223b. UNITED IRISH LEAGUE: Rules of the Young Ireland Branch of the United Irish League. Riaġlaċa Craoibe na hÉireannaċ nÓġ ve Ċumann na nGaeveal nAonċuiġċe. 19 pp. 8vo. *n.d.*

224. UNITED IRISH LEAGUE: The Irish party, what it has done for Ireland, from the Land League to Home Rule. Report of Standing Committee of the United Irish League . . . 12 pp. 8vo. Dublin, Freeman's Journal, [1915].

    Report read by Joseph Devlin, M.P., General Secretary, in the head offices of the League on January 12th, 1915, J. E. Redmond, M.P., presiding.

225. UNITED IRISHMAN, The, a national weekly review, 1899–1906. Pr. by Bernard Doyle, 9 Upper Ormond Quay, Dublin; in 1900 by P. C. D. Warren. Published at 17 Fownes Street.

    Edited by Arthur Griffith. William Rooney (1873–1901) was the principal contributor up to the time of his death. Rooney wrote the weekly notes headed "All Ireland." Afterwards, "almost single-handed, for a period, Griffith wrote and in part set up the type of his paper, week after week" (Sean-Ghall). Griffith used the pen-names, "Shanganagh" and "Cuguan." Distinguished Irish writers, scholars and economists contributed articles.

    Mr. P. S. O'Hegarty says: "The paper gave the [Separatist] movement expression, acted, so to speak both as secretary and organiser, and was very soon in touch with every club and every convinced Separatist in Ireland, holding them together, encouraging them, increasing them " (*Sinn Féin: an illumination*).

    In 1903 it was enlarged and taken over by a limited Publishing Co. with the original directors: Arthur Griffith (Managing Director), John O'Leary, Maude Gonne McBride, Thomas Kelly, T.C., Henry Dixon and Seumas MacManus, with J. D. Digges (Sec.). The political programme was thus explained in the issue of Dec. 26th, 1903: "In lieu of the present policy of Parliament, we have advocated the Hungarian policy for Ireland . . . Briefly it may be described as a policy of passive resistance to foreign government and national self-determination." *The United Irishman* was wound up after a libel action in 1906. Griffith resumed it as *Sinn Féin*.

    The United Irishman was several times suppressed. A collection of addressed wrappers, apparently of issues seized in the post in 1900, was transferred after 1921 from the Chief Secretary's Library, Dublin Castle, to the National Library of Ireland.

United States of America (*Irish people and political organisations in*), *see* 44 (Devoy, John); 83 (Higgins, P., and Connolly, F. V.); 194 (Roberts, E.); 212 (Splain, J. J.); 420 (Maguire, J. K.); 457 (*Orange lodges*); 549 (Sexton, Joseph); 849 (*Irische Blätter*); 876 (McCartan, P.). *See also* **1919–1921.**

226. VOICE OF IRELAND, The (Ġlór na hÉireann). A survey of the race and nation from all angles, by the foremost leaders at home and abroad. Edited by William G. FitzGerald. 612 pp. illustr. 4to. Manchester, Heywood, [1924].

    Statements relating to the Anglo-Irish settlement of 1921–1922 from well-known men and women at home and abroad, and essays on Irish history, politics, literature, social life, etc. Five sections in the book deal mainly with the period, 1912–1921, *i.e.*, *The Sinn Féin movement* (pp. 100-114); *Towards physical force* (pp. 116-142); *The reign of terror* (pp. 144-156); *The women's part* (pp. 158-175); *Ireland overseas* (pp. 210-266).

227. WALKER (Henry de Rosenbach): A review of the statute book. In *The new Irish Constitution*, ed. by J. H. Morgan. pp. 388–411. London, 1912.

228. WALSH (*Rev.* Patrick J.) : William J. Walsh, Archbishop of Dublin. 612 pp. pls. 8vo. Dublin, Talbot Press, 1928.

229. WARREN (Raoul DE) : L'Irlande et ses institutions politiques, leur évolution—leur état actuel. 496 pp. 8vo. Paris, Berger-Levrault, 1928.

> A survey of Irish history to 1921, with an examination of the constitutional and international status of the Irish Free State. Sections on the Home Rule Bill, Ireland, during the world war, the Anglo-Irish war, and the Ulster question. The author consulted Irish political leaders and officials in the collection of his material.

230. WELBY (Reginald E.) *1st Baron* : Irish finance. In *The new Irish Constitution*, ed. by J. H. MORGAN. pp. 112-156. London, 1912.

> Permanent Secretary of the Treasury, 1885-1894.

231. WELLS (Warre B.) : John Redmond, a biography. 210 pp. 8vo. illustr. London, Nisbet, 1919.

232. —— Irish indiscretions. 230 pp. 8vo. Dublin, Maunsel and Roberts, 1923.

> Reminiscences of Irish politics and journalism, 1914-1921. Of special interest for its account of the attitude of the " Southern Unionists " after 1916.

233. WILLIAMS (Basil) : Home Rule problems, edited by Basil Williams, with a preface by Viscount Haldane. 203 pp. 8vo. London, P. S. King, 1911.

> Papers read in 1911 at meetings of a small committee " formed of men keenly interested in the principle of Home Rule for Ireland, with the object of collecting information bearing on that subject, and of considering difficulties that must be faced in drafting a Home Rule Bill." The contributors include G. P. Gooch, W. P. Ryan, G. F.-H. Berkeley, Erskine Childers, Rev. James O. Hannay, Professor J. H. Morgan, Charles Roden Buxton, and Frank MacDermott.

2. FROM THE HOME RULE BILL (1912) TO 1916.

234. AMERY (Leopold Stennett) : Home rule and the colonial analogy; The economics of separatism. In *Against Home Rule*, ed. by S. ROSENBAUM. pp. 128-152, 282-294. London, 1912.

> M.P., (U.) from 1911.

235. AUDITOR TANTUM : The Home Rule Bill in Committee. *Fortnightly Rev.*, XCVIII (N.S.). pp. 214-222. Aug., 1914.

236. AUSPICIUM MELIORIS AEVI : Federalism and Ireland. *Empire Rev.*, VI. pp. 161-173. April, 1914.

237. BAGWELL (Richard) : The southern minorities. In *Against Home Rule*, ed. by S. ROSENBAUM. pp. 182-188. London, 1912.

238. BALFOUR (Arthur James BALFOUR) *1st Earl* : Nationality and Home Rule. 24 pp. 8vo. London, Longmans, Green, 1913.

> Repr. from the *University Magazine* (Montreal). *See also* 518.

239. BALFOUR (Gerald) : Unionist policy in relation to rural development in Ireland. In *Against Home Rule*, ed. by S. ROSENBAUM. pp. 225-248. London, 1912.
Chief Secretary for Ireland 1895-1900.

240. BATTERSBY (T. S. Frank), *K.C.* : A " modern eye "-opener. 60 points against Home Rule (a reply to the *Daily News* " 50 points in favour of Home Rule "). With a preface by the Rt. Hon. Sir Edward H. Carson, M.P. [70] pp. 16mo. Dublin and Belfast, Unionist Association of Ireland, 1912.

241. BAUMANN (Arthur A.) : Sir Edward Carson and the predominant partner. *Fortnightly Rev.*, CI. (N.S.). pp. 1-9. Jan., 1914.

242. BÉASLAÍ (Piaras) : Óglaigh na hÉireann and the Great War. An t-Óglác. Vol. IV. No. 3. N.S. Sept., 1931.
Gives an account of the division in the ranks of the Volunteers after the outbreak of the war, the Connolly-Clarke plan to prevent Asquith from speaking in the Mansion House (Sept., 1914) and the part played by the I.R.B.

243. BEWLEY (Charles) : If Home Rule is defeated. *Dublin Rev.*, CLIII. pp. 255-265. London, Oct., 1913.
Foretells a more vigorous national movement in Ireland if the Home Rule Bill is defeated.

244. BIRKENHEAD (Frederick Edwin SMITH) *1st Earl of* : Ulster and Home Rule. *National Rev.*, LIX. pp. 974-981. London, Aug., 1912.

245. BIRKENHEAD (Frederick Winston Furneaux SMITH) *2nd Earl of* : Frederick Edwin, Earl of Birkenhead : the first phase . . . 320 pp. 8vo. pls. London, Butterworth, 1933.
Chapters on the Home Rule Bill (1912) and the Ulster crisis (1913-1914).

See also 1025a.

246. BIROT (Georges) : Le home rule irlandais. Thèse pour le doctorat, présentée et soutenue le jeudi 28 mai 1914 . . . 184 pp. 8vo. Paris, Giard & Brière, 1914. (Faculté de droit de l'Université de Paris).

247. BLACKWOOD'S MAGAZINE : Home Rule for Ireland. Vol. CXCI. pp. 736-744. May, 1912.
English Unionist.

248. —— A page of history. *Blackwood's Mag.*, CXCV. pp. 713-722. May, 1914.
A comment on the Curragh army crisis. Supports the mutinous officers.

249. BLAKE (*Sir* Henry Arthur) : Peace or war ? *Nineteenth Century*, LXIII. pp. 1169-1177. June, 1913.

250. —— How is civil war to be averted. *Nineteenth Century*, LXIV. pp. 673-682. Oct., 1913

251. BLOXHAM (E.): North East Ulster. *Irish Rev.*, II. pp. 461-470. Oct., 1912.

252. BLÜCHER (Evelyn, *Princess*): An English wife in Berlin, a private memoir of events, politics, and daily life in Germany, throughout the war and the social revolution of 1918. 336 pp. portr. 8vo. Third impression. London, Constable, 1920.

> Refers to meetings with Sir Roger Casement in Germany. For Casement's own account see his *Diaries*.

253. BOYD (Ernest A.): Realism in Irish politics. *Forum*, New York, LI. pp. 26-37. Jan., 1914.

254. BRENTFORD (*Sir* William JOYNSON-HICKS) *1st Viscount*: The cost of Home Rule. *National Rev.*, LIX. pp. 446-458. London, May, 1912.

255. BROOKS (Sydney): Aspects of the " religious " question in Ireland. *Fortnightly Rev.*, XCI (N.S.). pp. 380-395. Feb., 1912.

256. —— Sir Horace Plunkett and his work. *Fortnightly Rev.*, XCI. (N.S.). pp. 1011-1021. June, 1912.

257. —— A glance at the Irish question, apropos of the present Home Rule Bill. *Century Mag.*, LXXXV. (O.S.). pp. 874-882. illustr. New York, Oct., 1912.

257a. —— Aspects of the Irish question. 8 + 255 pp. 8vo. Dublin, Maunsell, 1912.

258. BROWN (Stephen J.) *S.J.*: The question of Irish nationality. 44 pp. 8vo. Dublin, Sealy, Bryers and Walker, 1913. (Reprinted from " Studies ").

Buckingham Palace Conference (July, 1914), *see* (Carson, *Baron*); 81 (Healy, T. M.); 557 (Oxford and Asquith, *1st Earl of*); 70 (Redmond, J.); 575 (Ullswater, *1st Viscount*).

259. BUONAIUTI (*Very Rev.* Ernesto): Impressions of Ireland. By Very Rev. Ernesto Buonaiuti, D.D., Ph.D. Translated from the Italian by Rev. Bernard Maguire, C.C. . . . 32 pp. 8vo. Dublin, Gill, 1913.

260. BUXTON (Charles Roden): The ABC Home Rule handbook. Edited by Charles Roden Buxton. 276 pp. 8vo. London, Home Rule Council, 1912.

261. BYRNE (F. D.): The finance of Home Rule. *Catholic Bulletin*, VI. pp. 71-76, 146-152, 200-206. Feb.-April, 1916.

262. CALLWELL (*Major-General Sir* Charles Edward): Field-Marshal Sir Henry Wilson, Bart., G.C.B., D.S.O., his life and diaries. Vol. I., 364 pp. Vol. II., 388 pp. illustr. 8vo. London, Cassell, 1927.

> Vol. I contains extracts from the diaries of Sir H. Wilson (then Director of Military Operations at the War Office) relating to his conferences with leaders of the Unionist party, the Curragh army incident and the Ulster Volunteers. See also 1044.

263. CAMPBELL (Spencer): The real mind of Ulster. *Fortnightly Rev.*, CI. pp. 914-920. May, 1914.

264. CARSON (*Sir* Edward) *Baron, of Duncairn*: Introduction: *Against Home Rule*, edited by S. ROSENBAUM. pp. 17-38. London, 1912.

> A general statement of the case for legislative union, summarising the views of the other contributors to the same book.

265. ——— The position of Ulster. Speech . . . delivered at a meeting of the Ulster Unionist Council, held at Belfast, on 24 September, 1913. 14 pp. 8vo. Belfast, Ulster Unionist Council, [1913]. (U.U.C. Political Leaflets).

——— *See* General and Introductory Sect.; *and* 240 (Battersby, F.); 241 (Baumann, A. A.); 312 (Ervine, St. J.); 357 (Horgan, J. J.); 377 (Johnson, T.); 378 (Johnstone, J.); 397 (Legge E.); 479 (Peel, *Hon.* G.); 493 (Platt T. C.); 529 (Rosenbaum, S.); 543 (Samuel, A. W.).

266. [Casement (*Sir* Roger)]: Ireland, Germany and the next war. By "Shan van vocht" [*pseud.*, *i.e.*, Sir Roger Casement]. 8 pp. 8vo. Belfast, Davidson and M'Cormack, 1913.

> A reprint, for private circulation, from the *Irish Review* of July, 1913. This article was written in March, 1913, in reply to " Great Britain and the next war " by Sir A. Conan Doyle (*Fortnightly Rev.*, Feb., 1913), but not published until after Casement's retirement from the British Colonial service. It was translated and much discussed at the time in Germany.

267. ——— Ulster and Ireland. *Fortnightly Rev.*, C. pp. 799-806. Nov., 1913.

268. ——— From " coffin ship " to " Atlantic greyhound." By an Irish-American [*pseud.*, *i.e.*, Sir R. Casement]. *Irish Review*, III–IV. pp. 609-613, 1-11, 57-67. Feb.-April, 1914.

> A survey of the dealings of British steamship companies with Ireland since the Great Famine, with estimates of the profits made by them from Irish trade and emigration, in view of the Cunard Company's decision in 1913 to abandon Cóbh as a port of call.

268a. [———] Ireland, Germany and freedom of the seas: a possible outcome of the war of 1914. 39 pp. 8vo. New York and Philadelphia, Irish Press Bureau, September 1st, 1914.

> Contains the articles pr. in *The crime against Europe*, with the exception of " Ireland, Germany and the next war " and " The elsewhere Empire." There is a short introduction headed, " To free the seas, free Ireland."

268b. —— The crime against Ireland, and how the war may right it. 96 pp. 8vo. *n.p., n.d.* [Pr. in Germany, 1914-1915 ?].

269. —— The crime against Europe, a possible outcome of the war of 1914. Price 25 cents. 28 pp. 4to. Philadelphia, Celtic Press, 15 So. 9th St. 1915.

—— Second edition. 92 pp. 8vo. 1915.

> Seven articles " written at intervals between August 1911 and December 1913 without any thought of publication," *i.e.*, The keeper of the seas ; The balance of power ; The enemy of peace , The problem of the Near West ; the duty of Christendom ; The freedom of the seas ; Ireland, Germany and the next war ; together with " The elsewhere Empire " (first published in *Irish Freedom*).

270. —— Gesammelte Schriften. Irland, Deutschland und die Freiheit der Meere und andere Aufsätze, Casements Reden nach seiner Gefangennahme. 2te Auflage. 3 portrs. 248 + 8 pp. + 9 pp. facs. 8vo. Diessen vor München, Huber, 1917.

270a. —— Ireland and the war : the emerald isle and its giant parasite—ruthless and systematic ruin. *Gaelic American.* January 15-22, 1916.

> From the *Continental Times*, Berlin.

270b. —— Sir Edward Grey. *Gaelic American.* November 20-27, 1915.

> From the *Continental Times* (Berlin), Oct. 11, 1915.

270c. —— The causes of the war and the foundations of peace ; the keeper of the seas. 22 pp. 8vo. Munchen, Hubers, 1915.

270d. —— Objects of an Irish Brigade in the present war. Text of an address . . . delivered on 15 May to . . . Irish soldiers at Limburg. 8 pp. 8vo. [1915].

271. —— Sir Roger Casement's diaries. " His mission to Germany and the Findlay affair." Edited by Dr. Charles E. Curry, with foreword and preface. Three photographs and three facsimiles. 226 pp. 8vo. Munich, Arche Publishing Co., 1922.

272. —— Sir Roger Casement, seine Mission nach Deutschland und die Findlay-affaire. Auf grund seiner Tagebücher und Korrespondenz dargestellt von Dr. Charles E. Curry. Mit drei Portraits und drei Facsimiles. 256 pp. 8vo. München, 1922.

> Dr. Curry, an American, formerly resident in Germany, **says** in a foreword (Sept., 1921) that before going on board the submarine in April, 1916, Casement " entrusted to me all he possessed in this world, his personal effects and writings, and left me various written instructions chiefly regarding his diaries and their publication upon the close of the war . . ." Dr. Curry decided not to publish the portions dealing with the " Irish Brigade " and " the sad experiences and events of his last sojourn at Berlin." These portions (" The last page ") beginning March 17, 1916, were edited by Dr. William J. Maloney, and published in the *New York Globe* and other American journals, and in the *Irish Independent*, April 12—April 25, 1922.

—— *See also* General and Introductory Sect. ; Sect. **1916** ; *and* 252 (Blücher, *Princess*) ; 314 (*Fianna Handbook*) ; 324 (Gaffney, T. St. J.) ; 411 (MacKeogh, M.) ; 420 (Maguire, J. K.) ; 504 (Protestant protest, A) ; 509 (Quinn J.) ; 530 (Rothenfelder, F.).

273. CAVE (*Sir* George) 1*st* Viscount : The constitutional question. In *Against Home Rule*, ed. by S. ROSENBAUM. pp. 81-106. London, 1912.
   M.P. (U.).

274. CENSORSHIP : Army : Memorandum on the censorship. . . . 4to. 6 pp. H.M.S.O., 1915. [Cd. 7679].
   See also Memorandum on the Official Press Bureau (Cd. 7680).

275. CHAMBERLAIN (Austen) : Home rule finance. In *Against Home Rule*, ed. by S. ROSENBAUM. pp. 107-127. London, 1912.

276. CHARNWOOD (Godfrey Rathbone BENSON) 1*st* Baron : Federal Home Rule and the Government of Ireland Bill. *Nineteenth Century.*, LXXIII. pp. 834-845. April, 1913.

277. —— The federal solution. *Contemporary Rev.*, CV. pp. 772-782. June, 1914.

278. CHILDERS (Erskine) : The form and purpose of Home Rule : a lecture delivered at a public meeting convened by the Young Ireland branch of the United Irish League at the Mansion House, Dublin, on March 2nd, 1912. 34 pp. 8vo. Dublin, Ponsonby, 1912.

279. —— The real issue in Ireland. *Nineteenth Century*. LXXI. pp. 643-656. April, 1912.

280. —— The Home Rule Bill. *Fortnightly Rev.*, XCVI (N.S.). pp. 866-879. May, 1912.

281. —— The Home Rule Bill and the Unionist alternative : a contrast. *Contemporary Rev.*, CI. pp. 777-787. June, 1912.

282. —— Home Rule in parliament. *Contemporary Rev.*, CII. pp. 777-788. Dec., 1912.

282a. CHILDS (*Sir* Wyndham) : Episodes and reflections, being some records from the life of Major-General Sir W. Childs . . . portrs., pls. 8vo. London, Cassell, [1930].
   Contains recollections of the Curragh army crisis (1914) and Sir R. Casement (1916).

283. CHURCHILL (Seton) : A plea for Home Rule from the Protestant standpoint. *Fortnightly Rev.*, CI (N.S.). pp. 435-442. March, 1914.

284. CHURCHILL (Winston Spencer) : Mr. Winston Churchill's message to Ulster. Speech . . . at Belfast, on 8th February, 1912. Repr. from the *Daily Chronicle*. 12 pp. 8vo. [Westminster, Home Rule Council, 1912].

284a. CLAN-NA-GAEL : EMMET ANNIVERSARY MAGAZINE ; Academy of Music, Philadelphia. 32 pp. Philadelphia, Bradley Bros., 1914.

285. COLUM (Pádraic) : Sinn Féin and Irish Ireland ; Ulster's opposition to Home Rule ; Formation of the Irish Volunteers and the Irish Citizen Army ; The eve of the Great War ; Precipitating rebellion. In *The Irish rebellion of* 1916, ed. by M. Joy. New York, 1916.

Complete grammar of anarchy, The. [Selections from the speeches of Sir E. Carson, etc.], *see* 357 (Horgan, J. J.).

286. COMPTON-RICKETT (*Sir* Joseph) : The fortunes of Home Rule— and of Ulster. *Contemporary Rev.*, CV. pp. 457-464. April, 1914.
M.P. (Lib.)

287. CONNOLLY (James) : Labour in Dublin. *Irish Rev.*, III. pp. 385-391. Oct., 1913.

—— *See also* Sects. GENERAL AND INTRODUCTORY and **1916** ; 242 (Béaslaí, P.) ; 374 (*Irish Worker, The*) ; 450 [O'Casey (Seán)] ; 451 (Ó Donnabáin Rossa).

288. CORNFORD (Leslie Cope) : Home Rule, the real issue. *National Rev.* LVIII. pp. 722-731. London, Jan., 1912.

289. —— Home Rule and civil war. *National Rev.*, LX. pp. 436-443. Nov., 1912.
Editor of the literary department, Joint Unionist Associations of Ireland.

290. CORRESPONDENCE RELATING TO RECENT EVENTS IN THE IRISH COMMAND. Presented to Parliament . . . 4 pp. H.M.S.O., 1914. [Cd. 7318.]
The Curragh army incident, March, 1914.

291.—— (In continuation of Cd. 7318.) Presented to Parliament . . . 16 pp. 4to. H.M.S.O., 1914. [Cd. 7329].
Published on April 22, 1914, a few days after the Ulster Unionist Alliance had issued a statement to the Press, purporting to reveal the plan of military operations against the Ulster Volunteers.

292. COURTNEY OF PENWITH (Leonard Henry COURTNEY), *1st Baron* : Home Rule. *Contemporary Rev.*, CII. pp. 1-11. July, 1912.

293. CUMANN NA MBAN : Why Ireland is poor. English laws and Irish industries. 16 pp. 8vo. Dublin, Publication Committee of Cumann na mBann [*sic*] (Central Branch), [1915]. (National Series, No. 1).

294. CURIO : Ulster and the autumn campaign. *Fortnightly Rev.*, C. pp. 613-624. Oct., 1913.

295. —— The crisis and the détente. *Fortnightly Rev.*, CI. pp. 819-831. May, 1914.

Curragh army incident (1914), *see* 37 (Cushendun, *1st Baron*) ; 135 (Maxwell, *Sir* H.) ; 248 (*Blackwood's Mag.*) ; 11a (Blunt, W. S.) ; 262 (Wilson, *F.-M. Sir* H.) ; 282a (Childs, *Maj.-Gen. Sir* W.) ; 290-291 (Correspondence . . . H.M.S.O.) ; 295 (Curio) ; 416 (Macready, *Gen. Sir* C. F. M.) ; 444 (Northumberland, *8th Duke of*) ; 496 (Pollock, A. W.) ; 497 (Ponsonby, A., *1st Baron*) ; 528 (Roberts, *F.-M. Earl*) ; 467, 557 (Oxford and Asquith, *1st Earl of*) ; 536 (*Round Table*) ; 1136 (French, *F.-M., 1st Earl*).

Cushendun (Ronald McNeill) 1st *Baron*, see 37.

Daily Mail, The, *see* 322 (Fyfe, H. H.).

296. D'Arcy (*Most Rev.* Charles Frederick) *Archbp. of Armagh* : The religious difficulty under Home Rule : (i) The Church view. By the Rt. Rev. C. F. D'Arcy, Bishop of Down. In *Against Home Rule*, ed by S. Rosenbaum. pp. 204-211. London, 1912.

297. [Davidson (S. C.)] : Irish Manufacturers and the Home Rule Bill. 8 pp. 8vo. Belfast, M'Gowan and Ingram, [1914].

298. Deadlock, The : *Fortnightly Rev.*, ci. pp. 589-599. April, 1914.

299. Defence of the realm Act in Ireland, 1915. 32 pp. 8vo. Dublin, Committee of Public Safety, 1915.

> The aim of this pamphlet is to prove that " originally intended to meet the case of the invasion of Great Britain and Ireland by Germany," the D.O.R.A. " has in Ireland been used as an instrument of terrorism, of petty persecution and bullying " (Preface). *See also* 427.

See also Statutory Rules and Orders, 1914-1921 ; Restoration of Order in Ireland Act, 1920 ; 427 (Manual of emergency legislation).

300. Democritus : Home Rule and the Unionists. *English Rev.*, x. pp. 697-712. March, 1912.

301. De Vere (Robert Stephen) : Social aspects of Home Rule. *Nineteenth Century.* lxxii. Oct., 1912.

302. Department of Agriculture and Technical Instruction for Ireland : Food production in Ireland. Report of the Departmental Committee on food production in Ireland. Presented to both Houses of Parliament. . . . 22 pp. H.M.S.O. 1915. [Cd. 8046.]

303. —— Food production in Ireland. Minutes of evidence, minutes of deliberative conferences, and appendices. Presented to both Houses of Parliament. . . . 94 pp. H.M.S.O. 1916. [Cd. 8158.]

> The Committee was appointed to " consider and report what steps should be taken by legislation or otherwise for the sole purpose of maintaining and, if possible, increasing the present production of food in Ireland, on the assumption that the war may be prolonged beyond the harvest of 1916." The appendices include the views expressed by County Committees of Agriculture, agricultural statistics, production and disposal statistics, and some notes on measures adopted regarding food production by various European governments during the war. *See* 555a.
>
> See also *The Irish Homestead* (weekly journal of the Irish Agricultural Organisation Society); Bulletin of the Co-operative Reference Library, Dublin, 1914–1915 ; *Nationality* (440), and the journals, reports and other publications of the D.A.T.I.I. (see 40). " The War and Ireland's food supply," an address by Most Rev. Dr. Denis Kelly, Lord Bishop of Ross, was repr. in the Department's Journal, Oct., 1914 (pp. 20–24). " Ireland as a Food-Supplier of Great Britain " by J. R. Campbell (May, 1918) illustrates from statistics the dependence of Great Britain on Ireland for food supplies during the War.

304. Dicey (Albert Venn) : A fool's paradise, being a constitutionalist's criticism on the Home Rule Bill of 1912. By A. V. Dicey . . . formerly Vinerian professor of English law. 132 pp. London. Murray, 1913.

305. DREADNOUGHT : The navy and the plot. *National Rev.*, LXIII. pp. 562-571. London, June, 1914.

Unionist. A denunciation of the British Government for giving orders to the 3rd battle cruiser squadron to proceed to Ulster in March, 1914.

306. DUBLIN DISTURBANCES COMMISSION. Report of the Dublin Disturbances Commission. Presented to both Houses of Parliament . . . 16 pp. H.M.S.O. 1914. [Cd. 7269].

The Chief Secretary stated (in the House of Commons, Feb. 18, 1914) that he had been unable to get a judge or a representative of the police to serve on the Commission, and a representative of the working classes could not have been put on alone. He had, therefore, appointed lawyers of high character and position, previously engaged in police enquiries. The Report, issued Feb. 14, 1914, exonerated the police force generally.

307.—— Minutes of evidence and appendices. With index of witnesses. 452 pp. 4to. H.M.S.O., 1914. [Cd. 7272].

Report to the Lord-Lieutenant (signed by S. L. Brown, K.C., and Denis S. Henry, K.C.) on the disturbances in connection with Dublin Labour troubles on 30th, 31st Aug. and 1st and 21st Sept., 1913. " The year 1913 was a period of industrial unrest in Dublin."

308. DUNRAVEN (Windham Thomas WYNDHAM-QUIN) *4th Earl of* : The future of Ireland. *Nineteenth Century*. LXXIII. Jan., 1913.

309. —— Irish enigma. (1) A last plea for federation. *Nineteenth Century*, LXXIV. pp. 1125-1142. Dec., 1913.

310. EDINBURGH REVIEW, The : Home Rule or a United Kingdom. Vol. 215. pp. 515-534. April, 1912.

311. —— Home Rule economics. Vol. 216. pp. 216-234. July, 1912.

" Éire," 1914, *see* " Ireland " (359).

312. ERVINE (St. John Greer) : Sir Edward Carson and the Ulster movement. 126 pp. 8vo. Dublin, Maunsel, 1915, (Irishmen of To-day).

Regards Sir Edward Carson as " a stage Irishman," who " has no done anything to promote the well-being of Ireland."

313. FARRELL (H. William) : Ireland and the Empire, a plea for the commercial regeneration of Ireland. By H. William Farrell, organising secretary Irish League of the Empire. 8 pp. 8vo. Dublin, Humphrey and Armour, 1912.

314. FIANNA ÉIREANN, Na, Irish National Boy Scouts. [Constitution]. 8 pp. sm. 8vo. [Dublin, pr. Mahon, 1912].

" The Constitution of na Fianna Éireann as amended by the Ard-Fheis, 1912." *Irish Freedom* published the original constitution in October, 1911, and the constitution as revised in Sept., 1912.

314a. FIANNA HANDBOOK. Issued by the Central Council of na Fianna Eireann [*sic*] for the Boy Scouts of Ireland. 177 pp. 8vo. Dublin, Central Council of na Fianna Eireann, [1914].

The contributors include Madame de Markievicz, An Craoibhín Aoibhín, Sir Roger Casement and P. H. Pearse.

315. [FIFTY] 50 POINTS FOR HOME RULE : *Daily News* 1d. series. No. 16. 52 pp. 16 mo. London, *Daily News*, [1912 ?].

316. FIGGIS (Darrell) : Recollections of the Irish war. 310 pp. 8vo. London, Benn, 1927.

> Publisher's note : ' Darrell Figgis died on the 27th of October, 1925. The manuscript of " Recollections of the Irish war " was written, as far as can be traced, in 1921 to 1922. The book gives the author's personal impressions of . . . outstanding personalities . . . from the founding of the Irish Volunteers in 1913 to the truce in July, 1921.'

317. —— A nation in Ireland. *Forum*, LXIX. pp. 311-323—685-697. New York, March-June, 1913.

317a.—— Irish nationality. *English Rev.*, XIV. pp. 456-468. June, 1914. *See also* 810.

318. FILON (Augustin) : Histoire d'une constitution. Le " Home Rule " Irlandais. *Revue des deux mondes*. LXXXIII*i* année. pp. 122-148. Jan., 1913.

Finance (Irish), *see* Sect. GENERAL AND INTRODUCTORY ; *and* 254 (Brentford, 1*st Viscount*) ; 261 (Byrne, F. D.) ; 275 (Chamberlain, A.) ; 311 (*Edinburgh Review*) ; 330-334 (Govt. of Ireland Bill) ; 335 (Govt. of Irel. Act) ; 337 (Griffith, A.) ; 362 (Irish Co. Councils). 368 (Irish Taxpayer, An) ; 385 (Kettle, T. M.) ; 505 (*Quarterly Review*) ; 514 (Redmond, John) ; 525 (Revenue official, A) ; 542 (Samuel, *Sir* H.) ; 543-544 (Samuels, A. W.) ; 559 (Steel-Maitland, *Sir* A.) ; 566 (Ulster Liberal Unionist Assoc.) ; 577 (Ulster Unionist Council) ; 579 (Williams, W. M. J.).

319. FITZWALTER (Richard) : Ireland, a plea for a parley. *British Rev.*, II. pp. 47-60. Feb., 1913.

320.—— England, Ireland and Rome. *British Rev.*, II. pp. 16-27. March, 1913.

FOOD PRODUCTION IN WAR TIME, 1914-1918, *see* 40-43a, 302-303 (Dept. of Agriculture . . . Ireland).

320a. FORTNIGHTLY REVIEW, The : Why Ulster distrusts Roman Catholicism. *Fortnightly Rev.*, XCVII. (N.S.). pp. 1022-1036. June, 1912.

French (*Field-Marshal Sir* John Denton Pinkstone) 1*st Earl, of Ypres*, *see* 1136.

321. FULLER (*Sir* Joseph Bampfylde) : Psychology of the Irish question. *Nineteenth Century*, LXXIV. pp. 682-693. Oct., 1913.

322. FYFE (H. Hamilton) : Ulster to-day, the whole truth . . . Reprinted from the " Daily Mail." 48 pp. 8vo. London, Associated Newspapers, [1914 ?]. (Ulster Unionist Council Political Leaflets).

323. Ꞡaeʋeat, An, a weekly journal of stories, sketches, news notes, songs, etc. N.S. 1916. January 29th–March 18th, 1916. Edited by Eamon O'Duibhir, Ballagh, Co. Tipperary. Pr. Gaelic Press, 30 Upper Liffey Street, Dublin.

> Occasional articles in support of the Irish Volunteers. Sir M. Nathan in his evidence before the 1916 Rebellion Commission (*Minutes*, p. 5) says : " When, however, the Gael . . . produced in its issue of March 18th an article headed ' The Work Before Us,' urging insurrection, the police, acting on military warrant, searched the premises of the Gaelic Press, seized some thousands of copies of ' The Gael,' ' Honesty ' and ' The Spark,' and took away essential parts of the printing machinery."

324. GAFFNEY (Thomas St. John) : Breaking the silence ; England, Ireland, Wilson and the War. 358 pp. illustr. 8vo. New York, Liveright, 1930.

> The author was U.S. Consul-General at Munich to Oct., 1915. Afterwards associated with Sir Roger Casement's efforts to promote a German-Irish alliance. Account of conversations with Casement. Particulars of the Stockholm Conference (1917), the German-Irish Society (*Deutsch-Irische Gesellschaft*), and the German attitude towards Ireland in 1917–1918. For Mr. Gaffney's correspondence with the U.S. State Department see *Gaelic American*, Dec. 4, 1915.

Gill (Thomas Patrick), see 470.

325. GINNELL (Laurence) : D.O.R.A. at Westminster : being selections from Mr. Ginnell's parliamentary activities (reprint from Hansard), before Easter week, after Easter week. 622 pp. 8vo. Dublin, Irish Wheelman Printing and Publishing Co., 1918.

> L. Ginnell (Labras Mag Fionngail) was M.P. for N. Westmeath, 1906–1918, and T.D., 1918–1923. In the House of Commons he championed the cause of Sinn Féin and the Irish Volunteers.

326. GLENAVY (*Sir* James Henry CAMPBELL) *1st Baron* : A guide to the Home Rule Bill, edited by the Rt. Hon. J. H. Campbell, P.C., M.P. *Private and confidential.* 354 pp. 8vo. London, Union Defence League and National Unionist Association, 1912.

> Reprint of the Bill, with Unionist commentary page by page, comparison with previous Home Rule Bills, and detailed study of the Committee and Report stages of the Bill of 1893.

327. —— The control of judiciary and police. In *Against Home Rule*, ed. by S. ROSENBAUM. pp. 153-161. London, 1912.

328. GOBLET (Yann Morvran) : L'Irlande dans la crise universelle (3 Août 1914–25 Juillet 1917) . . . par Louis Tréguiz (*ps., i.e.*, Y. M. Goblet) . . . 280 pp. 8vo. Paris, Alcan, [1918].

> L'évolution des méthodes politiques (1893–1914) ; l'Irlande avec les alliés (depuis le 3 août 1914) ; la crise revolutionnaire (août 1914—avril 1916) ; les tentatives constitutionnelles (mai 1916—juillet 1917).

329. [——] L'Irlande dans la crise européene. Par Y. M. G. [*i.e.*, Yann Morvran Goblet]. Extrait de la *Revue de Paris* du 15 mai, 1917. 26 pp. 8vo. Paris, Pochy, 1917.
See also 58.

330. GOVERNMENT OF IRELAND BILL : Outline of financial provisions. Presented to the House of Commons . . . 8 pp. H.M.S.O. 1912. [Cd. 6154].

331. —— Further memorandum on financial provisions. Presented to the House of Commons . . . 6 pp. H.M.S.O., 1912. [Cd. 6486].

332. —— Memorandum on financial provisions, 1913. Presented to both Houses of Parliament . . . 6 pp. H.M.S.O., 1913. [Cd. 6844].

333. —— Memorandum on financial provisions, based on estimates of revenue and expenditure in the financial year 1913-14 . . . Presented to both Houses of Parliament by Command of His Majesty. 6 pp. H.M.S.O., 1913. [Cd. 6879].

334. —— Memorandum on financial provisions, based on revenue and expenditure in the financial year 1913-14. Presented to both Houses of Parliament . . . 8 pp. H.M.S.O., 1914. [Cd. 7400.]

334a. —— . . . Return " showing Government proposals in connection with the Government of Ireland Bill " . . . Ordered by the House of Commons, to be printed, 9th March, 1914. 4 pp. H.M.S.O., 1914 [H.C. 143].

> The plan for county option in Ulster [the first official proposal for the partition of Ireland].

335. GOVERNMENT OF IRELAND (AMENDMENT) BILL, 1914. 6 pp. H.M.S.O., 1914.

> This Bill provides for " county option " in Ulster on Home Rule. Any county in Ulster may secure " temporary exclusion " from the operation of the Government of Ireland Act, 1914, by a majority vote of the electors. A poll may be demanded by one-tenth of the electors by signing a petition to the Lord Lieutenant. The form of words on the ballot paper would be :
> " Are you in favour of the exclusion of —— from the operation of the Government of Ireland Act, 1914, for a period of six years ?
> " Are you against the exclusion of —— from the operation of the Government of Ireland Act, 1914, for a period of six years ? "
> The House of Lords amended the Bill so as to provide for the permanent exclusion without any poll of all nine Ulster counties.

336. GOVERNMENT OF IRELAND ACT, 1914 : An Act to amend the provision for the Government of Ireland Act. [18th September 1914]. 8vo. 56 pp. H.M.S.O. 1914.

> Along with the Government of Ireland Act, 1914, there was passed an Act to suspend its operation—the Suspensory Act—" until such date (not being later than the end of the present war) as may be fixed by His Majesty by Order in Council." The Government of Ireland Act, 1914, was repealed, as from December 23rd, 1920, by the Government of Ireland Act, 1920, and concurrently Orders in Council suspending the operation of the former Act expired.

—— *See also* Home Rule.

337. GRAVES (S. H. P.) : A Canadian view of the Home Rule bill. *Fortnightly Rev.*, c. (N.S.). pp. 817-827 Nov., 1913.

> Unionist. Maintains that the Protestant minority in Quebec has been treated unfairly, in spite of guarantees, and that the minority would fare likewise under an Irish Government. *See also Fortnightly Rev.*, Jan., 1914 : *Protestant guarantees in Quebec* : a reply, by Francis W. Gray.

337a. GREEN (Alice Stopford): L'Irlande et le Home Rule. *Revue de Paris*. 19ᵉ année. Tome 5ᵉ. pp. 425-448. 15 Sept. 1912.

337b. —— The Irish National Volunteers. *British Rev.*, VII. pp. 12-23. July, 1914.

337c. GREEN PAPERS, The. Ireland's attitude towards the warring powers . . . 23 pp. 8vo. [New York, 1914 ?].
    Arguments against Irish participation in the war.

337d. GREY (*Sir* Edward) 1*st Viscount* : Sir Edward Grey on Home Rule. Speech by the Rt. Hon. Sir Edward Grey, Bart., M.P., Secretary of State for Foreign Affairs, at Plymouth, on Tuesday, 5th December, 1911. [Repr. from the *Western Daily Mercury*. Westminster, Home Rule Council]. [1912 ?].

337e. GRIEVANCES IN IRELAND. By one of the tolerant majority. 32 pp. 8vo. Dublin, Duffy, 1913.

338. GRIFFITH (Arthur): Home Rule and the Unionists. *Irish Review*, II. pp. 113-118. May, 1912.

338a. —— The Home Rule Bill examined. 16 pp. 8vo. Dublin, Sinn Féin, 1912.

338b. —— The finance of the Home Rule Bill, an examination. *Sinn Féin*. Nos. 118-119. Vol. 3. N.S. May 4th-11th, 1912.
    In continuation of a lecture, " The Home Rule Bill examined," pr. in *Sinn Féin* of April 27th.

338c. —— When the Government publishes sedition. 12 pp. 8vo. Dublin, Irish Publicity League, [1915]. (Tracts for the Times, No. 4).

—— *See* sect. GENERAL AND INTRODUCTORY ; and 359 (*Ireland*); 440 (*Nationality*); 545 (*Scissors and Paste*). *See also* Sinn Féin.

339. GWYNN (Stephen): Home Rule and the House of Lords. *Nineteenth Century* LXXIII. pp. 580-596, March, 1913.

340. —— Protestants under Home Rule. *British Rev.*, IV. pp. 161-173. Nov., 1913.

341. HAMMOND (Thomas C.): The religious question in Ireland. *Nineteenth Century*, LXXIII. pp. 338-354. Feb., 1913.

342. HANNAY (*Rev.* James Owen): Ireland and the war. *Nineteenth Century*, LXXVIII. pp. 393-402. Aug., 1915.
    Maintains that anti-British feeling is " smouldering," and that Ireland is not providing a due proportion of recruits for the British army.

343. —— Ireland in two wars : (II). Recruiting in Ireland to-day. *Nineteenth Century*. LXIX. pp. 173-180. Jan., 1916.

344. HEALY (John Edward): Irish poor law reform. In *Against Home Rule*, ed. by S. ROSENBAUM. pp. 304-313. London, 1912.
    Editor of the *Irish Times*, 1908-1934.

345. HEALY (Timothy Michael) : Facts regarding the labour disputes, contained in the speech of Mr. T. M. Healy, K.C., M.P., at court of enquiry, held in Dublin Castle, on Wednesday, October 1st, 1913. 32 pp. 8vo. Dublin, Hely, [1913].

346. HOBSON (Bulmer) : A short history of the Irish Volunteers . . . with a preface by Eoin MacNeill. Vol. I (As passed by Censor). 206 pp. 8vo. Dublin, Candle Press, 1918.
> A record of events to September, 1914. The author, " in addition to being one of the Executive of the Volunteers from first to last, was for two years Hon. Secretary and Quarter-master to the organisation " (Publisher's note).

347. —— The origin of Óglaigh na hÉireann. An t-Óglác, Vol. IV. (N.S.). Nos. 1-2. pp. 1-8, 3-13. March–June, 1931.
> Gives an account of the gun-running for the Irish Volunteers at Howth and Kilcool and the differences on the Volunteer Executive in 1914.

348. —— Óglaigh na hÉireann before the 1916 insurrection. An t-Óglác IV. No. 4, N.S. pp. 1-7. Decr., 1931.

349. HOCKING (Joseph) : Is Home Rule Rome rule ? 192 pp. 8vo. London, Ward, Lock, 1912.
> The author, who believes that " Rome rule means corruption, decadence and ruin," was convinced, after a visit to Ireland, that Home Rule would not be Rome rule.

355a. HONESTY, an outspoken scrap of paper, edited by Gilbert Galbraith, Oct. 16, 1915—April 22, 1916. Dublin, Gaelic Press.

350. HOME RULE BILL, 1912. An outline of the Home Rule Bill of 1912, 16 pp. 8vo. London, Liberal Publication Department.

351. HOME RULE COUNCIL, The : Home Rule ?s answered. 64 pp. sm. 8vo. London, Home Rule Council, 1912.

351a. —— What the Home Rule Bill will do : a simple explanation of the Home Rule Bill of 1912. With a preface by the Rt. Hon. Herbert Samuel, M.P. 54 pp. 8vo. London, Home Rule Council, 1912.

352. HOME RULE FROM THE TREASURY BENCH : Speeches during the first and second reading debates, with an introduction by the Rt. Hon. H. H. Asquith, M.P. 320 pp. portrs. 8vo. London, Unwin, 1912.

353. " HOME RULE NOTES." 1911-1912 : A year's record of the Home Rule movement. Vol. 1. December, 1911, to November, 1912. 630 pp. + index (35 pp.) London, Home Rule Council, 1912.
> Published in monthly numbers.

HOME RULE, *see* Finance (Irish) ; 330-336 (Govt. of Ireland Bill), 95–96, 363–366 (Irish Press Agency) ; 178–185, 512–520 (Redmond, J. E.) ; Irish Unionist Alliance ; Sinn Féin ; Ulster.

354. HONE (Joseph Maunsel) : James Larkin and the nationalist policy. *Contemporary Rev.*, CIV. pp. 784-788. Dec., 1913.

355. —— Ireland during the war. *Contemporary Rev.*, CIX. pp. 360-368, March, 1916.

356. HOPE (James Fitzalan) : Home Rule for Ireland. *Dublin Review,* CL. pp. 353-369. London, April, 1912.

> Deputy-Speaker of the House of Commons. English Catholic Unionist view. Opposes Home Rule.

357. [HORGAN (John Joseph)] : The complete grammar of anarchy, by members of the War Cabinet and their friends. 44 pp. 8vo. Dublin, Maunsel, 1918. (Passed by Censor).

> Selections from statements against the Home Rule Bill in 1912-1914. Mr. Asquith called them "the complete grammar of anarchy" (author's foreword). Published at the time of the crisis brought about by the application of the British Conscription law to Ireland in 1918.

358. HOWARD GRITTEN (W. G.) : Should the Unionist party compromise on Home Rule ? *Fortnightly Rev.,* C. pp. 1027-1032. Dec., 1913.

HOWTH GUN-RUNNING (July, 1914), *see* 316 (Figgis D.) ; 346-347 (Hobson, B.) ; 371 (*Irish Volunteer*) ; 408 (Mac Donagh, T.) ; 446 (O'Brien, C.) ; 537-538 (Royal Commission).

> *See also* a letter from P. H. Pearse reproduced in facsimile in *An Phoblacht,* VIII. N.S., April 8th, 1933, and the *Irish Volunteer,* July 24th, 1915.

INDUSTRY AND TRADE, 1912-1916, *see* Sect. GENERAL AND INTRODUCTORY. [*For references to the effects of the Great War on industry and trade in Ireland see* 46 (Dublin Chamber of Commerce) ; 46a (Dublin Industrial Development Association) ; 36 (Cork Chamber of Commerce) ; 36a (Cork Industrial Development Association)].

359. IRELAND. Éire : Oct. 26th 1914-Dec. 4th 1914. Dublin, pr. by P. Mahon for the "Ireland Publishing Co." 12 D'Olier Street.

> The first number was published "in order to report the proceedings of the Irish Volunteer Convention." On Dec. 3rd, 1914, the printer was notified that in the opinion of the military authorities the paper was publishing matter contrary to the terms of regulations made under D.O.R.A. A notice signed by Arthur Griffith, editor, and Seaghan T. O Ceallaigh, manager, appears in the last number, announcing that owing to this development and the removal of printing machinery by police and military the printer has been unable to continue publication. Sir M. Nathan told the 1916 Rebellion Commission that " it was found necessary to give a second warning in the case of ' Ireland,' and that paper ceased to appear after the issue of December 4th " (*Minutes of Evidence,* p. 5).

360. IRISH CABINET-MAKER, An : Next year's Irish ministry. 24 pp. 8vo. Dublin, Ponsonby and Gibbs, 1913.

361. IRISH CHURCH QUARTERLY, The : The Church of Ireland and Home Rule. Vol. V. pp. 97-116. Dublin, February, 1912.

> Fears for Protestant rights and security under Home Rule. Contends that " the Irish people form two nations " (Protestants and Catholics)

Irish Citizen Army, 1912-1916, *see* Labour movement (Irish) ; 19 (Clarkson, J. D.) ; 199 (Ryan, D.) ; 203 (Ryan, W. P.) ; 306-307 (*Dublin Disturbances,* 1913) ; 450 (O Cathasaigh, S.) ; 578 (White, J. R.) ; Connolly J. ; Larkin, J. ; Markievicz, C.

See also Sect. **1916.**

362. IRISH COUNTY COUNCILS' GENERAL COUNCIL: Tables supplementary to draft report on national finance, presented by the standing committee on legislation. 24 pp. 8vo. Dublin, Cahill, 1912.

362a. IRISH NATIONAL VOLUNTEERS, Óglaiġ Ċioramla na hÉireann: Constitution and rules. Córuġaḋ ⁊ riaġlaca, 1915. 14 pp. 8vo. Dublin, Wood Printing Works, 1916.

> Dated December, 1915. J. E. Redmond, M.P., is given as chairman of the Irish National Volunteers.

Irish Parliamentary Party, *See* Sect. GENERAL AND INTRODUCTORY and 350-353 (Home Rule).

363. IRISH PRESS AGENCY, 1912: Letters from Irish Protestants. 8 pp. 8vo. London, Irish Press Agency, [1912] (Leaflet No. 39).

> Seventy letters sent to Jeremiah MacVeagh, M.P., in answer to a circular letter inviting expressions of opinion. The writers, including peers, privy councillors, merchants, clergymen, landowners and others, testify from experience to the absence of religious persecution or intolerance in Ireland.

364. —— Protestant opinion and Home Rule. How Protestants are treated in Ireland. 16 pp. 8vo. *n.d.* (Leaflet No. 15A.—Enlarged edition).

> Testimony of Protestant clergy, farmers, business men, etc., living in Ireland to the fairness and tolerance of the people.

365. —— Leaflets. London, 1912-1913.

> Published under the auspices of the Irish Parliamentary Party to show English readers the necessity for Home Rule. They include: " Home Rule and " Greater Britain " (No. 4); " The Ascendency spirit in Ireland " (No. 48); " Ulster " and the Provisional Government " by J. J. Clancy, K.C., M.P. (No. 49).

366. —— The Irish National Convention, 1912. List of delegates and report of proceedings. Repr. from the " Freeman's Journal." 96 pp. 8vo. London, Irish Press Agency, 1912.

> The Convention was called by the Irish Parliamentary party to consider the terms of the Home Rule Bill. The terms were approved and the meeting expressed unqualified confidence in the leaders.

Irish Race Convention (New York), March, 1916, *see* 44 (Devoy, J.) 549 (Sexton, J. P.); 631 (Egan, P. F.); 1140 (Friends of Irish' Freedom).

367. IRISH REVIEW, The, a monthly magazine of Irish literature, art, and science, Dublin. March, 1911-Sept.-Nov., 1914 (Vol. 4. No. 41).

> " The *Irish Review* has been founded to give expression to the intellectual movement in Ireland . . . The *Irish Review* will strive to speak for Ireland rather than for any party or coterie." Mr. Pádraic Colum says: " Professor Houston in the College of Science, with James Stephens, [Thomas] MacDonagh and myself started the *Irish Review*. MacDonagh was associate editor, first with the three of us, and after an interregnum, with his friend Joseph Plunkett " (See M. Joy: The Irish rebellion of 1916, p. 330). The publication of " Ireland, Germany and the next war " by Shan Van Vocht [Sir Roger Casement] in the issue of July, 1913, aroused much interest in England and Germany.

367a. —— Press cuttings, 1914. *Irish Rev.*, II. pp. 154-163. May, 1912.

368. IRISH TAXPAYER, An : The finance of the Home Rule Bill, 18 pp. 8vo. Dublin, Sealy, Bryers and Walker, 1913.

369. IRISH TRANSPORT AND GENERAL WORKERS' UNION, The : The facts concerning Larkin's departure to America [in 1914] . . . Repr. from the " Voice of Labour " of April 12, 1924. 12 pp. 8vo. [Dublin, Irish Transport and General Workers' Union, 1924].

369a. IRISH UNIONIST, An : The Home Rule " nutshell," examined by an Irish Unionist. (Being a reply to " Home Rule in a nutshell " by Mr. Jeremiah MacVeagh, M.P.). 112 pp. sm. 8vo. Dublin, and Belfast, Unionist Associations of Ireland, 1912.

See 132.

370. IRISH UNIONIST ALLIANCE, The : Home Rule : Nationalist " assurances and guarantees " : promise and performance— as evidenced by the Home Rule Bill of 1893. 8 pp. 8vo. Dublin, Irish Unionist Alliance, 1912. (No. 183).

371. IRISH VOLUNTEER, The : Óglác na h-Éireann. Feb. 7th, 1914– [Nov. 28th], 1914. Weekly. Printed by the North Wexford Printing and Publishing Co., [Enniscorthy] for the proprietors, Middle Abbey street, Dublin.

A new series began on Dec. 5th, 1914 (Vol. 2, No. 1. N.S). and continued to the week-end before the insurrection, April 22nd, 1916 (No. 72). Pr. for the proprietors by P. Mahon (Nos. 14-43 by the North Gate Printing Works, Belfast), and published at the Volunteer Headquarters, 41 Kildare street, Dublin, and, later, 2 Dawson street.

Official organ of the Irish Volunteers. Edited by Laurence De Lacey, Enniscorthy. Contributions by P. H. Pearse, Eamonn Ceannt, the O'Rahilly, M. J. Judge, Terence MacSwiney, etc. After the outbreak of the European war differences in national opinion were reflected in the columns of the paper and the Standing Committee of the Irish Volunteers disclaimed " all responsibility " for certain " articles and verses of an objectionable character."

The report of the Honorary Secretary (Bulmer Hobson) to the second Volunteer Convention on Oct. 31, 1915, says : " Towards the end of November, 1914, the proprietors of the *Irish Volunteer* informed Mr. MacNeill of their intention to discontinue publication of the paper. It was decided that it should be taken over, and since 5th December, 1914, it has been edited and managed at Headquarters, and has been most valuable as a propagandist organ throughout the year " (*Irish Volunteer*, November 6, 1915).

When the *Irish Volunteer* was revived " under new management " Professor Eoin MacNeill became editor. Among the contributors were E. MacNeill, Ua Rathgaille, and T. J. MacSwiney, and (of unsigned articles) J. J. O'Connell, Capt. J. R. White, Bulmer Hobson and Eimar O'Duffy.

Col. Edgeworth-Johnstone, Chief Commissioner, Dublin Metropolitan Police, in his evidence before the 1916 Rebellion Commission : ' Very clear and very good military articles were written every week in the " Irish Volunteer," giving instruction as to hedge fighting, taking trenches, and all that sort of thing ' (*Minutes of Evidence*, Par. 1294).

Irish Volunteers (Óglaigh na hÉireann), 1913-1916, see 10, 242 (Béaslaí, P.); 44 (Devoy, John); 45 (Donovan, T. M.); 128 (MacManus, L.); 316 (Figgis, D.); 334 (Green, A. S.); 346-348 (Hobson, B.); (Colum, P.); 379 (Judge, M. J.); 398 (Lennon, M. J.); 439 (*National Volunteer*); 455a (Ó Mórdha, M.); 459 (O'Rahilly, The); 460 (" Outis "); 471–478 (Pearse, P.); 537–538 (Royal Commission . . . landing of arms at Howth); 673 (Monteith, R.).

See also Irish Citizen Army; *Irish Freedom*; *Irish Review*; Sinn Féin.

372. IRISH VOLUNTEERS : Manifesto of the Irish Volunteers, promulgated at the Rotunda meeting, November 25th, 1913. *Irish Review.* pp. 503-505. December, 1913.

373. —— Manifesto to the Irish Volunteers, 24th Sept., 1914. *Irish Rev.*, IV. pp. 281-284. Sept.-Nov., 1914.

373a. —— The handbook for Irish Volunteers : simple lectures on military subjects. By " H." sm. 8vo. 100 pp. Dublin, Gill, 1914.

374. IRISH WORKER, The. People's advocate : Edited by Jim Larkin. Weekly. May 27th, 1911–Dec. 5th, 1914. Pr. for the Proprietor at the City Printing Works and published by him at 10 Beresford Place, Dublin.

James Connolly was a frequent contributor and wrote a weekly signed article in the early months of the Great War. Sir M. Nathan, in his evidence before the 1916 Rebellion Commission, said that on Dec. 4th, 1914, " ' The Irish Worker ' appeared with certain expurgations made by the printer, but as it still contained matter contravening the Regulations all ;copies that could be found were seized and the type and removable parts of the printing machinery were removed." One number of *Irish Work*, edited by Jim Larkin, appeared (on Dec. 19th, 1914). This was succeeded by the *Worker* and the *Worker's Republic*, both edited by James Connolly.

375. IRISHMAN, An : Intolerance in Ireland, facts not fiction, Second edition. 208 pp. 8vo. London, Simpkin Marshall, 1914.

Examples of alleged " Roman intolerance in Ireland," persecution of Protestants, etc., collected as arguments against Home Rule.

IRISHMAN, The, *see* 859.

376. JAMES (Lionel) : A vision of civil war. *Nineteenth Century*, LXXVI. pp. 268-280. Aug. 1914.

377. JOHNSON (Thomas) : A handbook for rebels, a guide to successful defiance of the British Government . . . Compiled by Thomas Johnson, a member of the Dublin Mansion House Conference, 1918. 32 pp. 8vo. Dublin, Maunsel, [1918]. (Passed by Censor).

Extracts from speeches made in 1912–1914 by Sir E. Carson, Sir J. H. Campbell, Mr. A. Bonar Law, Sir F. E. Smith, " and other organisers of rebellion in Ulster," in which they advocated violent measures against the British Government.

378. JOHNSTON (Joseph) : Civil war in Ulster, its objects and probable results. 200 pp. 8vo. Dublin, Sealy, Bryers and Walker, [1913].

A criticism of Ulster Unionism by a Fellow of Trinity College, Dublin.

379. JUDGE (Michael J.) : The inner history of the Volunteers. In th *Irish Nation* (weekly). Vol. I. July 22, 1916–April, 1917.

> A member of the original Volunteer Committee. Writing from an individual point of view describes formation of the Volunteers, the election of the Irish Parliamentary Party nominees (to which the author was opposed) and the split of 1914.

380. KEANE (*Sir* John) *5th Bart.* : A resident landlord's view of the Irish problem. *Nineteenth Century*, LXXV. pp. 479-488. March, 1914.

> Favours Home Rule and opposes the suggested partition of Ireland.

381. KENNEDY (J. M.) : Why Home Rule is unnecessary. *Fortnightly Rev.*, XCIX (N.S.). pp. 1082-1093. June, 1913.

382. KENNY (James David) : Irish nationalism, a humbug. *The Forum*. Vol. L. pp. 779-789. New York, Dec., 1913.

382a. —— : The Ulster Covenant, a humbug. *Forum*, LII. pp. 23-30. New York, July, 1914.

383. KERR (*Rev.* William Shaw) : Ireland and the war. *Irish Church Quarterly*, IX. pp. 108-118. April, 1916.

384. KERR-SMILEY (Peter) *M.P.* : Why Ulster objects to Home Rule. 32 pp. sm. 8vo. [Belfast, Ulster Unionist Council], [1914 ?] (Ulster Unionist Council Political Leaflets).

> M.P. (U.) North Antrim.

385. KETTLE (Thomas Michael) : The financial aspect of Home Rule. *British Rev.*, XVI. pp. 336-353. Jan. 1912.

386. —— The open secret of Ireland . . . with an introduction by J. E. Redmond, M.P. 172 pp. 8vo. London, Ham-Smith, 1912.

> Written mainly for English readers " in order to bring about a better understanding between the two countries " (J. Redmond).

387. —— The economics of nationalism. *Irish Eccles. Record*, I, 5th Series. pp. 12-18, 153-162. Jan., Feb., 1913.

388. —— The agony of Dublin. *Irish Review*, III. pp. 441-449, 1913.

> Member of the Industrial Peace Committee.

389. —— The business genius of " Ulster " ? *English Rev.*, XVII. pp. 540-551. July, 1914.

See also 107, 862.

390. KILLANIN (Martin Henry Fitzpatrick MORRIS) *2nd Baron* : The sickbed of Cuchuluin. *Nineteenth Century*, LXXVIII. pp. 159-182, 370-392. July, Aug,. 1915.

> Surveys Irish social conditions and national character.

391. KING (*Rev.* R. G. S.) : Ulster's protest. Her industrial, political, imperial reasons for refusing to submit to Home Rule. An appeal to Great Britain, by the Rev. R. G. S. King, M.A., Rector of Limavady, Co. Derry. 24 pp. 8vo. Derry, *Sentinel*, [1914].

>125,000 copies of this pamphlet were printed, in Dec., 1913—Jan., 1914.

392. —— Ulster's refusal to submit to a Roman Catholic Parliament, stated and justified . . . 22 pp. 8vo. Derry, *Pr. Sentinel*. 1914.

Labour movement (Irish), *see* Sect. GENERAL AND INTRODUCTORY; 26-35 (Connolly, J.); (Larkin, J.); 345 (Healy, T. M.); Irish Citizen Army; 354 (Hone, J. N.); 369 (Irish Transport Union); 583 (Wright, A.).

Larne gun-running (April, 1914), *see* 25 (Colvin, I.); 37 (Cushendun, *1st Baron*); 70 (Gwynn, D.); 557 (Spender, J. A.). *See also* Ulster.

393. LATHBURY (Daniel Conner) : Compromise or dissolution. *Nineteenth Century*, LXXV. pp. 19-33. Jan., 1914.

394. —— Exclusion the only compromise. *Nineteenth Century*, LXXVI. pp. 1-12. July, 1914.

395. LAW (Hugh Alexander) : Why is Ireland at war ? Second edition. 42 pp. 8vo. Dublin, Maunsel, 1916.

>M.P. (Nat.) W. Donegal, 1902-18.

396. LEES-SMITH (Hastings Bertrand) : The future of the Home Rule Bill. *Contemporary Rev.*, CV. pp. 331-339. March, 1914.

397. LEGGE (Edward) : The personality of Sir Edward Carson. *Fortnightly Rev.*, CI. (N.S.). pp. 600-607. April, 1914.

398. LENNON (Michael J.) : A retrospect. *Banba*, Vol. II. pp. 209-222. 297-311, 395-413. illustr. Dublin, Jan.-Mar., 1922.

>A well informed record of the progress of the national movement and the organisation of the Irish Volunteers, 1912-1916.

399. LIBERAL PUBLICATIONS DEPARTMENT : The Home Rule Bill of 1912. The full text with a summary outline and memorandum on financial provisions. 56 pp. 8vo. London, Liberal Publications Department, 1912.

400. LITTLE (Patrick John) : Rome Rule. A paper read at a meeting of the Young Ireland branch, U.I.L., 1911. 20 pp. 8vo. Dublin, Gill, 1913.

See also 442 (*New Ireland*).

401. LLOYD (Ernest T.) : When Ulster stood alone. 12 pp. 8vo. Shrewsbury. 1914.

>Repr. from the " Shrewsbury Chronicle."

402. LOCKER LAMPSON (Godfrey) : Irish education under the Union. In *Against Home Rule*, ed. by S. ROSENBAUM. pp. 314-331. London, 1912.
    M.P. (U.).

03. LONDONDERRY (Charles Stewart VANE-TEMPEST-STEWART) *6th, Marquess of* : The Ulster question. In *Against Home Rule*, ed. by S. ROSENBAUM. pp. 162-169. London, 1912.
    Lord-Lieutenant of Ireland, 1886-1889, Chairman, Ulster Unionist Council.

404. LONDONDERRY (Charles S. H. VANE-TEMPEST STEWART) *7th Marquess of* : The Ulster Volunteer Force. [By Viscount] Castlereagh, officer commanding North Belfast Regiment, U.V.F. *British Review*, VII. pp. 1-11. July, 1914.

405. LONG (Walter) *1st Viscount* : Private Bill legislation. In *Against Home Rule*, ed. by S. ROSENBAUM. pp. 295-303. London, 1913. 1912-1916.

406. MCCARTHY (Michael F.) : The nonconformist treason. 340 pp. 8vo. London, Blackwood, 1912.
    Anti-Catholic and anti-Nationalist. Expresses " amazement " and " grief " at the action of British Nonconformists in supporting Home Rule.

407. MCCULLAGH (Francis) : The Ulster Catholic. *Contemporary Rev.*, S.C. pp. 533-540. April, 1914.

408. MACDONAGH (Thomas) : Clontarf, 1914. By Thomas MacDonagh, Company commander. Supplement to the *Irish Review*, IV. [4] pp. July-Aug., 1914.

See also 367 ; 550 ; 663.

409. MACDONALD (John Archibald) and CHARNWOOD (Godfrey Rathbone BENSON) *1st Baron* : The federal solution. London, Murray, [1914].

410. MACDONALD (John Archibald Murray) : The Home Rule Bill. *Contemporary Rev.*, CI. May, 1912.

MACDONNELL (*Sir* Antony Patrick) *1st Baron, of Swinford, see* 124.

MACDONNELL (*Sir* John), *see* 125.

✓ **411.** MACKEOGH (Michael) : Roger Casement, Germany and the world war : From British imperial consul to Irish republican envoy. *Catholic Bulletin*, XVIII. Jan.–Nov., 1928.
    Served with the British Expeditionary Force in France, Aug., 1914, and was taken prisoner. Afterwards joined with Sir Roger to form an Irish Brigade in Germany. A narrative of events in the Irish prisoner of war camp at Limburg with details of the personnel of the Irish Brigade attached to the 203rd Brandenburger Regiment at Zossen. The author remained in the German army until 1919.

412. McL. (F.) : The Irish vote after Home Rule. *Socialist Rev.*, XI. pp. 203-210. May, 1913.

413. MacNeill (Eoin): Daniel O'Connell and Sinn Féin. Part I. O'Connell's alternative. 24 pp. 8vo. [Dublin, Irish Publicity League, 1915]. (Tracts for the Times. No. 6).

414. —— Daniel O'Connell and Sinn Féin. Part II. How Ireland is plundered. 24 pp. 8vo. [Dublin, Irish Publicity League, 1915]. (Tracts for the Times. No. 7).
See also 130; 371 (*Irish Volunteer*); 667a.

ᴍᴀᴄpιᴀʀᴀιs (pᴀ́ᴏʀᴀιc): ᴍo Cuᴀιʀιm ꜰéιn. In *Irish Volunteer*. Jan. 9–Feb. 27, 1915.
See also 471-478 (Pearse, P. H.).

415. Macready (*General Sir* C. F. Nevil): Papers relating to the appointment of Major-General Sir C. F. N. Macready, K.C.B., to command the troops in the province of Ulster and to be a Resident magistrate. Presented to both Houses of Parliament ... 4 pp. H.M.S.O. 1914. [Cd. 7330].

415a. —— Annals of an active life. Vol. I. 336 pp. illustr. 8vo. London, Hutchinson, [1924].
Gives an account of the author's visit to Ulster, as military commander and resident magistrate, in March–May, 1914. He was sent by the Government to investigate the situation at the time of the Curragh army crisis.

416. MacSwiney (Patrick, of Mashanaglass) *Marquis*: A propos du Home Rule et de la résistance de l'Ulster. 60 pp. 8vo. Paris, Auguste Picard, [1914 ?].

417. MacVeagh (Jeremiah) *M.P.*: The Conservative party and Home Rule ... Repr. from the *English Review*, June, 1912. 14 pp. 8vo. Westminster, Home Rule Council, 1912. (H. Leaflet. No. 86).

417a. —— "Home rule: Rome rule." An examination of religious intolerance in Ireland. With introduction by Rev. C. Silvester Horne, M.P. Fifth impression. 64 pp. 8vo. London, "The Morning Leader," 1912.
Compiled by Jeremiah Mac Veagh, M.P. 84 pp. 8vo. London, Irish Press Agency, [1912 ?].
Replies from "leading and representative non-Catholics in all parts of Ireland" to a circular letter inviting them to state their views from personal experience on religious toleration. Over one hundred replies are printed from clergymen, landowners, peers, military officers, merchants, university professors, etc., including prominent Ulster Unionists, testifying to the absence of unfair treatment of Protestants by Catholics.

418. Magistrates (Ireland) ... A return showing the names and addresses and occupations or descriptions of the persons appointed to the Commission of the Peace in Ireland since the preparation of the last Return, giving for each county and borough a summary of religions of those so appointed, a summary of religions of all now holding the Commission of the Peace in each county and borough ... ordered by the House of Commons to be printed, 16th December, 1912. 28 pp. H.M.S.O., 1913. [H.C. 396].

419. —— A Return showing the names, addresses, occupations or descriptions of the persons appointed to the Commission of the Peace in Ireland since the 30th day of November, 1912 . . . including all appointments to the end of 1913. 24 pp. 4to. H.M.S.O., 1914. [H.C. 461].

420. MAGUIRE (James K.) : The King, the Kaiser, and Irish freedom. 314 pp. 8vo. illustr. New York, Devin-Adair Co., 1915.

> Advocates friendship between Germany and Ireland. Particulars given of Sir Roger Casement's mission to Germany, the situation in Ireland, 1915 (with extracts from suppressed newspapers), and of Irish-American societies.

421. MAHAFFY (John Pentland) : Will Home Rule be Rome rule ? *Blackwood's Mag.*, CXCII. pp. 153-159. Aug., 1912.

422. —— Who wants Home Rule ? *Blackwood's Mag.*, CXCIII. pp. 244-253. Sept., 1913.

> Senior Fellow and (1915-1919) Provost of Trinity College, Dublin.

423. MAISONNIER (Louis) et LECARPENTIER (G.) : L'Irlande et le home rule. 320 pp. 8vo. Paris, Rivière (Librairie des sciences politiques et sociales).

425. " MANCHESTER COURIER " : Ulster will fight for unity of Empire. Home Rulers covet Ulster's wealth. Reprinted from " Manchester Courier " . . . March 9th, 1914. 8 pp. Maps. 8vo. [1914].

426. " MANCHESTER GUARDIAN " HISTORY OF THE WAR, The. Vol. III—1915. (Ireland and the War. pp. 321-332. illustr.). 4to. Manchester, Heywood, 1915.

427. MANUAL OF EMERGENCY LEGISLATION, COMPRISING ALL THE ACTS OF PARLIAMENT, PROCLAMATIONS, ORDERS, &C., PASSED AND MADE IN CONSEQUENCE OF THE WAR TO SEPTEMBER 30th, 1914. 572 pp. 8vo. H.M.S.O., Sept., 1914.

> For subsequent orders and regulations made under the Defence of the Realm Acts, see *Statutory Rules and Orders*, 1914-1921.

428. MARLOWE (Nathaniel) [pseud.] : Irish Volunteers. *Contemporary Rev.*, CVI. pp. 34-40. July, 1914.

429. —— The mood of Ireland. *British Rev.* pp. 1-12. July, 1915.

See also 744, 899.

430. MARRIOTT (*Sir* John Arthur Ransome) : The third edition of Home Rule. (I) A first impression of the Bill. *Nineteenth Century*, LXXI. pp. 829-848. May, 1912.

Mellows (Liam), *see* 135b, 434, 671a.

431. MEREDITH (James Creed) : Proportional representation in Ireland. 16 + 166 pp. 8vo. Dublin, Ponsonby, 1913.

432. METHODIST DEMONSTRATION COMMITTEE : Methodism and Home Rule, 1912. Resolutions unanimously adopted and speeches delivered by Rev. George R. Wedgwood, Professor Sir William Whitla, M.D., LL.D., J.P., and Rev. William Nicholas, D.D., LL.D., at the Methodist demonstration in Belfast, on March 14th, 1912. 24 pp. 8vo. Belfast, Methodist Demonstration against Home Rule, [1912]. (Ulster Unionist Council Religious Leaflets).

433. METHODIST DEMONSTRATION " CONTINUATION COMMITTEE " : Appeal. of the Irish Methodists to their co-religionists in Great Britain, 8 pp. 8vo. Belfast, " Continuation Committee " of the Methodist demonstration against Home Rule, Sept., 1913. (Ulster Unionist Council Religious Leaflets).

434. MILROY (Seán) : Memories of Mountjoy. An account of four months' prison experience by a Sinn Fein leader, with reminiscences of Sean MacDermott, Francis Sheehy-Skeffington, Seán Hegarty and Liam Mellowes. 89 pp. 8vo. Dublin, Maunsel, 1917.

MOLONY (*Sir* Thomas Francis) 1*st Bart. K.C.*, *see* 138.

434a. MOORE (Frank Frankfort) : The truth about Ulster. 286 pp. illustr. 8vo. London, Nash, 1914.
>Irish novelist. Unionist. Chapters on social and economic conditions, religious differences, the Orange Institution, etc.

435. MORGAN (John Hartman) : Home Rule and federalism. *Nineteenth Century*, LXXI. pp. 1230-1242. June, 1912.

436. ——— The future of Ireland. (II.) The Home Rule Bill re-considered. *Nineteenth Century*, LXXIII. pp. 212-230. Jan., 1913.

437. ——— Ulster. *Nineteenth Century*, LXXIV. pp. 889-907. Nov., 1913. *See also* 142-144.

438. MORRISON-BELL (Arthur Clive) : Redistribution before Home Rule. *Nineteenth Century*, LXXI. pp. 445-454. Sept., 1912.
M.P. (U.).

438a. MULDOON (John) *M.P.* : The story of a rigged " Convention." 20 pp. 8vo. Dublin, United Irish League, 1915.
>The Nationalist Convention held at Tullamore, 19th November, 1915, to select a candidate for a parliamentary bye-election.

National Council, *see* Sinn Féin.

439. NATIONAL VOLUNTEER, The. (Defence not defiance). Official organ of the National Volunteers. Oct., 17th 1914–April 22nd, 1916. Weekly. Pr. and published by the " National Volunteer " Co., 44 Parnell square, Dublin ; from Aug. 7th, 1915, pr. for the National Committee by the Wood Printing works).
>Supports the policy of John Redmond and the Irish Parliamentary paity in the " split " which followed the outbreak of the European war in 1914. " At the call of the governing body of the National Volunteers this journal has sprung into existence. It has been founded to save Ireland from the curse of dissension " (leading article in No. 1).

440. NATIONALITY, 1915-1916, 1917-1919. June 19th, 1915- March 25th, 1916. (No. 43). Weekly. Pr. for the proprietors at the Northgate Printing Works, Belfast, and published at the *Nationality* Office, 12 D'Olier Street, Dublin. New Series : Feb. 17th, 1917–Sept. 20th, 1919. Pr. by Patrick Mahon and publ. at the Offices, 6 Harcourt Street.

" Edited by Arthur Griffith " up to the time of his arrest in May, 1918. The articles written by Griffith, before and after the 1916 rising, defining the political and economic programme of Sinn Féin are of special interest. Major Ivor Price, Director of British Military Intelligence, Irish Command, at the 1916 Rebellion Commission said : ' In the case of one paper, " Nationality," which was supposed to have a circulation of 4,500, I found the circulation actually of 8,000, and that paper would go from hand to hand " (*Minutes of Evidence*, Parag. 1346).

441. NEVINSON (Henry Woodd) : Sir Roger Casement and Sinn Fein, some personal notes. The *Atlantic Monthly*, CXVIII. pp. 236-244. Boston, Aug., 1916.

442. NEW IRELAND, an Irish weekly. May 15th, 1915–Sept., 1919. *Pr.* Wood Printing Works, Dublin.

Edited by Denis Gwynn (to Feb. 1916) and afterwards by P. J. Little. The issue of Feb. 26th, 1916, in announcing that there has been a change in the editorship, says : " No change will take place in the national outlook of the paper, nor in its efforts to conserve the forces of a democratic Ireland, and to awaken new initiative for the benefit of the country." The circulation of the paper abroad through the post was prohibited in in Sept., 1916. *New Ireland* favoured the Irish Nation League in 1916, but afterwards adopted the policy of Sinn Féin. It was suppressed, along with other Sinn Féin weekly journals, in Sept., 1919. It was resumed by Mr. P. S. Little as *Old Ireland* in Oct., 1919 (see 1291).

443. " NORTHERN WHIG," The : Some arguments against Home Rule. Reprinted by permission from the " Northern Whig," Belfast. 22 pp. 8vo. Belfast, Ulster Unionist Council, 1912. (*Series U.C. 60*).

444. NORTHUMBERLAND (Alan Ian PERCY) *8th Duke of* : The " pogrom " plot : The case for the impeachment of ministers. *National Rev.*, LXIII. pp. 389-415. London, May, 1914.

An extreme Unionist comment on the Curragh army crisis. Reviews the military measures contemplated by the British Government in Ulster, and asserts that " they were to bombard the town [Belfast] from outside . . . an open town which the laws of civilised warfare do not permit troops to bombard."

445. —— Some impressions of the Ulster Volunteers. *National Rev.*, LXIII. pp. 754-764. July, 1914.

446. O'BRIEN (Conor) : From three yachts, a cruiser's outlook. 12 + 274 pp. portr. 8vo. London, Arnold, 1928.

Contains an account of gun-running for the Irish Volunteers in 1914.

449. O'BRIEN (William) *M.P.* : Grattan's Home Rule, Gladstone's, and Asquith's. An answer to a boast. 32 pp. 8vo. Cork, *Free Press* Office, 1915. (All-for-Ireland League Pamphlets).

Criticism of a claim made by Mr. John Redmond, in his letter to the Dublin Corporation, July 20th, 1915. See also 150.

450. Ó Cathasaigh (P.) [Seán] : The story of the Irish Citizen Army. 72 pp. 8vo. Dublin, Maunsel, 1919.

"The first account that has been given of the formation of the Irish Citizen Army during the Dublin strike of 1913-14, and the part played by it in the subsequent history of Ireland. . . . The book contains original character studies of Larkin, Connolly, Captain White and Madame Markievicz . . ." (Publisher's note). The author's initial was printed as "P" on the title page in error. See also 917.

450a. O'Connor (William J.) : The Irish ? a destroyer of pro-English arguments. 20 pp. 8vo. [New York, 1914 ?].

451. Ó Donnaháin Rossa (Diarmuid) : Ḋiaṙmuiḋ Ó Ḋonnaḃáin Rossa, 1831-1915. Souvenir of public funeral to Glasnevin cemetery, Dublin, August 1st, 1915. 24 pp. Pls. 4to. Dublin, [O'Donovan Rossa Funeral Committee, 1915].

451a. —— Second edition.

Contributions by P. H. Pearse, Thomas MacDonagh, Seán Ua Ceallaigh, Arthur Griffith, Northman, L. S. Ór., Seán MacGadhra, G, James Connolly, Ḃrian na Ḃanḃan. The second edition contains a description of the funeral ceremonies, the oration by Pearse, and several photographs, which are not in the first edition.

451b. O'Donovan Rossa (Mary J.) : [The death and funeral of Jeremiah O'Donovan Rossa]. *Gaelic American.* Sept. 11-Oct. 16. Nov. 6-Dec. 4, Dec. 25, 1915. Jan. 15, 1916.

An account of experiences in Ireland and of leading personalities in the Irish Volunteer movement.

Óglaiġ na hÉireann 1913-1916, *see* Irish Volunteers.

Óglaiġ Ṫioramla na h-Éireann, *see* Irish National Volunteers.

452. [O'Higgins (Brian F.)] and others : War, humour, and other atrocities. By Brian na Banban [*i.e.*, Brian F. O'Higgins], Myles Malone, and Will E. Wagtail. 76 pp. sm. 8vo. Dublin, "Spark" and son, [1915 ?].

Satires on the Irish Parliamentary Party and the recruiting campaign.

453. Oldham (Charles Hubert) : The record of Ulster in Irish patriotism. *Contemporary Rev.*, CIV. pp. 36-43. July, 1913.

See also 164-165.

454. Oliver (Frederick Scott) : The alternatives to civil war. 64 pp. 8vo. London, Murray, 1913.

455. —— What federalism is *not*. 132 pp. 8vo. London, Murray, 1914.

455a. Ó Móṙḋa (Muiris) : Tús aġus fás Óglác na hÉireann, 1913-1917. Tuairim : An Coronail Muiris Ó Móṙḋa, Seanaḋóir, Arḋ-Ċigire ḋÓglaiġ na hÉireann, 1914 aġus ḋÓglaiġ Náisiúnta na hÉireann, 1914-1917. Ḋ'aistriġ Liam Ó Rinn. 347 pp. 8vo. Baile Áta Cliaṫ, 1936.

The author, who was one of the founders of the Irish Volunteers, was appointed Inspector-General by the original committee (of which he was a member). After the division in the ranks in September, 1914, he was Inspector-General of the National Volunteers (who continued to accept the leadership of Mr. John Redmond).

456. O'NEILL (Hugh) : Who is the real foe of the Irish 12 pp. 8vo. n.p. [1916 ?].

457. [ORANGE] GRAND LODGE OF IRELAND : No surrender. The Orangemen of the world say " No Home Rule." 40 pp. 8vo. Dublin, Grand Lodge of Ireland, 1913.

> Resolutions and addresses against Home Rule by Orange lodges in the Dominions and the United States.

458. O'RAHILLY (The) : The secret history of the Irish Volunteers. 3rd edition, revised and enlarged. By the O'Rahilly, Treasurer of the Irish Volunteers. Dublin, Irish Publicity League, [1915] (Tracts for the Times. No. 3).

> Repr. of the first edition (8th April, 1915) with an additional note dated July 5th, 1915.

O'RIORDAN (*Rt. Rev. Mgr.* Michael), *see* 167.

459. O'Sullivan (*Rev.* P. P. : Dr. Blair ; or, I ish Protestants under Home rule. 204 pp. 8vo. Belfast, Carswell, 1912.

460. " OUTIS." The Irish National Volunteers. Can they defend the coasts of Ireland ? Will they enlist in Kitchener's army ? The answer is in the negative. *United Service Mag.* L (N.S.). Nov. 1914. pp. 170-176.

> Holds that offers from the Irish National Volunteers to co-operate in Irish coastal defence should be refused. " To train them to arms is but to establish a hostile force."

461. —— Has recruiting in Ireland been satisfactory ? *United Service Mag.*, LI. pp. 565-571. Aug., 1915.

> An anti-nationalist comment on the review of Irish National Volunteers held in Phœnix Park, Dublin, Easter Sunday, 1915.

462. OUTSIDER, An : Repeal or Home Rule. *Fortnightly Rev.* XCI. pp. 688-706. April, 1912.

463. —— " Ulsteria." *British Rev.*, IV. pp. 208-223. Nov., 1913.

464. —— The conciliation of Ulster. *Fortnightly Rev.*, C. (N.S.). pp 1017-1026. Dec., 1913.

465. OXFORD AND ASQUITH (Herbert Henry ASQUITH) *1st Earl of* : Mr. Asquith's speech in introducing the Home Rule Bill of 1912 . . . in the House of Commons, on April 11th, 1912. 32 pp. 8vo. [Westminster, Home Rule Council, 1912].

466. —— Mr. Asquith's first visit to Dublin. Speech by the Prime Minister at the Theatre Royal, Dublin, on July 19th, 1912. Introduction by Robert Harcourt, M.P. 16 pp. 8vo. London, Home Rule Council, [1912].

467. —— Fifty years of Parliament. Vol. II. 270 pp. illustr. 8vo. London, Cassell, 1926.

> Chapters in Vol. II on " Ulster " and the " Curragh incident." *See also* 557 (Spender, J. A.).

468. PAUL-DUBOIS (Louis) : Le drame irlandais. 250 pp. 8vo. Paris, Perrin, 1927

Ch. I : Les origines du Drame (1914-1918) ; Ch. II : Le " Sinn Fein " et la guerre anglo-irlandaise (1918-1921).

469. —— Le drame Irlandais. I. Les origines (1914-1918). *Revue des deux mondes.* XCI^e année. ; sixième periode. tome LXV. pp. 365-394. 1921.

470. —— The Irish struggle and its results. Translated from the French of L. Paul-Dubois and revised by T. P. Gill, late secretary of the Department of Agriculture and Technical Instruction, Ireland. 160 pp. 8vo. London, Longmans Green, 1934.

" The present book is a continuation of the work which was published over twenty years ago by the same author, under the title of *Contemporary Ireland and the Irish Question* " (*See* 170-171).

471. PEARSE (Pádraic Henry) : Collected works of Padraic H. Pearse. Political writings and speeches. 372 pp. frontisp. 8vo. Dublin, Maunsel and Roberts, 1922.

Containing the pamphlets by Pearse in the *Bodenstown* series and *Tracts for the Times*, and, in addition : The coming revolution (Nov., 1913) ; The psychology of a Volunteer (Jan., 1914) ; To the boys of Ireland (Feb., 1914) ; Why we want recruits (May, 1915) ; O'Donovan Rossa—character sketch (Aug., 1915) ; O'Donovan Rossa—graveside oration (Aug., 1915).

472. —— How does she stand ? Three addresses by P. H. Pearse. Second edition. 16 pp. 8vo. Dublin, " Irish Freedom " Office, 1915. (The Bodenstown series. No. 1).

An address on Theobald Wolfe Tone, delivered in Bodenstown Churchyard, 22nd June, 1913, and two addresses on " Robert Emmet and the Ireland of to-day," delivered at Emmet commemorations in New York on March 2nd and March 9th, 1914. The addresses are reprinted from verbatim reports in the *Gaelic American*, with a brief addendum, Aug., 1914.

473. —— From a hermitage. Second edition. 28 pp. 8vo. Dublin, " Irish Freedom " Office, 1915. (The Bodenstown series. No. 2).

Eight articles contributed to *Irish Freedom* from June, 1913, to January, 1914, reprinted with a few verbal changes and the omission of part of the open letter to Douglas Hyde (August, 1913). The author in his preface, dated 1st June, 1915, says : " They thus form a contemporary commentary on the period immediately preceding and covering the rise of the Irish Volunteers : a period which, when things assume their proper perspective, will probably be regarded as the most important in recent Irish history." " This pamphlet has been out of print for some months past, the original edition having been sold out almost immediately on publication " (*Irish Volunteer*, 27th Nov., 1915).

474. —— The murder machine. 20 pp. 8vo. Dublin, Whelan, 1916. (The Bodenstown series. No. 3).

Includes two articles on the English education system in Ireland reprinted from the *Irish Review*. " The rest of the pamphlet is a collection of notes made for a lecture which I delivered in the Dublin Mansion House in December, 1912 " (Author, 1st Jan., 1916).

475. —— Ghosts. 20 pp. 8vo. Dublin, Whelan, 1916. (Tracts for the Times. No. 10).

Preface dated Christmas Day, 1915, from St. Enda's College, Rathfarnham.

476. —— The separatist ideal. 20 pp. 8vo. Dublin, Whelan, **1916**. (Tracts for the Times. No. 11).

Preface dated 1st February, 1916.

477. —— The spiritual nation. 18 pp. 8vo. Dublin, Whelan, **1916**. (Tracts for the Times. No. 12).

Preface dated 13th February, 1916.

478. —— The sovereign people. 20 pp. 8vo. Dublin, Whelan, **1916**. (Tracts for the Times, No. 13).

Author's preface at St. Enda's College, Rathfarnham, 31st March, 1916 : ' This pamphlet concludes the examination of the Irish definition of freedom which I promised in " Ghosts." For my part I have no more to say.'

—— *See also* 173b, 371, and Sect. **1916**.

479. PEEL (*Hon.* George): The reign of Sir Edward Carson. 240 pp. 8vo. London, King, 1914.

A " connected account of the military and civil dispositions of Sir Edward Carson, from the date when he accepted or assumed authority at Craigavon in September, 1911." The author gives details of the war-like mobilisations and manœuvres carried out in Ulster and protests against the policy of opposing constitutional government by force of arms.

480. PHILALETHES : The chances of settlement. *Fortnightly Rev.*, CI. (N.S.). pp. 10-19. Jan., 1914.

481. —— The new situation. *Fortnightly Rev.*, CI. (N.S.) pp. 395-405. March, 1914.

482. —— The road to settlement. *Fortnightly Rev.*, CI. pp. 964-972. May, 1914.

483. —— Nearing the end. *Fortnightly Rev.*, CII (N.S.). pp. 212-223. Aug., 1914.

484. PHILLIPS (Justin): The Irish land bill, a criticism and a plea. *Irish Rev.*, III. pp. 450-457. Nov. 1913.

485. —— The new land bill and compulsory purchase. *Irish Rev.*, III. pp. 506-511. Decr., 1913.

486. —— Taxation of land values, the Irish standpoint. *Irish Rev.*, III. pp. 614-620. Feb., 1914.

487. [PIM (Herbert Moore)] : What Emmet means in 1915, a tract for the times. By A. Newman [*pseud., i.e.,* Herbert Moore Pim]. 16 pp. 8vo. Dublin, Irish Volunteer Headquarters, [1915]. [Tracts for the Times. No. 1].

488. —— Ascendancy while you wait. By A. Newman [*pseud., i.e.,* Herbert Moore Pim]. 16 pp. 8vo. Dublin, Irish Publicity League, [1915]. (Tracts for the Times. No. 5).

489. ——— What it feels like. By A. Newman. 28 pp. 8vo. Dublin, *n.p.* [September, 1915]. (Tracts for the Times. No. 8).
>The author was arrested and imprisoned in Belfast jail for refusing to obey a D.O.R.A. order to leave Ireland (1915). A narrative of his experiences, written in prison.

490. ——— Why the Manchester martyrs died. By A. Newman [*pseud.*, *i.e.*, Herbert Moore Pim]. 12 pp. 8vo. Dublin, Whelan, [1915 ?], (Tracts for the Times. No. 8).

491. ——— Three letters for Unionists only. 12 pp. 8vo. [Dublin, Sinn Fein n.d] (Leaflet No. 9).
——— See also 859 (*The Irishman*).

492. PIM (Jonathan) *K.C.* : The present position of the Irish land question. In *The new Irish constitution*, edited by J. H. MORGAN. pp. 166-214. London, 1912.

493. PLATT (T. Comyn) : The Ulster leader. *National Rev.*, LXII. pp. 236-245. Oct., 1913.
>" As one who has been with Sir Edward Carson through the recent Ulster campaign."

494. PLUNKETT (*Hon. Sir* Horace : A better way, an appeal to Ulster not to desert Ireland. 38 pp. 8vo. Dublin, Hodges, Figgis, 1914.

495. [POË (*Col. Sir* William Hutcheson)] : Irish Protestant's plea for Home Rule. 8 pp. 8vo. Westminster, Home Rule Council, [1912].
>Speech at a special General Synod of the Church of Ireland in Dublin, April 16th, 1912, protesting against an anti-Home Rule resolution before the meeting.

496. POLLOCK (Arthur Williamson Alsager) : The government and the army. *Fortnightly Rev.*, CI. pp. 783-792. May, 1914.
>Editor *United Service Magazine*.

497. PONSONBY (Arthur) *1st Baron* : The army crisis and Home Rule. *Contemporary Rev.*, CV. pp. 609-617. May, 1914.

498. PORRITT (Annie G.) : The Irish Home Rule Bill. *Political Science Quarterly*, XXXVIII. pp. 298-319. New York, June, 1913.

499. POSNER (Stanislaw) : Autonomia Irlandyi, Home Rule. 160 pp. 8vo. Warszawa, Nakladem Ksiegarni E. Wendeiska, [1913 ?].
>The author was afterwards a senator of Poland.

500. PRENTER (*Rev.* Samuel) : The religious difficulty under Home Rule : (ii) The Nonconformist view. In *Against Home Rule*, ed. by S. ROSENBAUM. pp. 212-221. London, 1912.

501. ——— Ulster and Home Rule, an address, delivered at Pitlorchry on September 22nd, 1913. By Rev. Samuel Prenter, ex-Moderator of the Presbyterian Church in Ireland. 14 pp. 8vo. Belfast, Belfast Steam-Printing Co., 1913 (Ulster Unionist Council Religious Leaflets).

502. PRESBYTERIAN CHURCH IN IRELAND, The : Home Rule : statement and appeal to the Free Churches of England and Wales, issued on behalf of the General Assembly of the Presbyterian Church in Ireland. [4] pp. *n.d.* (Ulster Unionist Council Religious Leaflets).

503. —— Castledawson outrage. Declarations by Rev. Robert Barron and injured persons, request of Belfast Presbytery for sworn public inquiry and Mr. Birrell's reply. 20 pp. 8vo. Belfast, " The Witness," 1913. (Ulster Unionist Council Leaflets).

503a. PRESS BUREAU : Army : Memorandum on the Official Press Bureau. . . . 4 pp. 4to. H.M.S.O., 1915 [Cd. 7680].

See also 274 (Censorship).

504. PROTESTANT PROTEST, A, 1913 : 54 pp. 8vo. *n.p.*, [1913].

Containing " an almost verbatim report of the principal speeches " made at a meeting of Protestants at Ballymoney, Co. Antrim, " to protest against the policy of Carsonism." The speakers included Captain J. R. White, Mrs. J. R. Green, Sir Roger Casement and Mr. Alec Wilson.

See also 3a (Armour, W. S.).

505. QUARTERLY REVIEW, The : Home Rule finance. Vol. 216. pp. 281-306. Jan., 1912.

506. —— The Home Rule Bill. Vol. 217. July, 1912.

506a. —— The Ulster covenant. *Quarterly Rev.* Vol. 217. pp. 559-598. Oct., 1912.

507. —— The Home Rule crisis and a national alternative. *Quarterly Rev.* Vol. 220. pp. 266-290. Jan., 1914.

508. —— The Home Rule crisis. *Quarterly Rev.* Vol. 220-221. pp. 570-590, pp. 275-294. April–July, 1914.

509. QUINN (John) : Roger Casement. *New Ireland*, II. Oct. 14th-28th, 1916.

Repr. from the *New York Times*, August 13th, 1916. The author, who met Casement in New York, advised him against undertaking the journey to Germany.

510. RECEPTION IN PARIS OF THE IRISH MEMBERS OF PARLIAMENT BY THE FRENCH DEPUTIES. 28 pp. 8vo. Paris, Chaix, 1916.

511. RECRUITING [for the British Army], 1916 : Report on recruiting in Ireland. Presented to both Houses of Parliament. 4 pp. 4to. H.M.S.O., 1916 [Cd. 8168].
> Dated 14th January, 1916. Signed by Lord Wimborne, Lord Lieutenant and Director of Recruiting for Ireland.

—— 1914-1918, *see* Army (British) ; Conscription crisis, 1918 ; Sinn Féin, 1914-1918 ; 215 ; 987 (Sullivan, A. M.) ; 342 (Hannay J. *Canon*) ; 786 (Crammond, E.) ; 800 (Dunraven, *4th Earl of*) ; 902a (*Men of military age*) ; 460-461 (" Outis ") ; 714-715 (Royal Commission on the rebellion) ; 1364 (Street, C. I. S.).

For anti-recruiting satires and verses see 452 ; 951 (O'Higgins, B. F., *and others*).

> See also *Estimate of Irishmen serving with the forces of the Crown*, 1916 (Cd. 8311). The figures for pre-war years may be found in the GENERAL ANNUAL REPORTS ON THE BRITISH ARMY, which give particulars of the recruits finally approved for the Regular Army in the different Irish regimental areas. Of the 55,602 N.C.Os. and men in the Special Reserve on October 1st, 1913, 12,462 were born in Ireland. The Regular Army at the same date included 20,780 N.C.O's and men who were born in Ireland. The total number of Irish N.C.Os. and men serving on the 15th April, 1916, with the military forces of the Crown was given by Sir Mathew Nathan as 150,183 (*Rebellion Commission Minutes*, p. 124).

512. REDMOND (John Edward) : Mr. Redmond on Ireland's hope. Speech . . . at the Eighty Club Banquet, Hotel Cecil, London, on Friday, 1st March, 1912. Authorised version. 8 pp. 8vo. [Westminster, Home Rule Council, 1912].

513. —— The justice of Home Rule. A statement of Ireland's claim for self-government. 62 pp. 8vo. London, Irish Press Agency, 1912.
> Ten articles, one reprinted from *McClure's Magazine*, one from *T. P.'s Magazine*, the remainder from *Reynold's Newspaper*.

514. —— The Home Rule Bill. 180 pp. 8vo. London, Cassell, 1912.
> Text and explanation of the Bill ; speeches by John Redmond on the first and second readings, at the National Convention in the Mansion House, Dublin, April 23, 1912, and the Eighty Club, March 1, 1912 ; outline of financial provisions and comparison with the Home Rule Bills of 1886 and 1893.

515. —— Orange threats . . . 16 pp. 8vo. London, Irish Press Agency, [1912 ?].

516. —— The " Ulster " question. Towards a united Ireland. *Rev. of Reviews*, XLVI. pp. 528-531. Nov. 1912.

517. —— Ulster and Home Rule. A speech delivered . . . at Newcastle-on-Tyne, November 14th, 1913. 12 pp. 8vo. London, Irish Press Agency, [1913]. (Leaflet No. 53).

518. —— Mr. Balfour on Nationality and Home Rule. A reply . . . 8 pp. 8vo. London, Irish Press Agency, [1913]. (Leaflet No. 54).

519. —— The Irish nation and the war. Extracts from speeches made in the House of Commons and in Ireland since the outbreak of the war. 38 pp. 8vo. Dublin, Sealy, Bryers and Walker, 1915.

520. —— Ireland and the war. Speeches delivered . . . at Dublin and Kilkenny, on September 25th and October 18th 1914, Repr. from the " Freeman's Journal." 12 pp. [Dublin, " Freeman's Journal," 1914 ?].

520a. —— Speech delivered by J. E. Redmond, M.P., Chairman, Irish Parliamentary Party, at the Waterford city and county convention. 22 pp. 8vo. London, Darling, 1915.
See also 178-185.

521. REDMOND-HOWARD (Louis George): John Redmond. *Forum*, LI. pp. 513-552. New York, April, 1914.

522. —— The new birth of Ireland. 264 pp. 8vo. London, Collins, [1914 ?].

523. REPINGTON (*Lieut.-Col.* Charles à Court): The first world war. Vol. 1, 18 + 621 pp. Vol. 2, 14 + 581 pp. London, Cassell, 1920.
Some references to Ireland: Ulster in 1914; the Convention (1917); the conscription crisis (1918).

524. RESIDENT MAGISTRATES (Ireland). Return " of the Resident Magistrates in Ireland on the 1st day of November, 1912," . . . ordered by the House of Commons to be printed, 2nd December, 1912. H.M.S.O., 1912. [H.C. 383].

Revenue and expenditure, *see* 192.

525. REVENUE OFFICIAL, A: Irish taxes under Home Rule. *Sinn Féin.* Vol. 3. June 8th-15th, 1912.

526. RIDGEWAY (*Sir* Joseph West): The Irish danger. (1) The responsibility. *Nineteenth Century*, LXXVI. pp. 256-267. Aug., 1914.
Under-Secretary for Ireland, 1887-1893.

527. RIGG (T. Galloway): The " wealthy Ulster " figment. *Westminster Rev.*, Vol. 217. pp. 357-365. Oct., 1912.

528. ROBERTS (*Field-Marshal* Frederick Sleigh ROBERTS) *1st Earl*: The army and civil war. *National Rev.*, XLIII. pp. 944-949. Aug., 1914.
Speech in the House of Lords, July 6, 1914. Defends the mutinous officers of the Curragh incident. *See* Curragh.

529. ROSENBAUM (S.): Against Home Rule, the case for the Union . . . With introduction by Sir Edward Carson, K.C., M.P., and preface by A. Bonar Law, M.P. Edited by S. Rosenbaum. 348 pp. 8vo. London, Warne, 1912.
Essays by British and Irish leaders of the Unionist party.

530. ROTHENFELDER (*Dr.* Franz): Casement in Deutschland. Mit einem Vorwort von Ferdinand Hansen, Kriegskorrespondent der " Isue and Events," New York. portrs. pl. facs. of handwriting. 124 pp. 8vo. Augsburg, Gebrüder Reichel, 1917.

531. ROUND TABLE, The : Home Rule. The other Irish question. *Round Table* [quarterly], II. pp. 422–446. London, June, 1912.

532. —— The Home Rule Bill. Map showing distribution of the non-Catholic population. *Round Table*, III. pp. 98-133. Dec., 1912.

533. —— The Irish question. *Round Table*, IV. pp. 1-61. Dec., 1913.
Also reprinted with a preface by Sir Horace Plunkett.

534. —— The Irish crisis. *Round Table*, IV. pp. 201-230. March, 1914.

535. —— The Home Rule Bill : the second reading and its sequel, *Round Table*, IV. pp. 518-532. June, 1914.

536. —— From Bradford to the Curragh. *Round Table*, IV. pp. 501-517. June, 1914.

537. ROYAL COMMISSION INTO THE CIRCUMSTANCES CONNECTED WITH THE LANDING OF ARMS AT HOWTH ON JULY 26th, 1914 : Presented to Parliament . . . 16 pp. H.M.S.O., 1914. [Cd. 7631].

538. —— Minutes of evidence with appendices and index. 78 pp. H.M.S.O., 1914. [Cd. 7649].
> Counsel appeared for the Dublin Corporation, the military authorities, Mr. Harrel (Assistant-Commissioner of Police), the Executive Committee, Irish National Volunteers ; the next-of-kin of the persons killed and wounded in Bachelor's Walk, and for the Crown. The report, signed by Lord Shaw of Dunfermline (Chairman), Rt. Hon. W. D. Andrews, and Mr. Justice T. F. Molony, found that the employment of police and military was illegal and the conduct of the troops unjustified.

539. RUSSELL (George William) : Imaginations and reveries. By A.E. [pseud., *i.e.*, George W. Russell]. 256 pp. 8vo. Dublin, Maunsel, 1915.

540. —— Imaginations and reveries. By A.E. Second edition. 316 pp. 8vo. Dublin, Maunsel, 1921.
> Essays, some on national politics and economics, including " Ulster," an open letter to Mr. Rudyard Kipling (1912). Among those added to the second edition are two essays, " Thoughts for a Convention " (1917) and " The new nation " (1917), which " made some little stir when they first appeared."

See also 959–962, 1334–1338.

540a. —— Co-operation and nationality. A guide for rural reformers from this to the next generation. 104 pp. 8vo. Dublln, Maunsel, 1912.

541. RYAN (William Patrick) : The Labour revolt and Larkinism. By W. P. Ryan. 32 pp. 8vo. London, " Daily Herald," 1913.

542. SAMUEL (*Sir* Herbert) : Mr. Herbert Samuel's speech in the debate on the introduction of the Home Rule Bill of 1912 . . . in the House of Commons, on April 15th, 1912. 26 pp. 8vo. [Westminster, Home Rule Council, 1912].
> Postmaster-General. Deals mainly with the finance of the Bill.

543. SAMUELS (Arthur Warren) *K.C.* : Home Rule finance, an examination of the financial bearings of the Government of Ireland Bill, 1916 . . . With a foreword by the Right Hon. Sir Edward Carson, M.P. 334 pp. 8vo. Dublin, Hodges, Figgis, 1912.

544. —— Possible Irish financial reforms under the Union. In *Against Home Rule*, ed. by S. ROSENBAUM. pp. 271-281. London, 1912.

Schiemann (Dr. Theodor), see 597, 968.

545. SCISSORS AND PASTE, 1914-1915 : Dec. 12th, 1914–Feb. 27th, 1915 (No. 27). Published on Wednesday and Saturday. Pr. P. Mahon and publ. at 67 Middle Abbey street, Dublin.
  Newspaper, edited by Arthur Griffith. Appeared a few days after the suppression of *Sinn Féin* and *Eire*. Mainly war news.

546. SEAGHAN ULTACH : Letters to Irish Unionists. *Sinn Féin.* May 11–June 22, 1912.

547. SELLAR (Robert) : Ulster and Home Rule, a Canadian parallel. . . . Repr. from " The Witness." 20 pp. 8vo. Belfast, Ulster Unionist Council, 1912.

548. SETON-KARR (*Sir* Henry) : The Irish enigma. (II) What is the next step ? *Nineteenth Century*, LXXIV. pp. 1143-1154. Dec., 1913.
  M.P. (Cons.) 1885-1906.

549. SEXTON (Joseph) : Irish republicanism in America. In *An Phoblacht (The Republic)*. N.S. VI. No. 38.-VIII. No. 8. July 18th, 1931–April 1st, 1933.
  The author, who was associate editor of the *Irish Press* (Philadelphia) is the son and grand-son of members of the Clan-na-Gael, and devotes special attention to the history and aims of that organisation. He gives details of the measures taken in America to arm the Irish Volunteers, and explains the relations of the various Irish-American groups—the Clan, A.O.H., supporters of John Redmond, etc.—with one another. Among other matters referred to are the attitude of President Wilson, the Irish Race Conventions (1916-1919), the preparations for the 1916 rising, the position of the Irish cause in the U.S. in 1917–1918. The narrative is continued to 1921.

550. SHEEHY SKEFFINGTON (Francis) : An open letter to Thomas MacDonagh. [4] pp. 8vo. Dublin, repr. from " Irish Citizen," 22nd May, 1915. Irishwomen's International League.

551. —— F. Sheehy Skeffington's speech from the dock. With letter from George Bernard Shaw . . . 12 + 4 pp. 8vo. Dublin, Irish Workers' Co-operative Society, [1915].

—— *See also* 86 (*Irish Citizen*) ; 434 (Milroy, S.) ; *and* Sect. **1916.**

552-553. SHOOTING OUTRAGES (Ireland) . . . A Return by counties, of all cases of Shooting and Bomb outrages, including firing at the person, into houses, etc., reported to the Police in Ireland since the Government dropped the Peace Preservation Act . . . ordered, by the House of Commons to be printed, 6th May, 1912. 6 pp. H.M.S.O., 1912. [H.C. 120].

554. SINCLAIR (Thomas) : The position of Ulster. In *Against Home Rule*, ed. by S. ROSENBAUM. pp. 170-181. London, 1912.
    A prominent Belfast merchant and a leader of the Unionist movement in Ulster since 1886.

555. SINN FEIN : ⱭN ҌeⱭʀnⱭ ҌⱭoꝫⱭıl, the national annual. Xmas. 1912. 18 pp. 4to. Dublin, Central Branch, Sinn Féin, 1912.
    The contributors include Arthur Griffith, Ald. Thomas Kelly, Patsy Patrick [Sean R. Etchingham], " Brian na Banban " [B. F. O'Higgins].

Sinn Féin, 1912-1916, *see* Sect. GENERAL AND INTRODUCTORY ; *and* 328 (Goblet, Y. M.) ; 336-338 (Griffith, A.) ; 359 (*Ireland*) ; 434 (Milroy, S.) ; 440 (*Nationality*) ; 468-470 (Paul-Dubois L.) ; (*Sinn Féin*) ; 555a (*Spark, The*) ; 562 (Ua Fhloinn, R.) ; 714-715 (*Royal Commission on the rebellion*, 1916).

555a. SMITH-GORDON (Lionel) : Food shortage and its remedy : the case against the Department. 56 pp. 8vo. Dublin, Hodges, Figgis, June, 1915.

555b. SPARK, The, 1915-1916 : Edited by Edward Dalton. [*pseud.*, *i.e.*, Seán Doyle]. Feb. 7, 1915 to April 23, 1916 (Vol. III. No. 64). Printed for the proprietors by the Gaelic Press, 30 Upper Liffey street, and published at 3 Findlater place, Dublin. ½d.
    Constance de Markeivicz is given in Sir Mathew Nathan's list of seditious weekly papers (*Rebellion Commission Minutes*, p. 118) as the " supposed " editor. " Edward Dalton," however, in *New Ireland*, August 26th, 1916, states that he was founder of the *Spark* and " editor of it from its first to its last number," and that Sir M. Nathan's estimate of the sale (2,382) was " 150 per cent. below the actual weekly sales at the time mentioned." Vol. II., No. 46, contains Pearse's article, " Peace and the Gael."

556. SPENDER (Harold) : Home Rule. With a preface by the Rt. Hon. Sir Edward Grey, Bart., M.P., Secretary for Foreign Affairs. 180 pp. 8vo. London, Hodder and Stoughton, [1912].

556a. —— The last stand. *Contemporary Rev.*, pp. 1-10. July, 1914.

557. SPENDER (J. Alfred) and ASQUITH (Cyril) : Life of Herbert Henry Asquith, Lord Oxford and Asquith. Vol. II [1912-1928]. 435 pp. illustr. 8vo. London, Hutchinson, 1932.
    Chapters by J. A. Spender on " Home Rule and Ulster " ; " The Ulster Challenge " ; " Ireland and the army " [1913-1914] ; " The Irish deadlock " [1914] ; " The Irish Rebellion " [1916] ; " Rallying the remnant " [1919-1921]. Extracts from Asquith's memoranda and letters on Ireland.

558. STANUEL (Charles A.) : The industrial awakening of Ireland. *Journal of the Statistical and Social Inquiry Society of Ireland*. Vol. XIII. pp. 99-112. Dublin.

559. STEEL-MAITLAND (*Sir* Arthur Herbert Drummond) : Finance of the Home Rule Bill. *National Rev.*, LIX. pp. 620-636. June, 1912.

559a. SWEETMAN (John) : Ireland and conscription . . . Notes of a speech delivered at the Dublin City Hall. 8 pp. 8vo. Dublin, 12 D'Olier Street, 1915.

560. TONE (Theobald Wolfe): The Spanish war. 20 pp. 8vo. Dublin. Cumann na mBann (Central Branch), 1915. (*National Series. No. 2*).
> First published by P. Byrne, Grafton St,. Dublin, in 1790.

561. TYNAN (Katharine): The years of the shadow. 344 pp. 8vo. London, Constable, 1919.
> Reminiscences, chiefly literary, of Ireland, 1912-1918. The author's sympathies are with the old *régime*. Chapters on the 1916 rising, including a description by an eye-witness, " The rebellion as seen by John Higgins."

Tracts for the Times, 1915-1916, *see* 338 (Griffith, A.); 413-414 (MacNeill, E.); 458 (O'Rahilly, The); 475-478 (Pearse, P. H.); 487-491 (Pim, H. M.).
> Over 23,000 of the first four tracts had been sold when No. 5 was published in 1915 (488). "When the screw of coercion began to tighten upon Ireland . . . Eoin MacNeill looked about him for some method by which a sound national opinion might be maintained. The precedent of the Oxford Movement instantly appealed to him" (*Irish Volunteer*, 10th April, 1915). Copies were examined by the Royal Commission on the Rebellion, 1916.

562. Uᴀ Ḟloinn (Rioḃáro): The ethics of Sinn Féin. 10 pp. 8vo. Limerick, An Ċoṁairle Ṅáisiúnta, Craoḃ Luimniġe [1912].
> *See also* 119, 221, 562, 872.

563. ULLSWATER (James William LOWTHER) *1st Viscount*: A speaker's commentaries. Vol. II. 312 pp. illustr. 8vo. London, Arnold, 1925.
> Speaker of the House of Commons, 1905-1921. Refers to Irish debates and gives an account of the Irish conference summoned by King George at Buckingham Palace in July, 1914, at which Lord Ullswater acted as chairman.

" ULSTER IMPERIALIST, An," *see* 579a (Wilson, Alec).

567. ULSTER LIBERAL ASSOCIATION: Facts and figures on the Irish question, including a summary of the " Government of Ireland Bill." 2nd edition, revised and enlarged. 18 pp. 8vo. Belfast Ulster Liberal Association, *n.d.*

568. ULSTER UNIONIST COUNCIL: Political leaflets. Belfast, 1911-1914.
> A collection of forty-six leaflets and pamphlets. Some of these are noticed separately.

569. —— Religious leaflets, 1911-1914. Belfast, Ulster Unionist Council,
> A collection of twenty-eight leaflets and pamphlets. Some are noticed separately.

570. —— The Government of Ireland Bill, 1912. Report on the measure by the Belfast Chamber of Commerce, together with the report of interview with the Prime Minister, and a copy of the deputation's reply to Mr. Asquith's speech. 30 pp. 8vo. Belfast, "Northern Whig," 1913 (Ulster Unionist Council political leaflets).

571. —— Labour conditions in Ireland. A series of articles on work, wages, opportunities of employment and the slums of Dublin and Southern cities of Ireland, showing . . . where Belfast leads . . . 18 pp. 8vo. Belfast, Ulster Unionist Council, [1913].

Repr. from " Belfast Evening Telegraph," Aug., 1913.

572. —— Ulster business men and Home Rule. 8 pp. 8vo. Belfast, (U.C.C. Political Leaflets), [1913].

573. —— Facts regarding the loyal Orange Institution. 12 pp. 16mo. n.d.

574. —— Nationalist " loyalty " ; or illustrations of openly avowed hatred of soldiers of the King. illustr. 8 pp. 8vo. (Series U.C.C. 65) [1914 ?].

575. —— The Ulster movement, its history and its lesson. 8 pp. 8vo. (Series U.U.C. 84) [1914 ?].

Ulster, 1912-1916, *see* Sect. GENERAL AND INTRODUCTORY. *See also* 244-245 (Birkenhead, *1st Earl of*); 251 (Bloxham, E.); 262 (Wilson, *Sir* H.); 263 (Campbell, S.); 264-265 (Carson, *Sir E. Baron*); 267 (Casement, *Sir* R.); 284 (Churchill, W.); 285 (Colum, P.); 286 (Compton-Rickett, *Sir* J.); 294 (Curio); 305 (Dreadnought); 320a (*Fortnightly Rev.*); 322 (Fyfe, H.); 335 (Govt. of Ireland Act, 1914); 357 (Horgan, J. J.); 377 (Johnson, T.); 378 (Johnstone, J.); 382a (Kenny, J. D.); 384 (Kerr-Smiley, P.); 389 (Kettle, T. M.); 391-392 (King, *Rev.* R. S. G.); 394 (Lathbury, D. C.); 401 (Lloyd, E. T.); 406 (Londonderry, *6th Marquess of*); 407 (McCullagh, F.); 415 (Macready, *Gen. Sir* C. F. N.); 417 (MacSwiney, *Marquis*); 425 (*Manchester Courier*); 434a (Moore, F. F.); 437 (Morgan, J. H.); 453 (Oldham, C. H.); 463-464 (Outsider); 467, 557 (Oxford and Asquith, *1st Earl of*); 479 (Peel, G.); 493 (Platt, T. C.); 494 (Plunkett, *Sir* H.); 501 (Prenter, *Rev.* S.); 503 (Presbyterian Church); 506a (*Quarterly Rev.*); 515-517 (Redmond, John); 527 (Rigg, T. G.); 541 (Russell, G. W.); 554 (Sinclair, T.); 579 [Wilson, Alec]; 580 (Woodburn, *Rev.* J. B.).

ULSTER VOLUNTEER FORCE 1912-1916, *see* ULSTER ; *and* 77 (*Hamilton, Lord* Ernest); 404 (Londonderry, *7th Marquess of*); 445 (Northumberland, *8th Duke of*); 479 (Peel, Hon. G.); 1075 (Crozier, F. P.).

576. WALSH (Louis J.) : Home Rule and English conservatism. *British Rev.*, IV. pp. 208-217. Aug., 1913.

577. WELLDON (*Rt. Rev.* James Edward Cowell) : The Home Rule Bill and Lancashire. *Nineteenth Century*, LXXV. pp. 465-478. March, 1914.

Dean of Manchester, 1906–1918. Forecasts that " if bloodshed " (over the Home Rule Bill) " occurs in Ulster it is practically certain to occur in Lancashire too."

578. WHITE (*Captain* James Robert) : Misfit, an autobiography. 352 pp. frontisp. 8vo. London, Cape, 1930.

> The author, an Ulster Protestant and ex-captain in the Gordon Highlanders, took a leading part in the organisation of the Irish Citizen Army during the Dublin Labour troubles of 1913.

—— *See also* 450 (Ó Cathasaigh, Seán), 504 (Protestant protest, A.)

579. WILLIAMS (William M. J.) : Imperial funds spent in Ireland, *Contemporary Rev.*, CI. pp. 213-222. Feb., 1912.

579a. [WILSON (Alec G.)] : An appreciation of the situation. By an Ulster Imperialist [pseud., *i.e.*, Alec G. Wilson]. *Irish Review*, II. pp. 1-11. Dublin, March, 1912.

579b. [——] On history repeating itself, or the Orangeman and the Pope. By an Ulster Imperialist. *Irish Rev.*, II. pp. 337-342. Sept., 1912.

579c. [——] "Half-time," a survey of the political situation. By an Ulster Imperialist. *Irish Rev.*, III. pp. 233-237. July, 1913.

WIMBORNE (Ivor Churchill GUEST) *1st Viscount, see* 511 (Recruiting); 714-715 (Royal Commission on the rebellion, 1916).

> Lord Lieutenant of Ireland, 1915-1918.

580. WOODBURN (*Rev.* James Barkley) : The Ulsterman. 8 pp. 8vo. [Belfast, Ulster Association for Peace with Honour], n.d.

581. WOODS (Maurice) : The future of Ireland. (III) the industrial aspect of Home Rule. *Nineteenth Century*, LXXIII. pp. 231-244. Jan., 1913.

582. —— The Irish crisis. *Fortnightly Rev.*, C (N.S.) pp. 807-816. Nov., 1913.

582a. WORKERS' REPUBLIC, The, 1915-1916. Pr. for the proprietors of the Irish Workers' Co-operative Society and published at Liberty Hall, Beresford Place, Dublin. May 29, 1915-April 22, 1916 (Vol. 1. No. 48).

> Edited by James Connolly, " Acting General Secretary of the Transport Union." Gives a weekly account of the activities of the Irish Citizen Army.

583. WRIGHT (Arnold) : Disturbed Dublin, the story of the great strike of 1913-14, with a description of the industries of the Irish capital. 338 pp. 8vo. London, Longmans, 1914.

> This book was the subject of a long criticism by James Connolly in the *Irish Worker*, 28th Nov., 1914.

584. WYNDHAM (George) : The completion of land purchase. In *Against Home Rule*, ed. by S. ROSENBAUM. pp. 249-270. London, 1912.

> Chief Secretary for Ireland, 1900-1905.

3.—THE INSURRECTION OF 1916.

585. ARTHUR (*Sir* George): General Sir John Maxwell. 10 + 330 pp. pls. facs. 8vo. [Chs. XXVII.–XXIX. The Irish rebellion]. London. Murray, 1932.

Sir John Maxwell was Commander-in-Chief of the British Forces in Ireland from Easter Thursday (April 27th) to Oct., 1916. Extracts given from his reports and letters to Mr. Asquith, Lord Kitchener and others, in which he comments on the Courts-martial and deportations, the mood of the people, the nature of his powers as Commander-in-Chief and the relationship of the military command with the civil authorities.

586. BEGLEY (Patrick): The mysterious motor car : a tragedy of Easter week. *The Nation*, Dublin, April 19, 1930.

586a. BIRKENHEAD (Frederick Edwin SMITH) *1st Earl of*: The trial of Sir Roger Casement. *In* Famous trials of history. pp. 249-255. London, Hutchinson, [1926].

587. BIRRELL (Augustine): ROYAL COMMISSION ON THE REBELLION (Evidence. pp. 21-27).
Chief Secretary for Ireland, 1907-1916.

588. BLACKWOOD'S MAGAZINE: Experiences of a V.A.D. at Dublin Castle during the rebellion. Vol. CC. pp. 814-840. Dec., 1916.

588a. BOUCH (Joseph J.) : The war bulletins of Easter week. In *Irish Press*, April 15-16, 1936.

See also " The Proclamation of Easter Week, 1916 " by J. J. Bouch (Bibliographical Society of Ireland, 1936).

589. BOYLE (John F.) : The Irish rebellion of 1916, a brief history of the revolt and its suppression. 300 pp. plan and map. 8vo. London, Constable, 1916.

590. [BRENNAN (Robert)]; The Wexford rising in 1916. By Selskar [*pseud.*, *i.e.*, Robert Brennan]. *Poblacht na hÉireann. The Republic of Ireland*. Special Easter number. April 20, 1922.

Took part in the rising. Director of Elections, 1918 and of Propaganda, 1919-1921, for Sinn Féin. Under-Secretary for Foreign Affairs (Dáil Éireann), 1921-1922.

591. BRENNAN-WHITMORE (*Commandant* W. J.) : I. The occupation of the G.P.O. : 1916. An t Óglác Vol. IV. No. 1. N.S. illustr. January 16, 1926.

592. —— Easter week, 1916. The occupation of the North Earl St. area. An t-Óglác, IV. Nos. 3-4. illustr. Jan 30–Feb. 6, 1926.

593. BROOKS (Sydney) : The Irish insurrection. *North American Rev.*, Vol. 216. pp. 57-69. New York, July, 1916.

594. BRUGHA (Cathal) : Biographies of the seven signatories : Pádraic Pearse. *Poblacht na hÉireann*. Dublin, April 20, 1922.

595. BURKE (*Captain* James J.): The Citizen Army in 1916. An t-Óglác. IV. N.S. No. 6. February 20, 1926.

595a. [CAHILL]: The Sinn Fein leaders of 1916. With fourteen illlustrations and complete lists of deportees, casualties, etc. 32 pp. 8vo. Dublin, Cahill, 1917.

595b. CAPUCHIN ANNUAL, 1936. 1916–1921. pp. 155–95. portrs. facs. Dublin, 1935.

596. CASEMENT (*Sir* Roger): The trial of Sir Roger Casement, edited by George H. Knott, M.A. (Edin.) of the Middle Temple, Barrister-at-law. 39 + 304 pp. illustr. 8vo. Edinburgh, Hodge, 1917.

See also 586a.

597. —— Der Casement-Prozess und seine Ursachen. Zusammengestellt und aus dem Englischen übersetzt von Antonie Meyer. Mit einem . . . Vorwort von. Dr. Th. Schiemann. 2te Auflage. portr. 62 pp. Berlin, Curtius [1916].

598. —— Speech of Roger Casement from the dock. 8 pp. 8vo. Dublin, Fergus O'Connor, [1916 ?].

599. —— Roger Casement's speech from the dock. 16 pp. 8vo. Cape Town, Irish Republican Association of South Africa. [1921 ?].

—— *See also* Sects. GENERAL AND INTRODUCTORY ; **1912-1916**; and 605a (Catholic Bulletin) ; 619 (Daly, M.) ; 641 (Gore-Booth, E.), 642 (Grabisch, A. M.) ; 647a (Joy, M.) ; 650 (Kavanagh, S.) ; 664 (McGarrity, J.) ; 673 (Monteith, R.) ; 726-728 (Spindler K.) ; 728a (Stack, A.) ; 735 (Thomson, Sir B.) ; 282a (Childs, *Maj.-Gen*) ; 996 (" Vigilant ") ; 586a, 1025a (Birkenhead, *Earl of*).

600. CATHOLIC BULLETIN, The: Events of Easter week. *Catholic Bulletin*, Vols. VI–IX. July–Dec., 1916. Dec., 1917. Jan., Feb., Dec., 1918. Feb.–March, 1919.

Biographical notes on about 100 men who died in the rising or shortly afterwards. Photographs of dead Volunteers and their families.

601. —— Events of Easter week: George Noble Count Plunkett [biographical note]. *Catholic Bulletin*, VII. pp. 53-57. Jan., 1917.

602. —— Events of Easter week. Eoin MacNeill [biographical note]. VII. pp. 57-60. Jan., 1917.

603. —— Events of Easter week. VII. pp. 125-130. Feb., 1917.

Brief biographical notes on some of the women, including relatives of leaders, who were associated with the rising.

604. —— Events of Easter week : A short account of some of the Irish prisoners sentenced to penal servitude or hard labour by secret courts martial, May and June, 1916. VII. illustr. March, July–Aug., 1917.

605. —— Events of Easter week. Jacobs and Stephen's Green area. VIII. pp. 452-456 ; St. Stephen's Green and College of Surgeons. pp. 502-504, 550-552. Sept.-Nov., 1918.

606. —— Events of Easter week. Vol. VI. pp. 513-517, 573-575. Sept.-Oct., 1916.

An account of Sir R. Casement's last moments in Pentonville Prison [in part written by Father Carey, prison chaplain], and a sketch of him as an Irish-Irelander by Alice Milligan.

—— See also 627 (Dublin priest, A) ; 643 (Grenan, J.) ; 693 (O'Farrell, E.) ; 707 (Reynolds, J. J.).

607. CEANNT (Eamonn): 1 ₅Cuimhne Air. 8 pp. 8vo. portr. Dublin, Cahill, [1917 ?].

> Programme of memorial concert, with biographical note on Eamon Ceannt and extracts from his writings. A reproduction in facsimile of a message which he wrote at Kilmainham, shortly before his execution, is given in An t-Óglác, N.S., Vol. V., No. 1, July 10, 1926.

— *See also* 8a (Barr Buadh, An) ; 619 (Daly, M.).

608. CEANNT (*Mrs.* Eamonn): Biographies of the seven signatories: Eamonn Ceannt. *Poblacht na hÉireann*, Special Easter number. April 20, 1922.

609. CHAMBERLAIN (*Sir* Neville) : ROYAL COMMISSION ON THE REBELLION [Evidence. pp. 43-51].

> Inspector-General of the Royal Irish Constabulary, 1900–1916.

609a. CHATTERTON (Edward Keble): Danger zone, the story of the Queenstown command . . . 434 pp. pls. maps. 8vo. London. Rich and Cowan, 1934.

> The author was commanding a ship in the British Auxiliary Patrol Service off the south coast of Ireland in 1916. In Chs. XII.–XIII. (Sinn Féin and Germany ; The Easter Rebellion) gives a detailed account of the Aud expedition. He says : " My authorities are the Commander-in-Chief himself [Admiral Sir L. Bayley] and some of the other naval officers who played conspicuous parts during those fateful days " and " my own notes, written down immediately after the actual happenings."

609b. [CHATTERTON-HILL (Georges)] : Gedanken zum Todestage Roger Casements. In *Irische Blätter*. 1. Jahr. Nr. 5. pp. 318-332. Berlin, August, 1917.

610. CHUMAILL (Eithne) : The history of Cumann na mBan : part played by the women of Ireland. *An Phoblacht*, VIII. Nos. 9-10. April 8th–15th, 1933.

> A brief account of the organisation from its foundation in May, 1913, and of its work in Easter Week.

Citizen Army, see Irish Citizen Army.

611. CLARKE (Kathleen) : Biographies of the seven signatories. Thomas J. Clarke. By Mrs. Clarke. *Poblacht na hÉireann*. Easter number, April 20th, 1922.

Clarke (Thomas J.), *see also* 18 (" Glimpses of an Irish felon's prison life ") ; 14 (Devoy, J.) ; 92 (Irish Freedom) ; 159 (O'Hegarty. P. S.) ; 706 (Reidy, J. J.).

612. " COILIN " : Patrick H. Pearse, a sketch of his life. 16 pp. 8vo. Dublin, Curtis, *n.d.*

613. COLGAN (*Commandant* P.) : The Maynooth Volunteers in 1916. An t-Óglác Vol. IV. No. 17. N.S. May 8, 1926.

614. COLLEY (Harry) : A human barricade. *An Phoblacht*, N.S. Vol. V. No. 33. June 7th, 1930.

> Was in F. Co. Batt. II (" MacDonagh's Own ").

615. COLUM (Padráic) : Padraic Pearse. In *The Irish rebellion of 1916 and its martyrs*, ed. by M. JOY. pp. 269-295. New York, 1916.

616. —— James Connolly. In *The Irish rebellion of 1916 and its martyrs*, edited by M .JOY. pp. 361-371. New York, 1916.

617. —— Francis Sheehy-Skeffington. In *The Irish rebellion of 1916 and its martyrs*, edited by M. JOY. pp. 380-392. New York, 1916.

Connolly (James), *see* 26-35 ; 287 ; *and* 616 (Colum P.) ; 685-6 (O'Brien, Nora Connolly).

618. CREGAN (Máirín) : Seán Mac Dermott—the worker. *Irish Press*, May 11, 1934.

—— Carrying the message in Easter week, a courier's thrilling story. *Irish Press* Christmas number, Dublin, 1934.

Cumann na mBan, *see* 610 (Chumaill, E.) ; 643 (Grenan, J.) ; 676 (Murray, M.) ; 691 (O'Daly, Nora) ; 693 (O'Farrell, Elizabeth) ; 711 (Reynolds, M.) ; 725 (Skinnider, M.).

619. DALY (Martin) : Memories of the dead. Some impressions of Roger Casement, Eamunn Ceannt, Tom Clarke, Peadar O'Meacin, Major MacBride, Sheehy-Skeffington, Thomas MacDonagh, The O'Rahilly, Padraic MacPiarais. 20 pp. 8vo. Dublin, Powell Press, *n.d.*

Desmond (Shaw), *see* 1109.

Devoy (John), *see* 44.

620. DONNELLY (Mary) : With the Citizen Army in Stephen's Green. *An Phoblacht*. N.S. v. No. 26. April 19th, 1930.

621. DONNELLY (Simon) : With the 3rd Battalion . . . The fighting at Boland's, Mount street and the neighbourhood. *Poblacht na hÉireann*. Easter number. April 20, 1922.

622. DOYLE (Séamus) : With Pearse in Arbour Hill. *Irish Press*. May 3 1932.
See also " The rising in Wexford " in the *People* (Wexford), May 2, 1936.

623. DOUGHERTY (*Sir* James Brown) : ROYAL COMMISSION ON THE REBELLION [Evidence. pp. 102-108].
Under-Secretary for Ireland, 1908-1914.

624. DUBLIN AND THE SINN FEIN RISING : Portraits, documents, pictures, volunteer relics, arms and accoutrements . . . [28] + 4 pp. [Dublin, 1916].
Reproductions in facsimile.

625. DUBLIN CASTLE FROM THE INSIDE, Easter week 1916 : The narrative of one who was there. An t-Óglác. N.S. IV. No. 5. February 13 1926.

✓ **626.** DUBLIN METROPOLITAN POLICE: Statistical tables of the Dublin Metropolitan Police for the year 1916 . . . 8 + 14 pp. H.M.S.O. 1916. [Cmd. 30].
> Containing statistics of persons killed and wounded in the Dublin Metropolitan Area during the rising, and of those arrested, tried and interned. For estimates of the casualties *see also* 589 (J. F. BOYLE).

—— *see also* 630 (Edgeworth-Johnstone, W.); 713 (Ross of Bladensburg, *Sir* J. F.).

627. DUBLIN PRIEST, A: Events of Easter week. The General Post Office area. *Catholic Bulletin*, VIII. pp. 405-408. plan. Aug., 1918.

628. DUBLIN SATURDAY POST. Vol. 12. No. 307. April 29-May 13, 1916.
> Accounts of the rising " compiled from various sources and from narratives by eye-witnesses."

629. [EASON]: The rebellion in Dublin, April, 1916. Oblong 8vo. [Dublin, Eason, 1916].
> Twelve mounted photographs.

630. EDGEWORTH-JOHNSTONE (*Lt.-Col.* Walter): ROYAL COMMISSION ON THE REBELLION [Evidence. pp. 51-56).
> Chief Commissioner of the Dublin Metropolitan Police, 1914-1923.

631. EGAN (*Hon.* Patrick Francis): What an Irishman thinks of the Irish-German alliance. New York, *Forum*, LVI. pp. 139-146. Aug., 1916.
> A Fenian and Treasurer of the Land League; afterwards U.S. Minister to Chile. Claims that the Irish Race Convention (New York, March, 1916) was " manipulated by the pro-German Clan-na-Gael " and that Clan-na-Gael has no title to speak for the Irish people. Deplores the Easter Week rising.

Enniscorthy (*the rising at*), *see* 590 [Brennan, R.]; 622 (Doyle, S.); 660 (Lyster, *Rev.* H. C.); 674 (Moore, M.); 698 (O'Neill, M.).

632. ERVINE (St. John Greer): The story of the Irish rebellion. *Century Magazine*, XCIII. pp. 22-39. illustr. New York, Nov., 1916.
> An eye-witness. Disapproves of the rebellion, but praises the sincerity and heroism of the leaders.

633. FITZGERALD (Desmond): The success of Easter week. In *The Star*. Dublin, Easter week, 1931.
> Personal recollections. Took part in the rising. Acting Director of Propaganda in the Dáil Ministry 1919-1921; Minister for Publicity, 1921-1922.

Fragment of 1916 history, A. *see* REYNOLDS (John J.).

634. FRIEND (*Maj.-Gen. Sir* Lovick Bransby): ROYAL COMMISSION ON THE REBELLION [Evidence. pp. 64-68].
> General Officer Commanding in Ireland, 1914–1916.

Frongoch internment camp, *see* 743 and Sect. **1916–1918.**

635. G.: Lighter side of Sinn Feinism. *National Review*, LXVIII. pp. 547-553. London, Dec., 1916.
> A facetious account of the rising.

635a. GAELIC AMERICAN, The : Graphic story of the Easter week rebellion told by a noncombatant who was in Dublin during the fighting . . . June 24, 1916.

635b. —— Inside history of the Easter week rebellion. Story of an eyewitness. *Gaelic American.* July 29, 1916.

635c. —— Graphic story of the battle of Ashbourne. *Gaelic American.* Sept. 23, 1916.
Told " by a young Dublin Volunteer officer."

635c. —— A Dublin woman's story of the rebellion. *Gaelic American.* Nov. 11-18, 1916.
A member of Cumann na mBan.

Galway (rising in) *see* 638 (Ṡaillṁeaċ); 667 (McNachain, A. O.); 671a (Mellows, L.); 692 (Ó hEidhin, P.).

636. GIFFORD (Sydney) : Countess de Markievicz. In *The Irish rebellion of 1916*, ed. by M. JOY. pp. 341-360.

637. GIFFORD-DONNELLY (Nellie) : The three printers of the proclamation : story of April 24th, 1916. *Irish Press*, April 24, 1934.

638. Ṡaillṁeaċ : Galway and the 1916 rising. An t-Óglaċ. Vol. v. No. 1. N.S. pp. 1-12. Feb., 1933.

639. GLENAVY (*Sir* James Henry CAMPBELL) *1st Baron*: ROYAL COMMISSION ON THE REBELLION [Evidence. pp. 69-72].
Attorney-General of Ireland in 1916.

Gore-Booth (Constance), *see* MARKIEVICZ (Constance).

640. GORE-BOOTH (Eva) : The Sinn Fein rebellion. *Socialist Review*, XIII. pp. 226-233.

641. —— For God and Kathleen ni Houlihan. *Catholic Bulletin*, VIII. 230-234. May, 1918.
The last moments of Roger Casement.

642. GRABISCH (*Dr.* Agatha M. Bullitt) : Roger Casement and the " German plot." In *The Voice of Ireland* (*See* 226, pp. 118–120).

643. GRENAN (Julia) : Events of Easter week : Miss Julia Grenan's story of the surrender. *Catholic Bulletin*, VII. pp. 396-398. June, 1917.

643a. [HELY] : The Sinn Fein revolt, illustrated. [34 pp.] Oblong 8vo. Dublin, Hely's, [1916].

644. HIGGINS (John) : " The rebellion as seen by John Higgins." *See* 561 (Tynan, K.).

644. HORNECK (A.) : The battle of Ashbourne. *Irish Weekly Independent*, Christmas number, 1934.

645. IRISCHE BLÄTTER: Martyrer der irischen Republik, 1916. In *Irische Blätter*. 1. Jahr. Nr. 2. pp. 73-92. illustr. Berlin, Mai, 1917.

645a. IRISH-AMERICAN VERDICT ON EASTER WEEK, The. [12] pp. 8vo. [Dublin, J. J. Walsh], [1916 ?].

> Report of the meeting held in the Carnegie Hall, New York, May 15th, 1916, "to protest against the continued executions of the Irish prisoners of war."

Irish Citizen Army, *see* Sects. GENERAL AND INTRODUCTORY; and **1912-1916**; *and* 595 (Burke, J. J.); 620 (Donnelly, Mary); 712 (Robbins, Frank).

646. IRISH LIFE: A record of the Irish rebellion of 1916. 64 pp. illustr. 4to. Dublin, Office of "Irish Life," [1916]. (Passed by the Press Censor).

> Tinged somewhat with contemporary prejudices, *e.g.*, that the rising was "chiefly financed by German money," but mainly attempts to give "a plain narrative of the events." Detailed account of the military operations from the British side, including a narrative by the officer commanding a machine gun section, who accompanied Pearse to Sir John Maxwell, brought Pearse's order for a surrender to James Connolly for his adherence, and "was present to receive the surrenders of all the Dublin Commandoes." Facsimiles of proclamations, bulletins, and orders of the day issued by the insurgents—some of them found on the body of The O'Rahilly.

646a. IRISH NATIONAL AID AND VOLUNTEER DEPENDENTS' FUND, Report of: *Catholic Bulletin*, IX. pp. 410-436. Aug., 1919.

> A detailed account of the steps taken to collect and administer a fund in aid of victims of the rising and their families.

Irish Parliamentary Party, *see* 738a.

Irish Republican Brotherhood, *see* Sect. GENERAL AND INTRODUCTORY.

646b. IRISH WAR NEWS: The Irish Republic. Vol. 1. No. 1. 4 pp. One penny. Dublin, Tuesday, April 25, 1916. [Pr. by the Gaelic Press].

> Issued by the insurgents. Under the heading "Stop Press" it is announced on page 4: '(Irish) "War News" is published to-day because a momentous thing has happened. The Irish Republic has been declared in Dublin, and a Provisional Government has been appointed to administer its affairs." The seven signatories of the Proclamation are named as the Provisional Government. "Commandant General P. H. Pearse is commanding in chief of the Army of the Republic and is President of the Provisional Government. Commandant General James Connolly is commanding the Dublin districts."

647. JOLY (John, F. R. S.): Reminiscences and anticipations. illustr. 8vo. [Ch. VIII. In Trinity College during the Sinn Fein rebellion. By one of the garrison]. London, Fisher Unwin, 1920.

648. JONES (Francis P.): History of the Sinn Fein movement and the Irish Rebellion. With an introduction by Hon. John W. Goff. portr. pp. 28 + 448. 8vo. New York, Kenedy, 1919.

649. Joy (Maurice): The Irish rebellion of 1916 and its martyrs: Erin's tragic Easter. By Padraic Colum, Maurice Joy, Sidney Gifford, Rev. T. Gavan Duffy, Mary M. Colum, Mary J. Ryan, and Seumas O'Brien 428 pp. pls. 8vo. New York, Devin-Adair Co., [1916].

> A survey of the Irish political movements leading up to the rising, with an account of the fighting and character sketches of the chief leaders. See under the names of writers.

650. —— Roger David Casement. In above work, pp. 296-308. New York, 1916.

651. Joyce (*Major* J.): The defence of the South Dublin Union . . . By Major J. V. Joyce, General Staff. An c-Óglác. N.S. IV, No. 22. June 12, 1926.

652. Judex: The Sinn Fein rising: a plea for mercy. *Fortnightly Rev.* cv (N.S.). pp. 989-996. June, 1916.

653. Kavanagh (Seán), *Sgt., Casement's brigade*: Last interview with Casement, before his departure for Ireland. *An Phoblacht*, N.S. VII. No. 26. August 6th, 1932.

> Captain Monteith (*see* 673) writes, in a prefatory note: "The narrative is substantially correct."

Knott (George H.), see 596.

654. Law and Procedure (Emergency Provisions) (Ireland) Act. 6-7 G. 5. C. 46. 4 pp. H.M.S.O., 1916.

> The period April 24 to May 8, 1916, not to be reckoned in computing time for legal proceedings.

655. Lawless (*Captain* Joseph): The fight at Ashbourne. Vicissitudes of the Fingal Volunteers in Easter week, 1916 . . . An c-Óglác, Vol. V. N.S. No. 4. illustr. July 31, 1926.

Kerry, Irish Volunteers in, see 586 (Begley, P.); Casement (*Sir* R.); 45 (Donovan, T. M.); 618 (Cregan, M.); 688 (Ó Cathail, P.); 728a (Stack, A.).

656. Lennon (Michael J.): A retrospect. *Banba.* Vol. II. pp. 478-493. III. pp. 33-52. illustr. facs. Dublin, April-May, 1922.

> The writer took part in the rising. A well-informed account of the fighting and subsequent experiences of captured Volunteers. Details of Volunteer movements in the provinces.

657. Leslie (Shane): The Irish scene in American eyes. *Dublin Rev.*, CLIX. pp. 234-249. London, Oct., 1916.

> Deplores the rising, but condemns the execution of the leaders.

658. Lynch (Diarmuid): My story of Easter week. In the *Echo*, Enniscorthy, January 3, 1931.

> Was a member of the Supreme Council, Irish Republican Brotherhood.

Lynd (Robert), see 119, 646b, 872.

659. LYONS (George A.) : Occupation of Ringsend area in 1916. *An Óglách.* Vol. IV. N.S. Nos. 13-15. illustr. April 10-24, 1926.
> A detailed narrative with photographs. Also gives facsimiles of letters from Thomas MacDonagh and Sir R. Casement.

660. LYSTER (H. Cameron) : An Irish parish in changing days. By H. Cameron Lyster, Canon of St. Patrick's Cathedral, Dublin, sometime Dean of Ferns. 144 pp. 8vo. London, Griffiths, 1933.
> Unionist. Gives an account of the " Rebellion in 1916 " and subsequent events in Enniscorthy, Co. Wexford

661. Mac Amlaoib Riscearo : A rebel's diary. Being extracts from the notes of an old Belvederian who fought in the rebellion of Easter week, 1916. *The Belvederian,* IV. pp. 14-25. illustr. Dublin, Kenny Press, 1917.
> A nephew of The O'Rahilly. On active service in the General Post Office. Gives a summary of Pearse's address to the men on Thursday, April 27th, in which he claimed that, having held out for three days, they were entitled to belligerent status.

662. MACDARA : The secret history of Easter week. *An Phoblacht,* VII. Nos. 16-27. N.S. illustr. May 28–August 13, 1932.
> This account of the events which led up to the rising was " pieced together," it is claimed (*An Phoblacht,* May 28th, 1932) from " narratives of surviving members of the I. R.B." and " from unpublished documents in the possession of relatives of the leaders."

663. MACDONAGH (Seán) : Biographies of the seven signatories. Thomas Mac Donagh. *Poblacht na hEireann. Easter number.* April 20, 1922.

MACDONAGH (Thomas), *see also* Sect. 1912-1916.

MacDermott (Seán), *see* (*Irish Freedom*) ; Irish Volunteers, The ; 618 (Cregan, M.) ; 720 (Ryan, Mary J.) ; 689 (Ó Ceallaigh, S. T.).

663a. [Mac Fionnlaoic (Peadar T.)] : bliadain na h-Aiséirige—1916. Cú Ulad do scriob. An t-Eireannác, Meadon Fogmair 7, 1935 —— .

664. MCGARRITY (Joseph) : Rory of the Gael. By his friend and comrade in U.S.A.—Joe McGarrity. *An Phoblacht,* VII. No. 27. Aug. 13th, 1932.

665. —— Twenty years ago in America. An Camán. Uimir na Cásga. Iml. III. Uim. 13. 1934.
> Memories of Pearse in Philadelphia with Bulmer Hobson, March, 1914.

666. MCKENZIE (Frederick Arthur) : The Irish rebellion, what happened and why. 112 pp. 8vo. London, Pearson, 1916.
> Selected as a representative of the Canadian Press to visit Ireland during the insurrection.

667. MCNACHAIN (Ailbhe O.) : Galway in Easter week. *Irish Press,* April 5, 1934.

Mac Neill (Eoin), *see* Sect. **1912-1916**; *and* 602 (*Catholic Bulletin*); 683 (O Briain, L.).
> See also an interview printed in "Michael Collins' own story" by Hayden Talbot (987a) referring to the Volunteer mobilisation, 1916.

668. MacSwiney (Mary): Easter week in Cork, 1916. *Poblacht na hÉireann.* Easter number. April 20, 1922.

Mallin (Michael) [Mícéál Ómaoláin,], *see* 684 (Ó Briain, L.).

669. "Manchester Guardian": History of the war. Vol. v.-1916. [pp. 29-56]. 4to. Manchester, Heywood, 1916.
> An account of the rising. Many photographs.

670. Markievicz (Constance): 1916. *Nation,* Dublin, April 23rd, 1927.

—— *See also* General and Introductory : Irish Citizen Army ; 636 (Gifford, S.) ; 724 (Skeffington, H. S.).

671. Mason (Thomas) : Photographs, 1916 rising. 51 pp. 4to. Dublin, 1916.
> An album containing 58 numbered photographs, illustrating the Easter Week Rising, 1916. They were on sale shortly after the rising by T. Mason, 53 Dame Street, Dublin. Photographic reproductions of important contemporary documents are included, *e.g.*, Irish Citizen Army Orders, signed by James Connolly ; Army orders, recruiting appeals and other documents of the Irish Volunteers ; letters by Sir R. Casement, Major J. MacBride ; proclamations and orders issued by the insurgents at headquarters during the rising ; martial law proclamations, etc.

Maxwell (*General Sir* John), *see* 585.

671a. [Mellows (Liam)]: True story of the Galway insurrection. By a Volunteer officer [*i.e.*, Liam Mellows]. *Gaelic American.* January 20, 1916.
> *See also* 135b, 692.

672. Midleton (St. John Brodrick) *9th Viscount*: Royal Commission on the Rebellion. Evidence. pp. 28-35.

673. Monteith (Robert): Casement's last adventure. By Captain Robert Monteith, first battalion, Dublin regiment, Irish Republican Army. 191 + 12 pp. illustr. 8vo. Chicago : " The Irish People Monthly " (for the author), 1932.
> The author, excluded from Dublin by a military order in Nov., 1914, then acted as organiser for the Irish Volunteers in Co. Limerick. He went to America in Sept., 1915, and thence to Germany, where he met Sir Roger Casement and helped to organise the Irish Brigade. He landed on Banna strand, Co. Kerry, along with Casement on April 21, 1916, and was " on the run " in Ireland until his escape to America in the following December. Treats only " of those incidents in which I took part, or which came directly under my notice."

674. [Moore (Myles)]: The inside story of Easter week . . . The organisation in Co. Wexford . . . Specially written for The *Echo* by " Nada," [*pseud., i.e.*, Myles Moore]. Enniscorthy, The *Echo*, April 19th and 10th, 1930.
> The writer took a part in the rising at Enniscorthy as a member of Fianna Éireann. He states that " the articles have been compiled from the narratives of responsible officers of the Irish Volunteers . . . They are a first attempt at . . . a coherent account of the organisation and preparations which preceded the Easter Rising of 1916 in Enniscorthy, and of the outstanding facts connected with the Rising itself."

675. MURPHY (T. W.) : Dublin after the six days' insurrection. Thirty-one pictures from the camera of Mr. T. W. Murphy (" The O'Tatur "), sub-editor, " The Motor News." 32 pp. oblong 8vo. Dublin, Macredy, Percy, [June, 1916]. (Passed for transmission abroad by the Official Press Bureau).

676. MURRAY (May) : A girl's experience in the G.P.O. *An Phoblacht na hEireann.* Easter number. April 20, 1922.

677. MURRAY (*Rev.* Robert Henry) : The Irish enigma. (III) The Sinn Fein rebellion. *Nineteenth Century,* LXIX. pp. 1203-1220. June, 1916.

   Opposed to the rebellion, its spirit and leaders.

678. NATHAN (*Lt.-Col. Sir* Mathew) : ROYAL COMMISSION ON THE REBELLION [Evidence. pp. 3-20].

   Under-Secretary for Ireland, 1914-1916. Evidence on " the movement which led up to the rebellion."

679. NATIONAL REVIEW, The : Wait-and-seeism in Ireland. The Hardinge Report. LXVII. pp. 876-899. London, Aug., 1916.

   An extreme Unionist criticism of the Report of the Royal Commission on the rebellion.

680. NORWAY (*Mrs.* Hamilton) : The Sinn Fein rebellion as I saw it. By Mrs. Hamilton Norway (wife of the Secretary for the Post Office in Ireland). 112 pp. illustr. 8vo. London, Smith, Elder. 1916.

   Letters to England, written during and immediately after the fighting.

681. NOTES FROM IRELAND. Published by the Irish Unionist Alliance. Special Number—the Sinn Féin revolt. No. 2a—Vol. 25. 8 pp. July 1st, 1916.

   " Published out of the quarterly order of the present series . . . as a summarised record of the insurrectionary events. . . ." The earlier numbers of the series review the progress of the revolutionary movement in a spirit of vigilant hostility (*see* 98).

682. O'BRENNAN (Lily) : One Easter Monday. *Irish Press,* April 2nd, 1934.

   Sister-in-law to Eamon Ceannt.

683. Ó BRIAIN (*Professor* Liam) : The historic rising of Easter week—1916. In the *Voice of Ireland* (see 226 pp. 132-139).
   Gives an account of the " inner developments " in the week before the rising and of the relationship between the Irish Volunteers and the I.R.B. Military Council.

684. —— Míceál Ó Maoláin, I.C.A. An t-Ollam Liam Ó Briain, do scríob. *Irish Press.* May 10, 1932.

685. O'BRIEN (Nora Connolly) : Easter. *Atlantic Monthly*, CXVIII. pp. 682-685. New York, July, 1916.

> An account by his daughter of an interview with James Connolly on the eve of his execution.

685a. —— Nora Connolly's graphic story of rebellion. *Gaelic American.* April 13, 1918.

686. —— Biographies of the seven signatories : James Connolly. *Poblacht na hÉireann.* Easter number. Dublin, April 20th, 1922.

686a. —— The rebellion of 1916, or the unbroken tradition. By Nora Connolly. 18 + 202 pp. illustr. 8vo. New York, Boni and Liveright, 1919.

686b. —— Portrait of a rebel father . . . With a preface by Robert Lynd. 327 pp. portr. 8vo. Dublin, Talbot Press, **1935.**

687. O'CARROLL (Kevin) : Memories of 1916. *An Phoblacht.* N.S. No. 26. April 19th, 1930.

688. Ó CATHAIL (Pádraig). *Editor " Kerry Champion "* : Last chapter of Easter week history. Who blundered in Ireland ? *An Phoblacht.* N.S. v. No. 47. Sept. 13th, 1930.

> The *Aud* off the Kerry coast.

689. Ó CEALLAIGH (Seán T.) : Seán MacDiarmada. *Poblacht na hÉireann.* Easter number. April 20, 1922.

690. —— When Easter week was planned. *Nation*, Dublin, February 15, 1930.

> Report of a lecture delivered in Dublin. The author was sent to the United States in 1915 to discuss the projected rising with the leaders of Clan-na-Gael. He was Ceann Comhairle (Speaker) of Dáil Éireann, 1919-1921 ; special envoy to seek a hearing for Ireland at the Peace Conference and envoy from Ireland in Rome 1920 and Paris 1920–1922

691. O'DALY (*Mrs.* Nora) : The women of Easter week. Cumann na mBan in Stephen's Green and in the College of Surgeons, An t-Óglác. Vol. IV. N.S. No. 12. illustr. April 3, 1926.

692. Ó hEIDHIN (Proinsias) : Liam Mellows in Galway, preparing for the rising. *An Phoblacht.* N.S. Vol. II. Nos. 31-35. Dec. 3rd–31st, 1927.

693. O'FARRELL (Elizabeth) : Events of Easter week. Miss Elizabeth O'Farrell's story of the surrender. *Catholic Bulletin*, VII. pp. 266-270, 329-334. April-May, 1917.

> Member of Cumann na mBan. Sent by Pádraic Pearse to treat with General Lowe. Visited the chief insurgent posts in the city with Pearse's order for a general surrender. A detailed narrative.

693. Ógláć, An t-: History of the Anglo-Irish war: 1916. Vol. iv. N.S. 1926.
   Narratives of the rising. An editorial note in the first of the series (January 16, 1926) says: " This series of articles will contain authentic records. . . . Data has been collected from the most reliable living participants ; and the scenes described are true in every particular." See names of writers.

693a. —— Amazing voyage of the " Libau " . . . Translated specially from the official German Naval History of the European War. An t-Ógláć. Vol. v. N.S. No. 3. July 24, 1926.
   The German arms ship, also known as the " Aud."

694. O'HIGGINS (Brian): The soldier's story of Easter week. 78 pp. 12mo. Third edition. Dublin, Brian Ó hUiginn, 1926.
   Took part in the rising.

695. O'LEARY (John J.): Sackville street, during the week of terror. *Dublin Saturday Post.* April 29–May 13, 1916.

Ó Meacain (Peadar), *see* 8 (*Barr Buadh, An*) ; 619 (Daly, M.).

696. ONE OF THEM : The magazine fort, 1916. *An Phoblacht.* N.S. II. No. 49. April 7th, 1928.

696a. O'NEILL (Brian): Easter week. 8 + 96 pp. 8vo. London, Laurence and Wishart, 1936.

697. O'NEILL (Charles): At the barricades in '16. *An Phoblacht.* N.S. v. No. 28. May 3rd, 1930.

698. O'NEILL (Moira): During the rebellion in Wexford. *Blackwood's Mag.*, CXCIX. pp. 819-827. June, 1916.
   Unionist. An account of the rising at Enniscorthy.

O'Reilly (Michael W.) : See Staines (Michael J.).

699. Ó RIAIN (Séamus): The six days, a doctor's experiences at the G.P.O. *Poblacht na hÉireann.* Easter number. April 20, 1922.
   Took part in the rising. T.D., S. Wexford, 1918–1921 ; Co. Wexford, 1921.

Oxford and Asquith (H. H. ASQUITH) *1st Earl of, see* 557.
   Extracts from letters written in Dublin to Mrs. Asquith in May, 1916.

700. PEARSE (Margaret): Biographies of the seven signatories. Pádraic Pearse. By his mother. *Poblacht na hÉireann.* Easter number. Dublin, April 20th, 1922.

Pearse (P.) see Sects. GENERAL AND INTRODUCTORY ; **1912-1916** ; *and* 594 (Brugha, C.); 612 (" Coilin "); 615 (Colum, P.); 619 (Daly, M.); 622 (Doyle, S.); 664a (McGarrity, J.); 665 (MacGarry, M.); 717-18 (Ryan, D.); 741 (Walsh, L. J.); 747 (Young, Ella).

702. PIM (Frederick W.): The Sinn Fein rising : a narrative and some reflections. 20 pp. 8vo. Dublin, Hodges, Figgis, 1916.

703. PLUNKETT (Grace): Biographies of the seven signatories. Joseph Plunkett. By Mrs. Plunkett. *Poblacht na hÉireann.* Easter number. April 20, 1922.

Plunkett (Joseph Mary), *see also* 44 (Devoy, J.); 595a; 647a (Joy, M.) and " Joseph Plunkett and his friends " by Geraldine Plunkett *Irish Press*, May 5, 1916.

703a. POKORNY *(Professor* Julius): Drei dichter-martyrer. *Irische Blätter.* 1. Jahr. pp. 280-302. Berlin, 1917.

704. PRICE *(Major* Ivor H.): ROYAL COMMISSION ON THE REBELLION *(which see*, pp. 56-60).

<small>Director of British Military Intelligence, Irish Command in 1916.</small>

Proclamation of the Provisional Government, *see* p. xix.

705. REDMOND-HOWARD (Louis George): Six days of the Irish republic: a narrative and critical account of the latest phase of Irish politics. 132 pp. 8vo. Dublin, Ponsonby, 1916.

<small>" An eye-witness of many of the incidents."</small>

706. REIDY (James): Thomas J. Clarke. *The Irish rebellion of 1916 and its martyrs*, ed. by M. JOY. pp. 393-412. New York, 1916.

707. [REYNOLDS (John J.)]: Events of Easter week: The defence of Mount street bridge. *Catholic Bulletin*, VII. Oct.-Dec., 1917.

<small>*See also* the *Irish Independent*, April 22, 1933: " The greatest fight of the rising . . ."</small>

708. ―― Events of Easter week: the fighting in the South Dublin area. *Catholic Bulletin*, VII. illustr. March-July, 1918.

709. [――] A fragment of 1916 history. 32 pp. map. 8vo. [Sinn Féin, 1918 ?].

<small>Deals with the " North King Street massacres " on April 29, 1916, said to have been perpetrated by the military. Statements of witnesses.</small>

710. ―― Four Courts and North King street area in 1916 . . . From statements made to the writer shortly after 1916, by actual participants in the fighting. An t-Óglác, IV. Nos. 18-20. N.S. illustr. May 15–May 29, 1926.

711. REYNOLDS (Miss M.): Cumann na mBan in the G.P.O. Heroic work of Irish girls during the fighting of Easter week, 1916. An t-Óglác. N.S. IV. April 3, 1926.

712. ROBBINS (Frank): The Citizen Army and Easter week, a first-hand account of the rising. In the *Irishman*. Vol. II. Nos. 20-26. Dublin, May 19–June 30, 1928.

713. ROSS-OF-BLADENSBURG *(Sir* John F.): ROYAL COMMISSION ON THE REBELLION [Evidence. pp. 87-92].

<small>Chief Commissioner, Dublin Metropolitan Police, 1901–1914.</small>

714. ROYAL COMMISSION ON THE REBELLION IN IRELAND : Report of Commission. 14 pp. [Cd. 8279]. 1916.

715. —— Minutes of evidence and appendix of documents. Presented to both Houses of Parliament . . . 126 pp. H.M.S.O., 1916. [Cd. 8311].

Terms of reference : " To enquire into the causes of the recent outbreak of rebellion in Ireland, and into the conduct and degree of responsibility of the civil and military executive in Ireland in connection therewith." Headings in the Report : The Irish Government ; Legal powers of the Irish Executive ; Causes of the outbreak ; Conclusions. The Report was signed by Lord Hardinge of Penshurst (Chairman), Montague Shearman, K.C., and Sir Mackenzie Dalzell Chalmers, June 26th, 1916.

The appendices include a list of seditious weekly papers circulating in Ireland in 1915–1916, with names of owners and editors and circulation figures, and (police) returns of the arms reported to be held by the Irish Volunteers at various periods in 1914–1916.

See also under names of chief witnesses.

716. ROYAL COMMISSION ON THE ARREST AND SUBSEQUENT TREATMENT OF MR. FRANCIS SHEEHY SKEFFINGTON, MR. THOMAS DICKSON, AND MR. PATRICK JAMES MCINTYRE : Report of Commission. Presented to both Houses of Parliament . . . 12 pp. 4to. H.M.S.O. 1916. [Cd. 8376].

Signed by Sir John Simon, Thomas F. Molony, Denis F. Henry, September 29th, 1916.

717. RYAN (Desmond) : Five portraits of P. H. Pearse. *Capuchin Annual*, 1931. pp. 188-197. illustr. Dublin, Father Mathew Record Office, Dec., 1930.

718. —— Margaret Pearse. *Capuchin Annual*, 1933. pp. 91-97. illustr. Dublin, Father Mathew Record Office, Jan., 1933.

See also 199-201 ; 173.

719. RYAN (John T.) : How the guns came to Ireland in 1916 : " The origin of the Aud expedition." *An Phoblacht*. N.S. VI. No. 26. April 25th, 1931.

Throws light on the communications which passed between Germany and America immediately before the rising.

720. RYAN (Mary Josephine) : Seán MacDermott. In *The Irish rebellion of* 1916 *and its martyrs*, ed. by M. Joy. pp. 372-379. New York, 1916.

721. ST. JOHN AMBULANCE BRIGADE : Report of work done by St. John Ambulance Brigade, No. 12 (Irish) district, during the Sinn Fein rebellion, April-May, 1916. 30 pp. illustr. 8vo. Dublin, Falconer, 1916.

722. SAURIN (*Commandant* Charles) : Hotel Metropole garrison. An t-Óglác. Vol. IV. Nos. 9-10. N.S. illustr. March 13-20, 1926.

722a. SCOLLAN (John J.) : A fight for an empty building, strange incident in the 1916 struggle. *Sunday Independent*. April 8, 1928.

723. SINN FEIN REVOLT 1916. Twelve interesting views, showing the ruins of Sackville Street and adjoining streets after the rising.

Sheehy Skeffington (F.), *see* Sect. **1912-1916**; *and* 617 Colum (P.); 619 (Daly, M.); 716 (*Royal Commission*).

724. SHEEHY SKEFFINGTON (Hanna): Constance Markievicz in 1916. *An Phoblacht*, N.S. II. No. 50. April 14th, 1928.

725. SKINNIDER (Margaret): Doing my bit for Ireland. 252 pp. 8vo. illustr. New York, The Century Co., 1917.

> A narrative of the insurrection. The author, " school-teacher, suffragist, nationalist, [was] wounded while fighting in the uniform of the Irish Volunteers."

726. SPINDLER (Kapitän Karl): Das geheimnisvolle Schiff : die Fahrt der " Libau " zur irischen Revolution . . . 264 pp. 8vo. Berlin, Scherl, 1921.

727. ——— Gun-running for Casement in the Easter rebellion, 1916. By Reserve-Lieutenant Karl Spindler of the German navy. Translated by W. Montgomery and E. H. McGrath. 242 pp. 8vo. London, Collins, [1921].

728. ——— The mystery of the Casement ship, with authentic documents. By the Commander of the 'Aud,' Captain Karl Spindler. 282 + 6 pp. illustr. facs. maps. 8vo. Berlin, Kaibe-Verlag, 1931.

> An enlarged and corrected edition of " Das geheimnisvolle Schiff " (which did not contain the reports of German naval conferences, etc.). The author claims to have given " a first authentic account of the Easter Week rising of 1916 and the part played by Roger Casement." He quotes from verbatim reports of German naval conferences at which he was present. (" I took copious notes at the time. After the war I compared these with the original documents, and was thus able to fill up the gaps in my account "). The appendices give extracts from cables and correspondence passing between the German Embassy at Washington and the German Government in 1915-1916.

728a. STACK (Austin) : The landing of Casement, the authentic narrative written by Austin Stack. In *Kerry Champion*. August 31– September 21, 1929.

> With notes by Mr. P. Ó Cathail (editor *Kerry Champion*).

729. STAINES (Michael J.) and O'REILLY (Michael W.) : The defence of the G.P.O. . . . From the narratives of M. J. Staines and M. W. O'Reilly. An c-Óglác. Vol. IV. No. 2. N.S. January 23, 1926.

730. STEINMAYER (*Lieutenant* Charles) : Evacuation of the G.P.O., 1916. An c-Óglác. Vol. IV. No. 7. N.S. illustr. February 27, 1926.

731. STEPHENS (James) : The insurrection in Dublin. 14 + 112 pp. 8vo. Maunsel, 1916.

> The author moved about in the streets during the fighting. He records his impressions from day to day and his memories of the leaders. The book was finished on May 8, 1916.

732. STUART-STEPHENS (*Major* Darnley): The secret history of Sinn Fein. *English Rev.*, XXII. pp. 487-496. May, 1916.
   The writer claims "a life-long acquaintance with Irish subterranean political movements."

733. —— How I foretold the Sinn Féin rebellion. *English Rev.*, XXII. pp. 548-561. June, 1916.

734. SWEENEY (P. Emmet): Recollections of a volunteer. *An Phoblacht*. N.S. v. Nos. 28-29. May 3rd-10th, 1930.
   Adjutant in F. Co., 2nd Batt. in 1916.

735. THOMSON (*Sir* Basil): Queer people. 10 + 320 pp. illustr. [Ch. VII.: The Germans and the Irish. Ch. VIII.: The Casement case]. pls. 8vo. London, Hodder and Stoughton, 1922.
   Assistant-Commissioner, London Metropolitan Police, 1913-1919; Director of Intelligence, 1919-1921. Interviewed the captured crew of the "*Aud*" at Scotland Yard, and (on Easter Sunday) Sir Roger Casement.

736. TIMES HISTORY OF THE WAR, The. Vol. VII. [Chs. CXXXIV.-CXXXV. The Irish rebellion of April, 1916]. 4to. illustr. [pp. 393-472]. London, The *Times*, 1916.

737. TURNER (*Captain* C.): The Kimmage garrison in 1916. By Captain C. Turner, Army Corps of Engineers. An t-Óglác. Vol. IV. No. 16. N.S. May 1, 1926.

738. —— The defence of Messrs. Hopkins and Hopkins, O'Connell St., Dublin, in Easter week, 1916. An t-Óglác. Vol. IV. No. 21. illustr. June 5, 1926.

738a. UNITED IRISH LEAGUE, 1916: Irish Party manifesto ... Denunciation of executions, martial law, and wholesale arrests, 4 pp. 4to. May, 1916.

V.A.D., Experience of a, *see* 588.

739. VANE (*Sir* Francis Fletcher): Agin the governments, memories and adventures ... Foreword by Æ. 8vo. illustr. London, Sampson Low, 1931.
   The author served in Ireland during the Great War and was at Portobello Barracks, Dublin, in Easter Week, 1916. He narrates the facts, which he helped to bring to light, regarding the murder of F. Sheehy Skeffington, and quotes a letter written to him on that subject by Theodore Roosevelt.

740. VETERAN: With an outpost in 1916. *An Phoblacht*. N.S. v. No. 26. April 19th, 1930.

740a. VOICE OF IRELAND, The: Being an interview with John Redmond, M.P. and some messages from representative Irishmen regarding the Sinn Féin rebellion. 55 pp. 8vo. London, Nelson, [1916].
   A statement made by Mr. Redmond to a London representative of the Central News of America expressing disapproval of the insurrection, with a selection from resolutions passed by Irish public bodies and messages from various Irish associations at home and abroad to the same effect.

741. WALSH (Louis J.) : P. H. Pearse. *Capuchin Annual, 1932.* pp. 110-114. illustr. Dublin, Father Mathew Record Office, Dec. 1931.

743. WEEKLY IRISH TIMES, The : Sinn Fein rebellion handbook, Easter, 1916 : a complete and connected narrative of the rising, with detailed accounts of the fighting at all points in Dublin and the county . . . Military despatches and official statements . . . Rebel proclamations and manifestoes . . . Casualties . . . Official lists of prisoners deported and released ; Reports of all public courts-martial ; Report and evidence of the Hardinge Commission ; Casement trial and sentence ; Work of the hospitals ; Work of the hospitals, etc. *Second edition.* 248 pp. illustr. 8vo. Dublin, *Weekly Irish Times*, 1916.

—— 1917 issue. [Third edition]. 286 pp. map. 8vo., 1917.

744. WELLS (Warre B.) and MARLOWE (N) [*pseud.*] : A history of the Irish rebellion of 1916. 272 pp. 8vo. Dublin, Maunsel, 1916.

745. WESTROPP (Thomas J.) : Photographs of the ruins of Dublin after the Sinn Fein rebellion, April 24th, 1916, taken by Thomas J. Westropp. May 17-18th, 1916. [20 pp.]. 8vo. [1916].

Wexford, Co., *see* Enniscorthy.

746. WIMBORNE (Ivor Churchill GUEST) *1st Viscount* : ROYAL COMMISSION ON THE REBELLION [Evidence. pp. 34-41, 101-103].

747. YOUNG (Ella) : Some impressions of Pádraic Pearse. *Poblacht na hÉireann.* Easter number. April 20, 1922.

748. YOUNG (*Captain* Thomas) : Fighting in South Dublin. With the garrison in Marrowbone Lane during Easter week, 1916. An t-Óglác. Vol. IV. No. 8. N.S. illustr. March 6, 1926.

4. MAY, 1916 TO DECEMBER, 1918.

749-750. ADDISON (Christopher) : Four and a half years : a personal diary from June 1914 to January 1919. Vols. I and II. 630 pp. illustr. 8vo. London, Hutchinson, 1934.

> Minister of Munitions (1916-1917) and of Reconstruction (1917-1918) in the British Government. In Vol. II refers frequently to the Irish policy of the War Cabinet in 1917-1918, the various proposals made for a settlement on Home Rule lines and the international reactions of the Irish question. Of special interest for the Irish conscription crisis of 1918.

751. ALPHEO : The book of the land of Ire, being a record of those things that were done by the men of Ire in the days when the men of Hun made war upon the earth . . . 36 pp. 8vo. Dublin, Talbot Press, 1919.

752. AMERY (Leopold Stennett): Irish grievances. (II). The demand for fiscal autonomy. *Nineteenth Century*, LXXXIII. pp. 1144-1156. June, 1918.

<blockquote>M.P. (U.) S. Birmingham. Assistant-Secretary, War Cabinet, 1917; Under-Secretary for the Colonies, 1919-1921.</blockquote>

753. AODH RUADH: Slí na saoirse, .i. Leabhar Drille d'Óglaigh na hÉireann. Aodh Ruadh do chuir le chéile. [72] pp. 8vo. [An dara chur]. Ath Cliath, Comhairle na nÓglach, [Meitheamh, 1918].

<blockquote>'Do leigh "Fiachra Eileach" agus Píaras Béaslaí an chuid is mó den tsaothar so, agus do léighfidís é go léir dá mb'ail liomsa foidhne bheith agam' (Reum-fhocal, Mí na Nodlag, 1917). An chéad chur, Márta, 1918; an dara chur Meitheamh, 1918.
This manual, which was approved by the Headquarters Staff, Óglaigh na hÉireann, contains instructions in rifle shooting, infantry drill, bayonet fighting, scouting, etc. The Irish terms are "largely based on those drawn up by a sub-committee of the Irish Volunteers" (An t-Óglác. Vol. I).</blockquote>

754. ASHE (James S.): The work before the Irish Convention, a final plea for lasting conciliation. 24 pp. 8vo. Dublin, Cahill, 1917.

755. ASHE (Thomas): Oration delivered by Commandant Thomas Ashe at Casement's fort, Ardfert, Co. Kerry, on Sunday, 5th August. 1917. 12 pp. 8vo. *n.p.*, [1917].

756. —— Death of Thomas Ashe. Full report of the inquest. 84 pp. illustr. 8vo. Dublin, J. M. Butler, 1917.

—— *See also* 918 (Ó Cathasaigh, S.); *and* "Tomas Aghas, the story of a noble life" by Austin Stack in the *Kerry Champion*, Sept. 29th, 1928.

757. ATHERLEY-JONES (Llewellyn): The Irish maze. (II) An English Home Ruler's viewpoint. *Nineteenth Century*, LXXXI. pp. 932-944. April, 1917.

758. AUDITOR TANTUM: Ireland and the ministerial changes. *Fortnightly Rev.*, CVI. (N.S.). Aug., 1916.

Banking, Irish, 1916-1918, *see* 842 (Horgan, J. J.); 874 (Lysaght, E.). *See also* Sects. **1919-1921** *and* GENERAL AND INTRODUCTORY.

759. BATES (Jean V.): Ulster and the Irish tangle. (II) the keepers of the door. *Nineteenth Century*, LXXXIII. pp. 1092-1100. May, 1918.

760. BATTINE (Cecil): The safety of Ireland *Fortnightly Rev.*, CIX (N.S.). pp. 462-469. March, 1918.

760a. BAUMGARTEN (Paul-Maria): Die politischen und nationalen Ziele Irlands. Von Monsignore Dr. . . . Baumgarten. In *Irische Blätter*. 1. Jahr.–2. Jahr Berlin 1917-1918.

761. [BEITH (John Hay)] : The oppressed English. By Ian Hay [*pseud.*, *i.e.* John Hay Beith). 88 pp. sm. 8vo. New York, Doubleday, Page, 1917.
   British war propaganda. Affirms the unreasonableness of the Irish demand for national freedom.

762. BENNETT (Louie) : Ireland and a people's peace. Paper read at a joint meeting of the Irishwomen's International League and the Irish section of the Union of Democratic Control, Feb. 27, 1918. Published for the Irish section of the Union of Democratic Control. 16 pp. 8vo. Dublin, Maunsel, 1918.

   Bernard (*Rt. Rev.* John Henry) *Archbp. of Dublin,* see 795 and 907.

763. BLÁCAM (Aodh de) : Towards the republic, a study of new Ireland's social and political aims . . . 110 pp. 8vo. Dublin, Kiersey, 1918. [As passed by Censor].

763a. —— Nationality in economics. *Irish Monthly.* Vol. 46. pp. 545-553. Oct., 1918.

   See also 1004, 1028.

764. BLAKE (*Sir* Henry Arthur) : A way out of the chaos in Ireland : some reflections of a Southern Unionist. *Nineteenth Century,* LXXX. pp. 734-739. Oct., 1916.
   Ex-police officer and resident magistrate in Ireland, and afterwards British Colonial Governor.

764a. BOSTON HERALD AND JOURNAL, The : The appeal for an Irish republic, Ireland's aspirations at this juncture in world history—precedents of other little peoples compared.
   Repr. from the Boston Herald and Journal, February 4, 1918.

765. [BOYD (Ernest A.)] : The sacred egoism of Sinn Féin. By Gnathaí gan iarraidh, *pseud., i.e.,* Ernest A. Boyd. 54 pp. 8vo. Dublin, Maunsel, 1918. (*As passed by Censor*).
   " Strong in the sacred egoism of Sinn Féin, the Irish nation is convinced that only in his own country can an Irishman usefully engage in the struggle for freedom."

766. BRENNAN-WHITMORE (William J.) : With the Irish in Frongoch. 211 pp. illustr. 8vo. Dublin, Talbot Press, 1917.
   Frongoch camp, North Wales, where 1,863 Irish prisoners were interned after the 1916 rising.

767. BRITON, A : The political psychology of Ireland, being notes by an English official in Ireland. *Fortnightly Rev.,* CVII. (N.S.). pp. 675-682. April, 1917.

767a. BROKEN TREATY, The : Lloyd George proposals, story of the collapse ; Irish Party's position defined by Messrs. Redmond, Dillon and Devlin. 55 pp. 8vo. Dublin, 1916.
   Report of speeches in the House of Commons, July 24 and 31, 1916.

768. BYRNE (Laurence P.) : Four years of Irish economics, 1914-1918. IV.—Irish Labour in war time. *Studies,* VII. pp. 319-327. June, 1918.

769. BYRNE (Joseph M.) : Prisoners of war : some recollections of an Irish deportee. 60 pp. 8vo. Dublin, The Art Depot (*pr.* Gaelic Press), 1917.

770. BURBAGE (*Rev.* Thomas H.) : The taxation riddle. *Catholic Bulletin*, VII. pp. 33-43. Jan., 1917.

771. CANBY (Henry Seidel) : The Irish mind. *Atlantic Monthly*, CXXIII. pp. 34-43. Boston, Jan., 1919.
>Visited Europe in 1918 " as a guest of the British Ministry of Information " (editorial note). Says : " I was in Ireland all through the excitements of March and April, 1918." Unsympathetic to the Irish national movement.

772. CANONISTA : Irish sovereignty : a study in international law. Dublin, *Catholic Bulletin*, VII. pp. 161-166. March-June, 1917.

773. CARTER (Bertram) : Another part of the platform. 238 pp. 8vo. London, Houghton Publishing Co., 1931.
>Impressions of life in Dublin, 1916-1919, by an English journalist, who went to Ireland " to escape the clamour of the war-mongers." Disapproves of patriotism.

773a. CATHOLIC BULLETIN, The : Events of Easter week. [Biographical note on Dr. E. O'Dwyer, Bishop of Limerick]. VII. pp. 587- Sept., 1917.

774. —— The plot—God help us ! *Catholic Bulletin*, VIII. pp. 268-274. June, 1918.

774a. CHATTERTON-HILL (Georges) : Irland und seine Bedeutung für Europa. Von Dr. Georges Chatterton-Hill. Mit einem Geleitwort von Eduard Meyer, Geheimem Regierungsrat, Ord. Professor an der Universität Berlin. 158 pp. 8vo. Berlin, Karl Curtius, 1916.

774b. —— Zweite umgearbeitete Auflage. 8vo. Berlin, 1917.

774c. —— Die wirtschaftliche Bedeutung Irlands. In *Irische Blätter*. 2, Jahr. Nr. 4. pp. 270-294. Juni, 1918.

775. CHESTERTON (Gilbert Keith) : Irish impressions. 244 pp. 8vo. London, Collins, 1919.
>An account of a visit to Ireland in 1918.

776. CLANCY (John Joseph) *K.C.*, *M.P.* : The Home Rule Act, a statement of its provisions. 28 pp. 8vo. Dublin, Dollard, 1917.
>M.P. (Nat.) North Co. Dublin to 1918.

777. CLANCY (*Rev.* J.) *P.P.* : The failure of ' Parliamentarianism ' . . . (Lecture delivered at Ennis, 13th December, 1917). Second edition. 16 pp. 8vo. Ennis, Sinn Féin, [1918]. Sinn Féin Pamphlets (Clare Series, No. 2).

778. CLAYTON (Bertram) : Sinn Fein II.—Sinn Fein and Labour. *Quarterly Rev.* Vol. 229. pp. 256-268. Jan., 1918.

779. CLEARY (Rev. Patrick) : Some questions regarding the morality of hunger-strikes. *Irish Eccles. Record,* XII (5th Series). pp. 265-273. Oct., 1918.

> A reply to Rev. John Waters (*whom see*), with an examination of hypothetical cases in which refusal to take food may be morally justifiable.

780. CLERY (*Prof.* Arthur E.) : Thomas Kettle. *Studies,* v. pp. 503-515. Dec., 1916.

781. [COFFEY (Diarmuid) and Cruise O'BRIEN] : Proposals for an Irish settlement. Being a draft bill for the Government of Ireland. By two Irishmen [*i.e.,* Diarmuid Coffey and Cruise O'Brien]. 32 pp. 8vo. Dublin, Maunsel, 1917.

782. COFFEY (*Rev.* Peter) : The conscription menace in Ireland. *Irish Ecclesiastical Record,* XI. (5th Series). pp. 484-498. June, 1918.

> Professor of Logic and Metaphysics, St. Patrick's College, Maynooth. Seeks to justify the organised resistance of the Irish people to the enforcement of conscription by the British Government.

783. —— Unionism and self-government, a study in "safeguards." *Catholic Bulletin,* VIII. pp. 337-344. July, 1918.

Comḋáil Cosanta Ꞡaeḋeal, 1918, *see* 896 (*Mansion House* Conference).

Conscription crisis, The, 1918, *see* 81 (Healy, T. M.) ; 215 (Sullivan, A. M.) ; 750 (Addison, C.) ; 773 (Carter, B.) ; 782 (Coffey, *Rev.* P.) ; 789 (De Valera, E.) ; 797 (Duffy, G. G.) ; 815 (Finlay, *Rev.* P.) ; 819 (Fisher, J. R.) ; 890 (Mahon, *Sir* B.) ; 896-897 (*Mansion House Conference, The*) ; 951 (Plunkett, *Sir* H.) ; 961 (Russell, G. W.) ; 989 (Ulster Unionist Council) ; 1136 (French, *Sir* J., Earl) ; 1229 (MacDonald, *Rev.* W.) ; 1287 (Óglác, An t-) ; 1364 (Street, C. J. S.) ; 876 (McCartan, Dr. P.).

Convention, The (1917), *see* IRISH CONVENTION.

784. CORKEY (*Rev.* William) : The Church of Rome and Irish unrest. How hatred of Britain is taught in Irish schools. Reprinted from the "Witness," Belfast. 42 pp. 8vo. Edinburgh, Bishop, 1918.

785. Cox (Harold) : Irish grievances. (1) Under-taxed Ireland. *Nineteenth Century,* LXXXIII. pp. 1144-1156. June, 1918.

786. CRAMMOND (Edgar) : Ireland's part in the war. *Nineteenth Century,* LXXXI. pp. 974-990. May, 1917.

Curzon (G. N.) *Marquess, of Kedleston, see* 1005 (Zetland).

787. CUSHENDUN (Ronald John MCNEILL) *1st Baron* : The Ulster viewpoint. *Nineteenth Century,* LXXXI. pp. 922-931. April, 1917.

788. D. : Ireland looks into the mirror. [14] pp. 8vo. Dublin, Whelan. [1916]. (Tracts for Irishmen. No. 1).

> Comparison between Ireland and Hungary.

789. DE VALERA (Eamonn) : Ireland's case against Conscription. 46 pp. 8vo. Dublin, Maunsel, 1918. *(Passed by Censor).*

>   Preface : "This statement of Ireland's case against Conscription which Mr. de Valera, at the instance of the Mansion House Conference, was preparing for presentation by the Lord Mayor of Dublin to President Wilson, was almost completed at the time of Mr. de Valera's arrest . . ." (Robert Brennan).

790. —— Eamonn De Valera states his case. Repr. from the "Christian Science Monitor," Boston, U.S.A. May 15th, 1918. [4] pp. 8vo. Dublin, Sinn Féin, [1918].

791. DICEY (Albert Venn) : An Irish settlement. (I) Is it wise to establish Home Rule before the end of the war ? *Nineteenth Century,* LXXXII. pp. 1-25. July, 1917.

792. —— Ireland as a dominion. *Nineteenth Century,* LXXXII. pp. 700-726. Oct., 1917.

>   Sets forth the " arguments in favour of Ireland's occupying the status of a dominion " and the " objections," assuming that British interests must be the first consideration in any Irish settlement.

793. DILLON (John) : East Cavan contest. Speech of Mr. Dillon, M.P. at Bailieboro' . . . 4 pp. Cavan, John F. O'Hanlon, 1918. May 26th, 1918.

>   *See also* 896.

794. DODD (William Huston) : Belfast prison inquiry. Report by the Right Honorable Mr. Justice Dodd of the proceedings at the inquiry directed by the Special Commission (Belfast Prison) Act, 1918. Presented to Parliament . . . 10 pp. H.M.S.O. [Cmd. 83].

>   Many Irish political prisoners were detained at Belfast prison in 1918. The inquiry was held as a result of persistent complaints of harsh and vindictive treatment. No representations were made on behalf of the prisoners, and the report favours the prison authorities.

795. DUBLIN (John Henry BERNARD) *Archbp. of* : Ireland in 1916. *National Rev.,* LXVIII. pp. 212–222. London, Oct., 1916.

>   Unionist.

796. [DUFFIN (Adam)] : Thoughts and facts for the consideration of the Irish Convention. By an Ulster Irishman [*i.e.,* A. Duffin). [Belfast, Baird, 17th August, 1917].

>   With a criticism of the financial proposals made by M. A. Ennis (803).

797. DUFFY (George Gavan) : The groundwork of conscription ; an epitome of the military service code in Great Britain, with the disciplinary measures, civil and military, for its enforcement. By G. Gavan Duffy, B.L. 32 pp. 8vo. Dublin, Talbot Press, 1918.

>   Written in view of the threatened enforcement of the code in Ireland (May, 1918), " in the belief that a general acquaintance with the exemplar will be found useful, if not necessary, by all who may ultimately have a closer concern in the new model."

798. DUN CAIRIN : The argument from Irish history. *Studies*, a quarterly review. VII. pp. 545–552. Dublin, Dec., 1918.
 Argues that " the people of Ireland have established beyond question their possession of all the qualities and attributes of a free nation."

799. DUNRAVEN (Windham Thomas WYNDHAM-QUIN) *4th Earl of*: Ireland's dilemma (II) The federal opportunity. *Nineteenth Century*, LXXXIV. pp. 622-634. Oct., 1918.

800. —— " Ireland, awake ! " An open letter to his countrymen. By the Earl of Dunraven. 16 pp. 8vo. Dublin, [Independent Newspapers], June, 1917.

801. EDINBURGH REVIEW, The : Sinn Fein. *Edinburgh Rev.* Vol. 224. pp. 114-136. July, 1916.

802. ENGLISH CATHOLIC, An : England, Germany and the Irish question. 44 pp. 8vo. London, Hodder and Stoughton, 1917.

802a. ENGLISHMAN, An : Dublin, explorations and reflections. By an Englishman [D. Goldring]. 272 pp. 8vo. Dublin, Maunsel, 1917.

802b. —— : A stranger in Ireland. 143 pp. 8vo. Dublin, Talbot Press, 1918.

803. ENNIS (Michael A.) : Some essentials of sound finance in an Irish constitution. 48 pp. 8vo. Dublin, Cahill, 1917.
 Published for the guidance of the author's colleagues, the representatives of the Irish County Councils' General Council on the Irish Convention. 1917.

804. ERGO : Should Irishmen be cons.ripted ? 32 pp. 8vo. London, Felix McGlennon, [1918].
 A comparison between the Irish crisis of 1780 and that of 1918.

805. ESCOUFLAIRE (Rodolphe C.) : L'Irlande ennemie . . . ? 272 pp. 8vo. Paris, Payot, 1918. (Bibliothèque Politique et Économique).

806. —— Ireland, an enemy of the allies ? : 40 pp. 8vo. London, Murray, 1919.
 Preface dated, at Paris, Aug. 15, 1918. A study of Ireland in modern times. Unsympathetic to the national movement.

807. EVANS (Richardson) : Ireland in the realm and Ulster in Ireland. 50 pp. 8vo London, Constable, 1917.

808. EVENING POST, The [New York] : The Irish Convention s proposed by Premier David Lloyd George : the opinions of prominent Americans of Irish blood. Reprinted from *The Evening Post*, New York. 36 pp. 8vo. New York, Friends of Irish Freedom, [1917].

808a. [EYRE (Edward)] : England's dilemma. 32 pp. 8vo. *n.t.p., n.d.* [1918 ?].
 A reply, in defence of the Irish people, to three articles in the *Nineteenth Century*, May, 1918.

809. Fáinne an Lae, An Claíḋeaṁ Soluis, 1918–1919. Cláruiġṫe mar páipéar nuaḋaċta. 12 eanair 1918–1920 Meaḋon Foġṁair 1919. ꝑr. p. Ó Maṫġaṁna.
> Suppressed in Sept., 1919, following the publication of a prospectus of the Dáil Loan. See also 17.

810. FIGGIS (Darrell) : The Gaelic State in the past and future or " the crown of a nation." 84 pp. 8vo. Dublin, Maunsel, 1917.

811. —— Sinn Féin Catechism. 30 pp. 8vo. *n.p.*, [1918].

812. —— The historic case for Irish independence. 78 pp. sm. 8vo. Dublin, Maunsel, 1918.

813. —— The freedom of the seas. 16 pp. 8vo. Dublin, [1918].

814. —— A chronicle of jails. 130 pp. 8vo. Dublin, Talbot Press, 1917.

814a. —— A second chronicle of jails. 102 pp. 8vo. Dublin, Talbot Press, 1919.

See also 316.

Finance (Irish) 1916-1918, *see* 752 (Amery, L.) ; 770 (Burbage, Rev. T. H.) ; 785 (Cox, H.) ; 803 (Ennis, M.A.) ; 842 (Horgan, J. J.) ; 851 (Irish Convention) ; 874 (Lysaght, E. E.) ; 930 (O'Herlihy) Rev. M.) ; 944-944a (Quin, M.).

See also Sects. GENERAL AND INTRODUCTORY ; **1912-1916.**

815. FINLAY (*Rev.* Peter) *S.J.* : The doctrinal authority of bishops. *Studies*, VII. pp. 193-209. June, 1918.
> Professor of Theology, Milltown Park, Dublin. A vindication of the pronouncement of the Irish bishops against the enforcement of conscription in Ireland by the British Government. Replies to a group of English Catholic laymen who complained to the Vatican of the bishops' action.

816. FISHER (Joseph R.) : The Irish enigma again. (I) What is wrong in Ireland ? *Nineteenth Century*, LXIX. pp. 1184-1189. June, 1916.

817. —— Ulster and the Irish tangle. (I) The ' unreasonableness ' in Ulster. *Nineteenth Century*, LXXXIII. pp. 1088-1091. May, 1918.

818. —— The federal panacea for Ireland. *Nineteenth Century*, LXXXIV pp. 59-67. July, 918.

819. —— Ireland's dilemma. (1) Ireland, America and the war. *Nineteenth Century*, LXXXIV. pp. 614-621. Oct., 1918.
> A criticism of the Mansion House anti-conscription conference appeal to the U.S.

820. FOGARTY (*Most Rev.* Michael), *Bp. of Killaloe* : The great bishop of Limerick. Panegyric delivered . . . at the month's mind of the dead prelate, in St. John's Cathedral, Limerick, 18 September, 1917. 22 pp. 8vo. Dublin, Gill, 1917.
> See also 925.

Food production in war time, 1914–1918, *see* 302

Frongoch internment camp, 1916, *see* **1916**.
  See also 10 (Béaslaí, P.); 766 (Brennan-Whitmore, W. J.); 769 (Byrne, Joseph M.).

Friends of Irish Freedom, the [U.S.A.], *see* 1137-1140.

821. GAYNOR (*Rev.* P.): The faith and morals of Sinn Fein. 8 pp. 8vo. Dublin, Art Depot, [1917 ?].

General Election, 1918, *see* 947 (Redistribution of seats); 750-752 (Representation of People Act, 1917); Sinn Féin; 993 (United Irish League); 1110 (de Valera, E.); 1102 (Dept. of Publicity).

822. GEORGE (David Lloyd): War memories of Lloyd George. Vols. I-II. 22 + 18 + 1038 pp. pls. 8vo. London, Nicholson and Watson, 1933.
  Vol. II (Ch. XXII) gives an account of the Home Rule negotiations of May-July, 1916 which were carried on by Mr. Lloyd George on behalf of the Prime Minister (H. H. Asquith). See 840 (*Home Rule*).

823. ——— Letter from the Prime Minister regarding Ireland. Presented to Parliament ... 4 pp. H.M.S.O., 1917.
  To John Redmond, dated 16th May, 1917.

823a. GERMANICUS: Quo vadis, Germania? In *Irische Blätter*. 1. Jahr. Nr. 6. pp. 406-419. Berlin, Oktober, 1917.

" German plot," The (19 8), *see* 774 (*Catholic Bulletin*); 867 (*Lector*); 980 (*Documents* . . .).

824. GERMANS IN CORK, The, being the letters of His Excellency, the Baron von Kartoffel (Military Governor of Cork in the year 1918) and others. 112 pp. 8vo. Dublin, The Talbot Press, [1917].

German-Irish Society, *see* 324 (Gaffney, T. St. John); 774 (Chatterton. Hill, G.); 846 (*Irische Blätter*).

Ginnell (Lawrence), *see* 325, 974.

" Gnathaí gan iarraidh," *see* 765 [Boyd, E. A.].

824a. GOLDRING (Douglas): Odd man out: the autobiography of a propaganda novelist. 324 pp. 8vo. London, Chapman and Hall, 1935.
  Includes recollections of literary and political life in Dublin, 1916–1918. See also 802a.

825. GOOD (James Winder): The spirit of Belfast. *Contemporary Rev.*, CXII. pp. 151-158. Aug., 1917.

826. ——— The Ulster nationalist. *Contemporary Rev.*, CXII. pp. 542-549. Nov., 1917.

827. GRAVES (Alfred Perceval): Ulster Home Rule: a proposal. *Contemporary Rev.*, CXIII. pp. 588-597. May, 1917.

828. GREEN (Alice Stopford) : Loyalty and disloyalty, what it means in Ireland. 14 pp. 8vo. Dublin, Maunsel, [1918 ?].

829. —— Thoughts on Irish industries. *Studies*, VII. pp. 385-399. Sept., 1918.

830. —— Ourselves alone in Ulster. 30 pp. 8vo. Dublin, Maunsel, 1918.

831. [GRIFFITH (Arthur)] : Arthur Griffith, a study of the founder of Sinn Fein. 24 pp. 8vo. Dublin, Cahill, [1917 ?].

832. GWYNN (Stephen) : John Redmond's last years. 352 pp. 8vo. frontisp. London, Arnold, 1919.

833. HAMBRO (C. J.) Irske streiftog og studier. 160 pp. 8vo. Kristiania, 1920.
>A member of the Norwegian Parliament. For a review of this book see *Young Ireland* (Dublin), March 26, 1921.

834. HARP, The, 1917. March 24th–July 7th, 1917. Weekly. Pr. for the proprietors (Waterford) at the *Kilkenny Journal* office, Kilkenny.
>Sinn Féin. Aims at " striking a definite and defiant National note " (March 24th).

835. HARRISON (Austin) : John Bull and his yoke. *English Rev.*, XXIII. pp. 237-246. Sept., 1916.

836. —— Home Rule is Ireland's opportunity. *English Rev.*, XXIII. pp. 425-434. Nov., 1916.

837. —— Ireland. *English Rev.*, XXV. pp. 272-284. Sept., 1917.

838. HARRISON (Marie) : Dawn in Ireland. 222 pp. 8vo. London, Melrose, 1917.
>" The author went on a special commission to study the people and their conditions at first hand, and the pictures she gives of agricultural, manufacturing and social progress of the last ten years are of the most rosy hue " (Publisher).

839. HERBERT (Arthur S.) : The Convention, or else ? *Nineteenth Century*, LXXXII. pp. 1216-1233. Dec., 1917.

840. HOME RULE, 1916 : Proposed Home Rule settlement. Irish public opinion. Nos. 1-5. 224 pp. Dublin, Humphrey and Armour, [1916].
>" These pages are published with the object of showing from day to day the tendency of public opinion in Ireland in reference to the Proposals for Settlement of the Home Rule question made through Mr. Lloyd George, M.P., on behalf of the Government." Extracts from speeches and letters, Irish newspapers, resolutions of public bodies, etc.

>*See also* 37 (Cushendun, *1st Baron*) ; 70 (Gwynn, D. : *Life of John Redmond*) ; 81 (Healy, T. M.) ; 117 (Long, W., *1st Viscount*) ; 150 (O'Brien, W.) ; 767a (" Broken Treaty, The ") ; 822 (George, D. Lloyd).

841. HORGAN (John Joseph): William Redmond: some personal memories. *Studies*, VI. pp. 417-423. Dublin, Sept., 1917.

842. —— The peaceful penetration of Ireland. *Studies*, VI. pp. 635-641. Dec., 1917.
> Noting the absorption of Irish by English banks as signs and portents of . . . the control of Irish commerce and industry in the interests of England." See also 46; 874; 1216; 1351.

843. —— The world policy of President Wilson. *Studies*, VII. Dec., 1918.
> With special reference to Ireland's claim for self-determination.

See also 357.

Hunger-strikes, 1917-1921, see 756 (Ashe, T.); 1143 (Gallagher, F.); 1245 (MacSwiney, T.).
For discussions of the ethics of hunger-striking see 1027 (Bishops of Ireland); 779, 1063a (Cleary, *Rev.* P.); 1145 (Gannon, *Rev.* P. J.); 1215 (Kelleher, *Rev.* J.); 1000, 1383 (Waters, *Rev.* J.).

844. INDIAN NATIONALIST COMMITTEE (EUROPEAN CENTRE): Roger Casement and India. 24 pp. sm. 8vo. Stockholm, Dahlbergs Förlags A-B., 1917.

845. INTERNATIONAL MAGNA CHARTA, An: Repr. from *The English Review* (August, 1917). 16 pp. 8vo. Dublin, Cahill, 1917.

846. IRISCHE BLÄTTER, 1917-1918. Im Auftrage der Deutsch-Irischen Gesellschaft, herausgegeben von Georges Chatterton-Hill. 1 Jahr., 8 + 690 pp. 2 Jahr., 614 pp. Berlin, Karl Curtius. April 1917–Oct. 1918.
> Organ of the *Deutsch-Irische Gesellschaft* (German-Irish Society). The presidents of the society were: Herr Mathias Erzberger, Baron von Richthofen, and Count Westarp. The members included many Germans eminent in learning and public affairs.
> The inaugural address, published in Vol. I, stresses the importance to Germany of Irish friendship and the value of Irish organisations in the United States in joining with the "politically unorganised" German-Americans to strive for "true neutrality." The "heroic rebellion of 1916" commended. Quotations from comments on Irish affairs in German newspapers. Articles on Irish history, politics, economics, literature, folk-lore.
> See also under names of principal contributors.

847. —— Deutschland und die irische Frage. 1. Jahr. Nr. 1. pp. 11-26. April, 1917.

848. —— Irland, Amerika und die Friedenskonferenz. 1. Jahr. Nr. 2. pp. 151-162. May, 1917.

849. —— Irland, Deutschland und die Irische-Amerikaner. In *Irische Blätter*. 2. Jahr. Nr. 5. pp. 400-411. August, 1918.

850. IRELAND'S APPEAL TO AMERICA 1917. Address presented to Congress, Washington, July 23rd. Also America's appeal to Ireland, 1775. . . . 16 pp. 8vo. Dublin, Kiersey, 1917.
> Repr. from the *Irish World* of two documents presented at the Capitol by Dr. P. McCartan, one (dated June 17th) on behalf of "the Provisional Government of the Irish Republic," the other by 26 officers of the Irish Volunteers (June 18th) after their release from imprisonment.

851. IRISH CONVENTION, 1917 : Report of the proceedings of the Irish Convention. Presented to Parliament . . . 176 pp. H.M.S.O. 1918. [Cd. 9019].
> In addition to the main Report the documents printed include : Report of the Ulster Unionist delegates ; Report by twenty-two Nationalist members ; Note by the majority of the Nationalist members ; Note by the majority of the Labour representatives ; Note by the Southern Unionists. In the appendices are given lists of members, secretariat, committees and divisions, and reports of sub-committees.

—— *see also* 36 (Cork Chamber of Commerce) ; 37 (Cushendun, *1st Baron*) ; 70 (Redmond, J.) ; 81 (Healy, T. M.) ; 136 (Midleton, *1st Earl of*) ; 150 ; 913, 916 (O'Brien, W.) ; 796 (Duffin, A.) ; 804 (Ergo) ; 839 (Herbert, A. S.) ; 851 (*Report of the proceedings*) ; 937 (Orchelle, R. L.) ; 940 (Plunkett, *Sir* H.) ; 960 (Russell, G. W.) ; 983 (Stack, *Rev.* T.) ; 1002 (Wells, W. B. *and* Marlowe, N.) ; 1003 (Windle, *Sir* B.) ; 808a (New York " Evening Post.")

852. IRISH K.C., An : Ulster's opportunity : a united Ireland. 36 pp. 8vo. Dublin, Duffy, [1917].

853. IRISH LEAGUE OF NATIONS SOCIETY : International reconstruction. Views of the Rt. Revd. the Bishop of Kilmore and Professor Eoin MacNeill. 12 pp. 8vo. Dublin, Repr. by the Irish League of Nations Society, March, 1918 (I.L.N.S.—Series 'A' No. 11).

854. —— Proposed non-British tribunal. The international reference movement. List of supporters . . . [24] pp. 8vo. Dublin, Irish League of Nations Society, July, 1918. (I.L.N.S.—Series A—No. 16).

855. IRISH NATION, The : June 24th, 1916 to Dec. 22nd, 1917 (Vol. II. No. 25). [Edited by M. J. Judge]. Printed by Cahill for the Irish nation Publishing Co., Dublin.
> Policy : repeal of the Act of Union. Opposed to the Irish Parliamentary Party, but also disapproves of Sinn Féin.

Irish Nation League, 1916, *see* 442 (*New Ireland*) ; 855 (*Irish Nation*) ; 921 (O'Connor, F. J.).

856. IRISH OPINION, 1916-1917 : a weekly newspaper and review. June 17, 1916–April 28, 1917. Printed for the Irish Opinion Publishing Co. by the Wood Printing Works.
> Moderate Sinn Féin.

857. IRISH OPINION, 1917–1918 (N.S.) : a weekly journal of industrial and political democracy. N.S. 1917-1918. Dec. 1st 1917–April 13th, 1918 (Vol. 1. No. 20).
> Extract from an advertisement, signed Thomas Johnson, in *Nationality* (Dec. 7th, 1917) : " Since Easter, 1916, the demand on the part of Irish Trade Unionists and friends of Labour for a Labour Newspaper has steadily grown . . . With a view to meeting this demand it is proposed to resume publication of the journal known as " Irish Opinion," with the addition as a sub-title of " The Voice of Labour " . . . The editorship will be undertaken by Mr. Andrew E. Malone . . . The general direction and responsibility will be in the hands of the undersigned."

Irish Parliamentary Party, 1916-1918, *see* 776 (Clancy, J. J.); 793 (Dillon, John); 851 (Irish Convention); 864-865a (Law, H. A.); 896 (Mansion House Conference); 906 (Murphy, W. M.); 911-916 (O'Brien, W.); 70 (Redmond, John); (Sinn Féin); Ulster; 991-993 (United Irish League); 1014 (Peace Conference).

See also GENERAL AND INTRODUCTORY.

858. IRISH PRIEST, AN: In Maryboro' and Mountjoy, the prison experiences and prison-breaking of an Irish volunteer (Padraic Fleming). 32 pp. 8vo. n.p., [1917].

Irish World (Dublin), *see* 963.

859. IRISHMAN, The, 1916-1919: Monthly from Jan. to Sept., 1916. Weekly, Sept., 1916–Sept., 1919. Printed by Northgate Printing Works, Belfast, to Dec., 1917; by Wood Printing Works, Dublin from Jan. 4th, 1918. Edited by "A. Newman" [*pseud.*, i.e., Herbert Moore Pim], by "Herbert Moore Pim" to May, 1918; later by P. S. O Flannagain.

860. IRLAND UNTER ENGLAND. Tatsachen und Ziffern. 16 pp. illustr. 8vo. Berlin, Karl Curtius, [1916 ?].

861. JOINT COMMISSION ON THE PROBLEMS OF THE INTERNATIONAL SETTLEMENT: Memoranda on some crucial questions. IV. Ireland. 14 pp. 8vo. London, [1918 ?].
   "Special Note. The following memorandum on the Irish Question has been prepared in co-operation with a small group in Dublin, and has been approved by several well-known Irish writers."

862. KETTLE (Thomas Michael): The ways of war. By Professor T. M. Kettle, Lieut. 9th Dublin Fusiliers. With a memoir by his wife, Mary S. Kettle. 240 pp. portr. 8vo. Dublin, Talbot Press, 1917.
   The cause of European liberty, as represented by Great Britain and her allies in the Great War, was synonymous for the author with the cause of national freedom in Ireland. The War Office refused to grant permission for the publication of this book during his life time. See also 107, 385–389.

Labour movement (Irish), 1916-1918, *see* Sects. GENERAL AND INTRODUCTORY; **1912-1916**.
   See also 768 (Byrne, L. P.); 778 (Clayton, B.); 857 (*Irish Opinion*); 896 (*Mansion House Conference*, 1918); 887 (MacDonagh, M.); 884 (MacKenna, R.); 955 ("Ronald"); 969 (Sigerson, S.); 981 (Spálpín); 998 (*Voice of Labour, The*).

864. LAW (Hugh Alexander): Pacata Hibernia. *Contemporary Rev.*, CIX. pp. 690-700. June, 1916.

865. —— Ireland, 1918. *Contemporary Rev.*, CXIII. pp. 601-609. June, 1918.

865a. —— The travail of Ireland. I. John Redmond: a remembrance. *Dublin Review,* CLXIII. pp. 1-11. July, 1918.

866. LECTOR : The Plot : German or English ? By Lector [*pseud.*, *i.e.*, Professor Alfred O'Rahilly]. (as passed by censor). 16 pp. 8vo. Dublin, New Ireland Publishing Co., 1918. (New Ireland Pamphlets. No. 2.)

867. —— The issue ; the case for Sinn Fein. As passed by censor. 14 pp. 8vo. Dublin, New Ireland Publishing Co., 1918. (New Ireland Pamphlets. No. 3.)

868. LENNON (Michael J.) : A retrospect. *Banba*, III. pp. 222-235. Dublin, July-Aug., 1922.
> A well-informed study of Irish public opinion and of the reorganisation of Sinn Féin to Dec. 1917.

869. LESLIE (Shane) : The travail of Ireland. (III). Burnt offerings *Dublin Rev.*, CLXIII. pp. 20-27. July, 1918.

870. —— The German and Irish element in the American melting pot. *Dublin Rev.*, CLXIII. pp. 258-283. Oct., 1918.

Lloyd George (David), *see* George (D. Lloyd).

871. LOCAL TAXATION (Ireland) 1917-1918. Returns of local taxation in Ireland for the year 1917-1918, collected and compiled by desire of His Excellency the Lord Lieutenant by the Local Government Board for Ireland . . . Presented to Parliament. 28 pp. H.M.S.O., 1919 [Cmd. 133].

Long (Walter) *1st Viscount*, see 117.

872. LYND (Robert) : If the Germans conquered England. 158 pp. 8vo. Dublin, Maunsel, 1917.
> Essays, some on Irish affairs and political personalities. See also 646b.

873. LYONS (George A.) : A Christmas ghost story. By George A. Lyons (interned in Usk Prison). Dublin, Manico, *pr.* [1918 ?].

874. LYSAGHT (Edward E.) : Self-government and business interests ; a memorandum on the economic and fiscal aspect of the question. 34 pp. 8vo. Dublin, Maunsel, 1918.
> Repr. from *Studies*, Dec., 1917. Maintains that "Ireland . . . is not in a position to stand the financial strain involved in partnership with a large and wealthy state of long-standing prosperity like Great Britain."

875. —— Four years of Irish economics, 1914-1918. III.—Irish agriculture. *Studies*, VII. pp. 314-319. Dublin, June, 1918.

876. MCCARTAN (*Dr.* Patrick) : With de Valera in America. By Patrick McCartan, F.R.C.S.I., Envoy of the Irish Republic to the United States, 1917-1920. 284 pp. illustr. 8vo. Dublin, Fitzpatrick, 1932.
> Dr. McCartan arrived in New York on July 1st, 1917, as an envoy from the Supreme Council of the I. R. B. He gives a valuable account of the connection between the Irish organisations at home and those in America. Chapters on the Irish Race Convention (1919) ; the American mission of President de Valera (1919-1920) ; the American-Irish organisations (Clan-na-Gael, the Friends of Irish Freedom, the American Association for the Recognition of the Irish Republic, etc.) and their differences ; the American Commission on Ireland (1920-1921). Appendices contain the communications addressed by Dr. McCartan to the U.S. Congress and Government in 1918.

876a. —— Dr. McCartan's note to the President and Congress of the United States. 4 pp. 8vo. *n.p.* [1918].

876b. —— Memorandum on the pending Anglo-American treaty. Presented to the State Department of the United States. . . . February 17, 1918. *n.p.*, 1918.

876c. —— Memorandum addressed to the Secretary of State for the United States and to the allied ambassadors concerning the violation of principle involved in conscription of the manhood of Ireland by England. By Patrick McCartan, Envoy of the Provisional Government of Ireland. 8 pp. 8vo. [New York?]. May 1, 1918.

877. MacDonagh (Michael): Sinn Fein and Labour in Ireland. *Contemporary Rev.*, CXIII. pp. 424-433. April, 1918.

878. McGrath (John): Agrarian reform in Ireland. *Fortnightly Rev.*, CVII (N.S.) pp. 1060-1074. June, 1917.

879. —— Sir Horace Plunkett, Sinn Fein, and the Irish situation. *Fortnightly Rev.*, CVIII (N.S.). pp. 865-874. Dec., 1917.

880. —— Mr. Redmond as Irish leader: and his legacy. *Fortnightly Rev.*, CIII. pp. 744-754. May, 1918.

881. —— Irish national leaders and a federal solution. *Fortnightly Rev.*, CIII (N.S.). pp. 924-933. June, 1918.
A member of the staff of "The Freeman's Journal."

883. McIntyre (*Most Rev.* John), *Archbp.-Auxiliary of Birmingham*: Catholics and the war. A speech delivered at St. Patrick's reunion, June 24th, 1918. 12 pp. 8vo. London, *The Universe*, 1918. (Universe Pamphlet, No. 4.)

884. MacKenna (Rose): A plea for social emancipation in Ireland. 16 pp. 8vo. Manchester, National Labour Press, [1917].

MacKeogh (Michael), *see* 1237.
Experiences as a soldier in the German-Irish Brigade, 1915-1918.

885. MacNeice (*Rev.* Frederick J.): A plea for unity and peace in Ireland. Address to Orangemen . . . at a service in Carrickfergus Parish Church . . . 8th July, 1917. 12 pp. 8vo. [Carrickfergus, Bell, *pr.*, 1917].

886. MacNeill (Eoin): War and reconstruction: Irish settlement. By Professor John MacNeill. *English Rev.*, XXV. pp. 253-262. Sept., 1917.

887. MacNeill (John Gordon Swift), *M.P.*: Irish rights and British honour. *Contemporary Rev.*, CXIII. pp. 499-508. May, 1918.

MacSwiney (*Marquis*), *see* 939 (P. J. F.).

888. MAGENNIS (*Rev. Peter E.*), *Order of Calced Carmelites*: **Peter Golden, orator-poet-patriot.** *Catholic Bulletin*, XVI. pp. 526-533. May, 1926.
> Claims that [in 1917-1918] " the Irish cause [in America] centred around Peter Golden."

890. MAHON (*General Sir Bryan*): The Irish welter as I found it. In the VOICE OF IRELAND, (*which see*, pp. 125-128).
> General officer commanding the British forces in Ireland, 1916-1918.

891. MALONEY (*Dr.* William J. M. A.): Ireland's plea for freedom. In the *Irish question*, pp. 106-126.
> See 994 (U.S. Congress) and 876 (McCartan, *Dr.* P.).

892. MANCHESTER GUARDIAN HISTORY OF THE WAR, The : Vol. VIII.—1917-19. illustr. 4to. [Ireland in the fourth year. pp. 254-265]. Manchester, Heywood, 1919.

893. MANNIX (*Most Rev. Dr.* Daniel) *Archbp. of Melbourne*: The case of Ireland. 12 pp. 8vo. *n.p., n.d.*
> A speech delivered at Melbourne, November 5, 1917.

894. —— Archbishop Mannix and his critics. *Catholic Bulletin*, VIII. pp. 3-11. Dublin, Jan., 1918.

895. —— Ireland's voice at the antipodes. *Catholic Bulletin*, VIII. 1918.
> See also 1254.

896. MANSION HOUSE CONFERENCE, 1918: To the President of the United States of America. 4to. 12 pp. 1918.

897. —— No conscription ! Ireland's case re-stated. Address to the President of the United States of America from the Mansion House Conference, 16 pp. 8vo. Dublin, Mansion House Conference, 1918.
> Dated June 11th, 1918. Signed by Laurence O'Neill, Lord Mayor of Dublin (Chairman), Joseph Devlin, John Dillon, T. M. Healy, William O'Brien, Michael Egan, Thomas Johnson, William O'Brien (the last three representing Labour), and by Thomas Kelly and John MacNeill (acting in the place of E. de Valera and Arthur Griffith, members of the conference, who had been deported to English prisons on May 18th).

898. MARKIEVICZ (Constance de): A call to the women of Ireland. Being a lecture delivered to the Student's National Literary Society, Dublin, under the title of " Women, Ideals, and the Nation." 16 pp. 8vo. Dublin : Fergus O'Connor, 1918.
> See also 134.

899. MARLOWE (N.) : A week in Clare. *Contemporary Rev.*, CXIII. pp. 434-439. April, 1918.

900. —— The Irish bishops, the war and Home Rule. *Contemporary Rev.*, CXIV. pp. 402-406. Oct., 1918.

901. MARRIOTT (*Sir* John Arthur Ransome) : Prussia, Poland and Ireland. *Edinburgh Rev.*, 225. pp. 158-177. Jan., 1917.

902. MASSINGHAM (Henry William): Ireland, 1916— and beyond. *Atlantic Monthly*, CXVIII. pp. 839-845. Dec., 1916.

902a. MEN OF MILITARY AGE, 1916. Statement giving particulars, regarding men of military age in Ireland. Presented to both Houses of Parliament. . . . [4] pp. H.M.S.O., 1916 [Cd. 8390].

Military service Act, 1918, *see* 511 (Recruiting for the British army); 797 (Duffy, G. Gavan); *and* Conscription crisis, 1918.

903. MOORE (Alfred S.): Ireland's hold-back. *Forum*, LX. pp. 191-199. New York, Aug., 1918.

904. [MOORE (Myles)]: The inside story of Easter week. Specially written for the *Echo* by " Nada " [pseud., *i.e.*, Myles Moore]. Enniscorthy, The *Echo*. May 17th-June 21st, 1930.

905. [———] In the days of the Volunteers . . . Specially written for *The Echo* by " Nada," *pseud.*, *i.e.*, Myles Moore. *The Echo* (Enniscorthy). June 28th–Sept. 30th, 1930.

>A record of Irish Volunteer activities in 1916-1921, with special reference to Enniscorthy and North Co. Wexford. The writer states that " the articles have been compiled from the narratives of responsible officers of the Irish Volunteers."

906. MURPHY (William Martin): The Home Rule Act 1914 exposed. 18 pp. 8vo. Dublin, [Independent Newspapers], 1917.

>Repr. from " Irish Independent " 30th March and 24th April, 1917, and " Times," 2nd May. Advocates Dominion Home Rule.

907. MURRAY (*Rev.* Robert H.): Archbishop Bernard, professor, prelate and provost. 392 pp. portr. 8vo. London, Society for Promoting Christian Knowledge, 1931.

>Illustrates Southern Unionist opinion in the period. Dr. Bernard was Protestant Archbishop of Dublin, 1915-1919, and Provost of T.C.D., 1919-1927. Extracts from his letters to the Archbishop of Canterbury on the proceedings of the Irish Convention (1917).

908. NATION, The: Some reflections of a soldier. Repr. from " The Nation " of Oct. 21st, 1916. 8 pp. 8vo. London, Nation Publishing Co., [1916].

National Aid (1916-1917), *see* Irish National Aid.

Nationality, 1917-1919 [N.S.]. Edited by Arthur Griffith, *see* 440.

New Ireland, 1916-1919. [Edited by P. J. Little], *see* 442.

909. NEW IRELAND PAMPHLETS (No. 1): Is the Irish party nationalist ? Our policy on the parliamentary question. 12 pp. 8vo. Dublin, New Ireland Publishing Co., *n.d.*

>For Nos. 2-3 see 866-867 (Lector).

910. NORTHCLIFFE (*Sir* Alfred HARMSWORTH) *Viscount*: The remaking of Ireland. 16 pp. 8vo. London, Clement Shorter (privately printed), March, 1917.

>Repr. from the *Times* report of a speech before the Irish Club on March 17, 1917. Twenty-five copies of the reprint were issued.

911. O'BRIEN (William) *M.P.*: Is there a way out of the chaos in Ireland? *Nineteenth Century*, LXXX. pp. 489-506. Sept., 1916.

912. —— The Irish sybil's books. *Nineteenth Century*, LXXXI. pp. 945-960. April, 1917.

913. —— The Irish cause and the Irish "Convention." Authorised report of speech delivered on May 21, 1917, in the House of Commons, in the debate on Mr. Lloyd George's Irish proposals. 16 pp. 8vo. Dublin, Maunsel, 1917.

914. —— "The Party," who they are and what they have done. 40 pp. 8vo. Dublin, Maunsel, 1917.

   A criticism of the Irish Parliamentary Party.

915. —— Sinn Féin and its enemies. 16 pp. 8vo. Dublin, 1917.

   A speech delivered in the House of Commons, 23rd Oct., 1917.

916. —— The downfall of parliamentarianism; a retrospect for the accounting day. (*As passed by Censor*). 62 pp. 8vo. Dublin, Maunsel, 1918.

   Written at Mallow, October, 1918.

—— *See also* 150 ("The Irish revolution").

   Gives an account of the author's conversations with Mr. Lloyd George, Mr. Bonar Law and Sir E. Carson in May, 1916, regarding the proposals then made for an Irish settlement.

917. Ó CATHASAIGH (Seán): The story of Thomas Ashe. 16 pp. 8vo. Dublin, Fergus O'Connor, *n.d.*

   Another edition, entitled "The sacrifice of Thomas Ashe," is dated 1918.

918. O'CONNELL (*Sir* John Robert): An Irish nationalist's plea for self-government for Ireland . . . Published in the "Overseas" Magazine, June, 1917. 8 pp. 8vo. Dublin, Valentine W. Miley . . . Election agent for Sir John R. O'Connell, *n.d.*

919. —— What Ireland wants. *Fortnightly Rev.*, CVIII. pp. 101-110. July, 1917.

920. —— The foundations and growth of Dominion self-government: an examination of the origins and development of the principles of self-government in the British Empire. 43 pp. 8vo. Dublin, Sealy, Bryers and Walker, [1917.].

921. O'CONNOR (Francis J.): Ireland's opportunity. 16 pp. 8vo. Omagh, North-West of Ireland Printing and Publishing Co., [1916].

   Outlines the attitude of the Irish Nation League (1916).

922. O'CONNOR (*Major* G. B.) : The Irish muddle and its solution, Passed by censor. 8 pp. 8vo. Cork, Shandon Printing Works, [1918 ?].

923. O'CONNOR (Thomas Power) : Mr. T. P. O'Connor, M.P. in Chicago . . . Fellowship club reception. *n.p.*, [1917 ?].

924. [O'Doherty (*Rev.* Philip)] : Through corruption to dismemberment ; a story of apostacy and betrayal, by " Red Hand " [*ps.*, *i.e.*, Rev. Philip O'Doherty of Carndonagh]. 41 pp. 8vo. Derry, Chambers, 1916.

925. O'Dwyer (*Most Rev.* Edward Thomas) *Bp. of Limerick* : Pastoral letter to the clergy and laity of the diocese of Limerick for Quinquagesima Sunday, 1917 . . . 16 pp. 8vo. *n.p.*, [1917 ?].

See also 773a *and* 820.

926. —— Letters of the late Bishop O'Dwyer. 16 pp. 8vo. *n.p. n.d.*

927. —— Speech made by his lordship . . . on the occasion of the conferring of the freedom of the city of Limerick on him, on the 14th September, 1916. Full report. [4] pp. 8vo. *n.p. n.d.*

928. O'Flanagan (*Rev.* Michael) : The Roscommon election. *Catholic Bulletin*, VII. pp. 146-151. March, 1917.
Vice-President of Sinn Féin, Oct., 1917.

929. —— Father O'Flanagan's suppressed speech. [4] pp. 8vo. *n.p.* [1918].
" A verbatim report of the speech delivered . . . at Ballyjamesduff on Sunday, May 26, 1918."

Óglaiġ na h-Éireann, 1916-1918, *see* 160 (Brugha, C.) ; 10, 151, 987a. (Collins, M.) ; 51, 71, 154 (de Valera, E.) ; 753 (*Leabhar Drille* . . .) ; 904-905 (Moore, Myles) ; 1364 (Street, C. J.) ; 1091 (Dalton, C.) ; 1287 (Óglác, An t-).

930. O'HERLIHY (*Rev.* P.) : Independence the remedy for taxation. By another clerical student of finance. *Catholic Bulletin*, VII. pp. 102-108. Feb., 1917.

931. [O'HIGGINS (Brian F.) and others] : War humour and other atrocities. By Brian na Banban [Brian F. O'Higgins], Myles Malone and Will E. Wagtail. VII + 76 pp. 8vo. Dublin, " Spark " and son, [Whelan ?], *n.d.*

932. OLIVER (Frederick Scott) : Ireland and the Imperial Conference. Is there a way to a settlement ? 16 pp. 8vo. London, Macmillan, 1917.

933. O'LOUGHRAN (*Rev.* Robert) : Redmond's vindication. 212 pp. 8vo. frontisp. Dublin, Talbot Press, 1919.

934. O'NEILL (Colmann) : Das Unuberwindliche Irland. *Irische Blätter*. 1. Jahr. Nr. 2. Berlin, pp. 186-194.

935. O'NEILL (Hugh) : Who is the real foe of the Irish ? 11 pp. 8vo. *n.p.*, [1916 ?].

A reprint in yellow wrappers. A note printed on the cover says : " The accompanying leaflet was dropped from a German aeroplane into the English lines in France." *See* 456.

936. ORAGE (Alfred R.) : An Englishman talks it out with an Irishman. With a preface by John Eglinton [*i.e.*, W. K. Magee]. 32 pp. 8vo. Dublin, Talbot Press, 1918.

937. ORCHELLE (R. L.) : England und die Irische Konvention. *Irische Blätter.* 1. Jahr. Nr. 3. pp. 206-213. April, 1918.

938. PHŒNIX, The, 1916-1917 : a weekly national review. December 9th, 1916—[Feb. 24th, 1917. No. 12]. Pr. by the *Kilkenny Journal*, Kilkenny. Publ. at 1 College Street, Dublin.

939. P. J. F. : The Marquis MacSwiney of Mashanaglass. His services to the Papacy and Ireland. 16 pp. 16mo. [Dublin, " Irish Catholic " Office], *n.d.*

940. Plunkett (*Sir* Horace) : A defence of the Convention. 14 pp. 8vo. Dublin, Maunsel, 1917.

A speech delivered at Dundalk, June 25, 1917.

See also 120a (Lysaght, E.).

941. —— Home Rule and conscription. 32 pp. 8vo. Dublin, Talbot Press, 1918.

"A revised reprint of three articles published in the press last week " (Author's preface, July 18, 1918).

942. PROCLAIMED DISTRICTS, IRELAND : Proclamation, dated June 14, 1918, declaring sections 3 and 4 of the Criminal Law and Procedure (Ireland) Act, 1887 (50 and 51 Vict., c. 20) relating to Special Jury and removal of Trial in force within certain counties and county boroughs. *Statutory Rules and Orders . . .* issued in 1918. Vol. II. pp. 675-688. H.M.S.O., 1919.

943. QUARTERLY REVIEW, The : The Irish rebellion. *Quarterly Rev.* Vol. 226. pp. 244-265. July, 1916.

944. QUINN (M.) : The finance of freedom. *Catholic Bulletin*, VIII. pp. 235-240. May, 1918.

944a. —— The finance of servitude. *Catholic Bulletin*, VIII. pp. 286-291. June, 1918.

945. " RAJAH OF FRONGOCH," The : Topical ditties. 8 pp. 8vo. Dublin, The Art Depôt, *n.d.*

946. REDDY (Louis George) : Count Plunkett, the man and his message. 40 pp. 8vo. [1917]. *n.p.*

947. REDISTRIBUTION OF SEATS (IRELAND) ACT, 1918 : An Act to provide for the Redistribution of Seats at Parliamentary Elections in Ireland and for purposes connected therewith. Ch. 65. 7 & 8 Geo. 5. 10 pp. H.M.S.O., 1918.

Redmond (John), 1916-1918, *see* Sects. GENERAL AND INTRODUCTORY ; **1912-1916.**
See also 832 (Gwynn, S.) ; 865a (Law, H. A.) ; 880 (McGrath, J.) ; 933 (O'Loughran, *Rev.* P.) ; 982 (Spender, H.) ; and *Irish Convention.*

948. REDMOND (William Hoey Kearney) *M.P.* : Major William Redmond. London, Burns and Oates, [1918].
" Memories " by Mgr. Arthur Ryan ; " From the trenches, a plea and a claim " and " Last things " by Major Wm. Redmond, and Postscript.

949. REDMOND-HOWARD (Louis George) : Ireland, the Peace Conference and the League of Nations. 132 pp. 8vo. Dublin, Thomas Kiersey, [1918].

950. REPRESENTATION OF THE PEOPLE BILL, 1917 : Conference on the redistribution of seats in Ireland. Letter from Mr. Speaker to the Prime Minister. Presented to Parliament. 4 pp. H.M.S.O., 1918. [Cd. 8919].

951. —— Redistribution of seats. Report of the Boundary Commission (Ireland). Presented to Parliament . . . Maps. [46] pp. H.M.S.O., 1917 [Cd. 8830].
With the names and populations of the existing and proposed parliamentary constituencies in Ireland, and Schedule containing statements showing the determination of the Commissioners, illustrated by large maps of the Counties of Down, Dublin, Galway, Kilkenny, Tyrone and Waterford, and the Boroughs of Belfast and Dublin.

952. REPRESENTATION OF THE PEOPLE ACT, 1918 : An Act to amend the Law with respect to Parliamentary and Local Government Franchises, and the Registration of Parliamentary and Local Government Electors, and the conduct of elections, and to provide for the Redistribution of Seats at Parliamentary Elections, and for other purposes connected therewith. 7 & 8 Geo. 5. Ch. 64. 159 pp. H.M.S.O., 1918.

953. [Richardson (James)] : The Germans at Bessbrook, a dream. 32 pp. 8vo. Newry, Magowan, 1917.

954. RIORDAN (Edward Joseph) : Four years of Irish economics. II. Restraint of industry. *Studies*, a quarterly review, VII. pp. 306-314. Dublin, June, 1918.

955. —— A fragment of Irish industrial history. *Studies*, VII. pp. 633-643. Dec., 1918.
History of the efforts (1913-1918) to procure a War Office Receiving Depot for Ireland. Estimates the value of War Office contracts placed with Irish firms since the beginning of the war at over £20,000,000.

955a. ROLLESTON (Thomas William) : Ireland and Poland, a comparison. 22 pp. 8vo. London, Unwin, 1917.
Also in Danish, " Irland og Polen " (Copenhagen, 1917) and South African Dutch, " Ierland en Polen : een vergelijking " Cape Town, 1918.

955. " RONALD " : Freedom's road for Irish workers. 16 pp. 8vo. Manchester, National Labour Press, [1917].

956. ROUND TABLE, The : Ireland and the Empire. *Round Table*, v. pp. 614-651. London, Sept., 1916.
Federal imperialist.

957. —— The Irish crisis. *Round Table*, VIII. pp. 496-525. June, 1918.

958. " RUSSELL (Charles)" : Should the workers of Ireland support Sinn Fein ? 24 pp. 8vo. Dublin, W. H. West, 1918.

959. [RUSSELL (George W.)] : The national being, some thoughts on an Irish polity. By A.E. [*pseud., i.e.* George W. Russell]. 176 pp. 8vo. Dublin, Maunsel, 1916.
Second edition in 1918.

960. —— Thoughts for a Convention. Memorandum on the state of Ireland. By A.E. 32 pp. 8vo. Dublin, Maunsel, 1917.

961. —— Conscription for Ireland : a warning to England. 4 pp. [Dublin, Mansion House Conference, 1918].
Repr. from the " Manchester Guardian " of May 11th, 1918.

962. —— Four years of Irish economics, 1914-1918. I.—The self-supporting community. *Studies*, VII. pp. 301-306. June, 1918.

963. Saoġal Ṡaeḋealaċ An. The Irish World and Industrial Advocate. September 7, 1918-September 20, 1919 (Vol. III. No. 2. N.S.). Dublin, Wood Printing Works.
Organ of the Irish Republican Brotherhood. Edited and for the most part written by Mr. P. S. O'Hegarty.

Sexton (Joseph), *see* 549.

964. SHAW (George Bernard) : How to settle the Irish question. 32 pp. 8vo. Dublin, Talbot Press, [1917].
Reprint of a series of articles which " were published simultaneously in London and Dublin, Cork and Belfast, on the 27th, 28th and 29th November " [1917].

965. SHEEHY-SKEFFINGTON (Hanna) : Impressions of Sinn Féin in America. An account of eighteen months' Irish propaganda in the United States. Passed by censor. 30 pp. 8vo. Dublin, Davis Publishing Co., 1919.
See also 980a.

966. SHERIDAN (J. Clerc) : The Irish enigma again. (II) An appeal for an Irish entente . . . *Nineteenth Century*, LXIX. pp. 1190-1202. June, 1916.

967. SHORTER (Dora Sigerson) : West Britain and Ireland. *Catholic Bulletin*, VIII. pp. 183-188. April, 1918.

968. SICHEL (Walter) : Germany and Ireland : ' England's Achilles-heel.' *Nineteenth Century*, LXXIX. pp. 966-976. May, 1916.
Review of Theodor Schiemann's : *Die Achilles-ferse Englands*.

969. SIGERSON (Selma) : Sinn Féin and Socialism. With foreword by Aodh de Blácam. 56 pp. 16mo. Dublin, [1918].

970. SINN FÉIN, 1916 : Sinn Fein tracts : How to form Sinn Fein clubs (No. 3) ; The nature of Sinn Fein (No. 4) ; Spectacles for Ulstermen (No. 5). [Dublin, 1916 ?].
    Advertised as "Constitutional Sinn Fein Tracts," to be obtained from the *Irishman* offices.

971. SINN FÉIN, 1917 : Leaflets. Dublin, National Council of Sinn Féin, 6 Harcourt street, [1917].
    [No. 1] : Colonial Home Rule : would it settle anything ? ; No. 2 : Farmers ! your turn now ; No. 3 : Work for a Sinn Féin branch ; No. 4 : Robbery under arms ; No. 5 : The small nations ; No. 6 : The ethics of Sinn Féin, our moral obligations ; No. 7 : War on the cattle trade ; No. 8 : The land question. By Labṙas Maġ Ḟionnġail No. 9 : Three letters for Unionists only. By H. M. Pim.

972. ⸺ Scheme of organisation, rules, &c. (to be proposed by Eamonn de Valera). 4 pp. pr. P. Mahon.
    This Scheme, which recommends a large Executive Committee, was adopted in preference to 973.

973. ⸺ Scheme of organisation proposed by Caṫal Bruġa. 4 pp. [1917 ?].

974. ⸺ [Árd-Fheis, an Clár, 1917].
    At this Convention held in the Mansion House, Dublin on October 25-27, 1917, Sinn Féin was reorganised and the majority of the twenty-four members elected to the Executive Committee were participants in the 1916 rising. Mr. E. de Valera was elected President of the organisation, the Rev. M. O'Flanagan and Mr. A. Griffith, Vice-Presidents, Mr. W. T. Cosgrave and Mr. L. Ginnell Hon. Treasurers. In the agenda it is stated that the " chair will be taken by Mr. A. Griffith, President of Sinn Féin." For a report of the proceedings see " The tenth Convention of Sinn Fein " in *Nationality* (edited by Arthur Griffith) Nov. 3-10, 1917.

975. ⸺ Coruġaḋ. Constitution. 8 pp. 8vo. [1917 ?].

976. SINN FEIN, 1918 : *Leaflets* : General election fund ; Irish prison atrocities : what about the Belfast inquiry ? English horrors in Irish jails ; What Sinn Féin must meet and beat ; Sinn Féin : Éire abú ; Robbery under arms ; The policy of abstention.

976a. SINN FÉIN : Coruġaḋ. Constitution. 8 pp. 8vo. *n.p.* [1917, 1918 ?].
    The Scheme of organisation and Rules included in this pamphlet was also published separately in a revised form, printed by the Wood Printing Works, Dublin.

977. SINN FÉIN ÁRD-FHEIS, AN CLÁR, 1918 : An t-aonṁaḋ Árd Ḟeis ḋéaġ a ḃéiḋ ar siuḃal i ḋTiġ an Árd-Ṁaoir Aṫ-Cliaṫ, aġ cosnuġaḋ ar a ḋeiċ a ċloġ ḋíreaċ ar maiḋin an 29aḋ lá ḋeireaḋ Ḟoġṁair, 1918. 24 pp. 8vo. Aṫ Cliaṫ, Sinn Féin, 1918.
    Agenda of the eleventh Ard-Fheis of Sinn Féin, held in the Mansion House, Dublin, 29th October, 1918, with the constitution, list of the officer board and executive committee, elected at the Ard-Fheis, October, 1917, the names of Directors in charge of special departments, the appointments to fill the places of those who were arrested, and copies of the resolutions to be moved at the meeting.

978. ──── 1918: Registration instructions, issued by the Sinn Fein election department. 16 pp. 8vo. [Dublin, Sinn Féin, 1918].

979. [────] Two years of English atrocities in Ireland. 64 pp. 8vo. [Dublin, Sinn Féin, 1919).

> Statistics of homicides, raids, suppressions of public meetings and other " hostile acts committed against the people of Ireland " and lists of " Irish men and women arrested and imprisoned for ' political offences ' in 1917-18," collected to illustrate the unjust and aggressive character of British rule in Ireland. The account for printing furnished to Dáil Éireann by the Secretary for Finance (Michael Collins) on August 20th, 1919 contains an item of £190 12s., being ' half-cost " Atrocities " pamphlet '.

Sinn Féin, *see* GENERAL AND INTRODUCTORY; **1912–1916**; 1916–1918. *See also* 760a (Baumgarten, P. M.); 763 (De Blácam, A.); 765 (Boyd, E. A.); 777 (Clancy, *Rev.* J.); 790 (De Valera, E.); 805-806 (Escouflaire, R. C.); 810-814a (Figgis, D.); 821 (Gaynor, Rev. P.); 834 (Harp, The); 856 (*Irish Opinion*); 847 (Irische Blätter); 859 (*Irishman, The*); 868 (Lennon, M. J.); 928-929 (O'Flannagan, *Rev.* M.); 938 (*Phœnix, The*); 942 (*Proclamations against*); 1003 (Western priest, A.); 1109 (Desmond, S.); 1306 (Pim, H. M.); 1364 (Street, C. J. S.).

980. SINN FÉIN MOVEMENT, 1918: Documents relative to the Sinn Féin movement. Presented to Parliament . . . H.M.S.O., 1921. [Cmd. 1108].

> This paper appeared early in 1921 at an acute stage of the Anglo-Irish conflict with the following explanation [The statement to which it refers was published in the daily press, May 25, 1918]: " In May, 1918, His Majesty's Government published a statement which, so far as was then expedient in the public interest, summarised without disclosing sources of information and channels of communication, evidence and documents in the possession of the Government showing the active connection between the leaders of the Sinn Fein movement and the German Government. The following statement amplifies the previous narrative and reveals (as far as seems at present expedient) in greater detail certain of the documents proving the intrigues between Sinn Fein and Germany." A considerable part of the " Statement " is occupied with the communications said to have passed between the Irish-American leaders and the German Government before the insurrection of 1916.
>
> An official reply on behalf of Dáil Éireann from President de Valera appeared in the *Irish Bulletin*, Vol. 4. No. 6. Jan. 11th, 1921, in the course of which he says : " There was no such thing as this German Plot of 1918 . . . From July, 1917, I was intimately in touch with all the major activities both of the Sinn Féin political organisation and of the Irish Volunteers, and so I speak with knowledge and authority." He examines the Report in detail, refers to its " total untrustworthiness," and claims that its purpose is " to bring to play on the side of the authors of the present military frightfulness in Ireland all the prejudices and hatreds of the past war."

980a. SKEFFINGTON (Francis Sheehy) and Hanna Sheehy SKEFFINGTON : A forgotten small nationality, Ireland and the war. By F. Sheehy Skeffiington. British militarism as I have known it. By Hanna Sheehy-Skffiington. 32 pp. illustr. 8vo. New York, Donnelly Press, [1916].

981. SPÁLPÍN : Sinn Féin and the Labour movement. 24 pp. 8vo. Dublin, Mahon, *n.d.*

982. SPENDER (Harold) : John Redmond : an impression. *Contemporary Rev.*, CXIII. April, 1918.

983. STACK (*Rev.* Thomas L. F.) : Convention or covenant (A sermon preached before the Orangemen in Lower Langfield Church, on Sunday, 8th July, 1917). 8 pp. 8vo. *n.p.* [1917].

984. STRAHAN (James Andrew) : Easters in Ireland. *Blackwood's Mag.*, CCXI. pp. 368-375. May, 1922.
> Impressions of political changes, 1913-1919, noticed on visits to Dublin and Belfast by an Ulster Unionist.

[STREET (*Major* Cecil John C.)] : see 1364 (The administration of Ireland, 1920). [Ch. II. From the rebellion to the end of 1919].
> Quotes freely from unpublished police reports, 1916-1919, relating to political conditions in the different counties—the strength of national feeling, progress of recruiting for the British army, membership of Sinn Féin clubs, etc. Gives of a copy of a pamphlet stated to have been issued from the Irish Volunteer Headquarters in 1918, entitled, "Measures for combating Conscription."

985. STUART-STEPHENS (*Major* Darnley) : The secret constitution of Shinn Fane (*sic*). *English Rev.*, XXIII. pp. 55-64. July, 1916.

986. —— God save Ireland ! *English Rev.*, XXV. pp. 79-88. July, 1917.

987. SULLIVAN (Alexander M.) : The road to Irish liberty. By A. M. Sullivan, *H.M. Second Serjeant-at-Law*. 32 pp. 8vo. Maunsel, 1918.

See also 215.

987a. TALBOT (Hayden) : Michael Collins' own story 256 pp. frontisp. London, Hutchinson [1923].
> An American journalist. Views of Michael Collins, on the national struggle, 1916-1921. Stated to have been expressed at interviews. Unreliable.

988. TWO IRISHMEN : Proposals for an Irish settlement : being a draft bill for the government of Ireland. 32 pp. 8vo. Dublin, Maunsel, 1917.

Ulster (*with special reference to the Unionist movement*), *see* Sects. GENERAL AND INTRODUCTORY ; **1912-1916. 1916-1918.**

> *See also* 759 (Bates, J. V.) ; 787 (CUSHENDUN, *Baron*) ; 807 (Evans, Richardson) ; 817 (Fisher, J. R.) ; 825-826 (Good, J. W.) ; 827 (Graves, A. P.) ; 828, 830 (Green, A. S.) ; 852 (Irish K.C., An).

989. ULSTER UNIONIST COUNCIL, 1918 : Unionist manifesto : Mansion House claims refuted . . . 4 pp. [Belfast, 1918].

990. " UNIFICUS " : Ireland's opportunity, a plea for settlement by conference. By " Unificus," scholar of Trinity College, Dublin, with an introduction by W. F. Trench, Litt. D. . . . 74 pp. 8vo. London, King, 1916.

991. UNITED IRISH LEAGUE : Appeal to the people : Irish Party manifesto. Dublin, January, 1918.

992. —— 1918. Leaflets : Ireland's appeal to President Wilson : Irish Parliamentary Party reiterates the national demand. An Irish Republic ! difficulties in the way ; The abstention or Hungarian policy ; Ireland and Germany.

993. —— 1918. The issues of the election : address to the Irish people, from the Irish Party and National Directory. 4 pp. [Dublin, 1918].

994. UNITED STATES OF AMERICA. CONGRESS : The Irish question. Hearings before the Committee on Foreign Affairs, House of Representatives, sixty-fifth Congress, third session on H. J. Res. 357, requesting the Commissioners plenipotentiary of the United States of America to the international Peace Conference to present to the said Conference the right of Ireland to freedom, independence and self-determination. December 12, 1918. 158 pp. 8vo. Washington, Government Printing Office [House Documents. Vol. 107. No. 1832].
> Statement's by members of Congress, representatives of Irish organis..-tions in U.S. and others interested in the Irish question, including Dr. P. McCartan, M.P., Diarmuid Lynch (Nat. Sec., Friends of Irish Freedom), Pádraic Colum (Irish Progressive League, New York), George A. Fox, Katherine Hughes (Irish Women's Council of America), Rev. John E. Fenlon (Irish Societies, Montana), P. J. Lennox, D. Litt. (Catholic University of America), with the text [pp. 106-126] of " Ireland's plea for freedom " by Dr. Wm. J. M. A. Maloney, and appendix, giving names of many Irish associations in U.S.A., which sent messages supporting the resolution. See also Sect. 1919-1921.

995. VICTORY SONG BOOK. 32 pp. 8vo. Seventh edition. ḃaile Áta ḃreatnaċ , [1921 ?].

996. VIGILANT : Sinn Fein and Germany. *Quarterly Rev.*, Vol. 229. pp. 239-256 ; Vol. 230. pp. 214-235. Jan., July, 1918.
> A commentary on the associations of the Irish revolutionary movement with Germany, before and after the 1916 rising. Quotations from Irish journals and the writings of Sir Roger Casement.

997. VMD : The road to Irish prosperity. 16 pp. 8vo. London, Vacher, [1916].

998. VOICE OF LABOUR, The, 1918-1924. Irish Labour Press.
> In continuation of *Irish Opinion*. Beginning with the issue of Oct. 22, 1921 (Vol. IV. N.S. No. 1) became the " official organ of the Irish Transport and General Workers' Union."

999. WALKER (Henry De Rosenbach) : Home Rule and Irish administration. *Contemporary Rev.*, CIV. pp. 836-846. Dec., 1913.

1000. WATERS (*Very Rev.* John Canon) : The morality of the hunger-strike. *Irish Eccles. Record*, XII. (5th Series), pp. 89-108. Aug., 1918.
> Concludes that " the hunger-strike is immoral on every test that can be applied to a human act," and regrets its association " with the time-honoured cause of a nation."
> For other views see 779, 1063a Cleary (*Rev.* P.), 1145 Gannon (*Rev.* P. J., *S.J.*) and 1215 (Kelleher *Rev.* J.).

1001. WELLS (Warre B.) : An Irish apologia, some thoughts on Anglo-Irish relations and the war. 82 pp. small 8vo. Dublin, Maunsel, 1917.

1002. WELLS (Warre B.) and MARLOWE (N.) *pseud.* : The Irish Convention and Sinn Fein. In continuation of, " A history of the Irish rebellion of 1916." 196 pp. 8vo. Dublin, Maunsel. 1918.

> The authors " endeavour to exhibit, not to criticise, conflicting tendencies in present day Ireland " (Prefatory note). See also 231.

1002a. WESTERN PRIEST, A : The two policies, Sinn Fein or Parliamentarianism. 16 pp. 8vo. *n.p.* [1918].

1003. WINDLE (*Sir* Bertram A.) : The travail of Ireland. II. The Convention : a member's after-thoughts. *Dublin Rev.*, CLXIII. pp. 12-19. July, 1918.

1004. YOUNG IRELAND, 1917-1921 : Pr. by Mahon, and (from Nov : 1920) by Cahill and Co., Ormond Quay, for Miss Mahon.

> Until January 28th, 1918 it was " the paper for the young people of Ireland." No. 12, Vol. II (N.S.) January 28th, 1918 announces : " Our future issues will be political and will advocate the security and the complete independence of Ireland." Mr. Aodh de Blácam was editor then and for some time afterwards.
> *Young Ireland* was one of the few Sinn Féin periodicals which escaped the general suppression in September, 1919. It was published under increasing difficulties after the closing of Sinn Féin headquarters in November, 1919 during the whole period of hostilities and until after the Treaty. Arthur Griffith was editor up to the time of his arrest (November, 1920).
> The printer was warned by British military headquarters on Sept. 28, 1920, that statements in the paper were liable to cause disaffection and was referred to the new " Restoration of Order " Act. The manager was arrested on Oct. 2 ; on Nov. 6 the printer was arrested and parts of the machinery taken away : these were subsequently restored. The new editor and members of the staff were arrested, and on Jan. 6, 1921, all books, papers, files, etc. were taken by the Auxiliary Police ; on Jan. 19 the machinery was dismantled. Nevertheless, the paper continued to appear.

1005. ZETLAND (Lawrence J. DUNDAS) *2nd Marquess of* : The life of Lord Curzon . . . By the Rt. Hon. the Earl of Ronaldshay. Vol. 3. pp. 177-190. 8vo. London, Benn, [1929].

> Ireland 1916-1918.

5. 1919-1921.

1006. ACKERMAN (Carl W.) : Ireland from a Scotland Yard note-book, *Atlantic Monthly,* CXXIX. pp. 433-444, 603-614, 801-812. Boston, April-June, 1922.

> Foreign correspondent, United Press Association. Claims to have acted as an intermediary in Anglo-Irish peace negotiations, 1920-1921 : "At the joint request of Col. House and Sir Basil [Thomson] I went to Dublin to explore the possibilities of peace " [on June 30th, 1920]. " This was the beginning of an almost endless number of journeys between London and Dublin."

ADDRESS TO THE REPRESENTATIVES OF FOREIGN NATIONS, 1921, *see* 1083 (Dáil Éireann).

1007. AMERICAN COMMISSION ON IRISH INDEPENDENCE, 1919 : Report on conditions in Ireland with demand for investigation by the Peace Conference. 24 pp. 8vo. Paris, American Commission on Irish Independence, 1919.

> Messrs. Frank P. Walsh (Chairman), Edward F. Dunne, former Governor of Illinois, and Michael J. Ryan of Philadelphia were appointed by a Committee of the Irish Race Convention, held in Philadelphia, 22-23 Feb., 1919, " to obtain for the delegates selected by the people of Ireland a hearing at the Peace Conference, and to place before the Conference, if that hearing be not given, the case of Ireland ; her insistence upon her right of self-determination ; and to international recognition of the republican form of government established by her people." The report is dated from Paris, June 3, 1919. A reply to the statements made by the delegates with reference to conditions in Ireland was issued from the Chief Secretary's Office, 14th June, 1919.

1008. —— Correspondence in case of Ireland's claim for independence, American Commission to negotiate peace, and representatives of other Governments. Before Senate Committee on Foreign Relations. 66 pp. 8vo. New York, American Commission on Irish Independence, [1919].

1009. —— Another edition. [30] pp.

> With " a reply to the statement of the Hon. Ian MacPherson, Chief Secretary for Ireland, by Frank P. Walsh."

See also 876 (McCartan, P.) ; 1095 (Délégation Irlandaise, La) ; 1120 (Dunne, E. F.) ; 1272 (Murphy, J. A.) ; 1283 (Ó Ceallaigh, S. T.) ; 1340 (Ryan, M. J.) ; 1375 (U.S. Congress) ; 1378 (Walshe F. P.) ; 1379-1380 (Walsh, J. C.).

1010. AMERICAN COMMISSION ON CONDITIONS IN IRELAND, The [1920-1921] : evidence on conditions in Ireland, comprising the complete testimony, affidavits and exhibits presented before the American Commission on conditions in Ireland. Transcribed and annotated by Albert Coyle, official reporter to th Commission. 14 + 1105 pp. 8vo. Washington, 1921.

> " The American Commission on conditions in Ireland was selected by and derives its authority from a committee of distinguished Americans brought together through the efforts of the editors of the New York *Nation* to perform the service of ascertaining for the American people the truth about conditions in Ireland, which increasingly menace the friendly relations that have existed between Great Britain and the United States " (Secretariat of the Commission). Among those who consented to act were U.S. senators and congressmen, State governors, city mayors, and dignatories of the Churches. Evidence was given by Irish, British and American witnesses. Subject index of 37 pp. See also under names of principal witnesses.

1011. —— Interim report. 144 pp. Map and illustrs. 8vo. Washington; 1921.

> The contents include : personnel, history, purpose and method of the Commission ; review of the situation and statement of findings. The interim report was " signed by the whole of the Commission at Washington on March 5, 1921." It was published simultaneously in the United States, Canada and England on March 31st, 1921, and 100,000 copies were distributed to libraries, newspapers, members of parliament, etc. A French translation by Xavier Moisant, arranged for by the Irish delegation in Paris, appeared soon afterwards and was widely circulated in France, Belgium and Switzerland.

1012. —— Interim report (British edition). 72 pp. 8vo. London, Harding and More, 1921.

> No appendices.

1013. AMERICAN COMMITTEE FOR RELIEF IN IRELAND. Part I:
Suggested plan for national organisation. 8 pp. 4to. Part II :
State Committee accounting. 8 pp. 4to. American Committee
for relief in Ireland. Part III : Local Committee Accounting.
[New York ? 1920 ?].

1013a. AMERICAN COMMITTEE FOR RELIEF IN IRELAND : Distress in
Ireland ; a survey . . . 14 pp. 8vo. New York.

1013b. —— The need for relief. 8 pp. illustr. 8vo. New York, [1921].
See *Irish Bulletin*, Vol. 6, No. 18, (14th November, 1921),
and 1931 (Irish White Cross).

1014. ANNIVERSARY OF THE GENERAL ELECTION, 1918, The : Promise
and performance ; what Sinn Fein declarations are worth ;
Peace Conference myth. 24 pp. *n.p.* [1919 ?].

Extracts from speeches by members of Sinn Féin and of the Irish
Parliamentary party, arranged by a supporter of the latter.

1015. ARRAN (Arthur J. C. GORE) *6th Earl of* : A plea for the southern
Irish loyalists. *National Rev.*, LXXVIII. pp. 209-217. Oct., 1921.

1016. ASTON (E. A.) : An Irish Constituent Convention : the Sligo
" mouse " and the Paris " lion." 33 pp. 8vo. Dublin, Kenny
Press, [1920].

AUSTRALASIAN IRISH RACE CONVENTION, 1919, *see Catholic Bulletin*,
x. pp. 77-81. Dublin, Feb., 1920.

1017. AUSTRALIAN ROMAN CATHOLIC, An : A mad dog from Maynooth.
National Review, LXXVI. pp. 642-659. London, Jan., 1921.

A criticism of the Most Rev. Dr. Mannix, Archbishop of Melbourne,
formerly President of St. Patrick's College, Maynooth.

1018. BAEZA (Ricardo) : La isla de los santos (Itinerario en Irlanda).
310 pp. 8vo. Madrid, Compañía Ibero-Americana de Publicaciones (S.A.) Renacimiento, [1930].

Contains some comments on Irish affairs in 1920-1922, repr. with
additions from *El Sol* (Madrid).

1019. BAGENAL (Philip H.) : Irish unrest reviewed. *Edinburgh Rev.*,
Vol. 233. pp. 178-195. Jan., 1921.

Irish Unionist. Argues that Irish efforts to resist English rule have
been " always of the same barbarous character."

BALLYKINLAR INTERNMENT CAMP, Co. Down, *see* 1023 (*Belvederian*) ;
1050 (*Catholic Bulletin*) ; (Walsh, L. J.), and *Irish Bulletin*.

BANKING (Irish), *see* GENERAL AND INTRODUCTORY ; **1916-1918** ;
and 1216 (Kelly, R. J.) ; 1351 (Smith-Gordon, L.). *See also*
FINANCE.

1021. BELFAST TELEGRAPH, The : The Terror in Ireland. Murder,
outrage, intimidation. Reprinted from " Belfast Telegraph."
12 pp. 8vo. Belfast, W. and G. Baird, [1921].

1022. BELVEDERIAN, The : Under the terror : I. In a Sinn Fein court.
By Cionnaith Ó Roideáin. II. In Ballykinlar. By Michael
Ó Briain. III. In an English prison. By Feargus Mac
Murchadha. *The Belvederian*, VI., 1922. pp. 89-97. Dublin,
1922.

1023. BENJAMIN FRANKLIN BUREAU, 1921 : Torture and terror : The torture of Kevin Barry. 2. The torture of Tom Hales. 3. Frightfulness in Thurles. 4. The burning of Balbriggan. 24 pp. 8vo. Chicago, Benjamin Franklin Bureau, [1921].

1024. BENNETT (Louie), *Secretary, Irish Women Workers' Union*: Evidence . . . presented before the AMERICAN COMMISSION ON CONDITIONS IN IRELAND (*which see*, pp. 979-1015, 1019-1029, 1036-1052). Washington, 1921.
> With special reference to Irish Labour conditions and the attitude of the British and Irish Labour parties towards the Anglo-Irish political question.

1025. BEUQUE (Etiennette) : Pour l'Irlande. 110 pp. 8vo. illustr. Paris, Éditions de l'Ame Gauloise, *n.d.*
> A review of the Irish Republican movement from 1916.

1025a. BIRKENHEAD (Frederick Winston Furneaux SMITH) *2nd Earl of* Frederick Edwin, Earl of Birkenhead : The last phase. By his son . . . 320 pp. portrs. 8vo. London, Butterworth, 1935.
> Chapters on the trial of Roger Casement (1916) and the Irish Treaty (1921). See also 245.

1026. BIRMINGHAM POST, The : Disaffected Ireland, a survey of present conditions. 34 pp. 8vo. Birmingham, " Birmingham Post," February, 1920.
> Repr. of articles, January 16-February 9, 1920, by the Parliamentary representative of the " Birmingham Post ", the outcome of an investigation made in Ireland.

1027. BISHOPS OF IRELAND : Statement issued by the Cardinal Primate and the Archbishops and Bishops of Ireland on the present condition of their country. 12 pp. 8vo. Dublin, Browne and Nolan, [1920].
> From St. Patrick's College, Maynooth, Oct. 19th, 1920.

—— *See also* Sects. GENERAL AND INTRODUCTORY ; **1916-1918** ; *and* 1103 (Dept. of Publicity) ; 1223 (Logue, M., *Cardinal*) ; 1229-1231 (Macdonald, *Rev.* W.).

1028. BLÁCAM (Aodh de) : What Sinn Féin stands for : the Irish republican movement ; its history, aims and ideals, examined as to their significance to the world. 248 pp. 8vo. Dublin, Mellifont Press, 1921.

1029. BLACKWOOD'S MAGAZINE : Experiences of an officer's wife in Ireland. *Blackwood's Mag.*, CCIX. pp. 552-598. May, 1921.

1030. BODKIN (Matthias McDonnell) *K.C.* : A considered judgment. Report of Judge Bodkin . . . County Court judge of Co. Clare, forwarded to the Right Hon. Sir Hamar Greenwood, Chief Secretary for Ireland, and read in open court at Ennis, Co. Clare, on Saturday, 5th February, 1921. 16 pp. 8vo. Dublin, Talbot Press, 1921.

1031. —— Another considered judgment. Second report of Judge Bodkin . . . 8 pp. 8vo. Dublin, Talbot Press, 1921.

1031a. BOLETIN IRLANDES, 1921-1922. Madrid. Nr. 1, 28 de Mayo de 1921.

>A bulletin of Irish news circulated in Spain, 1921–1922, by the Press Bureau established in Madrid by the Dáil Department of Foreign Affairs. The Bureau was directed by Miss M. O'Brien.

1032. BOLSHEVISM AND SINN FEIN. Intercourse between Bolshevism and Sinn Fein. Presented to Parliament . . . 6 pp. H.M.S.O., 1921. [Cmd. 1326].

>Includes a copy of " the draft of a proposed treaty between the Russian Socialist Federal Republic and the Republic of Ireland," stated to have been captured in Dublin [1920-1921].

1033. BOURGEOIS (Maurice) : L'Irlande du dedans et du dehors. Par " Æ ". Reimprimé par autorisation spéciale du *Pearson's Magazine* américain. Traduit de l'anglais par Maurice Bourgeois. 22 pp. 8vo. [Paris, *La Démocratic*, 1921 or 1922].

1034. BOYD (Ernest A.) : Ireland versus " Ulster." New York, *Century Magazine*, XCVIII (O.S.). pp. 584-587. Sept., 1919.

1035. BRADY (Edward M.) : Ireland's secret service in England. 160 pp. 8vo. illustr. Dublin, Talbot Press, [1928].

1036. BREEN (Daniel) : My fight for Irish freedom . . . with an introduction by Joseph McGarrity (Philadelphia). 258 pp. 8vo. illustr. Dublin, Talbot Press, 1924.

>A personal narrative of hostilities in Ireland, 1919-1923.

1037. BRIGHT (John Hampden) : What's wrong with Ireland ? 30 pp. 8vo. *n.p.* [1920 ?].

1038. —— What's wrong with Ireland ? No. 2. 24 pp. 8vo. *n.p.* [1920 or 1921].

1039. BRINE (Blanche Marie) : Sinn Fein, an epitome. By Blanche Marie Brine, Librarian, Friends of Irish Freedom National Bureau of Information. 8 pp. 8vo. Washington, Friends of Irish Freedom, June, 1920. (No. 16).

Briollay (S), *see* Chauviré (R).

1040. BRODERICK (Daniel J.) : Evidence . . . presented before the AMERICAN COMMISSION ON CONDITIONS IN IRELAND (*which see*, pp. 665-683).

>An account of incidents, mainly in the neighbourhood of Abbeyfeale, Sept.-Dec., 1920.

1041. BROWN (Stephen J.) *S.J.* : Ireland through foreign eyes. *Studies*, Vol. XX. pp. 621-628. Dublin, Dec., 1921.

Brugha (Cathal), *see* (p. 3)

BULLETIN, OFFICIAL (Irish), *see* 1078-1081 (Dáil Éireann) ; 1186 (*Irish Bulletin*).

1042. CADDEN (John Joseph): Evidence . . . presented before the AMERICAN COMMISSION ON CONDITIONS IN IRELAND (*which see*, pp. 407-420).
    Experiences in the R.I.C. in Co. Galway, 1920.

1043. CAILLIET (Emile): Les origines du mouvement sinn-fein en Irlande. Par M. Emile Cailliet, Directeur du Cours complémentaire de Morhange. 64 pp. 16 mo. Metz, " Le Messin," 1921.

1044. CALLWELL (*Major-Gen.* Sir Charles Edward): Field-Marshal Sir Henry Wilson, G.C.B., D.S.O., his life and diaries. Vol. II. 388 pp. illustr. London, Cassell, 1927.
    Gives extracts from the diary of Sir H. Wilson, when Chief of the Imperial General Staff (1918-1921) illustrating the measures adopted or recommended with a view to the suppression of the Irish national movement by military force. See also 262.

1045. CAMPBELL (H. A.): The crucifixion of Ireland. By H. A. Campbell, Labour organiser of Australia and New Zealand. Third and revised edition. 48 pp. 8vo. Glasgow, Scottish Workers' Committees, 1920.

1046. CARSON (*Sir* Edward) *Baron, of Duncairn* : Ireland and Home Rule. Has the Union failed? a convincing answer. Sir Edward Carson's review. 8 pp. 8vo. [Belfast Ulster Unionist Council, 1919]. (U.C. 123).
    Address at a special meeting of the Ulster Unionist Council, Belfast, 2nd September, 1919.

1047. CATHOLIC BULLETIN, The : Ireland's claim : Statement of claim of the Irish nation to the exercise of its natural sovereign independence, addressed to the nations of the world and the high contracting parties of the Peace Congress. Dublin, *Catholic Bulletin*, IX. April-July, 1919.
    Mainly historical. " Does not purport to have any official authority whatever."

1048. —— Ireland's trinity of martyred priests [Rev. Canon Magner, Rev. Michael Griffin, Rev. James O'Callaghan]. *Catholic Bulletin*, XII. April-May, 1922.

1049. —— Events of Easter week—and after. The first martyred Lord Mayor of Cork. *Catholic Bulletin*, x. pp. 328-336. illustr. May, 1922.
    Brief memoir of Tomás Mac Curtain, with letters written to his wife and son. See also MACCURTAIN (T.).

1050. —— British treatment of Irish prisoners. Dublin, *Catholic Bulletin*, XII. pp. 232-235. 306-310. April-May, 1923.
    A critical account of the conditions at Ballykinlar internment camp, Co. Down, where about 2,000 men were interned in 1921.

1051. —— Events of Easter week—and after. The second martyred Lord Mayor of Cork. *Catholic Bulletin*, XII. pp. 405-416. June, 1922.
    A brief memoir of Terence MacSwiney.

1052. —— Events of Easter week—and after. Michael O'Callaghan, Mayor of Limerick. *Catholic Bulletin*, XII. pp. 477-480. July, 1922.

See also O'Callaghan (Michael).

1052a. —— Seoirse mac𝔣lanncaoá (George Clancy, Mayor of Limerick). *Catholic Bulletin*, XII. pp. 711-722. illustr. Nov., 1922.

Gives Mrs. Clancy's account of the murder of the Mayor of Limerick on March 7, 1921.

See also 1107.

1053. CESSATION OF ACTIVE OPERATIONS. Arrangements governing the cessation of active operations in Ireland which came into force on July 11, 1921. Presented to Parliament. [2] pp. H.M.S.O., 1921. [Cmd. 1534].

See also *Irish Bulletin*.

1054. [CHAUVIRÉ (Roger)]: L'Irlande insurgée. 136 pp. 8vo. Par Sylvain Briollay [*pseud.*, *i.e.*, Roger Chauviré]. 5e édition; Paris, Plon-Nourrit, 1921. (Les Problèmes d'aujourd'hui).

1055. [——] Ireland in rebellion. Translated from the French of Sylvain Briollay. 144 pp. 8vo. Dublin, Talbot Press, 1922.

From the prefatory note : " The author is a distinguished Frenchman resident in Ireland since the beginning of 1919, who saw and judged for himself, noted events as they appeared in the Irish newspapers, and had many opportunities of seeing prominent members of all the Irish parties." Professor of French, University College, Dublin, since 1919.

1056. CHILDERS (Erskine) : Might and right in Ireland. *English Rev.*, XXVIII. pp. 512-520. June, 1919.

1057. —— Law and order in Ireland. *Studies*, Vol. VII. pp. 598-607. Dec., 1919.

1058. —— Military rule in Ireland. A series of eight articles contributed to the *Daily News*, March-May, 1920, with notes and an additional chapter. 48 pp. illustr. 8vo. Dublin, The Talbot Press, 1920.

March 29th-May 20th, 1920. The additional chapter is entitled, " The situation in July, 1920."

1059. —— Second edition—revised. 50 pp. 8vo. Dublin, Talbot Press, 1920.

With another chapter : " The situation in August, 1920."

1060. [——] Is Ireland a danger to England ? The strategical question examined. [Repr. from the *Irish Bulletin* of 29th July, 1921]. 8 pp. 8vo. [Dublin, Dáil Éireann, 1921].

See also 15, 1085 (Constructive work of Dáil Éireann) and 1188 (*Irish Bulletin*).

1061. CHURCHILL (Winston Spencer) : The world crisis : the aftermath. 474 pp. 8vo. [Ch. XIV. The Irish spectre ; Ch. XV. The Irish settlement]. London, Butterworth, 1929.

> An account of the British Government's Irish policy after the Great War and of the negotiations for a settlement in 1921. The author was Secretary for War, 1918-1921 and one of the five British representatives at the conference between the two countries, Oct.-Dec., 1921.

1062. —— Thoughts and adventures. 320 pp. pls. 8vo. [pp. 219-226. The Irish treaty]. London, Butterworth, 1932.

CLAN-NA-GAEL, *see* 1140.

1063. CLARKE (John Charles) : Evidence . . . presented before the AMERICAN COMMISSION ON CONDITIONS IN IRELAND (*which see*, pp. 699-715). Washington, 1921.

> An American citizen.

1063a. CLEARY (*Rev.* Patrick) : Some further questions regarding the morality of the hunger-strike. *Irish Eccles. Record*, XIII (5th Series). pp. 219-229. Dublin, March, 1919.

> Undertakes to prove that Canon Waters (1383) has failed to show the hunger-strike to be essentially immoral.

1064. COCKRAN (William Bourke) : Treaty of Peace with Germany. Hearings before the Committee on Foreign Relations, United States Senate . . . [Statement of Hon. W. Bourke Cockran. pp. 879-903. August 30, 1919]. Senate Documents. Vol. 10. No. 106. Washington, Government Printing Office, 1919.

1065. COHALAN (Daniel F.) : Treaty of peace with Germany : Hearings before the Committee on Foreign Relations, United States Senate . . . [Statement of Hon. Daniel F. Cohalan, Justice of the Supreme Court of New York. pp. 757-794. August 30, 1919]. Senate Documents. Vol. 10. No. 106. Washington, Government Printing Office, 1919.

1066. —— *To provide for the salaries of a Minister and Consuls to the Republic of Ireland.* Statement of Hon. Daniel F. Cohalan, taken from the Official report of the hearings before the Committee on Foreign Affairs, House of Representatives, on the Mason resolution (H.R. 3404). December 12, 13, 1919. 16 pp. 8vo. Reprinted. New York, Friends of Irish Freedom, *n.d.*

1067. —— The indictment. By Hon. Daniel F. Cohalan, Justice of the Supreme Court, State of New York. 20 pp. 8vo. New York, Friends of Irish Freedom, [1919].

1068. —— The freedom of the seas. By Hon. Daniel F. Cohalan, Justice of the Supreme Court, State of New York. 20 pp. 8vo. New York, Friends of Irish Freedom, [1920 ?].

1069. —— Our economic interest in Ireland. *The Forum*, LXV. pp. 59-67. New York, Jan., 1921.

—— *See also* 1137 (Friends of Irish Freedom).

COLLINS (Michael), see GENERAL AND INTRODUCTORY ; **1916-1918**.
See also 1078 (Dáil Éireann) ; 1287 (Óglách, An t-) ; 1300a (Pakenham, F.) ; 1348 (Sinn Féin).

1070. COLQUHOUN (John J.) : The Irish as fighters. *National Review*, LXXV. pp. 623-632. London, July, 1920.
> Argues that " the native Irish " have no sense of fair play and have never been good soldiers, and that the Irish regiments fought badly in the Great War.

COMMISSION OF INQUIRY INTO THE RESOURCES AND INDUSTRIES OF IRELAND [Dáil Éireann], see 1086-1087.

1071. CONDRON (J. F.) : Archbishop Mannix, prelate, patriot and scholar . . . who he is and what he has done. 16 pp. 8vo. Dublin, Nugent, 1920.

CONNAUGHT RANGERS, see 1212a.

CONSTRUCTIVE WORK OF DÁIL ÉIREANN, The, see 1085 (Dáil Éireann).

CORK (fires in the city, Dec., 1920), see 1075 (Crozier, *Brig-Gen.* F. P.) ; 1186 (*Irish Bulletin*) ; 1194 (Irish Labour Party) ; 1218 (British Labour Party) ; 1281 (O'Callaghan, D.) ; 36 (Cork Chamber of Commerce annual report, 1920).

1072. CORKERY (Daniel) : Terence MacSwiney : Lord Mayor of Cork. *Studies*, a quarterly review. XIX. pp. 512-520. Dublin, Dec., 1920.

CORRESPONDENCE RELATING TO . . . AN IRISH SETTLEMENT, see 1203-1206 (Irish settlement).

COSGRAVE (William T.) [mac Cosgair, l. t.], *Minister for Local Government*, see 1078-1086. (Dáil Éireann) ; 1116 (Dublin Corporation).
> Took part in the rising 1916. Hon. Treasurer of Sinn Féin 1917. Minister for Local Government in Dáil Éireann, 1919-1922. President of the Executive Council, Saorstát Éireann, 1922-1932.

COURTS OF JUSTICE (Irish Republican), see 1085 (Dáil Éireann) ; 1188 (*Irish Bulletin*) ; 1226 (McCormick, W.) ; 1341 (Saorstát na hÉireann : Judiciary, 1921).

COYLE, Albert, see 1010 (American Commission on conditions in Ireland).

CRAIGAVON (*Sir* James Craig) *1st Viscount*, see ULSTER, **1912-1916** ; **1919-1921** ; and 1276 (Northern Ireland).

1072a. CRAWFORD (Lindsay) : The problem of Ulster. By Lindsay Crawford, President of the Independent Order of Grand Lodges . . . President of the Protestant Friends of Ireland; and Editor of " The Statesman," Toronto, Canada. 15 pp. 8vo. New York, Protestant Friends of Ireland, [1920 ?].

1073. CRIMINAL INJURIES (IRELAND) ACT, 1920 : An act to amend the enactments relative to compensation for criminal injuries in Ireland [23rd December, 1920]. Ch. 66. 10 & 11 Geo. V. 6 pp. H.M.S.O., 1920.

1074. CROWLEY (Daniel Francis) : Evidence . . . presented before the AMERICAN COMMISSION ON CONDITIONS IN IRELAND, (which s:e, pp. 376-389).
Experiences in the R.I.C. Joined the force in 1916, resigned in 1920.

1075. CROZIER (Frank Perry) : Impressions and recollections. By Brig.-Gen. F. P. Crozier . . . 330 pp. illustr. 8vo. London. Laurie, 1930.
Chapters on the Ulster Volunteers, the Ulster Division in the Great War, and the author's experiences as Commandant of the Auxiliary Division, R.I.C., from Aug., 1920 to Feb., 1921. Details of the military and police reprisals.

1076. —— A word to Gandhi, the lesson of Ireland. 142 pp. 8vo. London, Williams and Norgate, 1931.
Details of the Irish hostilities, 1920-1921.

1077. —— Ireland for ever. By Brigadier-General F. P. Crozier, C.B., C.M.G., D.S.O., (Commandant, Auxiliary Division, Royal Irish Constabulary, 1920-21). 302 pp. 8vo. London, Cape, 1932.
Personal recollections.

Cumann Leigeactaí an Phobail, 1921-1922.
A series of lectures on Irish economics, industrial development, social problems, history, biography and art projected for the winter of 1921–1922, Mrs. Alice Stopford Green was President of the Cumann and Mr. Erskine Childers Vice-President. Only a few of the series were published.

1078. Dáil Éireann, 1919-1921 : Iris Dáil Éireann. An ceud tionól 21 Ianuar, 1919. Rolla na Dála, bunreact na Dála, an faisnéis neamspleadcuis, Toscairí cum comdála na síotcána. Sceul ón Dáil cun saornaisiún an domain. Clár oibre poblacánaige. Ar n-a cur fá cló le hugdaras Dáil Éireann. 32 pp. 8vo. 1919.

1079. —— Miontuairisc an Chéad Dála, 1919-1921. Minutes of proceedings of the first Parliament of the Republic of Ireland, 1919-1921. Official record. 292 pp. 8vo. Dublin, pr. Wood Printing Works, n.d.
Six sessions of the First Dáil were held in 1919 (January, April, May, June, August, and October), three in 1920 (June, August, September), and three in 1921 (January, March, and May). Some of the meetings in January and April, 1919 were held in public, all the meetings from June, 1919 in private, and, towards the end of the period, in great secrecy.
The record of the public session held on April 11th, 1919 has the following note : " The minutes of the Proceedings of this day were destroyed owing to enemy action. The following is a press report taken from the *Irish Independent* of the 12th April, 1919."
The Irish newspapers in 1919-1921 have no reports of the proceedings at the secret sessions. Summaries appeared in the *Irish Bulletin* (see 1186).
An "Order of the Lord Lieutenant in Council, dated September 10, 1919, under the Criminal Law and Procedure (Ireland) Act, 1887 (50 & 51 Vict. c. 20), prohibiting and suppressing the Dail Eireann association as a dangerous association within every county and county borough throughout Ireland " was published in the *Dublin Gazette*, September 11th, 1919.

1080. —— 1919. Tuairisc Inferoṁeaċ ar seisean an ṁeitim 17aṫ-19aṫ 16pp. 8vo. [1919].

Official Bulletin, in Irish and English, of the fourth session of 1919.

1081. —— Iris Dháil Éireann. Tuairisg oifigiuil. Díosbóireacht ar an gConnradh idir Eire agus Sasana, do signigheadh i Lundain ar an 6adh lá de Mhí na Nodlag, 1921.
Official Report. Debate on the Treaty between Great Britain and Ireland, signed in London on the 6th December, 1921. 424 pp. 8vo. Dublin, Talbot Press.

1082. —— The authority of Dáil Éireann. 8 pp. 8vo. [Dublin, Department of Publicity,?] [1919].

Asserts that of the two bodies which " claim governmental authority"— Dublin Castle and *An Dail*—" Dáil Éireann is in fact the constitutionally elected National Government of Ireland."

1083. —— 1921 : Address to the representatives of foreign nations, adopted at the January session of Dail Eireann, 1921. 40 pp. 4to. [London, *pr.* Woodgrange Press, 1921].

With appendices : (A) Democratic foundation of the Republic ; (B) Depopulation of Ireland ; (C) Destruction of wealth and financial robbery ; (D) English aggression in Ireland ; (E) List of 270 Irish citizens murdered ; (F) Map of wrecked Irish towns, with index ; (G) Letter of President de Valera to English M.P.s.

The Report on the Department of Foreign Affairs, submitted to Dáil Éireann by Count Plunkett, 17 August, 1921 (Dáil Reports, 1921–1922, p. 16), referring to the Address, says : " This document was forwarded to our Foreign Representatives with instructions to have it translated into the different languages and delivered to each elected representative in the following countries : France, Spain, Germany, Portugal, Italy, Greece, Bulgaria, Austria, Czecho-Slovakia, Hungary, Rumania, Switzerland, Turkey, Jugo-Slavia, Belgium, Holland, Sweden, Norway, Denmark, Russia, Japan, China, Phillipines, the British colonies and all the countries on the American continent."

1084. —— 1921. Official correspondence relating to the peace negotiations, June-September, 1921. Part I. Preliminary correspondence, June 24th to July 9th, 1921. Part II. Correspondence arising from the conversations at London, between President de Valera and the British Prime Minister, July 20th to September 30th. 24 pp. 4to. Dublin, 1921.

1085. —— The constructive work of Dáil Éireann. No. 1. The National Police and Courts of Justice. [Ministry for Home Affairs]. 32 pp. 8vo. Talbot Press, 1921.

Contents : I. The first civil court. II. The rise of the Republican Police. III. The Land agitation. IV. The National Arbitration Courts, May, 1920. V. Civil and criminal justice in the summer of 1920. VI. New Constitution of the Courts, August-September, 1920. VII. War on the Republican Courts, July, 1920–July, 1921.

1086. —— 1921. The constructive work of Dáil Éireann. No. 2. *In three sections*: I.—The Department of Agriculture and the Land Settlement Commission. II.—The Commission of Inquiry into the resources and industries of Ireland. III.—The Department of Trade and Commerce. 36 pp. 8vo. Dublin, Talbot Press, 1921.

A brief history of the civil government of Dáil Éireann (1919-1921) which, the preface says, " has been carried on under unprecedented conditions by Ministers and officials hiding from arrest, and, for the last year-and-a-half—up to the date of the Truce of July 11th, 1921—in the midst of a war." Published with the authority of the Dáil Ministry during the truce of 1921. The preface notes that the circumstances at the time of publication made it impossible " to record the whole story of the administration." These two pamphlets (edited by Mr. Erskine Childers) were reprinted with some alteration from the Irish Bulletin.

See the IRISH BULLETIN, in which appeared the official proclamations, decrees, orders and statements of Dáil Éireann and the Irish Government, official reports of the meetings of the Dáil and details of the constructive work of the Departments of Government.

1087. —— Coimisiun Fiafruigte maom is tionnscal Éireann. Commission of Inquiry into the resources and industries of Ireland. Minutes of evidence. 197 + 256 + 14 pp. Chart. 8vo. Dublin, [1921].

Part I. City Hall, Dublin. 2nd, 3rd, and 4th December, 1919. Milk-production and milk products ; Fishing.

Part II. City Hall, Dublin. 9th, 10th and 11th December, 1919. Co-operative organisation ; Meat trade ; Milk production ; Coal ; Water power ; Peat ; Industrial alcohol ; Mineral resources ; Harbour development.

The Commission was set up by a decree of the Dáil (1919) : " That a Select Commission be appointed to inquire into the Natural Resources and the present condition of Manufacturing and Productive Industries in Ireland and to consider and report by what means those Natural Resources may be more fully developed, and how those Industries may be encouraged and extended." Offices were acquired in O'Connell street, Dublin. " Mr. Darrell Figgis was appointed Secretary to the Commission and invitations were sent to a number of representatives of industry, labour and science . . . Political opinions were ignored in appointing the Commissioners " (see 1086).

Acting-President Arthur Griffith opened the first session, September 21st, 1919. The Irish press was prohibited by the British authorities from publishing the evidence, and the municipal buildings in Cork were occupied by armed police to prevent the public session announced there in February 1920. Similar incidents took place in Limerick. The work of the Commission, although thus hampered, was nevertheless carried on.

[The publications of the Commission include : Report on dairying and the dairy industry ; Memoir on the coal fields of Ireland ; Report on industrial alcohol ; Milk production : ad interim report ; Report on peat ; Report on sea fisheries ; Report on stock breeding ; Report on water power.]

1088. —— Aireacht na Trachtála. Trachtas ar Iasg Leasuithe na hÉireann. Sliocht as Cúntas an Phriomh-Chonsuil i Nua Eabhrac, i. D. L. Fausitt, [1920 ?].

—— *See also* 11b (Brugha, C.) ; 24 (Collins, M.) ; 43b (de Valera, E.) ; 68 (Griffith, A.) ; 119 (Lynd, R.) ; 213 (Stack, A.) ; 1102-1107 (Dept. of Publicity) ; Óglaigh na hÉireann ; 1188 (*Irish Bulletin*).

1089. DALTA : An Irish Commonwealth. 236 pp. 8vo. Dublin, Talbot Press, 1920.

1090. —— National land policy. 38 pp. 8vo. Dublin, Talbot Press, 1920.

A plea for a national land policy, with a scheme for the taxation of land values.

1091. DALTON (Charles) : With the Dublin brigade (1917-1921). 178 pp. 8vo. illustr. map of Dublin. London, Davies, 1929.

" Mr. Dalton, as an ex officer of the Intelligence Department of the Irish Republican Army (1918-21), deals vividly with the activities of the decisive phase of the Irish Revolution " (Publisher).

1092. DANGEROUS ASSOCIATIONS, IRELAND, 1919 : Proclamations. In Statutory rules and orders . . . issued in 1919. pp. 228-236. H.M.S.O., 1920.

Order of the Lord Lieutenant in Council, dated Sept. 10th, 1919, suppressing Dáil Éireann, and orders dated July 4th to Nov. 25th, suppressing in various districts the Sinn Féin organisation, Sinn Féin clubs, the Irish Volunteers and the Gaelic League.

1093. DAVIDSON (Randall) *Archbp. of Canterbury* : The situation in Ireland ; reprisals. [4] pp. 8vo. London, Peace with Ireland Council, 1921.

Extracts from a speech in the House of Lords, February 22, 1921.

1094. DAWSON (Richard) : Red terror and green. 272 pp. 8vo. London. Murray, 1920.

Purports to reveal " many startling facts of the alliance between Sinn Fein and Germany, and of Irish Revolutionaries with the Bolsheviki of Russia and Great Britain."

1095. DEADLY PARALLEL, The : 1914—Germany, 1920—England. 8 pp. 8vo. London, Burt, 1920.

Quotations from the Bryce Report (1915), with comparisons between the outrages attributed to the German army in Belgium and those alleged to have been committed by the British forces in Ireland.

1096. DÉLÉGATION IRLANDAISE, La, Paris : Memorandum à l'appui des revendications de l'Irlande, á l'effet d'être reconnue comme État souverain et indépéndant. Presenté par Seán T. O Ceallaigh et Georges Gavan Duffy, envoyés à Paris du Gouvernement élu de la République Irlandaise. 12 pp. 8vo. Abbeville, *impr.* F. Paillart, Juin, 1919.

1096a. —— Trois mois de représailles anglaises en Irlande, d'après un journaliste anglais. [Extrait du *Daily News*, Londres, du 15 novembre, 1920 par Hugh Martin]. 12 pp. 8vo. Paris, La Délégation Irlandaise, [1921 ?].

1097. —— Une tentative d'escroquerie. Le home rule act ou loi d'autonomie pour l'Irlande de 1920. 14 pp. 8vo. Paris, La Délégation Irlandaise, [1921 ?].

1098. —— Rapport de la Commission envoyée en Irlande par le Parti Travailliste Anglais, traduit de l'anglais par J. Gros. 40 pp. 8vo. Paris, La Délégation Irlandaise, [1921 ?] (Rapports sur l'Irlande).

1099. —— Rapport sur la situation en Irlande par le Lieutenant-General Sir Henri Lawson, K.C.B., envoyée du "Conseil de la Paix avec l'Irlande." 8 pp. 8vo. Paris, La Délégation Irlandaise, [1921 ?]. (Rapports sur l'Irlande).

1099a. —— Ce qu'un grand écrivain catholique anglais pense de la guerre Anglo-Irelandaise [G. K. Chesterton]. 8 pp. 8vo. Paris, [1921 ?].

1100. DEMPSEY (Frank), *Chairman Mallow Urban Council* : Evidence . . . presented before the AMERICAN COMMISSION ON CONDITIONS IN IRELAND (*which see*, pp. 893-935).
With special reference to the burning of Mallow by the military, Sept., 1920.

1101. DENNIS (Alfred Lewis P.) : Ireland and the outside world. *Atlantic Monthly*, CXXV. pp. 234-244. Boston, Feb., 1920.
Reproves the Irish people for not showing greater enthusiasm in the European war : " In 1916, while the French held at Verdun, Sinn Fein leaders struck at Dublin in a fashion to aid and comfort the men who sank the Lusitania."

1102. [DEPARTMENT OF PUBLICITY, DÁIL ÉIREANN] : The voice of Ireland. 12 pp. 8vo. [1919].
An analysis of the general election results, Dec., 1918.

1103. —— Irish bishops on English rule. 8 pp. [1919].
Extracts from the Lenten pastoral letters of the Irish Catholic bishops.

1104. —— England's fair words and—Ireland. 12 pp. 8vo. Dublin [*pr.*, Mahon], 1919.

1105. —— Irish Councils for Irish freedom. 24 pp. maps. 8vo. [1920 ?].
A survey of the County and Rural Council elections in June, 1920.

1106. —— The first of small nations. 32 pp. 8vo. [1920 ?].

1107. —— [Leaflets, 1919-1921] : Can Ireland pay her way ? [1919 and 1921] ; The cost of slavery [1919] ; England's " goodwill " [1919] ; The Limerick curfew murders [1921].
Some of the printed literature issued by the Department of Publicity had previously been published by the Sinn Féin organisation. For an account of certain pamphlets published under official auspices in 1919 see Dáil Eireann : Miontuairisc an Chéad Dála, 1919-1921 : Report of the Acting-President, October 27th, 1919.

1108. DERHAM (John), *Town Councillor of Balbriggan* : Evidence . . . presented before the AMERICAN COMMISSION ON CONDITIONS IN IRELAND (*which see*, pp. 92-120).

1109. DESMOND (Shaw) : The drama of Sinn Fein. 424 pp. 8vo. London, Collins, 1923.
An account of the national movement from the 1916 rising (with a description of the fighting) to the Dáil debate on the Treaty. The author is " an Irishman, born in Ireland, but of an English mother and coming from a Southern Protestant Unionist family." Sympathetic to the national cause.

1110. DE VALERA (Eamonn) : The foundation of the Republic of Ireland, in the vote of the people. Results of the General Election of December, 1918—a national plebiscite held under British law and British supervision . . . 16 pp. map. 8vo. New York, [Friends of Irish Freedom ?], *n.d.*

1111. —— Presidential statement of policy, delivered at the public session of Dáil Éireann, April 10, 1919. [4] pp. 8vo. *n.p.*, [1919.]

The Irish newspapers at the time were prohibited by the press censor from publishing this statement.

—— *See also* Sect. GENERAL AND INTRODUCTORY : 972-977 and 1348 (Sinn Féin) ; *and* 1078-1086 (Dáil Éireann).

DEVOY (John), *see* FRIENDS OF IRISH FREEDOM.

1112. DICKIE (John) : A New Zealand sidelight on the Irish question. *National Review*, LXXVIII. pp. 556-566. London, Dec., 1921.

1113. DORBENE (Kevin Stroma) : Ireland beats Wilson. By Kevin Stroma Dorbene, an American. 32 pp. 8vo. Dublin, Whelan, [1920].

Repr. of a series of articles from *New Ireland* (Dublin, 1920).

1114. DOWNING (Rossa F.) : Men, women and memories : a review of thirty years' sympathy and labour for the Irish cause . . . In the *Voice of Ireland* (*see* 226, pp. 215-222).

Elected President of the Friends of Irish Freedom in Dec., 1918. Gives an account of the work done for Ireland in the U.S.A. by that organisation and others. Photographs of prominent U.S. citizens who supported the Irish cause.

1114a. —— American Association for the Recognition of the Irish Republic. A report presented to the Patrick H. Pearse branch of the Friends of Irish Freedom . . . November 28th, 1920. 24 pp. 8vo. Washington, [1920].

1115. DUBLIN CHAMBER OF COMMERCE : The Dublin Chamber of Commerce and the Government of Ireland Bill, 1920. Report of the special committee and reports of the various sub-committees, together with a memorandum on the finance of the bill, prepared by Professor C. H. Oldham. 54 pp. 8vo. Dublin, Sealy, Bryers and Walker, 1920.

1116. DUBLIN CORPORATION, 1921 : Report and printed documents of the Corporation of Dublin . . . Letter from the Minister for Local Government, setting forth the reasons which led to the definite severance of the relations between Irish Local Authorities and English Local Government Board . . . Dublin Corporation Reports. Vol. II. 1921. pp. 455-460.—No. 208.

Headed : " LOCAL GOVERNMENT DEPARTMENT—DÁIL ÉIREANN. *9th September*, 1921. To each County Council, County Borough Council, Corporation, Urban Council, and Poor Law Board . . ." and signed L. T. MAC COSGAIR, *Minister for Local Government*.

1117. DUFF (Douglas V.): Sword for hire, the saga of a modern free companion. 16 + 338 pp. pls. 8vo. London, Murray, 1934.

    The author joined the R.I.C. in London in 1920. Two chapters describe his experiences at Gormanstown, Dublin and Galway.

1118. DUFFY (Georges Gavan), *Envoyé à Paris du Gouvernement Élu de la République Irlandaise* : La République d'Irlande et la presse Française. 86 pp. 8vo. Paris, Délégation du Gouvernement élu de la République Irlandaise, Novembre, 1919.

    Articles on the Irish question form *Le Temps, Le Journal des Débats, L'Action Française, L'Information, L'Europe Nouvelle, La Croix, Le Journal de Genève*, and other journals, published between February and July, 1919.
    T.D. 1918 ; Irish representative in Paris during 1919 and in Rome 1920-1921 ; one of the Irish plenipoteniaries at the Anglo-Irish conference in London, 1921.

1119. DUKE OF NORTHUMBERLAND'S FUND, [1921]: Plight of Southern Irish loyalists. Sinn Fein terrorism . . . 8 pp. 8vo. London, Publicity Office, Duke of Northumberland's Fund, *n.d.*

1120. DUNNE (Edward F.): Treaty of Peace with Germany. Hearings before the Committee on Foreign Relations, United States Senate . . . [Statement of Hon. Edward F. Dunne. pp. 860-865. Aug. 30, 1919]. Senate Documents. Vol. 10. No. 106. Washington, Government Printing Office, 1919.

1121. DUNRAVEN (Windham Thomas WYNDHAM-QUIN) *4th Earl of*: The urgency of Ireland. *Nineteenth Century*, LXXXVI. pp. 237-244. Aug., 1919.

1122. —— The crisis in Ireland : federal union, through devolution . . . 40 pp. 8vo. London, Hodder and Stoughton, 1920.

    Report of a speech in the House of Lords, July 1st, and repr. of three letters in the *Times*.

—— See also 50.

Eaglaiseac Gaedealac, An t- see 1142 (*Gaelic Churchman*).

1123. EDMOND (James): Is Ireland important ? *National Rev.*, LXXVI. pp. 492-502. London, Dec., 1920.

    Ex-editor Sydney *Bulletin*. Pleads for abandonment of Ireland by England on the ground that Ireland " isn't one-tenth as important as it imagines it is."

1124. ENGLISH OFFICER'S SON, An: Ireland to-day under England. 16 pp. 8vo. London, B. Delaney, O.P. [1921]. (Blackfriars reprints, No. 1).

1126. EVANS (Richardson): Ireland and the realm. *Nineteenth Century*, LXXXIX. pp. 574-586. April, 1921.

1127. EWART (Wilfrid): A journey in Ireland, 1921. By Wilfrid Ewart, Captain, late Special Reserve, Scots Guards. With an introduction by Major the Earl Winterton, M.P., Under-Secretary of State for India. 170 pp. 8vo. London, Putnams, 1922.

1128. FAWSITT (Jeremiah L.) [Diarmuid] *Irish Consul-General, New York*: Evidence presented before the AMERICAN COMMISSION ON CONDITIONS IN IRELAND. (*which see*, pp. 935-978).

Reviews Irish local government, finance, trade, industrial development, and the decrees of the Dáil Government.

1129. FERRIS (*Rev.* William): The Gaelic Commonwealth. *Catholic Bulletin*, IX pp. 69-80. February, 1919.

1130. FIGGIS (Darrell): The economic case for Irish independence. 8 + 92 pp. 8vo. Dublin, Maunsell, 1920.

—— *see also* 316 ("Recollections of the Irish war"); 810 and 1087 (Commission of inquiry into the resources of Ireland).

1131. FIGGIS (Darrell) and CHILDERS (ERSKINE) : La tragedia de Irlanda : sus orígenes, su desarrollo histórico, su fase actual. Trad. de A. Ruiz y Pablo. 294 pp. 8vo. Barcelona, Industrias Gráficas Seix & Barral Herms., S.A., 1921.

Translation of "The historic case for Irish independence," and "The economic case for Irish independence" by Darrel Figgis, and "The military terror in Ireland" by Erskine Childers. (See 812, 1058, 1131).

Finance (Irish), 1919-1921, *see* Sect. GENERAL AND INTRODUCTORY.

See also 1078-1087 (Dáil Éireann); 1163 (Anglo-Irish Treaty, 1921); 1159 (Govt. of Irel. Act, 1920); 1166 (Griffith, A.); 1290 (Oldham, C. H.); 1359 (Stamp, *Sir* J.).

1132. FITZGERALD (Desmond): Mr. Pakenham on the Anglo-Irish Treaty. *Studies*, an Irish quarterly review, XXIV. pp. 406-414. Dublin, September, 1935.

See also 633 (Insurrection of 1916); 1078-1086 (Dáil Éireann); 1102 (Dept. of Publicity); 1188 (*Irish Bulletin*); and 1300a (Pakenham, F.).

1133. Fitzgerald (Edmund B.): Fiddling amid the flames. 16 pp. 8vo. "The Red Hand" Magazine pamphlet series. Belfast, Ulster Information Bureau, 1920.

Ulster nationalist.

1134. FORREST (Sir George W.): Irish administration. *Fortnightly Rev.*, CX. (N.S.) pp. 907-916. Dec. 1921.

1135. Fox (George L.), *New Haven, Conn.*: More light on the Irish question : arguments to prove that the Irish Sinn Feiners are secessionist traitors to the United Kingdom and the United States, consummate liars and Bolshevistic advocates of wholesale robbery and spoliation. [8] pp. 8vo. *n.p.*, [1919 ?].

1136. FRENCH (*Major Hon.* Gerald): The life of Field-Marshal Sir John French, first Earl of Ypres . . . 432 pp. pls. 8vo. London, Cassell, 1931.

A chapter on the 'Curragh "insurrection"' (1914) and three chapters on Lord French as Viceroy of Ireland (May 11, 1918-April 30, 1921), Extracts from his letters.

Friends, Society of, *see* 1141 (Furnas P.); 1389 (Wilkins, G.).

1137. FRIENDS OF IRISH FREEDOM, The, 1919-1922 : News letter of the Irish National Bureau. No. 1, July 4th, 1919. Washington.

    Published weekly. From No. 15 (Oct. 10, 1919) the F.O.I.F. " assumed direct management over the Bulletin." From No. 28 (Jan. 9, 1920) the title became : NEWS LETTER OF THE NATIONAL BUREAU OF INFORMATION, FRIENDS OF IRISH FREEDOM.

1137a. —— Constitution and branch by-laws of the Friends of Irish. Freedom. Revised by the Irish Peace Convention, February 22 and 23, 1919. 40 pp. sm. 8vo. New York, Diarmuid Lynch, *National Secretary*, [1919 ?].

1138. —— 1920-1921. Leaflets : Are you a member of the F.O.I.F. for 1920 ? ; Ireland's economic situation (Arthur Griffith) ; Theology, some theologians and the hunger strike ; Irish independence . . . Idle thoughts of an idle fellow (Jerome K. Jerome) ; Ireland and America, a comparison (Willard De Lue) ; Ireland and the French press.

1139. —— Ireland's part in the world war, the greatest contribution of any unfree nation . . . 8 pp. 8vo. Washington, Friends of Irish Freedom, [1919 ?].

1140. —— Ireland's elected government, a history of Dáil Éireann, being an official account of its establishment and growth . . . published at Dublin, Ireland . . . 8 pp. 8vo. Washington Friends of Irish Freedom, National Bureau of Information. No. 22. Aug., 1920.

    Repr. from the *Irish Bulletin*, July 1st, 1920.
    The " Friends of Irish Freedom " organisation was established in New York at the Irish Race Convention, March 4-5, 1916, and was controlled by Clan-na-Gael.
    For references to its history and activities and to the differences with President de Valera which developed in 1920.

—— *See also* 44 (Devoy, John) ; 212 (Splain, J.) ; 549 (Sexton, J.) ; 876 (McCartan, *Dr.* P.) ; 1065 (Cohalan, D.) ; 1114 (Downing, Rossa) ; 1144 (Gallagher, *Rt. Rev.* M. J.).

1140a. IRELAND'S REQUEST TO THE GOVERNMENT OF THE UNITED STATES OF AMERICA FOR RECOGNITION AS A SOVEREIGN INDEPENDENT STATE. 136 pp. 8vo. Washington, Irish Diplomatic Mission, [1920].

    Preface, signed by President de Valera, October 27, 1920. Appendices include War Aims, Ireland a nation, Ireland's exercise of the right of self-determination, the " Ulster " question, English ruthlessness in Ireland, the commercial ruin of Ireland, Continental Congress address to the people of Ireland.

1141. FURNAS (Paul J.) : Evidence . . . presented before the American Commission on conditions in Ireland (*which see*, pp. 517-528.) Washington, 1921.

    Account of an investigation in Ireland made by the English Society of Friends in Sept., 1920.

1142. GAELIC CHURCHMAN, The. An t-Eaglaiseac Gaedealac, 1919-1928. Monthly. March, 1919–March, 1928.

    Organ of the Irish guild of the Church, formed to promote Irish ideals in the Church of Ireland. Protests against the " identification of the Church of Ireland with one political party."

1143. GALLAGHER (Frank) : Days of fear. 176 pp. 8vo. London, Murray, 1928.
  A personal record, written by a prisoner in Mountjoy jail, Dublin, during the hunger-strike in April, 1920. "At the time this protest by imprisoned men attracted world-wide attention."
  The author was assistant to the Director of Publicity in the Dáil Ministry 1919-1921 and acting editor of the *Irish Bulletin* (1919-1921) during the greater part of its career.

1144. GALLAGHER (*Rt. Rev.* Michael J.) *Bp. of Detroit* : Statement by Rt. Rev. Michael J. Gallagher, D.D., National President, Friends of Irish Freedom, dealing with matters which arose out of the visit to the United States of America of the Hon. Eamon de Valera, President of the Republic of Ireland. [12] pp. 8vo. [New York, Friends of Irish Freedom, April, 1921].
  Correspondence between President de Valera and Mr. Justice Cohalan, Feb., 1920, and a letter from John Devoy " to a colleague," together with Dr. Gallagher's own statement, in which he sets forth " the three principal reasons why the Friends of Irish Freedom refused to accept and to follow the leadership of President de Valera."
  For further references to the differences between President de Valera and the other Irish envoys on one hand, and the Clan-na-Gael F.O.I.F. group on the other, see FRIENDS OF IRISH FREEDOM.

1145. GANNON (*Rev.* Patrick Joseph) *S.J.* : The ethical aspect of the hunger-strike. *Studies*, XIX. pp. 448-454. Sept., 1920.
  Professor of Dogmatic Theology, Milltown Park, Dublin. Inquires " on what grounds should any moral obloquy attach to the hunger-protest of the Irish political prisoners ? "

1146. GAY (Francisque) : L'Irlande et la Société des Nations. 164 pp. 12 mo. Paris, Bloud & Gay, 1921.
  A plea for arbitration of the Anglo-Irish quarrel by the League of Nations, with annexe : " Une enquête à Dublin sur la Société des Nations, 1921."

1147. G. B. : [The] situation in Ireland : a short history. 14 pp. 8vo. London, Peace with Ireland Council, [1921 ?].

1148. GEARY (*Rev.* James A.) : The Irish land question. The story of a confiscated country. 8 pp. 8vo. Washington, Friends of Irish Freedom, 1920. (No. 13).

1149. George (David Lloyd) : Is it peace ? 291 pp. 8vo. Second edition. [Some Irish memories, pp. 267-275]. London, Hodder and Stoughton, [1923].
  Papers on the European situation, with a brief account of the signing of the Anglo-Irish Treaty, Dec., 1921, when the author was Prime Minister.

1150. GIBBS (Philip) : The anarchy in Ireland from the view of the average Englishman. *Harper's Mag.*, CXLII. pp. 409-418. New York, March, 1921.

1151. —— The hope of Europe. 344 pp. 8vo. [Ch. III. The truth about Ireland]. London, Heinemann, 1921.
  Pleads for Anglo-Irish friendship.

1152. —— An appeal to the Irish people. *Rev. of Reviews*, LXIV. pp. 165-169. Sept., 1921.

1153. GINNELL (Laurence), *T.D.* : Evidence . . . presented before the AMERICAN COMMISSION ON CONDITIONS IN IRELAND (*which see*, pp. 462-505). Washington, 1921.

> See also 1252.

1153a. —— A glance back at the time of our harmony. By Labhras Mag Fhinnghail [*i.e.*, L. Ginnell]. *Catholic Bulletin*, XII. pp. 768-770. Dublin, December, 1922.

> A brief account of the writer's official mission to South America on behalf of Dáil Éireann in 1921.

1154. GOBLET (Yann Morvran) : L'évolution politique irlandaise de 1914 à 1920. *Revue de Paris*. 27e année. Tome 3e, pp. 201-224. 1er Mai, 1920.

> A series of lectures on this subject was delivered by M. Goblet at l'École Interalliée des Hautes Études Sociale, Paris, in December, 1919.

1155. —— Possibilities of Franco-Irish commerce. In *Young Ireland*. Dublin, March 20th, 1920.

> Translated report of a lecture at the Commerical club, Paris.

1156. —— L'Irlande dans la crise universelle (1914-20) . . . 462 pp. 8vo. Deuxième edition, revue et augmentée. Paris, Alcan, 1921. (Bibliothèque d'histoire contemporaine).

> The sections which have been added to the first edition include : La décadence du parti parlementaire (Juillet 1917–Décembre 1918) ; Le bilan de la crise universelle en Irlande (1919) ; La nouvelle question d'Irelande (1920). See 328.

1157. GOOD (James Winder) : British Labour and Irish needs. *Studies*, a quarterly review, XIX. pp. 551-560. Dublin, Dec., 1920.

> A criticism of the inactivity of the British Labour movement during the war against Ireland.

See also 59.

1158. GOUGH (*General Sir* Hubert) : The situation in Ireland. *Rev. of Reviews*, LXIII. pp. 35-39. Jan.-Feb., 1921.

1159. GOVERNMENT OF IRELAND ACT, 1920. [10 & 11 Geo. 5. Ch. 67]. An Act to provide for the better Government of Ireland. 82 pp. 8vo. H.M.S.O., 1920.

> This Act gave the sanction of British law to the division of Ireland which is described in the preamble as " partition." It sets up a Parliament for an area to be known as " Northern Ireland " (Antrim, Armagh, Down, Fermanagh, Londonderry and Tyrone) and another Parliament for " Southern Ireland " (the rest of Ireland), though the two Parliaments are empowered " by mutual agreement and joint action to terminate partition and to set up one Parliament and one Government for the whole of Ireland." The legislative powers of both Parliaments are subject to great and numerous limitations. If a majority of the members in either Parliament refuses to take the oath of allegiance, that Parliament is to be dissolved and the area administered by the Lord Lieutenant, assisted by a nominated Council and Assembly.
>
> The Act was to come into operation " on Aug. 2nd, 1921, or on such dates (either generally or as regards any particular provisions) between Jan. 2nd, 1921, and March 2nd, 1922, as might be fixed by H.M. by Order in Council . . ."

1160. —— Summary of main provisions. 8 pp. H.M.S.O. [1921 ?].
> An official laudation of the Act, claiming that it "recognises the aspirations of the great bulk of the Irish people," and warning Ireland that the consequences of a refusal to "work the Act" would be "a system analogous to Crown Colony Government."

1161. —— Appointed days under the 1920 Act. Orders in Council fixing appointed days for certain purposes. *Statutory Rules and Orders . . . issued in the year* 1921. pp. 349-358. H.M.S.O., 1922.

—— *See* 36 (Cork Chamber of Commerce); 1115 (Dublin Chamber of Commerce); 1164 (Green, A. S.); 1168, 1169 (Gwynn, S.); 1186 (*Irish Bulletin* [Vol. 4, No. 17, 18th April, 1921]); (Long, W., *1st Viscount*); 1097 (Délégation Irlandaise); 1208 (*Irish Statesman*); 1259 (Marriott, J. A.); 1271 (Moyne, W. E. Guinness, *1st Baron*); 1317 (Quekett (Sir A.)).

1162. GRASTY (Charles H.): Irish realities. *Atlantic Monthly*, CXXVI. pp. 383-394. Boston, Sept., 1920.
> Foreign correspondent of the New York *Times*. Unsympathetic to Sinn Féin.

1163. GREAT BRITAIN AND IRELAND, 1921 : Articles of agreement for a treaty between Great Britain and Ireland, 1921. Presented to Parliament by Command of His Majesty. H.M.S.O., 1921 (Cmd. 1560).

See also 1084 (Dáil Éireann); 1186 (*Irish Bulletin*).

1164. GREEN (Alice Stopford): The Government of Ireland. By Mrs. J. R. Green. Foreword by George Russell (Æ). 16 pp. 8vo. London, Labour Publishing Co., 1921. (Labour Booklets, No. 5).
> A criticism of the Government of Ireland Act, 1920.

1165. GRIFFITH (Arthur): To re-build the nation. 8 pp. 8vo. [Dublin, Mahon], [1919 ?].

1166. —— Local taxation. *Young Ireland*. August 28th–September 11th, 1920.

See Sects. GENERAL AND INTRODUCTORY; **1912–1916**; **1916–1918**. *See also* 1078–1088 (Dáil Éireann); 1348 (Sinn Féin).

1167. GROS (J.): La terreur militaire en Irlande, par le Commandant Erskine Childers, D.S.C., traduit de l'Anglais par J. Gros. 72 pp. 8vo. Paris, Beauchesne, 1920.

1168. GWYNN (Stephen): The Irish situation. 96 pp. 8vo. Cape, 1920.
> "A reasoned survey of the situation in Ireland up to and including the elections of June, 1921 " (Publisher).

1169. —— "The better government of Ireland." *Contemporary Rev.*, CXVII. pp. 477-486. April, 1920.

1170. HACKETT (Francis) : Evidence . . . presented before the American Commission on conditions in Ireland. (*which see*, pp. 137-173). Washington, 1921.

> Associate editor, *New Republic* (New York). Investigated conditions in Ireland for the New York *World* in July-Sept., 1920.

1171. —— The silver lining in Ireland. *Harper's Mag.*, CXLIII. pp. 1-8, New York, June, 1921.

1172. [HAGAN (*Rev.* John)] : Notes from Rome. By Scottus [*i.e.*, Mgr. John Hagan, Vice-Rector of the Irish College, Rome]. *Catholic Bulletin*, Vols. I-IX. Dublin, 1913-1919.

> Vice-Rector, Irish College, Rome, 1904-1919, and Rector, 1919-1929. The notes throw light on Irish affairs in Italy and on the attitude of the Vatican towards the Irish national question.

—— *See also* 1247, 1251 (Magennis, *Rev.* P. E.).

1173. HAMMOND (John Lawrence) : a tragedy of errors. (Reprinted from " The Nation " of January 8th, 1921). 32 pp. sm. 8vo. London, British Periodicals, [1921].
Second printing [1921].

1174. —— The terror in action. By J. L. Hammond. (Reprinted from " The Nation and the Athenaeum " of April 30th, 1921, with an appendix). 64 pp. 8vo. London, British Periodicals, [1921].

> These two pamphlets had a large circulation in England in 1921. They review the Irish situation from 1914 and the condition of Ireland under the military régime of 1920-1921. Sympathetic to the Irish national resistance.

1175. HARRISON (Austin) : Ireland before the Imperial Conference. *English Rev.*, XXXII. pp. 57-66. June, 1921.

1176. HARRISON (Henry) : The Irish case considered A remonstrance, addressed to the British public . . . with preface by the Rt. Hon. Sir Horace Plunkett . . . 18 pp. 8vo. London, Irish Dominion League, 1920.

1176a. —— The Irish peace conference, 1920, and its betrayal. Does the Government want a genuine peace ? 12 pp. 8vo. Dublin, Irish Dominion League, [January], 1921.

1177. —— Mr. George Russell ("Æ") and his Court of Conscience for Ireland and the Empire, an intervener. 8 pp. 8vo. Dublin Irish Dominion League, 1921.

1178. HAYES (S.) : The story of *an t-Óglách*. By the manager—Captain S. Hayes. ᴀn t-Óglác. N.S. Vol. v. No. 1. pp. 1-7. April, 1932.
See 1287.

Healy (Timothy Michael), see 81.

Henry (Robert Mitchel), see 82.

1179. HERCÉ. En Irlande. [5 novembre 1919]. *Revue de Paris.* 27e année. Tome 4e. pp. 521-553. 1er Aout 1920.

1180. —— La réaction anglasie contre le mouvement irlandais. *Revue de Paris.* 27e année. Tome 6e. 15 Déc. 1920.

1181. HERDMAN (J. O.) : Sinn Fein trials and parliamentary disqu lification. *Contemporary Rev.*, CXV. pp. 177-182. Feb., 1919.

1182. HIBERNICUS : The government's opportunity in Ireland. *Fortnightly Rev.*, CVI. (N.S.). pp. 983-995. Dec., 1919.

1183. HOARE (*Sir* Samuel) : The Prime Minister and the chances of an Irish settlement. *Nineteenth Century,* LXXXVIII. Oct., 1920.

1184. —— Irish war and English peace. The *Forum,* LXVI. pp. 91-102. New York, Aug., 1921.

M.P. (C.), since 1910.

1185. HORGAN (John J.) : Precepts and practice in Ireland, 1914-1919. In *Studies,* VIII. pp. 210-226. Dublin, June, 1919.

1185a. HUGHES (Katherine) : English atrocities in Ireland ; a compilation of facts from court and press records . . . With a foreword by Hon. James D. Phelan. 64 pp. 8vo. New York, Friends of Irish Freedom, [1920].

Hunger-strikes, 1917-1921, *see* Sect. **1916-1918**.

Iceland, *see* 1223 (McGill, A.).

1186. IMPERIAL DANGER, An : The Sinn Fein menace, the Irish problem in a nutshell, the only safe course. 12 pp. 8vo. Dublin, Ponsonby and Gibbs, 1919.

Ireland and Great Britain : Articles of agreement for a treaty between Ireland and Great Britain. In *Irish Bulletin* December 7, 1921. See also 1081, 1084 (Dáil Éireann) ; 1163 (Great Britain) ; 1203-1206 (Irish settlement) ; 1276-1277 (Northern Ireland).

1187. IRELAND'S DECLARATION OF INDEPENDENCE and other official documents including letters to the President of the Peace Conference and the General Memorandum submitted in support of Ireland's claim as a sovereign independent state. 20 pp. 8vo. [Washington ?] [1919 ?].

Containing the Declaration of independence by Dáil Éireann of Jan. 21st, 1919, the message to the nations and democratic programme adopted at the same session, and letters from the delegates appointed by Dáil Éireann to present Ireland's case.

Iris Dáil Éireann, *see* 1078 (Dáil Éireann).

1188. IRISH BULLETIN, 1919-1921. [No. 1] 11th November, 1919 to Vol. VI. No. 39, 13th December, 1921. [The system of numbering began with Vol. II. No. 1. 3rd May, 1920]. [Dublin, Department of Publicity, Dáil Éireann].

"The publication of the *Irish Bulletin* was made necessary by the circulation from Dublin Castle of official statements misrepresenting the situation in Ireland and by the fact that the National Movement was allowed to have no organ in the Press. In order to contradict the official misrepresentations and to acquaint people resident outside Ireland with the case for Irish Independence, the *Irish Bulletin* was established. To prevent suppression it was, and has since been, published secretly" (*Irish Bulletin*. Vol. 3. No. 52. 29th Nov., 1920). In the same number the sources from which the *Irish Bulletin* gets its information are given as : (1) The daily press ; (2) Eye-witnesses and victims of military and constabulary outrages ; and (3) The English Government in Ireland. Eye-witnesses "are personally examined by members of the Bulletin staff, or if living at a distance swear affidavits before the Commissioner of Oaths." Secret [intercepted] orders and reports of the British Government were frequently published. "In no case has the authenticity of these documents been challenged."

Mr. Frank Gallagher, in an account of "Literature of the conflict" ("Irish Book Lover," XVIII., pp. 69-71. May-June, 1930), writes : "The *Irish Bulletin* was the daily organ of the Irish Government during the War of Independence. It was first published (in the cyclostyled form it always kept) in November, 1919. It seems to have originated with a typewritten sheet issued to the press about once a fortnight in the spring and summer of 1919 from the Dáil Éireann Publicity Department, giving a summary of British acts of aggression. This was first compiled under Lawrence Ginnell's Directorship of Publicity. I was then his assistant. In November, 1919, Mr. Robert Brennan, then Director of Publicity for Sinn Féin, thought of a regular organ for the Government, and the *Irish Bulletin* was the result. Afterwards it became the daily organ, and published elaborate statements of the Irish case, and a full history of the contemporary growth and development of the Republican Government." It was mainly compiled by Mr. Gallagher under the general editorship of the Director of Publicity for Dáil Éireann—Mr. Desmond FitzGerald (1919–1921), and, for some months in 1921, Mr. Erskine Childers.

According to an official statement issued from Dublin Castle a few days later, "several tons of files, books and literature were removed in the Government lorries ... The office furniture was of an elaborate character including a 'Roneo' duplicator, typewriters and desk which had been used by the clerks." A list of the addresses to which the *Irish Bulletin* was being regularly sent was also seized. Shortly afterwards, spurious Irish Bulletins and typewritten proclamations purporting to emanate from Dáil Éireann, began to reach these addresses. (See "The forged issues of the Irish Bulletin," an investigation of the typescript and subject matter of these spurious issues in the *Irish Bulletin*, April 7, June 1, July 1, 1921, and House of Commons Debates [answers to questions], April 7, 12, 20, 28, 1921). The first of the forged issues is dated March 30. The compilers apparently were not then aware that the production of the genuine *Irish Bulletin* had continued without interruption from other premises. The genuine issues henceforth bore a stamp, "Official Copy" in green ink.

1189. IRISH CENTRE PARTY, The : Objects of the party. 4 pp. 8vo. *n.p.* [1919].

Irish Councils [for local government], see DAIL ÉIREANN.

1190. IRISH COMMONWEALTH, The, 1919 : a monthly review of social affairs, politics and literature. Dublin, Kiersey. 176 pp. 8vo. March-May, 1919.

Three numbers published.

1191. IRISH DOMINION LEAGUE, The . . . Founded, June, 1919. Dissolved, November, 1921 . . . : Official report, setting forth a summary of results achieved, together with the proceedings on dissolution. 24 pp. 8vo. Dublin, Irish Dominion League, 1921.

—— *See also* 232 (Wells, W. B.); 1175-1177 (Harrison, H.); 1207 (*Irish Statesman*); 1308-1312 (Plunkett, *Sir* H.); 1313 (Pope-Hennessy L.).

1192. IRISH EXILE, The. Ðeoṛaiḋe Ṡaoḋlaċ, An, 1921: An organ of Irish movements in and around London. Monthly. Vol. 1. March-Oct., 1921. Vol. II. Nov., 1921–Jan., 1922. London, London District Committee of the Irish Self-Determination League.

Official organ of the Irish Self-Determination League of Great Britain.

1193. IRISH LABOUR PARTY : Ireland at Berne, being the reports and memoranda presented to the International Labour and Socialist Conference held at Berne, February, 1919. Issued by the authority of the National Executive of the Irish Labour party and Trade Union Congress. 52 pp. 8vo. Dublin, Talbot Press, [1919].

See also Labour movement.

1194. IRISH LABOUR PARTY AND TRADE UNION CONGRESS : Who burnt Cork ? A tale of arson, loot and murder. The evidence of over seventy witnesses. 68 pp. map. illustr. 8vo. Dublin, Irish Labour party and Trade Union Congress, January, 1921.

1195. IRISH LEAGUE OF NATIONS SOCIETY : International sacrifice—or chaos. 12 pp. 8vo. Dublin, Repr. by Irish League of Nations Society, [1918]. (I.L.N.S.—Series 'A'—No. 10).

1196. IRISH RECONSTRUCTION ASSOCIATION, The : The scope of reconstruction. 16 pp. 8vo. Dublin, Roberts, [1919 ?].

Irish Republican Army (I.R.A.), The, 1919-1921, *see* Óglaigh na hÉireann.

1197. IRISH REPUBLICAN PRISONERS' DEPENDENTS' FUND, 1921 : Fête in aid of Irish Republican Prisoners' Dependents' Fund, September 29th–October 9th, 1921. 32 pp. 8vo. illustr. Dublin, 1921.

1198. IRISH SELF-DETERMINATION LEAGUE OF GREAT BRITAIN, An Cumann um Saoirse Ṡaeḋeal. Constitution and rules. [8] pp, 8vo. London, pr. Woodgrange Press, [1920 ?].

1199. —— Souvenir programme. Mass meeting, Irish residents in London, Albert Hall, 11th Feb., 1920. [8] pp. illustr. 8yo. [London, Irish Self-Determination League of Great Britain, 1920].

1200. —— First annual conference, to be held at Manchester, on Saturday, November 27th, 1920. Agenda. 28 pp. 8vo. London, *pr.* Woodgrange Press, 1920.

1201. —— Second annual delegate conference, to be held at London, on Saturday, June 25th, 1921. Agenda, 16 pp. 8vo. [London, pr. National Labour Press, 1921].

1202. —— Reception to the Irish republican delegation, by the Irish-Ireland societies in London, Albert Hall, Wednesday, 26th Oct., 1921. [8] pp. illustr. 8vo. London, [Irish Self-Determination League of Great Britain, 1921].

1203. IRISH SETTLEMENT, 1921 : Correspondence relating to the proposals of His Majesty's Government for an Irish settlement. Presented to Parliament . . . H.M.S.O., 1921 [Cmd. 1470].

> The British Government's proposals of July 20, with letters subsequently exchanged between Mr. de Valera and Mr. Lloyd George (Aug. 15).

1204. —— Correspondence relating to the proposals of His Majesty's Government for an Irish settlement. Presented to Parliament. 8 pp. H.M.S.O., 1921. [Cmd. 1502].

> July 20–Aug. 26.

1205. —— Further correspondence relating to the proposals of His Majesty's Government for an Irish settlement . . . Presented to Parliament . . . 12 pp. H.M.S.O., 1921. [Cmd. 1539].

> August 24–September 30.

1206. —— Correspondence between His Majesty's Government and the Prime Minister of Northern Ireland relating to the proposals for an Irish settlement. Presented to Parliament. 12 pp. H.M.S.O. 1921. [Cmd. 1561].

> November 10–December 5, 1921.

See also 1078-1084 (Dáil Éireann).

1207. IRISH STATESMAN, The, 1919-1920. Weekly. O.S. June 28, 1919–June 19, 1920 (Vol. II. No. 52). Pr. by George Roberts, 50 Lower Baggott St., and published by the Irish Statesman, 13 St. Stephen's Green.

> Sir Horace Plunkett, who says : " I had a good deal to do with its inception," explains in the last issue that the policy of the *Irish Statesman* " was embodied in a Manifesto adopted by the Organisation which called itself the Irish Dominion League." Warre B. Wells, who acted as editor, says : " It was started eventually, after certain negotiations for funds had miscarried, on a capital of precisely five hundred pounds provided by Plunkett himself . . . For a year it kept in being with an increasing influence but diminishing funds, supplemented by some capital from American sympathisers, until finally it was compelled to suspend publication with the prospect of settlement as remote as ever."

1208 —— The finance of the Government of Ireland Bill, critically examined by some Irish men of business and affairs. [12] pp. 4to. Supplement to the *Irish Statesman*, May, 8th 1920.

> The contributors include G. F. H. Berkeley, Sir John R. O'Connell, Nicholas J. Synnott, Major Erskine Childers, G. A. Tulloch, John Mackie, J. X. Murphy.

1209. Irish Transport and General Workers' Union, 1919: Annual report for 1919. 48 pp. 8vo. Dublin, Executive Committee, I.T. and G.W.U., [1919].

1209a. —— Annual report for 1920. 40 pp. 8vo.

1210. —— Annual report for 1921. 40 pp. 8vo.

1211. IRISH UNIONIST ALLIANCE, The : The revolutionary movement in Ireland, its aims and methods . . . Repr. from " Notes from Ireland," 1st May, 1921, for the Irish Unionist Alliance. 12 pp. 8vo. Dublin, Humphrey and Armour, 1921.

1212. IRISH WEEKLY INDEPENDENT, The, 1925-1934.

Narratives, mainly by participants, of events in 1919-1921 have been published in the St. Patrick's Day and Christmas numbers of the *Irish Weekly Independent* each year since 1925.

1212a. IRISH WEEKLY INDEPENDENT, The : The Connaught Rangers' mutiny, its history and sequel. By one who knows. *Irish Weekly Independent.* Feb. 21-April 18, 1925.

The 1st Batt. of the Connaught Rangers, after service in the Great War on the Western front and in Mesopotania, Egypt and Palestine, arrived at Jullundur in the Punjab on November 24, 1919. According to the writer, some of the men informed the Commanding Officer on June 28, 1920, that, as a protest against the actions of the Black and Tans in Ireland, they were refusing to parade. The Irish tri-colour was hoisted over the barracks. The mutinous troops were surrounded by battalions from other regiments and disarmed in the following week. One man was afterwards sentenced to death by court-martial and executed and forty-five men were sentenced to terms of imprisonment, ranging from life to three years.

See also the *Irish Press*, Christmas number, 1934.

Irish White Cross, see 1391 (Williams, W. J.).

1212b. JONES (George Garro) : Ventures and visions. illustr. 8vo. London, Hutchinson, 1935.

Judiciary (Saorstát na hÉireann, 1921) *see* Courts.

1213. JUNIUS JUNIOR : The truth about Ireland, the priests, pests and perils. 192 pp. 8vo. Guernsey, Gair, [1921].

1214. KEANE (Patrick) : Strife and victory in Canada. By Patrick Keane (Vice-President of the Canadian Ancient Order of Hibernians). In the *Voice of Ireland* (see 226). pp. 257-259.

1214a. KEARNS (Linda) : In times of peril ; leaves from the diary of Nurse Linda Kearns from Easter week, 1916, to Mountjoy, 1921. Edited by Annie M. P. Smithson. 62 pp. portr. 8vo. Dublin, Talbot Press, 1922.

1215. KELLEHER (*Rev.* J.) : The lawfulness of the hunger strike. *Irish Theol. Quarterly.* XVI. pp. 47-64, 262-264. Jan., July, 1921.

Reviews what has been written on this question in the *Irish Theological Quarterly, Irish Ecclesiastical Record, Studies, Catholic Times, Tablet, America,* etc. Considers that the conclusion has been left in doubt " with as it appears to me a decided preponderance of opinion in favour of the morality of the hunger strike."

1216. KELLY (Richard J.) *K.C.* : The recent British bank amalgamations in Ireland. Irish banks and amalgamation. *Journ. of the Statistical and Social Inquiry Society of Ireland.* Part XCVII. pp. 642-674.

A paper read on March 21st, 1919.

1217. KENSIT (J. A.): Rome behind Sinn Fein. 3rd edition. 64 pp. 8vo. illustr. London, Protestant Truth Society, 1921.

Labour movement (Irish), *see* 1193-1194 (Irish Labour Party); 1209-1211 (Irish Transport and General Workers' Union); 1024 (Bennett, L.).

See also Sect. GENERAL AND INTRODUCTORY.

1218. LABOUR PARTY [British] The : Report of the Labour Commission to Ireland. 120 pp. 8vo. illustr. London, The Labour Party. 1921.

The Commission was set up by the Labour Party in consequence of the British Government's refusal to hold an enquiry into the " reign of violence " of the British forces in Ireland. The Rt. Hon. Arthur Henderson, M.P. acted as chairman. The Commission arrived in Dublin on Nov. 30, 1920, visited some of the principal scenes of violence in Dublin, Cork and the South-West, and reported on its investigations to a special conference of the party on December 29, 1920. The report condemns the British Government's Irish policy. Statements by witnesses and copies of police documents are given in the appendices.

1218a. LABOUR PARTY INQUIRY. Parliamentary Labour Party Commission of inquiry into the present conditions in Ireland. (*Private and confidential*). 10 pp. 8vo. *n.p.* [1921 ?].

—— *See also* Clarkson (J. D.); 1157 (Good, J. W.); 1352 (Somerville, H.); 1373 (Ulster Unionist Council).

1219. LA FOLLETTE (Robert Marion): Seantor La Follette's speech on the 25th and 26th April, 1921 in support of the joint resolution in favour of recognition of the Irish Republic. Repr. from the Congressional Record in *Young Ireland* [weekly]. May 24th-September 3rd, 1921.

1220. LAWSON (*Lt.-Gen. Sir* Henry): A report on the Irish situation. 8 pp. 8vo. [London, Peace with Ireland Council, 1921].

See also DÉLÉGATION IRLANDAISE, (Paris).

1221. —— A second report on the Irish situation. 8 pp. 8vo. London, Peace with Ireland Council, [1921].

1222. LESLIE (Shane): The Irish issue in its American aspect, a contribution to the settlement of Anglo-American relations during and after the war. 208 pp. 8vo. London, Fisher Unwin, 1919.

Little (Patrick James), *see* 442 (*New Ireland*); 1291 (*Old Ireland*),

Local Government elections, 1920, *see* 1105 (Dáil Publicity Dept.); 1188 (*Irish Bulletin*); 1227 (McCormick, W.).

1223. LOGUE (Michael) *Cardinal, Archbp. of Armagh* : Cardinal Logue and the terror in Ireland. [4] pp. London, Peace with Ireland Council.

Passages from pastoral, November 28, 1920.

Long (Walter) *1st Viscount*, see 117.

1224. LYNCH (*Col.* Arthur) : Ireland and Empire, the solution. *English Rev.*, XXXI. pp. 65-71. July, 1920.

Lynd (Robert), *see* 119.

1225. LYNN (Robert John) : Ulster and Sinn Fein. *Edinburgh Rev.*, Vol. 230. pp. 279-296. Oct., 1919.

M.P. (U.), Woodvale, Belfast ; editor, *Northern Whig*.

1226. MCBRIEN (Peter) : The renascence of Ireland. *Studies*, Vol. VIII. pp. 46-58. Dublin, March, 1919.

1226a. MCCORMICK (Wright) : Irish republican arbitration courts : Their work in combating land and emigration evils. 8 pp. 8vo. [Washington], Friends of Irish Freedom, 1920. (*No.* 17).

1227. —— Irish electors again proclaim the republic : Results of Rural District Council elections demonstrate passing of British rule. Compiled by Wright McCormick, Managing Editor, News Service. 8 pp. 8vo. Washington, Friends of Irish Freedom, August, 1920. (*No.* 24).

1228. —— Ireland under English intrigue : British responsibilities for Ulster disturbances. 8 pp. 8vo. Washington, Friends of Irish Freedom, National Bureau of Information, 1920. (*No.* 25).

Mac Curtain (Tomás), *Lord Mayor of Cork*, 1920, *see* 1049 (*Catholic Bulletin*) ; 1243 (MacSwiney, M.) ; 1377 (Walsh, A.) ; 1381 (Walsh, S.).

1229. MACDONALD (*Rev. Dr.* Walter) : Some ethical questions of peace and war, with special reference to Ireland. 220 pp. 8vo. London, Burns and Oates, 1919.

Prefect of the Dunboyne Establishment, St. Patrick's College, Maynooth, 1888-1920. Defends the British administration of Ireland on moral and material grounds. Disapproves of the new national movement, criticises the Mansion House Conference (1918), and justifies the application of conscription to Ireland by the British Government.

1230. —— Some ethical questions of peace and war ; postscript in reply to certain criticisms. 32 pp. 8vo. London, Burns, Oates and Washbourne, 1920.

A reply to reviews of the author's book in the *Catholic Times, Dublin Review, Leader*, etc.

1231. —— Reminiscences of a Maynooth professor . . . edited by Denis Gwynn. 416 pp. portr. 8vo. London, Cape, 1925.

In the later pages the author writes of the 1916 rising, Sinn Féin, and the criticisms of his book, " Some ethical questions of peace and war."

1232. McDOWELL (William Wallace): Hearings before the Committee on Foreign Relations, United States Senate . . . [Statement on Ireland by Hon. W. W. McDowell, Lt.-Gov. of Montana. pp. 865-867. Aug. 30th, 1919]. Senate Documents, Vol. 10 No. 106. Washington, 1919.

1233. McGILL (Alexander): The independence of Iceland. A parallel for Ireland. 32 pp. 8vo. Glasgow, P. J. O'Callaghan, 1921.

1234. McGRATH (John): The Sinn Fein tragedy. *Fortnightly Rev.*, CXI (O.S.). pp. 771-778. May, 1919.

1235. —— United Ireland—a plea for. *Fortnightly Rev.*, CXII (O.S). pp. 467-478. Sept., 1919.

1236. McGUINNESS (Charles John): Nomad: memoirs of an Irish sailor, soldier, pearl-fisher, pirate, gun-runner, rum-runner, rebel, and Antarctic explorer . . . 290 pp. pls. 8vo. London, Methuen, 1934.
> Adventures with the Irish Republican Army—rescuing prisoners, gun-running, etc. See also " Gun-running for the I.R.A." [in 1921] by R. J. Kenny in *An Phoblacht*, March 18th, 1933.

1237. MACKEOGH (Michael): Roger Casement, Germany and the world war. Ch. XIII.—The third German plot. Catholic Bulletin, Vol. XVIII. pp. 1281-1292. Dublin, Dec., 1928.

1238. McKNIGHT (W. A.): Ireland and the Ulster legend, or the truth about Ulster. Statistical tables, compiled from parliamentary blue books and white papers, etc., by W. A. McKnight, with notes and observances by the compiler and foreword by Sophie Bryant, D.Sc., Litt. D. 96 pp. map. 8vo. London, King, 1921.
> The author's purpose is to " dispel the illusion that Ulster is superior in things moral and material to the rest of Ireland " (Preface).

1239. MACNEILL (Eoin): " The Ulster difficulty." 24 pp. 8vo. n.p. [1921 ?].
> See also 130.

1240. MACNEILL (John Gordon Swift): An Irish settlement and public opinion. *Contemporary Rev.*, CXVI. pp. 264-273. Sept., 1919.
> M.P. (Nat.) 1887-1918; Prof. of Constitutional Law, National University of Ireland.

1241. MACREADY (*General Sir* Charles F. Neville): Annals of an active life. Vol. II. pp. 337-694. illustr. 8vo. London, Hutchinson, [1924].
> The greater part of this volume is devoted to the author's experiences as Commander-in-chief of the British forces in Ireland from April, 1920 to the evacuation of the Irish Free State in December, 1922. Takes an unfavourable view of Irish political movements and of the Irish people generally. See also 415a.

1242. McSWEENEY (Edward F.): Ireland is an American question. By Edward F. McSweeney, member of the Advisory Committee of the Irish Victory Fund and National Officer Friends of Irish Freedom. 48 pp. 8vo. New York, Friends of Irish Freedom, [1919].

1243. MACSWINEY (Mary): Evidence ... presented before the American Commission on conditions in Ireland (*which see* pp. 183-264, 303-365), Washington, 1921.

Reviews the Anglo-Irish struggle to 1920. Refers to Easter week, 1916 in Cork; the murder of Tomás MacCurtain, Lord Mayor of Cork; the early life of Terence MacSwiney, his trial and hunger-strike.

1244. MACSWINEY (Muriel): Evidence ... presented before the AMERICAN COMMISSION ON CONDITIONS IN IRELAND (*which see* pp. 265-302). Washington, 1921.

An account by his widow of the life and character of Terence MacSwiney and of his last weeks in Brixton prison.

1245. MACSWINEY (Terence): A brief anthology. [8] pp. 8vo. Washington, Friends of Irish Freedom, 1920. (*No.* 29).

—— *See also* 1243, 1244 *and* 92 (*Irish Freedom*); 158 (O'Hegarty, P. S.); 371 (*Irish Volunteer*); 1051 (*Catholic Bulletin*); 1072 (Corkery, D.).

Madrid, see 1031a (*Boletin Irlandes*).

1246. MAGENNIS (*Rev.* Peter E.), *Prior-General of the Order of Calced Carmelites*: Monsignor Hagan, Rector of the Irish College, Rome. *Catholic Bulletin*, x. pp. 82-87. Feb., 1920.

1247. —— Irish America—a contrast. *Catholic Bulletin*, x. pp. 23-31. Jan., 1920.

1248. —— Woodrow Wilson: an appreciation. *Catholic Bulletin*, xi. pp. 106-115. Dublin, Feb., 1921.

With special reference to Ireland.

1249. —— An Irish priest in America [Rev. D. O'Connor]. *Catholic Bulletin*, xii. pp. 312-320.

Sidelights on the Irish cause in the U.S., 1914-1921.

1250. —— Catherine Hughes—a memory. *Catholic Bulletin*, xii. pp. 1045-1054. Oct. 1925.

Identified with Irish organisations in Canada and the U.S.

1251. —— Monsignor John Hagan. *Catholic Bulletin*, xix. pp. 296-304. June, 1929.

An obituary notice.

1253. MALONEY (William J. M. A.): The Irish issue. By William J. M. A. Maloney, M.D., Captain in the British army, August, 1914–August, 1916. 32 pp. 8vo. New York, The Donnelly Press, 1919.

Also printed in U.S. Congress records—Hearings before the Committee on Foreign Affairs, House of Representatives, Dec. 12, 1918. ("Ireland's plea for freedom") pp. 106-126 and in "America" (New York) Oct. 16–Nov. 14, 1918.

1253a. —— The recognised Irish republic. By Wm. J. M. A. Maloney, M.D. 32 pp. 8vo. New York, Statesman Press, [1920].

1253b. —— Tres puntos de vista del problema irlandes, capitulos traducidos del folleto intitulado *The Irish issue*, ... 27 pp. map. 8vo. New York. American Commission on Irish Independence, 1919.

Manchester Guardian, The, 1919-1921, see 78.

1254. MANNIX (*Most Rev. Dr.* Daniel) *Archbp. of Melbourne* : Extracts from speeches at Melbourne and San Francisco before leaving for Ireland. *Catholic Bulletin,* x. pp. 441-448. Dublin, Aug., 1920.

1255. —— Archbishop Mannix's speech, at the reception in the Cannon Street Hotel, London, September 23rd, 1920. *Catholic Bulletin,* x. pp. 670-679.

1256. —— Archbishop Mannix at Harrowgate. *Catholic Bulletin,* xi. pp. 29-38. Jan., 1921.
 A speech describing his arrest at sea on his way to Ireland.

1257. —— Archbishop Mannix's farewell address at the banquet given by the clergy resident in England, Wales and Scotland, at the Cannon Street Hotel, London, May 12, 1921. *Catholic Bulletin,* xi. pp. 343-350.

—— *See also* **1916-1918**; *and* 1017 (Australian Roman Catholic); 1071 (Condron, J. F.); 1279 (O Briain, C.); 1295 (O'Sheehan, J.); 1331 (Ronayne, *Rev.* C.).

1258. MARRIOTT (*Sir* John Arthur) : The heel of Achilles. *Nineteenth Century,* LXXXVII. pp. 1100-1110. June, 1920.

1259. —— The government of Ireland : the fourth Home Rule bill. *Fortnightly Rev.,* CXIII (O.S.). pp. 572-583. April, 1920.

1260. MARTIN (Hugh) : Ireland in insurrection, an Englishman's record, of fact. With a preface by Sir Philip Gibbs. 223 pp. 8vo. map. London, O'Connor, 1921.
 An account of the author's experiences as special correspondent of the *Daily News* in 1920.

1261. M.M. : France and Ireland. In *Young Ireland.* Dublin, July, 1919–Dec., 1921.
 A weekly letter from an Irish correspondent in Paris. Notes the progress of the Irish national cause in French public opinion. Gives summaries of articles about Ireland in the French newspapers and reviews.

1262. MOHAN (*Mrs.* Michael) : Evidence . . . presented before the AMERICAN COMMISSION ON CONDITIONS IN IRELAND (*which see,* pp. 684-698). Washington, 1921.
 Refers mainly to conditions in Cobh, May-November, 1920.

1263. MOISANT (Xavier) : Pour comprendre l'Irlande. 56 pp. 8vo. Paris, Beauchesne, 1920.

1264. —— L'ame de l'Irlande. 164 pp. 8vo. Paris, Beauchesne, 1920.

1265. —— Commission d'enquête Américaine sur la situation de l'Irelande. Premier rapport. Traduit de l'anglais par Xavier Moisant. 202 pp. 8vo. Paris, La Démocratic, [1921].
 A translation of the Commission's interim report. See 1010 (AMERICAN COMMISSION ON CONDITIONS IN IRELAND).

1266. —— : La volonté de l'Ulster. 68 pp. 8vo. Paris, ' La Démocratie,' [1922 ?].

1267. MOLES (Thomas) *M.P.* : Ulster facts and " Ulster legend." Statistical " discoveries " ! ! Amazing misstatements refuted. 16 pp. 8vo. Belfast, Ulster Unionist Council, [1921].
 A reply to " Ireland and the Ulster legend " by W. A. McKnight, (1238).

1268. MONTGOMERY (K. L.) : Ireland's psychology, a study of facts. *Fortnightly Rev.*, CXII (O.S.). pp. 572-584. Oct., 1919.

1269. MONTEAGLE (Thomas Spring Rice) *2nd Baron* : The Irish problem. *Contemporary Rev.*, CXVIII. pp. 305-314. Sept., 1920.

1270. MORGAN (Denis), *Chairman of the Urban Council of Thurles* : Evidence . . . presented before the AMERICAN COMMISSION ON CONDITIONS IN IRELAND (*which see*, pp. 6-52). Washington, 1921.

1271. MOYNE (Walter Edward GUINNESS) *1st Baron* : The vivisection of Ireland. *National Rev.*, LXXV. pp. 324-332. London, May, 1920.

An Irish Unionist criticism of the Government of Ireland Bill (1920), with special reference to partition and safeguards for Southern Unionists.

1272. MURPHY (John Archdeacon) : Treaty of Peace with Germany; Hearings before the Committee on Foreign Relations, United States Senate . . . [Statement by John Archdeacon Murphy. pp. 867-873. August 30, 1919]. Senate Documents. Vol. 10. No. 106. Washington, Government Printing Office, 1919.

Fourth member of the AMERICAN COMMISSION ON IRISH INDEPENDENCE. Reached Paris from U.S. on June 30 (after the departure of Messrs. F. P. Walsh and E. F. Dunne).

1273. NEVINSON (Henry Woodd) : The Anglo-Irish war. *Contemporary Rev.*, CXX. pp. 20-26. July, 1921.

1274. —— Last changes, last chances. [Ireland pp. 168-200]. 8vo. illustr. London, Nisbet, 1928.

Impressions of visits to Ireland in 1919-1921. Criticises Black-and-Tan methods.

1275. NORTHCLIFFE (Alfred Charles William HARMSWORTH) *1st Viscount* : Ireland and the world's peace. *Nineteenth Century*, LXXXIX. pp. 566-573. April, 1921.

Calls for a truce and a settlement on the basis of an all-Ireland Dominion. See also 1360 (H. Wickham STEED) and 1370 (The *Times*).

1276-1277. NORTHERN IRELAND, 1921 : Parliamentary Debates : Senate and House of Commons. Belfast, H.M.S.O., 1921.

See also 1317 (Queckett, *Sir* A.)

1278. NORTHUMBERLAND (Alan Ian PERCY) *8th Duke of* : International revolutionary propaganda. The situation in Ireland. No. 62 (New Series). 8 pp. 8vo. [London, Reconstruction Society, 1920].

1279. Ó BRIAIN (Cearball) : Dr. Mannix in Australia : the brief story of seven strenuous years under the southern cross. 40 pp. 8vo. Dublin, Mahon, *n.d.*

1280. O'BRIEN (William) *M.P.* : The responsibility for partition, considered with an eye to Ireland's future. 62 pp. 8vo. Dublin, Maunsel, 1921.

1281. O'CALLAGHAN (Donal), *T.D.*, *Lord Mayor of Cork* : Evidence . . . presented before the AMERICAN COMMISSION ON CONDITIONS IN IRELAND (*which see*, pp. 718-852). Washington, 1921.

An account of the situation in Ireland in 1920, with particular reference to Local government problems and the British military régime in Cork city. Details, accompanied by affidavits, of raids, burnings, shootings and other excesses stated to have been committed by the police and military.

1282. [O'CALLAGHAN (Mrs. Kate)]: The Limerick curfew murders of March 7th, 1921. The case of Michael O'Callaghan (Councillor and ex-Mayor), presented by his widow. 32 pp. 8vo. [1921]. See also *Catholic Bulletin*.

1283. Ó CEALLAIGH (Seán T.): Reminiscences of a Republican envoy abroad . . . The *Nation*. N.S. Dublin, February 15th–March 15th, 1930.

> A lecture describing the author's experiences as representative of Dáil Éireann in Paris and Rome, 1919-1921—his efforts to secure a hearing for Ireland at the Peace Conference and to arouse interest in the Irish question in France and on the Continent generally, and his audience with Pope Benedict XV. in 1920.

1284. O'CONNELL (Daniel T.): Owen Wister, advocate of racial hatred . . . By Daniel T. O'Connell, LL.D. . . . Director, Friends of Irish Freedom National Bureau of Information. 12 pp. 8vo. Washington, Friends of Irish Freedom, May, 1920. (*No.* 14).

1285. —— An answer to Rev. Walter McDonald, Dunboyne establishment, Maynooth, apologist for English rule. 12 pp. 8vo. Washington, Friends of Irish Freedom, 1920.

O'Connor (*Sir* James), see 153.

Ó Faoláin (Seán), see 154.

1286. O'FLAHERTY (Daniel C.): Treaty of Peace with Germany: Hearings before the Committee on Foreign Relations, United States Senate . . . [Statement by Daniel C. O'Flaherty. pp. 873-878. August 30, 1919]. Senate Documents. Vol. 10. No. 106. Washington, Government Printing Office, 1919.

1287. Óglác an t-, 1918-1922 [O.S.]: The official organ of the Irish Volunteers. No. 1. August 15th, 1918. 8vo. Dublin, Headquarters Staff, Ógláig na h-Éireann.

> This was the only nationalist journal in Ireland which was published continuously without censorship from 1918 to 1921. The first number announced that an t-Óglác "will enable the Headquarters Staff to keep officers and men in touch with their views on general Volunteer topics, to give authoritative directions on any points which may arise, and detailed instructions on the various branches of Volunteer work." Piarais Béaslaí acted as editor; weekly organisation notes were written by Michael Collins, training notes by J. J. O'Connell, and engineering notes by Rory O'Connor.
> The paper was printed at the Gaelic Press, Liffey street, Dublin, until the Gaelic Press was compelled to close down on account of continuous military raids and intervention. Two issues were printed by the Wood Printing works; the printing was then carried on by Mr. P. Mahon (who was afterwards sentenced by a British court-martial to two years' imprisonment). The editor was imprisoned in March, 1919; one issue was edited by Mr. Ernest Blythe, who was also arrested, and Mr. Béaslaí, having escaped from prison, edited two more issues before being rearrested.
> In 1920-1921 an t-Óglác was printed on a platen machine, worked by a treadle, in a small windowless room muffled with sacking behind a tobacconist's shop in Aungier street, Dublin. The first printer to operate this machine was Commandant Richard McKee, O.C., Dublin Brigade, Óglaigh na hÉireann. The paper was issued irregularly, about once a month, up to April, 1921, and then weekly. It had a large circulation among Volunteers in spite of the danger attached to the possession of copies. See also 10 (P. Béaslaí: Life of Michael Collins) and 1178 (Captain S. Hayes: The story of an t-Óglách).

Óglaiġ na h-Éireann. 1919-1921 [The Irish Volunteers or Irish Republican Army], *see* Sects. GENERAL AND INTRODUCTORY; **1912-1916**; **1916**; **1916-1918** (Brugha, C.; Collins, M.; de Valera, E.; Griffith, A.; Stack, A.; Irish Volunteers; etc.).

See also 1035 (Brady, E. M.); 1036 (Breen, Dan); 1079-1081 (Dáil Éireann); 1091 (Dalton, C.); 1092 (Dangerous associations); 1188 (*Irish Bulletin*); 1212 (*Irish Weekly Independent*); 1236 (McGuinness, C.); 1364-1365 (Street, C. J.); 159 (O'Hegarty, P.S.).

> The principal contemporary sources for the history of the armed forces of the Irish Government in 1919-1921 are An t-Óglác and the *Irish Bulletin*, which during 1921 published a weekly supplement "compiled from the official reports of the I.R.A. commandants in the field."

1288. O'HEGARTY (Patrick Sarsfield): Ulster: a brief statement of fact. 48 pp. 8vo. Dublin, Maunsel, 1919.

See also 157.

O'Kelly (John Joseph), *see* 160-163 and 1078 (Dáil Éireann).

1289. OLDHAM (Charles Hubert.): The public finances of Ireland. *Economic Journal*, XXX. London, March, 1920.
> Professor of National Economics in the National University of Ireland. A paper read before the Statistical and Social Inquiry Society of Ireland, January 23rd, 1920. Also printed in the Journal of the Society, Vol. XIV. pp. 15-28.

1290. —— The present "taxable capacity" of Ireland. By Professor C. H. Oldham, Vice-President. *Journal of the Statistical and Social Inquiry Society of Ireland*. Vol. XIV. 30 pp.
> A paper read on June 28th, 1921. Professor Oldham concludes (1) That the taxable capacity of Ireland to Great Britain is now relatively 1 : 31, and relatively to the United Kingdom is 1 : 32. (2) That of the £50,615,000 "contributed" to the Revenue in 1919-1920 by Ireland (the Treasury estimate), a sum equal to £18,516,000 was "over-taxation"—contrary to the Act of Union.
> See also 1115.

1291. OLD IRELAND, 1919-1922. Oct. 18th, 1919—[Jan., 1922]. Pr. by Socialist Labour Press, Glasgow for the "Old Ireland" Publishing Co., Glasgow, Oct. 19th, 1919–Jan. 1920; from Feb. 7th, 1920 pr. by Cahill for the proprietors, 13 Fleet St., Dublin, and from March 13th, 1920 by the National Labour Press, Manchester.
> Edited by P. J. Little. In continuation of 442 (*New Ireland*).

1292. O'MORDHA (Muiris): The historical case for Irish independence. 8 pp. sm. 8vo. (Capetown, Irish Republican Association of South Africa, 1921].

1293. [O'NEILL (Henry)]: The Irish case stated. 12 pp. 8vo. [Baywater. Burt, *n.d.*].
> Reprinted from *The New World* and revised by the author.

1294. O'RAHILLY (Alfred): Some theology about tyranny. *Irish Theological Quarterly*, XV. pp. 301-320. Oct., 1920.
> Professor of Mathematical Physics, University College, Cork. A discussion of the right of revolt.

1295. O'SHEEHAN (John) : Archbishop Mannix, his life and work. 32 pp. 8vo. Dublin, Emton Press, [1925].

1296. Ó SUILLEABHÁIN (Proinnseas) : Aus Irlands Leidensgeschichte. *Schweizerische Monatshefte für Politik und Kultur.* Jahrg. I. Heft 4. pp. 157-164. Juli 1921.

1297. OUTRAGES (IRELAND) : Return showing by monthly periods the outrages attributed to the Sinn Fein movement from 1st January, 1919, to 30th April, 1920. [2] pp. H.M.S.O., 1920. [Cmd. 709].

1298. ── Return showing the number of serious outrages in Ireland reported by the Royal Irish Constabulary and the Dublin Metropolitan Police for the months of May and June, 1920 . . . [2] pp. H.M.S.O., 1920. [Cmd. 859].

1299. ── Return showing the number of serious outrages . . . . during the months of July, August and September, 1920. Presented to Parliament . . . [4] pp. H.M.S.O., 1920. [Cmd. 1025].

1300. ── Return showing the number of serious outrages in Ireland reported by the Royal Irish Constabulary and Dublin Metropolitan Police during the months of October, November and December, 1920. Presented to Parliament . . . 4 pp. H.M.S.O., 1921. [Cmd. 1165].

> The figures furnished, it is stated [Cmd. 1025], do not include destruction or casualties in the " Ulster riots " or in military or police reprisals. Among the occurrences classified as " outrages " are the casualties and injuries to property resulting from engagements between *Óglaigh na hÉireann* and the British forces, in connection with the defensive campaign of the Irish Government.
> For a commentary with an analysis of these figures see the *Irish Bulletin*, February 2nd, 1920, according to which the " outrage " returns are " political manifestoes against the Castle opponents," the lists having been constructed by a process of taking the ordinary criminal offences for the period and attributing them without justification to Sinn Féin : " They are based upon a system of expansion and contraction, varying according to the pressure of the political barometer . . . for instance, preparatory to coercive measures a list of crimes reaching to large dimensions is forthcoming. This is effected . . . by classifying under several distinct headings what is in reality one offence." See also *Irish Bulletin*, April 4th, 1920.

1300a. PAKENHAM (*Hon.* Francis) : Peace by ordeal, an account from first-hand sources, of the negotiation and signature of the Anglo-Irish Treaty, 1921. By Frank Pakenham. 400 pp. 8vo. London, Cape, 1935.

> The author has had access " to a large mass of documents never before published or made the basis of published work. They include copies of correspondence that passed between President de Valera and Arthur Griffith, Chairman of the Irish Delegation, during the Treaty negotiations of October to December, 1921. Also copies of the official Irish records of all the Downing Street Plenary Sessions, and a great deal of other matter indicative of the proposals put forward by both sides and of the discussions concerning them . . . I have had interviews with nearly all of the principal living actors of this period in some detail with Sir Austen Chamberlain " (Preface).

See also 1132 (Fitzgerald, D.).

Paris (*the Irish cause in*), 1919-1921, see 1007 (American Commission) : 1096-1099a (Délégation Irlandaise) ; 1118 (Duffy, G. Gavan) ; 1187 (Ireland's declaration) ; 1261 (M. M.) ; 1283 (Ó Ceallaigh, S. T.).

1301. PARRY (M. Sidney) : The avenue to peace in 1921. Ireland's claim to independence ; how England met this claim in 1782. 24 pp. 8vo. London, Burt and sons, *pr.* [1921 ?].

1302. PAUL-DUBOIS (Louis) : Le drame Irlandaise. II : Le Sinn Fein et la guerre Irlandaise (1918-1921). *Revue des deux mondes* . . . 6^e periode. Tome LXV. pp. 584-619. 1er Oct. 1921.

See also 468.

Peace Conference (Paris), 1919-1920, see Paris.

1303. PEACE WITH IRELAND COUNCIL, 1920-1921 : *Leaflets* : The Sinn Fein fellowship (*Mrs.* F. Acland,) ; What are reprisals ? (G. K. Chesterton,) ; The delusion of the double policy (G. K. Chesterton,) ; Irish reprisals : Auxiliary division's record (*Sir* J. Simon,) ; The state of South Ireland, a Unionist M.P.'s tour (A. Baldwin Raper,) ; Cardinal Logue and the terror in Ireland ; Peace or ——— ? (A. Clutton-Brock,) ; The situation in Ireland (*Archbp. of* Canterbury,) ; The Auxiliary Police (R. C. Grey,) ; The right to shoot (*Hansard*, 1920) ; Stop the terror (A. G. Gardiner,) ; Some moderate and non-party views on affairs in Ireland, 1921 ; Peace with Ireland Council, appeal for funds.

A leaflet circulated in 1920-1921 explains that the Peace with Ireland Council " has been founded on non-party lines with the following objects :

1.—To acquire and disseminate accurate information on Ireland.
2.—To appeal to public opinion to vindicate the fundamental British principles of Law and Liberty.
3.—To protest against the lawless policy of reprisals countenanced by the Government.
4.—To assist in providing relief in cases of distress from whatever cause in Ireland.

The Chairman was Lord Henry Bentinck and the Honorary Secretary Mr. Oswald Moseley. The other members of the Council included Mr. Ramsay Macdonald, Sir John Simon and several English bishops, clergymen, military officers, university professors and men of letters. On March 16, 1921 the Council demanded the immediate withdrawal from Ireland of the " Black-and-Tans " and Auxiliaries, a truce and an Anglo-Irish conference.

Peace negotiations (Anglo-Irish), 1920-1921, see Sect. GENERAL AND INTRODUCTORY (Birkenhead, 1*st Earl of* ; Collins, M. ; de Valera, E. ; Griffith, A. ; Healy, T. M.).

See also 1061-1062 (Churchill, W.) ; 1079-81, 1084 (Dáil Eireann) ; 1149 (George, D. Lloyd) ; 1186 (*Irish Bulletin*) ; 1277-1278 (Northern Ireland) ; 1300a (Pakenham, F.).

The *Irish Bulletin* in several numbers during 1921 gave the history of the peace negotiations in chronological form.

1304. PERISCOPE : The last days of Dublin Castle. *Blackwood's Mag.,* pp. 137-190. Aug., 1922.
   Anti-Sinn Féin. A well-informed record of the British administration of Ireland, 1919-1921. Character studies of the chief personages in the " Castle " government, including Earl French of Ypres (" Power had gone from his hands, and he was kept in ignorance of most things that were happening "), Sir Hamar Greenwood, Sir John Taylor, Sir John Anderson (" No civil servant has ever wielded . . . such power as he did during his twenty-one months' tenure of office as Under-Secretary "), Sir A. W. Cope (" His career in Ireland was a long struggle against militarism, ") Sir Henry Wynne (Chief Crown Solicitor), Rt. Hon. James McMahon, Maj.-Gen. Sir H. Tudor etc.

Phillips (Walter Alison), *see* 173.

1305. PIM (Frederick W.) : Home Rule through federal devolution. With an introduction by Frederick Harrison. 30 pp. 8vo. London, T. Fisher Unwin, 1919.

1306. PIM (Herbert Moore) : Sinn Fein : past, present and future. *Nineteenth Century,* LXXXV. pp. 1165-1174. June, 1919.
   Describes his part in the organisation of Sinn Féin and his reasons for leaving it.

1307. —— Unconquerable Ulster . . . With foreword by Sir Edward Carson. 98 pp. 8vo. Belfast, Carswell, 1919.

1308. PLUNKETT (*Sir* Horace) : Dominion self-government. A copy of a letter to " The Times " published on April 15th, 1919. 8 pp. 8vo. Dublin, [Roberts, 1919].

1309. —— The Irish Peace Conference and after. Memorandum to the members of the Irish Dominion League, by the President. 8 pp. 8vo. [Dublin, Irish Dominion League, September 15th, 1920].

1310. —— Speech of Sir Horace Plunkett on the Irish situation in America, at Westminster and in Ireland, delivered at a public banquet given in his honour in the Aberdeen Hall, Dublin, Thursday, March 4, 1920. 8 pp. Supplement to the *Irish Statesman,* May 8th, 1920.

1311. —— Irish chaos, the British cause and the Irish cure, being a letter published in " The Times " of June 2nd, 1920. 8 pp. 8vo. Dublin, The Irish Dominion League, 1920.

1312. —— England's Irish policy during and after the war . . . Being two letters published in " The Times " of November 8 and 17, 1920. 12 pp. 8vo. Dublin, Irish Dominion Laegue, 1920.

Pollard (*Major* H. B. C.), *see* 176.

1313. POPE-HENNESSY (*Col.* Ladislaus Herbert Richard) : The Irish Dominion. A method of approach to a settlement. 32 pp. 8vo. London, Nisbet, [1919].
   With the manifesto of the Irish Dominion League.

1314. " PRO TANTO QUID " : A Christmas day in an English prison in Ireland. *Red Hand Mag.,* I. pp. 19-26. Glasgow, Dec., 1920.

1315. QUARTERLY Review, The : Ireland and federalism. Vol. 231. pp. 445-470. April, 1919.

1316. —— Ireland. Vol. 237. pp. 155-171. July, 1921.

1317-1318. QUEKETT (Sir Arthur S.) : The constitution of Northern Ireland By Sir Arthur S. Quekett, LL.D., . . . Parliamentary draftsman to the Government of Northern Ireland. In two parts. Part 1 : The origin and devilopment of the constitution. 90 pp. Part II : The Government of Ireland Act, 1920, and subsequent enactments. 660 pp. 8vo. Belfast, H.M.S.O., 1928-1933.

1319. QUIRK (James) : Evidence . . . presented before the AMERICAN COMMISSION ON CONDITIONS IN IRELAND, (which see, pp. 852-869). Washington, 1921.
> An account of conditions in Co. Galway in Aug. 1920, and of the shootings in Croke Park, Dublin, Nov. 1920.

1321. RASHAD (Ibrahim) : An Egyptian in Ireland. Preface by Susan L. Mitchell. 318 pp. map. London, privately printed for the author, [1920 ?].
> Description of a tour of Ireland with special reference to the co-operative movement. Shows sympathy with the spirit and aims of Sinn Fein.

1322. RED HAND MAGAZINE, The, 1920. Edited and published by W. Forbes Patterson at Belfast and Glasgow. Sept.-Dec., 1920.
> Irish republican. Four numbers published.

1323. REGAN (John X.) : Ireland and the Presidents of the United States. 16 pp. 8vo. Boston, Advisory Committee. Irish Victory Fund, 1919. (Irish Independence series, No. 1).

Relief of distress, 1920-1921, see 1013 (American Committee) ; 1391 (Williams, W. J. M.) ; and *Irish Bulletin* (Nov. 14, 1921).

1324. RESTORATION OF ORDER IN IRELAND ACT, 1920. An Act to make provision for the restoration and maintenance of order in Ireland. [9th August, 1920]. Ch. 31. 10 & 11 Geo. 5. 4 pp. H.M.S.O., 1920.

1325. —— Orders in Council making amending regulations under the Restoration of Order in Ireland Act, 1920. *Statutory rules and orders* . . . *issued in the year* 1920. pp. 1008-1027. H.M.S.O., 1921.

1326. —— Orders in Council making amending regulations under the Restoration of Order in Ireland Act, 1920. Statutory rules and orders . . . issued in the year 1921. pp. 430-439. H.M.S.O., 1922.
> Provide that the Defence of the Realm regulations in force in Ireland on August 13th, 1920, subject to specified modifications, " shall apply for the purpose of the restoration and maintenance of order in like manner as they apply for the defence of the Realm." The Orders in Council purport to give legal sanction to the British military régime in Ireland. They facilitate the process of making arrests, and provide for the constitution of courts of summary jurisdiction, the procedure at courts-martial, the prohibition of unlawful associations, the abolition of coroners' inquests, the suspension of grants payable to local authorities, etc., and empower the military authorities to regulate, require, restrict or prohibit transport by road or rail.
> For the Irish view of these measures, see the *Irish Bulletin*, Vol. 2. No. 78. Aug. 23rd, 1920.

1327. REVUE DE PARIS. La question Irlandaise. [33] pp. 8vo. Extract from " Revue de Paris," 23 Juillet, 1919.

1328. ROBINSON (*Mrs.* Arnott Erskine): Evidence . . . presented before the AMERICAN COMMISSION ON CONDITIONS IN IRELAND (*which see,* pp. 530-578).
> One of a committee sent to Ireland by the British section, Women's International League n Oct., 1920. Deals largely with social and economic conditions in Belfast.

Robinson (*Sir* Henry), see 195.

1329. ROLLESTON (T. W.): Ireland's vanishing opportunity. 19 pp. 8vo. Dublin, Talbot Press, 1919.

1330. —— The Irish malady. *Nineteenth Century,* Aug., 1920.

Rome, see 1172 (Hagan, Rev. J.); 1283 (Ó Ceallaigh, S. T.).

1331. RONAYNE (*Rev.* Charles F.), *O.C.C.* : The Archbishop of Melbourne. *Catholic Bulletin,* XI. pp. 148-154. March, 1920.

Royal Irish Constabulary [R.I.C.] 1919-1921, see Sect. GENERAL AND INTRODUCTORY ; and 1040 (D. J. Broderick) ; 1042 (J. J. Cadden) ; 1075 (D. F. Crowley) ; 1075-1077 (*Brig-Gen.* F. P. Crozier); 1117 (D. V. Duff) ; 1304 (Periscope) ; 1241 (Macready, *Gen. Sir* C. F. N.) ; 1303 (Peace with Ireland Council).

1332. RUSSELL (Ruth): What's the matter with Ireland ? 160 pp. 8vo. New York, Devin-Adair Co., [1920].
> With a prefatory letter to the author from President de Valera, January 29th, 1920.

1333. —— Evidence . . . presented before the AMERICAN COMMISSION ON CONDITIONS IN IRELAND (*which see* pp. 428-462).
> Visited Ireland in March-June, 1919, as representative of the *Chicago Daily News.* Refers mainly to Irish social and economic conditions as affected by English rule.

1334. RUSSELL (George W.): A plea for justice : being a demand for a public inquiry into the attacks on Co-operative Societies in Ireland. By Geo. W. Russell, " Æ." 24 pp. 8vo. Dublin, The Irish Homestead, 1920.
> A report, furnished to the Irish Agricultural Organisation Society, of co-operative creameries and agricultural societies " stated to have been destroyed or damaged by armed forces of the crown."

1335. —— Thoughts for British Co-operators : being a further demand for a public enquiry into the attacks on Co-operative Societies in Ireland. By Geo. W. Russell, "Æ." 36 pp. 8vo. Dublin, The Irish Homestead, 1921.
> A report of the co-operative creameries and agricultural societies " stated to have been destroyed or damaged by armed forces of the crown " to April, 1921.

1336. —— The economics of Ireland and the policy of the British Government. With an introduction by Francis Hackett. 32 pp. 8vo. New York, Huebsch, 1921.

1337. [——] The inner and outer Ireland. By A.E. Reprinted . . . from *Pearson's Magazine*, U.S.A. 16 pp. 8vo. Dublin, Talbot Press, 1921.

1337a. [——] Another edition. 28 pp. 8vo. London, Fisher Unwin, 1921.

1338. [——] Ireland and the Empire at the court of conscience. By A.E. 16 pp. 8vo. Dublin, Talbot Press, 1921.
> Repr. from the *Manchester Guardian*, September 22nd, 1921.

Ryan (Desmond), see 199.

1339. RYAN (*Rev.* John A.) : The principle of non-intervention in relation to Ireland. Studies, xx. pp. 205-217. Dublin, June, 1921.
> Maintains that the United States has not only a right but a moral obligation to intervene in the Anglo-Irish struggle and advocates " formal recognition of the Republic of Ireland by the Government of the United States."

1340. RYAN (Michael J.) : Treaty of Peace with Germany : Hearings before the Committee on Foreign Relations, United States Senate . . . [Statement of Mr. Michael J. Ryan. pp. 854-860. August 30, 1919]. Senate Documents. Vol. 10. No. 106. Washington, Government Printing Office, 1919.

1341. SAORSTAT NA hÉIREANN, 1921 : Judiciary. Rules and forms. Parish and District Courts. 40 pp. 8vo. Dublin, ᴀɪʀeᴀċc ṡnotᴀí ᴅúɪcċe. (Department of Home Affairs), 1921.
> Contains " the Provisional Constitution of the courts of justice of the Irish Provisional Constitution," setting forth the jurisdiction of the Supreme Court, District Courts and Parish Courts, the Legal Code, Rules of Court, forms, etc. " The law, as recognised on the 21st January, 1919, shall, until amended, continue to be enforced, except such portion thereof as was clearly motived by religious or political animosity " (Legal Code).

1342. SERENA : Letters to an Englishwoman on Sinn Féin and coercion. *Irish Statesman*. March 13th–April 3rd, 1920.

Sexton (Joseph), see 549 (*An Phoblacht*).
> An account of the movement in support of the Irish republic in U.S.A., 1919-1921. Takes an unfavourable view of the Clan-na-Gael (Devoy-Cohalan) group in the controversy which began in 1920.

1343. SHERWOOD (Isaac R.) : An appeal for free Ireland. Speech of Hon. Isaac R. Sherwood of Ohio in the House of Representatives, Monday, January 5, 1920. 8 pp. 8vo. Washington, [Government Printing Office], 1920.

1344. SIMON (*Sir* John) : Frightfulness in Ireland, an analysis of Government admissions. 8 pp. 8vo. London, Liberal Publication Department, 1921.
> Repr. from " The Times " of April 25, 1921.

1345. SINN FEIN, 1919 : Annual Ard Fheis, 16th October, 1919 : Instructions to Secretaries of Cumainn. 4 pp. [Dublin, 1919].

1346. Sinn Féin, [1919 ?] : The case of Ireland. 8 pp. 8vo. Dublin, Sinn Féin series. No. 12.
   With coloured map showing the results of the General Election of 1918.

1347. ——, 1920 : Instructions to Sinn Féin Cumainn, regarding programme of work, 1920-1921. [4] pp. 8vo.

1348. ——, 1921 : Clár. An 13adh Árd-Fheis, a bheidh ar siúl sa Seomra Cruinn i dTig an Árd Mhéire, Áth Cliath, Diardaoin, an 27adh Deire Foghmhair, 1921. 18 pp. 8vo. Áth Cliath, an Árd-Fheis.

—— 1919-1921, *see* Sects. GENERAL AND INTRODUCTORY ; **1912-1916** ; 1916-1918 ; *and* in Sect. **1919-1921** Dáil Éireann.
   See the *Irish Bulletin*, Vol. 6, No. 11, 3rd November, 1921 : " The Sinn Féin organisation : its relationship to Dáil Éireann."

1349. SINN FEIN AND THE PEACE CONFERENCE : promises and performances. 8 pp. 8vo. *n.p.* [1919 ?].
   Hostile to Sinn Féin.

1349a. SINN FEINER, The, 1920-1921. Bi-weekly. June 19, 1920–[Oct. 29, 1921 ?]. New York, Sinn Fein Publishing Co.
   Edited by Patrick Walsh. Jeremiah J. O'Leary was among the associate-editors. Opposed to Clan-na-Gael group.

1350. SMITH (Thomas F.) : American recognition of Irish independence. Speech of Hon. Thomas F. Smith of New York in the House of Representatives, June 1, 1920. 8 pp. 8vo. Washington, [Government Printing Office], 1920.

1351. SMITH-GORDON (Lionel) : The place of banking in the national programme. 14 pp. 8vo. Dublin, Cumann Leigeactaí phobail, 1921 (Series A.—Economics. No. 3).

1352. SOMERVILLE (Henry) : The political impotence of British Labour. *Studies*, x. pp. 1-18. Dublin, Jan., 1921.
   Comments on the failure of the British Labour party to follow up the REPORT of its Commission of Inquiry in Ireland, (1218) and concludes that the party is " a negligible factor in British politics."

1353. SOUTHERN LOYALIST : In Ireland to-day. *Blackwood's Mag.*, CCVI. pp. 814-827. Dec., 1919.

1354. Spálpín : Sinn Fein and the Labour movement. 24 pp. Dublin, *pr.* Mahon, *n.d.*

1355. SPEDDING (Rosamond F.) : The Call of Democracy : a study of the Irish question. 24 pp. 8vo. Dublin, Maunsel, 1919.

1356. SPENDER (Harold) : Ireland : a plea for conciliation. *Contemporary Rev.*, CXIX. pp. 299-309. March, 1921.

1357. —— Ireland under the truce, the story of a tour. *Contemporary Rev.*, CXX. pp. 585-592. Nov., 1921.

1358. SPLAIN (John J.) : Under which king ? . . . By John J. Splain, of New Haven, Conn., National Vice-President of the Friends of Irish Freedom. in the *Voice of Ireland (which see).* pp. 242-254. Manchester, 1924 (*see* 226).

> A criticism of President de Valera and the other Irish envoys who supported him in the dispute with Clan-na-Gael and the Friends of Irish Freedom (1920).

Stack (Austin), *see* 213.

1359. STAMP (*Sir* Josiah Charles) : The taxable capacity of Ireland. *Economic Journal,* XXXI. pp. 335-348. Sept., 1921.

1359a. STATESMAN PRESS, The : The re-conquest of America : full text of the most astounding document ever discovered in the history of international intrigue . . . Has this nation been betrayed and, Who's Who among the betrayers ? . . . 32 pp. 8vo. New York, Statesman Press, [1919 ?].

1360. STEED (Henry Wickham) : Through thirty years, 1892-1922 : a personal narrative. Vol. II. 8 + 418 pp. 8vo. [Ch. XIX. The power of " The Times " (1919-1922)]. London, H. inemann, 1924.

> Editor of the *Times,* 1919-1922. Explains the attitude of Lord Northcliffe towards an Irish settlement.

1361. STRAHAN (James Andrew) : Opposites. *Blackwood's Mag.,* CCVII. pp. 826-833. June, 1920.

> A criticism of the Irish people, with special reference to James Larkin and James Connolly.

1362. —— The recent events in Ulster. *Blackwood's Mag.,* CCVIII. pp. 354-361. Sept., 1920.

1363. —— The isle of saints. *Blackwood's Mag.,* CCVIII. pp. 823-831. Dec., 1920.

> Prof. of Jurisprudence at Queen's University, Belfast. Writes from an intensely Unionist point of view.

1364. [STREET (*Major* Cecil John C.)] : The administration of Ireland, 1920. By " I.O." [*ps.,* i.e., Major C. J. Street]. 468 pp. 8vo. London, Allan, 1921.

> Published in April, 1921. Seeks to explain and justify the Irish policy of the British Government at that time. The author quotes freely from unpublished police and military reports and from documents alleged to have been captured from Dáil Éireann and Irish political organisations. The police reports apparently belong to the class of documents said to have been destroyed in Dublin Castle by the British authorities in January, 1922 (See 173). They give statistics of the membership of Sinn Féin clubs and attempt to guage political feeling in the different counties and the degree of support accorded to Dáil Éireann.

1365. —— Ireland in 1921. 320 pp. 8vo. London, Allan, 1922.

> An account of the hostilities and the negotiations leading to the Truce and the Treaty. The documents printed include extracts from correspondence alleged to have been captured in raids on Dáil Éireann offices, Mr. Lloyd George's long letter on Irish policy to the Bishop of Chelmsford, dated April 19th, 1921, in which he expounds the British Government's Irish policy at the time, and a detailed statement setting forth, in a spirit hostile to Sinn Féin, the situation throughout the country during the truce (Sept., 1921).

Sullivan (A. M.), *K.C.*, see 215.

1366. SYKES (Edith) : Ireland, a contrast. *Dublin Rev.* Vol. 168. pp. 209-218. London, June, 1921.

Impressions of Ireland in 1903 and 1921 contrasted.

1367. 'TALES OF THE R.I.C.', Author of : Ulster in 1921. *Blackwood's Mag.*, CCXII. pp. 425-451. Oct., 1922.

1368. TANGNEY (John) : Evidence . . . presented before the AMERICAN COMMISSION ON CONDITIONS IN IRELAND (*which see*, pp. 390-402). Washington, 1921.

Experiences in the R.I.C., 1915-1920.

1369. TÉRY (Simone) : En Irlande, de la guerre d'indépendance à la guerre civile (1914-1923). 284 pp. Paris, Flammarion, [1923].

Thomson (*Sir* Basil), *see* 735 and 1006.

1370. TIMES, The : Irish peace, a test of British statesmanship : a series of special articles, together with four leading articles, reprinted from " The Times." 34 pp. 8vo. [London, " The Times, 1919].

June-July, 1918.

1370a. —— Irish number. London, November 4, 1919.

Articles, written by leading authorities, on various phases of Irish life : the Churches ; Ireland in the War ; History and Sociology ; Education ; Touring ; Land Purchase ; Agricultural development ; Agriculture and Industry ; Manufactures ; Communications ; Literature and Art ; Sport.

See also 1276 (Northcliffe, *Viscount*) ; 1360 (Steed, H. W.).

1371. TOKSVIG (Signe) [Mrs. Francis Hackett] : Evidence . . . presented before the AMERICAN COMMISSION ON CONDITIONS IN IRELAND (*which see*, pp. 174-181). Washington, 1921.

Visited Ireland in July-Sept., 1920.

(Truce July, 1921), *see* 1053 Cessation of hostilities.

Treaty (December, 1921), *see* Ireland and Great Britain.

1372. [TRUE IRISHMAN, A] : Pampered Ireland, fact, not fiction. 8 pp. 8vo. Belfast, T. H. Jordan, [1919].

1373. ULSTER UNIONIST COUNCIL : Labour party and Ireland. The deputation's report. Analysis and criticism. Belfast, Ulster Unionist Council, [1921 ?]. (U.C. 127).

See LABOUR PARTY (British).

1373a. ULSTER UNIONIST COUNCIL LEAFLETS, 1919-1921 : The position of Ulster (J. A. Strahan), 1919 ; Belfast cathedral, special service, 28th Sept., 1919 ; The Ulster situation, answers to mis-statements ; Dominion Home Rule, what it really means [1921 ?] ; Ulster and Ireland, some useful facts [1921 ?] ; What American Protestants say [1921 ?].

Ulster, 1919-1921, see Sect. GENERAL AND INTRODUCTORY ; and 1367 (Blackwood's Mag.) ; 1046 (Carson, Baron) ; 1225 (Lynn, R. J.) ; 1238 (McKnight, W. A.) ; 1239 (MacNeill, E.) ; 1260 (Moisant, X.) ; 1267 (Moles, T.) ; 1280 (O'Brien, W.) ; 1288 (O'Hegarty, P. S.) ; 1307 (Pim, H. M.) ; 1317-1318 (Quekett, *Sir* A.) ; 1328 (Robinson, E. A.) ; 1362 (Strahan, J. A.) ; *and* NORTHERN IRELAND.

1374. UNITED IRISH LEAGUE : Parliamentary and Local Government registration in Ireland. Claims and objections. 16 pp. 8vo. Dublin, United Irish League, 1919.

1375. UNITED STATES OF AMERICA : CONGRESS : Hearings before the Committee on Foreign Relations, United States Senate . . . on the Treaty of Peace with Germany, signed at Versailles on June 28, 1919 and submitted to the Senate on July 10, 1919 by the President of the United States. Senate Documents. Vol. 10. No. 106. 66th Congress. 1st Session. Washington, Government Printing Office, 1919.

   Statements heard or submitted in writing from American citizens, (August 30, 1919) on behalf of the Irish in America in support of Ireland's claim to national independence. The documents filed and printed include numerous memorials from Irish organisations in the United States ; as memorial against the League of Nations ; the Declaration of independence by Dáil Éireann (1919) ; Correspondence between the American Commission on Irish independence and the American Peace Commission in Paris, and a brief from other American citizens protesting against the statements put forward in support of the Irish cause.

1376. —— The struggle of the Irish people : Address to the Congress of the United States, adopted at the January session of Dail Eireann, 1921. Presented by Mr. Borah, May 2, 1921— Referred to the Committee on Foreign Relations and ordered to be printed. Senate Document. Vol. 9. No. 8. 67th Congress. 1st session. 32 pp. 8vo. Washington, Government Printing Office, 1921.

—— *See also* 876 (McCartan, P.) ; 994 (Irish question hearings, Dec., 1918) ; 1007-1009 (American Commission . . .) ; 1064 (Cockran, W. Burke) ; 1064-1065 (Cohalan, *Justice* D. F.) ; 1114 (Downing, R.) ; 1219 (La Follette, *Senator* R. M.) ; 1343 (Sherwood, I. R.) ; 1350 (Smith, T. F.) ; *and* Joseph Sexton (In *An Phoblacht*, Feb. 25th, 1933).

1377. WALSH (Anna) : Evidence . . . presented before the AMERICAN COMMISSION ON CONDITIONS IN IRELAND (*which see*, pp. 653-664).

   Sister-in-law of Tomás MacCurtain, Lord Mayor of Cork. Gives an account of his murder.

1378. WALSH (Frank P.): Treaty of Peace with Germany: Hearings before the Committee on Foreign Relations, United States Senate . . . [Statement of Hon. Frank P. Walsh. pp. 794-854. August 30, 1919]. Senate Documents. Vol. 10. No. 106. Washington, Government Printing Office, 1919.

> With ex-President Taft, acted as Joint Chairman, U.S. War Labor Board. Chairman of the American mission (to the Peace Conference) on Irish independence. An account of his journey to France and Ireland, with "Correspondence in the case of Ireland's claim for independence between the American Commission on Irish independence, the American Commission to negotiate peace, and representatives of other governments," and an account of an interview between President Wilson and Messrs. Edward F. Dunne and Frank P. Walsh at the President's house in Paris, June 11, 1919.

1379. WALSH (J. C.): Ireland at the peace conference. *Studies*, VII. pp. 177-188. Dublin, June 1919.

> Correspondent of "America". A well-informed study of the Irish cause in the United States, 1916-1919, and of the Irish efforts to secure representation at the Peace Conference. See Dr. P. McCartan: "With de Valera in America."

1380. —— The invincible Irish. 202 pp. 8vo. New York, Devin-Adair Co., [1919].

> Comments on the Irish case at the Peace Conference and the attitude of President Wilson. The author came to Ireland from Paris and visited various districts in the early months of 1919. Pleads for American support of Ireland. Appendix: Ireland's right to freedom, a speech delivered in New York, March 17, 1919 by Martin Conboy.

1380a. WALSH (Louis J.): "On my keeping" and in theirs: a record of experiences "on the run," in Derry gaol and in Ballykinlar interment camp. Foreword by Mrs. Cecil Chesterton. 16+112 pp. 8vo. Dublin, Talbot Press, 1921.

1381. WALSH (Susanna): Evidence . . . presented before the American Commission on conditions in Ireland (*which see*, pp. 627-653).

> Sister-in-law of Tomás MacCurtain. Family history, 1916-1920, and account of his murder.

1382. WARD (*Lt.-Col.* John): The army and Ireland. *Nineteenth Century*, LXXXIX. pp. 1-7. Jan., 1921.

Warren (Raoul De), *see* 229.

1383. WATERS (*Very Rev.* John *Canon*): The morality of the hunger-strike, a rejoinder. *Irish Ecclesiastical Record*. XIII (5th Series). pp. 14-26. Jan., 1919.

> In reply to Rev. Dr. P. Cleary (1063).

1384. —— The morality of the hunger-strike, a further rejoinder. *Irish Eccles. Record*, XIII (5th Series). pp. 391-410. May, 1919.

1384a. —— The lawfulness of the hunger-strike. *Irish Theol. Quarterly*, XVI. pp. 130-146. April, 1921.

> A reply to Rev. J. Kelleher (1215.)

1385. WATSON (*Sir* William): Ireland arisen. 24 pp. 8vo. London, Richards, 1921.

1385a. WEEKLY SUMMARY, The, 1920-1921 : [Dublin Castle Press Bureau]. Aug. 13, 1920- July 1, 1921].

A weekly journal defending the British military régime, circulated mainly among the police. For the official account of its purpose and direction, see Brit. Parl. Debates, 24th November, 1920 and 19th March, 1921 (Sir Hamar Greenwood). For criticism, see the *Irish Bulletin*. See also a letter from Sir Basil Clarke (editor of the *Weekly Summary*) in the *People* (Wexford), January 27, 1934.

1386. WHITE (Albert C.) : Ireland : a study in facts. (1920 series, IV). 28 pp. 8vo. London, Hodder and Stoughton, [1920].

1387. —— The Irish Free State : its evolution and possibilities. By Albert C. White, late editor *Lloyd George Liberal Magazine*, with a preface by Sir Alfred W. Cope, K.C.B. 160 pp. 8vo. London, Hutchinson, [1923].

Comments on the events leading to the Anglo-Irish Treaty.

1388. WHITE (James Robert) : The significance of Sinn Fein—psychological, political and economic. 30 pp. 8vo. Dublin, Martin Lester, 1919.

Written immediately after the General Election of Dec., 1918.

1389. WILKINS (*Alderman* W. G.) : A history of Ireland and its people . . . with an introduction by Mr. A. G. Gardiner and a full report of the deputation sent by the society of friends upon the state of Ireland. 92 pp. 8vo. London, " The Daily News," [1920].

1390. WILKINSON (Ellen C.) : Evidence . . . presented before the American Commission on conditions in Ireland (*which see*, pp. 578-620). Washington, 1921.

1391. WILLIAMS (William J.) : Report of the Irish White Cross to 31st August, 1922 . . . prepared by W. J. Williams, M.A., for the Managing Committee of the Irish White Cross. 142 pp. 8vo. illustr. Dublin, Lester, [1923].

" The Irish White Cross Society was organised to cope with the distress and destitution resulting in Ireland from the war caused by the determination of the Irish people to assert their right to nationhood . . . Towards the end of 1920 a body of men and women came together, on the invitation of and under the chairmanship of the Lord Mayor of Dublin, to see how far it was possible to alleviate the great amount of suffering that, even at that date, had resulted from the Irish conflict." Up to August 31st, 1922 the Society had received £1,374,795 in subscriptions— almost entirely from the United States.
See also IRISH RELIEF.

1392. WOMAN OF NO IMPORTANCE, A : As others see us. 320 pp. 8vo. illustr. London, Jenkins, 1924.

Appreciations of British soldiers, politicians and others, including Sir Hamar Greenwood and Major-General Sir H. Tudor.

1393. WOMEN'S INTERNATIONAL LEAGUE : A " sort of war " in Ireland. Report of mission to Ireland by the Women's International League, October, 1920. 8 pp. 8vo. [London, Women's International League, 1920]. (Index No. 31).

INDEX

The numbers refer to the numbered entries. When the reference is to the page it is given in brackets.

Aberdeen, Marquess and Marchioness of, 1
Ackermann, C. W., 1006
Acland, Mrs. F., 1303
Addison, Dr. C., 749
"Address presented to Congress" (1917), 850
"Address to representatives of foreign nations" (1921), 1083
"Address to the Congress of the U.S." (1921), 1375
"Administration of Ireland, The" (1920-21). *See* Street, C. J. S.
A.E. See Russell, G. W.
"Against Home Rule," 264
Agriculture. See Department of . . . See also Co-operative movement, Land settlement and 875, 962, 1370a
Aireacht na Trachtála, 1088
All for Ireland League, (p. 1)
Alpheo, 751
American Association for Recognition of the Irish Republic (1921), 876, 1114a
American Commission on conditions in Ireland (1920-21), (p. xxvi), 876, 1010-12, 1265
American Commission on Irish independence (1919), 1007-09, 1379-80.
"American recognition of Irish independence," 1350
"America's appeal to Ireland" (1775), 850
Amery, L. S., 254, 752
Ancient Order of Hibernians, (p. 1), 549
Anderson, Sir John, 1304
Anderson, R. A., (1a)
Andrews, W. D., 538
"Anniversary of the General Election, The," 1014
"Annual Register, The," 2
Aodh Ruadh, 753
"Appeal for an Irish republic" (*Boston Herald*), 764a
"Appeal to the people" (U.I.L.), 991
Appointed days under the Govt. of Ireland Act (1920), 1161
"Argument from Irish history, The," 794
Armour, Rev. J. B., 3-3a
Armour, W. S., 3a
Army: Memo on the Official Press Bureau, 503a
Army (British). See also (p. 1), 557
Arran, Earl of, 1015
Arrangements governing the cessation of active operations (1921), 1053
Arthur, Sir George, 585
Articles of agreement for a Treaty . . . (1921). See Great Britain, Ireland, Irish settlement

Ashbourne (fighting at, 1916), 635c, 644, 655
Ashe, J. S., 754
Ashe, Thomas, 755-56, 918
Asquith, Cyril, 557
Asquith, H. H. See Oxford and Asquith, Earl of
Aston, E. A., 4, 1016
Atherley-Jones, L., 757
Aud, The (Arms ship, 1916), 693a, 719, 735
Auditor Tantum, 235, 758
Auspicium melioris aevi, 236
Australasian Irish Race Convention (1919), (p. 119)
Australia: Parliamentary debates, 5
Australian Roman Catholic, An, 1017
"Authority of Dáil Éireann," 1082
Auxiliary Division, Royal Irish Constabulary. See R.I.C.

Baeza, R., 1018
Bagenal, P. H., 1019
Bagwell, R., 237
Balbriggan (burning of), 1023
Balfour, A. J., 9a, 238, 518
Balfour, G., 239
Ballykinlar internment camp, 1022, 1050, 1380a
Banking (Irish), 43a, 46, 842, 874, 1216, 1351
Barker, E., 6-7
Barr Buadh, An (1912), 8
Barry, K., 1023
Barton, Sir D. Plunkett, 9
Bates, J. V., 9a, 759
Battine, C., 760
Battersby, T. S. F., 240
Baumann, A. A., 241
Baumgarten, P.-M., 760a
Bayley, Sir L., 609a
Bearna Bhaoghail, An, 555
Begbie, H., 10a
Begley, P., 586
Beith, J. H., 761
Belfast Chamber of Commerce, 570
Belfast Industrial Development Association, 10b
Belfast prison inquiry (1918), 794
Belfast Telegraph, 1021
Belvederian, The, 661, 1022
Benjamin Franklin Bureau, 1023
Bennett, L., 762, 1024
Bentinck, Lord H., 1303
Bergin, J. J., 10c
Berkeley, G. F.-H., 233, 1208
Bernard, J. H., Archbp., 795, 907
Best, R. I., (p. VIII)
Beuque, E., 1025
Bewley, C., 243

(165)

INDEX

Birkenhead, 1st Earl of, (p. xviii), 11, 244-45, 377, 586a, 1025a
Birkenhead, 2nd Earl of, 245, 1025a
Birmingham Post, 1026
Birot, G., 246
Birrell, A., (p. xvii), 306, 503, 587
Bishops of Ireland, 116, 228, 801, 815, 900, 1027, 1103, 1223, 1229
Blácam, A. de, 763-63a, 969, 1004, 1028
Blackwood's Magazine, 247-48, 588, 1029
Blake, Sir H. S., 249-50, 764
Bloxham, E., 251
Blücher, E., Princess, 252
Blunt, W. S., 11a
Blythe, E., 92, 1287
Bodenstown series, 471-74
Bodkin, M. McD., 1030-31
Boletin irlandes (1921), 1031a
"Bolshevism and Sinn Fein," 1032
Bonar Law, A. See Law, A. Bonar
Bonn, M. J., 11b
"Book of the land of Ire," 751
Boston Herald and Journal, 764a
Borah, Senator, 1376
Bouch, J. J. (p. xix), 588a
Bourgeois, M., (p. viii), 1033
Boyd, E. A., (p. viii), 233, 765
Boyle, J. F., 589
Brady, E. M., 1035
Breen, D., 1036
Brennan, R., 590, 789, 1188
Brennan-Whitmore, Comdt. W. J., 591-92, 766
Brentford, Viscount, 254
Bright, J. H., 1037-38
Briollay, S. (pseud., R. Chauviré), 1054
"British treatment of Irish prisoners," 1050
Briton, A, 767
Broderick, D. J., 1040
"Broken Treaty, The" (1916), 767a
Brooks, S., (11c), 255-57a, 593
Brown, Rev. S. J., (p. viii), 258, 1041
Brown, S. L., 306-07
Brugha, C., (p. 3), 160, 594
Bryant, Sophie, 1239
Buckingham Palace Conference (1914), (p. 37)
Buckmaster (Sir S.), Lord, (p. xvii)
Bulkley, M. E., (p. viii)
Bulletin (Irish) see *Irish Bulletin*
Buonaiuti, Rev. C., 259
Burbage, Rev. T. H., 770
Burke, Capt. J., 595
Burns, E., 12
Butler, M., 12a
Buxton, C. R., 233, 260
Byrne, F. D., 261
Byrne, J. M., 769
Byrne, L. P., 768, 857

Cadden, J. J., 1042
Cahill, 595a
Cailliet, E., 1043
Callwell, Maj.-Gen. Sir C. E., 262, 1044
Campbell, Sir J. H. See Glenavy, Lord
Campbell, H. A., 1045
Campbell, J. R., 303
Campbell, S., 263
Canada (Irish in), 1214, 1250

Canadian view of Home Rule, A, 337
Canby, H. S., 771
Canqnista, 772
Capuchin Annual, 39, 595b, 717-18, 741
Carnegie Endowment for International Peace, (pp. viii-ix)
Carson, Sir Edward, Lord, (pp. xiii-xiv), (p. 108), (p. 3), 9a, 11, 25, 37, 112, 133, 223, 240-41, 264-65, 312, 357, 377-78, 397, 479, 493, 529, 543, 1046
Carter, B, 773
"Case for Ireland, The," 1346
Casement, Sir Roger, 44, 73, 132b, 169a, 252, 266-72, 282a, 314, 324, 367, 411, 420, 504, 509, 530, 586a, 596-99, 605a, 619, 641-42, 647a, 650, 664, 671, 673, 726-28a, 735, 996, 1025
Castledawson outrage (1913), 503
Castlereagh (Viscount), See Londonderry, Marquess of
Catholic Bulletin, 160-163, 600-06, 627, 643, 646a, 693, 707, 772-774, 1047-52a
Cave, Sir George, Lord, 273
Ceannt, Eamonn, 8a, 371, 607-08, 619, 682
Censorship (Press), (p. viii), (pp. xvii-xxv), 274, 503a
Census of Ireland (1911), 13-14, 57, 146, 209, 217-18
Cessation of active operations (July 11, 1921), 1053, 1186
Chalmers, Sir M. Dalzell, 714-15
Chamberlain, A., 275, 1300a
Chamberlain, Sir N., 609
Chanel (*pseud.*, i.e. A. E. Clery, whom see)
Charnwood, Lord, 276-77
Chatterton, E. A., 609
Chatterton-Hill, G., 609b, 774a-74b
Chesterton, Ada (Mrs. Cecil), 1380a
Chesterton, G. K., 775, 1099a, 1303, 1380a
Childers, E., (p. xiii), 15-16, 233, 278-82, 1056-60, 1085, 1131, 1208
Childs, Maj.-Gen. Sir W., 282a
Chumaill, E., 610
Churchill, S., 283
Churchill, W. S., 132, 284, 1061-62
Claidheamh Soluis, An (p. xiv), 17
Clan-na-Gael, 44, 56a, 212, 284a, 549, 631, 690, 876, 1114, 1144, 1349a, 1358
Clancy, G. [S. MacFhlannchadha], 1052a, 1107
Clancy, Rev. J., 777
Clancy, J. J., 365, 776
Clarke, Sir B., 1385a
Clarke, J. C., 1063
Clarke, K., 611
Clarke, T. J., (p. xv), (p. xix), 4, 18, 92, 611, 619, 706
Clarkson, J. D., (p. xvi), 19
Clayton, B., 778
Cleary, Rev. H. W.
Cleary, Rev. P., 77a, 1063a
Cleary, P. S., 19b
Clery, A. E., 20-22, 780
Clutton-Brock, A., 1303
Cockran, W. Bourke, 1064
Coffey, D., 781
Coffey, Rev. P., 23, 782-83

INDEX

Cohalan, D., 781, 1065-69, 1144
" Coilin," 612
Coimisiun Fhiafruigthe maom is tionnscal Éireann (Commission of inquiry into the resources and industries of Ireland), 1086-87
Colgan, *Comdt.* P., 613
Collins, Michael, 10, 24, 68, 151, 162, 979, 987, 1287, (p. 125)
Colum, M. M., 649
Colum, Pádraic, 24a, 285, 367, 615-17, 649, 994
Colvin, Ian, 25
Comhdháil Chosanta Gaedheal (1918). See Mansion House Conference
Commission d'enquête américaine sur la situation de l'Irlande, 1265
Committee of Public Safety (1915), 299
"Complete grammar of anarchy, The," 357
Compton-Rickett, Sir J., 286
Conboy, M., 1380
Condron, J. F., 1071
Conference on the redistribution of seats (1917), 950
Congested Districts Board, 135c, 137
Congress (U.S.). See U.S.A.
Connaught Rangers (1920), 1212
Connolly, F. V., 83
Connolly, James, (p. xvi), (p. xvii), (p. xix), 19, 26-35, 45b, 127, 152, 199, 242, 287, 374, 450-51a, 582a-83, 616, 646b, 671, 685-86
Conscription crisis (1918), (p. 95)
" Constructive work of Dáil Éireann, The," 1085-86
Continental Times (Berlin), 270a
Convention, The (1917-18), see Irish Convention
Cooper, Bryan, (p. xxiii), 195a
Co-operative movement, 1a, 211a, 1321. See also Finlay (Rev. T. A.), Plunkett (Sir H.), Russell (G. W.)
Cope, Sir A. W., 1304, 1387
Cork Chamber of Commerce, 36
Cork (Easter week in), 668
Cork (fires in, Dec. 1920), (p. 125)
Cork Industrial Development Association, 36a
Corkery, Daniel, 158, 1072
Corkey, Rev. W., 784
Cornford, L. P., 288-89
" Correspondence between His Majesty's Government and the Prime Minister of Northern Ireland," 1206
" Correspondence in case of Ireland's claim for independence " (1919), 1008
" Correspondence relating to . . . an Irish settlement " (1921), 1203-06
" Correspondence relating to recent events in the Irish command " (1914), 290-91
Cosgrave, W. T., 974, 1116, (p. 125)
Cousins, J. H., 89
Courtney of Penwith, Lord, 292
Courts of Justice (Dáil Éireann), 1085, 1186, 1226, 1341
Cork Chamber of Commerce, 36

Covenant, The (1912). See Ulster Covenant
Coyle, A., 1010
Cox, H., 785
Craigavon, Lord (Sir J. Craig), (p. 7), 9a, 1206. See also Northern Ireland, Ulster
Crawford, L., 1072a
Creel, G., 36b
Cregan, M., 618
Criminal Injuries Act (1920), 1073
Criminal Law and Procedure Act, (p. xxiii)
Crozier, Brig.-Gen. F. P., 1075-77
Cumann na mBan, 293, 610, 643, 676, 691, 693, 711, 725
Cumann na nGaedheal (1902), (p. xi)
Cumann Léigheachtai an Phobail (1921), (p. 126)
Curio, 294-95
Curragh army incident (1914), (p. xiv), (p. 41)
Curry, Dr. C. E., 271-72
Curzon, G. N., Marquess of, 1005
Cushendun, Lord, 37, 387
Cú Uladh, 663a

D, 788
Dáil Éireann (1919-22), (pp. xxiii-xxvi), 10, 11b, 24, 43b, 68, 119, 159, 213, 1078-88, 1092, 1102, 1116, 1187-88, 1364, 1375
Daily Chronicle, (p. xvi)
Daily Express (Dublin), (p. xviii)
Daily Mail, 322
Daily News, 315, 1096
Dalta [pseud., *i.e.*, C. Llewelyn-Davies, whom see]
Dalton, C., 1091
Dalton, E., 70
D'Alton, Rev. E. A., 38
Daly, M., 619
Dangerous associations (proclamations against), (pp. xxii-xxiii), 1092
D'Arcy, C. F., Archbp., 296
Davidson, R., Archbp., 1093
Davidson, S. C., 297
Dawson, R., 1094
" Deadly parallel, The," 1095
Dearle, N. B., (p. ix)
" Death of Thomas Ashe, The," 756
Defence of the Realm Act, (pp. xvii-xxiv), 297, 325, 427, 1324-26
" Defensive warfare," 211
De Lacey, L., 371
Délégation irlandaise, La (Paris), (p. xiv), 797, 1096-99a, 1118, 1283
De Lue, W., 1138
Democritus, 300
Dempsey, F., 1100
Dennis, A., 39
Dennis, A. L. P., 1101
Deoraidhe Gaodhlach, An, 1192
Department of Agriculture and Technical Instruction, 40-43a, 302-03
Department of Agriculture (Dáil Éireann), 1079, 1086-87, 1188
Department of Finance (Dáil Éireann), 10, 24, 1079, 1188

Department of Foreign Affairs (Dáil Éireann), (pp. XXIV–XXVI), 1079, 1083, 1188
Department of Defence (Dáil Éireann). See Óglaigh na hÉireann
Department of Local Government (Dáil Éireann), 1079, 1116, 1188
Department of Publicity (Dáil Éireann), (p. XXV), 1079, 1102–07
Department of Trade and Commerce (Dáil Éireann), 1079, 1086–88
Derham, J., 1108
Desmond, S., 1109
Deutsch-Irischen Gesellschaft, 846
"Deutschland und die irische Frage," 847
De Valera, E., 8, 134, 789–90, 876, 896–97, 972–77, 980, 1078–86, 1110–11, 1140a, 1203–05, 1300a, 1358
De Vere, R. S., 301
Devlin, J., (p. 9), 224, 767a, 896–97
Devoy, John, 44, 56a, 1144. See also Clan-na-Gael, Friends of Irish Freedom
Dicey, A. V., 304, 791–92
Dickie, J., 1112
Dickson, T., 716
Dillon, John, (p. XX), 767a, 793
"Disaffected Ireland," 1026
"Distress in Ireland, a survey," 1013a
Dix, E. R. McC., (p. VIII)
"Documents relating to the Sinn Fein movement," 980
Dodd, W. H., 794
Donnelly, Mary, 44a, 620
Donnelly, Simon, 621
Donovan, T. M., 45
D.O.R.A. See Defence of the Realm Act
"D.O.R.A. at Westminster," 325
Dorbene, K. S., 1113
Dougherty, Sir J. B., 623
Downey, A., 12a
Downing, Rossa F., 1114–14a
Doyle, S., 622
"Dublin after the six days' insurrection," 675
"Dublin and the Sinn Fein rising," 624
Dublin Castle. See Ireland (government of)
Dublin Chamber of Commerce, 46, 1115
Dublin Corporation, 1116
Dublin Disturbances Commission (1913–14), 306–07, 345, 388
Dublin Industrial Development Association, 46a
Dublin Magazine, (p. VIII), 173b
Dublin Metropolitan Police, 197–98, 713, 626, 630
Dublin priest, A (1916), 627
Dublin Saturday Post (1916), 628
Dublin Trades Council, 46b
"Dublin woman's story of the rebellion," A, 635c
Duff, D. V., 1117
Duffin, A., 796
Duffy, G. Gavan, 797, 1096, 1118
Duffy, Rev. T., 649
Duke of Northumberland's Fund. See Northumberland, Duke of
Dun Cairin, 798
Dungannan club, 47
Dunne, E. F., 1009, 1120

Dunraven, Earl of, 48–50, 308–09, 799–800, 1121–22
Dwane, D. T., 51

Eaglaiseach Gaedhealach, An t-, 1142
Eason, 629
East Cavan election (1918), 793
Echo, The (Enniscorthy), 674
Economic history, Irish (Bibliography), (p. VIII)
Edgeworth-Johnstone, Lt.-Col. W., 371, 630
Edinburgh Review, 310–11, 801
Egan, M., 896–97
Egan, P. F., 631
Eglinton, John [pseud., i.e. W. K. Magee, whom see]
Eighty Club, The, 142, 512
Eire, 359
Emergency legislation, 427
"Emmet anniversary magazine," 284a
"England's fair words—and Ireland," 1104
Englishman, An, [D. Goldring], 802a–02b
"Englishman, An, talks it out with an Irishman," 938
English officer's son, An, 1124
Ennis, Michael A., 803
Enniscorthy (1916 rising at), 590, 622, 660, 674, 698
Ergo, 804
Ervine, St. John G., 312, 632
Erzberger M., 846
Escouflaire, R. C., 805–06
"Estimate of Irishmen serving with the forces of the Crown" (1916), 511
Evans, R., 807, 1126
Evening Post (New York), 808a
Ewart, W, 1127
"Experiences of an officer's wife in Ireland," 1029
"Experiences of a V.A.D. at Dublin Castle" (1916), 588
Exports (Irish), 41, 165
Eyre, Edward, 808
Events of Easter week and after (*Catholic Bulletin*), 600–06, 627, 643, 707–08, 773a–74, 1049–52a

"Facts and figures on the Irish question," 567
"Facts of radical misgovernment," 101
"Facts regarding the loyal Orange Institution," 573
Fainne an lae, 17, 809
Falls, C., (p. VIII)
"Farmers, your turn now!" (Sinn Féin), 971
Farrell, H. W., 313
Fawsitt, J. L. [D. Fausitt], 1088, 1128
Ferris, Rev. W., 1129
Fiachrach Eilgeach. See Field, W., 52
"50 points for Home Rule," 315
Figgis, D., 316–17a, 810–14a, 1087, 1130–31
Filon, A., 318
Finance (Irish), (p. 10), (p. 44), (p. 98), (p. 133)
"Financial relations of Ireland with the imperial exchequer," 205
Finlay, Rev. P., 815
Finlay, Rev. T. A., 54, 1087

"First of small nations, The," 1106
Fisher, J. R., 222, 816–19
FitzGerald, D., 633, 1132, 1188
FitzGerald, E. B., 1133
FitzGerald, W. J., 226
Fitzmaurice, Lord E., 55
Fitzwalter, R., 319–20
Fleming, P., 858
Fogarty, M., Bp., 820
Food production (1914–18), 40 43a, 302–03
Foreign Affairs (Dáil Éireann). See Dept. of Foreign Affairs
Forrest, Sir G., 1134
Fortnightly Review, 320a
"Foundations of the Republic of Ireland," 1110
Fox, G. L., 1135
"Fragment of 1916 history, A," 709
"France and Ireland," 1231
"Freedom's road for Irish workers," 955a
Freeman's Journal, (pp. XVI, XVIII)
French, F.-M. Sir J., Earl, 1136
Friend, Maj.-Gen. Sir L. B., 604
Friends of Irish Freedom, (p. XXVI), 103, 1114–14a, 1137–40, 1284–85
Friends, Society of, 133, 1141, 1389
Frongoch camp (1916), 743, 766, 769
Fuller, Sir J. B., 321
Furnas, P. J., 1141
Fyfe, H., 56, 322

G, 451a
G, 635
G.B., 1147
Gaedheal, An (The Gael), 323
Gaelic American, (p. XXVI), 56a, 451b, 635a–35c. See also Clan-na-Gael, Cohalan (D. F.), Devoy (J.), Friends of Irish Freedom, McCartan (P.)
Gaelic Churchman, 1142
Gaelic League, The, (pp. X–XII), 17, 22, 109, 209
Gallagher, F., 1088, 1143
Galway (1916 rising in), 638, 667, 671, 692
Gallagher, Most Rev. M. J., *Bp.*, 1144
Gannon, Rev. P. J., 57, 1145
Gardiner, A. G., 1303, 1389
Gay, F., 1146
Gaynor, Rev. P., 821
Geary, Rev. J. A., 1148
General alphabetical index to parliamentary and command papers, (p. VIII)
General Post Office (1916), 591, 627, 633, 643, 661, 676, 693, 699, 711, 729–30
General election (1918), (p. XXIII), 1014
George, D. Lloyd, (p. XX), (p. XXII), 36, 767a, 808a, 822–23, 840, 1084, 1149, 1183, 1203–03, 1365, 1387
German-Irish Brigade. See Casement (Sir R.)
German-Irish Society (Deutsch-Irischen Gesellschaft), 324, 774, 846, 996
"German plot, The," (1918), 774, 867, 980
Germanicus, 823a
Germany and U.S.A. (Treaty of Peace, 1920), 1065–66, 1120, 1272, 1286, 1340, 1378

"Germans at Bessbrook, The," 959
"Germans in Cork, The," 824
Gibbs, Sir P., 1150–52, 1260
Gifford, S., 636, 649
Gifford-Donnelly, N., 637
Gill, T. P., 470
Ginnell, L., 325, 971, 974, 1153–55, 1186
Glenavy, Lord, 326–27, 377, 639
Gnathaí gan iarradh [pseud. See Boyd, E. A.]
Goblet, Y. M., 58, 328–29, 1154–56
Goff, J. W., 648
Golden, P., 888
Goldring, D., 802a–02b, 824a
Gooch, G. P., 233
Good, J. W., 59–59a, 92, 825–26, 1157
Gordon, E., Lady, 60
Gore-Booth, Constance. See Markievicz (C. de)
Gore-Booth, E., 134, 640–41
Gough, Gen. Sir H., (p. 41), 1158
Government of Ireland. See Ireland (Government of)
Government of Ireland Act (1914), 46, 776. See also Home Rule, Ulster
Government of Ireland Act (1920), (p. XIII), 137, 1159–61, 1317–18
Government of Ireland Bill (1912–14), (p. XIII), 330–34a, 351a, 449, 568–70. See also Home Rule, Ulster
Government of Ireland (Amendment) Bill, 335
Grabisch, A. M. Bullitt, 642
"Graphic story of the battle of Ashbourne," 635c
"Graphic story of Easter week rebellion," 635a
Grand Orange Lodge of Ireland, 168a, 457
Grasty, C. H., 1162
Graves, A. P., 827
Graves, S. H. P., 337
"Great bishop of Limerick [Dr. E. O'Dwyer], The," 820
Great Britain and Ireland (Articles of agreement for a Treaty, 1921), 1084, 1163
Green, A. S., 61–62, 337a–37b, 504, 828–30, 1164
Green papers, The, 337c
Greenwood, Sir Hamar, 36, 1030, 1212b, 1304, 1385a, 1392
Gregory, Lady A., 11a
Grey, Sir E. (Viscount), 270b, 337d, 556
Grey, R. C., 1303
Grievances in Ireland, 337e
Griffin, Rev. M., 1048
Griffith, A., (pp. XI–XII), (p. XVI), (p. XX), 63–68, 106, 109–11, 120, 161, 209, 214, 225, 338–38c, 359, 440, 451a, 545, 831, 974, 1087, 1107, 1138, 1165–66, 1300a
Gros, J., 1167
Guinness, W. E. See Moyne, Lord
Gwynn, D., 69–73, 442, 1231
Gwynn, S., (p. XIV), 74, 96, 339–40, 832, 1168–69

H, 373a
Hackett, F., 75–76, 1170–71, 1336
Hagan, Rev. J., 76a, 1172, 1247, 1251

Hailsham, Viscount, 133
Hales, T., 1023
Hambro, C. J., 833
Hamilton, Lord E., 77
Hammond, J. L., 78
Hammond, Rev. T. C., 341
" Handbook for Irish Volunteers " (1914), 373a
" Handbook of the Ulster question," 146
Hannay, Rev. J. O., 78a, 233, 342–43
Hanson, F., 530
Hardinge of Penshurst, Lord. See Royal Commission on the rebellion, 1916
Harmsworth, Sir A. See Northcliffe, Viscount
Harmsworth, C., 79
Harp, The (1917), 834
Harrison, A., 835–37, 845, 1175
Harrison, M., 838
Hayden, M. T., 80
Hayes, M., 1055
Hayes, S., 1178
Headquarters Bulletin (*Irish Volunteer*), (p. xviii)
Healy, J. E., 344
Healy, T. M., 9, 11, 81, 150, 156, 345
Hegarty, S., 434
Hely, 643a
Henderson, A., 1218
Henry, D. S., 307, 716
Henry, R. M., (p. xi), 82
Herbert, A. S., 839
Hercé, 1179–80
Herdman, J. O., 1181
Hibernicus, 1182
Higgins, J., 644
Higgins, P., 83
Hirst, F. W., (p. xvii)
Hoare, Sir S., 1183–84
Hobhouse, L. T., 84
Hobson, B., (p. xii), (p. xviii), 47, 85–86, 92, 191, 211, 346–48, 371, 665
Hocking, J., 349
Home Rule Act. See Government of Ireland Act (1914)
Home Rule Bill (1886), (p. x), 16, 91, 179, 449
Home Rule Bill (1893), (p. x), 91, 179, 326, 370, 449
" Home Rule Bill of 1912, The," 399
Home Rule Council, (p. xiv), 351–52
" Home Rule from the Treasury bench "
" Home Rule notes " (1911–12), 353
" Home Rule problems," 233
Home Rule. See also Finance, Government of Ireland Bills, Irish Parliamentary Party, Irish Press Agency, Irish Unionist Alliance, Sinn Féin, Ulster, United Irish League
Hone, J. M., 354–55
Hope, J. A., 356
Horgan, J. J., 357, 841–43, 1185
Horne, Rev. S., 417a
Horneck, A., 644
How to form Sinn Fein clubs, 971
Howard-Gritten, W. G., 358

Howth Gun-running (July, 1914). See Figgis (D.), Hobson (B.), *Irish Volunteer*, MacDonagh (T.), O'Brien (C.), Royal Commission on the landing of arms . . .
Hughes, K., 994, 1185a, 1250
Hull, E., 87
Hungarian policy, The, 63–65, 107a, 788. See also Sinn Féin
Hunger-strikes (1917–21), 756, 779, 1000, 1027, 1063a, 1215, 1383
Hyde D. [An Craoibhín Aoibhinn], 473

Iceland, 1223
" Imperial danger, An," 1186
Imperial Parliament, 169
Imperial revenue, 88
Independent Order of Grand Lodges, 1072a
Indian Nationalist Committee, 844
Industry (Irish), (p. 15), (p. 49), 193, 954–55, 829, 1370a
" Instructions to Sinn Fein Cumainn " (1920), 1374
" International Magna Charta " (1917), 845
International reconstruction (1918), 853
International reference movement (1918), 854
" International revolutionary propaganda . . .", 1278
" Intercourse between Bolshevism and Sinn Fein," 1032
" I.O." [pseud., *i.e.* Street, C. J. S., whom see]
" Ireland at Berne," 1193
Ireland : Census of (1911), 13–14
Ireland (Government of), (pp. xii–xiii), (p. 15)
Ireland overseas, 226
" Ireland to-day under England," 1124
" Ireland's appeal to America " (1917), 850
" Ireland's case against conscription," 789
" Ireland's claim " (1919), 1047
" Ireland's declaration of independence," 1187
" Ireland's elected government," 1140
" Ireland's part in the world war," 1139
" Ireland's request to the U.S. . . . ", 1140
" Ireland's trinity of martyred priests," 1048
Iris Dáil Éireann, 1081
Irische Blätter (1917–18), 847–48
" Irish-American verdict on Easter week," 645a
" Irish bishops on English rule," 1103
Irish bishops. See also Bishops of Ireland
" Irish boy scouts " [na Fianna Éireann], 135b
Irish Bulletin, (p. xxv), (p. 153), 1079, 1188, 1300
Irish cabinet-maker, An, 360
Irish Centre Party (1919), 1189
Irish Church Quarterly, 361
Irish Citizen, 89
Irish Citizen Army, (p. xvi), (p. xviii), (p. 49), (p. 80), 5, 114, 285, 450, 595, 620, 684, 712
Irish Commonwealth, The, 1190
" Irish councils for Irish freedom," 1105
Irish County Councils General Council, 362, 803

Irish Daily Independent, (p. xviii), 1079
Irish Dominion League, 1191, 1313
Irish economic history, (p. viii)
" Irish electors again proclaim the republic," 1227
Irish exile, The, 1192
Irish Finance (Report of Committee on), 90–91
Irish Finance. See also Finance (Irish)
Irish Freedom, (pp. xiv–xvii), 92
Irish Homestead, 303
" Irish in America, The," 83
" Irish in Great Britain, The," 153a
Irish Industrial Development Association, (p. xii), 92b, 193, 209
Irish industry. See Industry (Irish)
Irish K.C., An, 852
Irish Labour movement. See Labour movement (Irish)
Irish League of the Empire, 313
Irish Life (1916), 146
" Irish manufacturers and the Home Rule Bill," 297
Irish Nation, 855
Irish Nation and Peasant, The, 94
Irish Nation League, (p. 102)
Irish National Aid and Volunteer Dependents' Fund, 646a
Irish National Boy Scouts. See Fianna Éireann
Irish National Bureau (New York), 1137
Irish National Convention (1912), 366
Irish National Volunteers, 362a, 439, (p. 52)
Irish Opinion, 856–57
" Ireland or Westminster," 86
Irish Parliamentary Party, 224, 738a, 991–93. See also Ancient Order of Hibernians, Devlin, J., Dillon, J., Gwynn, S., Home Rule, Irish Press Agency, Irish Unionist Alliance, Lynch, A., MacVeagh, J., O'Brien, W., O'Connor, T. P., O'Malley, W., Redmond, J., Redmond, W., United Irish League
Irish peace (*The Times*), 1370
Irish peace conference (1920), 1176a, 1309
Irish Press (Philadelphia), (p. xxvi)
Irish Press Agency, (p. xiv), 83–84, 95–96, 363–66
Irish priest, An, 858
Irish question, The (U.S.A. Congress), 994
Irish Race Convention (1916), (p. 50), 1140
" Irish rebellion of 1916 and its martyrs," 649
Irish Reconstruction Association (1918), 1196
Irish republican arbitration courts, 1226a
Irish Republican Army. See Óglóigh na hÉireann
Irish Republican Brotherhood, (p. xv), (p. xix), 114, 154, 159, 242, 190, 658, 662, 683. See also Clarke (T. J.), Clan-na-Gael, Collins (M.)
Irish Republican Prisoners' Dependents Fund (1921), 1197
Irish Review (1912–14), (p. xiv), 367
Irish Self Determination League of Great Britain, 1192, 1198–1202

Irish settlement : Correspondence ... (1921), 1078–84, 1203–06. See also p. 153
Irish Statesman (1919–20), 1207–08
Irish taxpayer, An, 368
Irish Times, The, (p. xviii)
Irish Transport and General Workers Union, (p. xv), (p. 7), 369, 1209–10
Irish Unionist, An, 369a
Irish Unionist Alliance, The, (p. x), 98–103, 195a, 370, 681, 1211
Irish Volunteer (1914–16), (pp. xv–xviii), 371, 473
Irish Volunteer officer, An, 135b
Irish Volunteers, handbook for, 374
Irish Volunteers, manifestoes (1913–14), 372–73
Irish Volunteers, (pp. xiv–xxiv), (p.52), (pp. 74–91). See also Óglaigh na hÉireann
Irish War News (1916), (p. xix), 643b
Irish Weekly Independent, 1212–12a
Irish White Cross, 1391
Irish Work, 374
Irish Worker, (pp. xiv–xv), 374
Irish World (Dublin), 963
Irish World (New York), (p. xxvi), 103
Irish Year Book (Sinn Féin), (p. xii), 109–111
Irishman, An, 104
Irishman, The, 859
Irishwomen's International League, 762
" Irland, Amerika und die Friedenskonferenz," 847
" Irland unter England," 860
" Is the Irish Party nationalist ? " 909
" Issue, The," 867
" Issues of the election " (1918), 993

James, L., 376
Jerome, J. K., 1138
Johnson, T., 377, 857
Johnston, J., 378
Joint Commission on ... international settlement, 861
Joly, J., 647
Jones, F. P., 648
Joy, M., 649
Joyce, J. V., 651
Joynson-Hicks, Sir W. See Brentford, Viscount
Judex, 652
Judge, M. J., 371
Judiciary (Saorstát na hÉireann, 1920), 1341
Junius Junior, 1213

Kavanagh, S., 653
Keane, Sir J., 380
Keane, P., 1214
Kearns, L., 1214a
Kelleher, Rev. J., 1215
Kelly, D., Bp., 303
Kelly, R. J., 1216
Kennedy, J. M., 381
Kenny, J. D., 382–82a
Kenny, H. E., 105
Kensit, J. A., 1217
Kerr, W. S., 383

Kerr-Smiley, P., 384
Kerry (Irish Volunteers in), 45, 73, 169a, 586, 618, 688
Kettle, M., 862
Kettle, T. M., (p. XIII), 107–09, 171, 385–89, 780, 862
Killanin, Lord, 390
Kimmage garrison in 1916, 737
King, Rev. R. S. G., 391–92
Knott, S. H., 596

Labour movement, Irish, (pp. XV–XVI), (p. 18), (p. 54), (p. 103), (p. 144)
Labour party, British, 1157, 1218, 1352, 1373
Land Settlement Commission (Dáil Éireann), 1085
Larkin, James, (p. XV), 354, 369, 374, 450, 541, 1361
Larne gun-running, The (1914), (p. XIV), (p. 54)
Law, A. Bonar, 529
Law and Procedure (Emergency Provisions) Act, 654
Lawless, J., 655
Lawson, Sir H., 1220–21
"Leabhar na hÉireann," (p. XII), 109–11
Leader, The, 11a, 141
Lecarpentier, G., 423
Lector, 866–67
Leech, H. B., 13
Lees-Smith, H. B., 396
Legge, E., 397
Lennon, M. J., 398, 656, 868
Le Roux, L. N., 113–14
Leslie, S., 656, 869–70, 1222
" Letter from the Prime Minister regarding Ireland " (1917), 823
" Letters from Irish Protestants," 363
" Letters of . . . Bishop O'Dwyer," 926
Liberal Publications Department, 399
Libre Belge, La, (p. XXV)
" Limerick curfew murders of 1921," 1281
Little, P. J., 400, 442, 1291
Llewelyn-Davies, C., 1089–90
Lloyd, E. T., 401
Local Government Board, 114a. See also Dept. of Local Government (Dáil Éireann)
Local government elections (1920), 1105, 1227
Local government registration, 1374
Locker-Lampson, G., 402
Logan, J., 115
Logue, M., Cardinal, 116, 1223
Londonderry, 6th Marquess of, 403
Londonderry, 7th Marquess of, 404
Long, W., Viscount, (p. X), 117, 405
Lynch, A., 118, 1224
Lynch, D., 658, 994
Lynd, R., 119, 646b, 872
Lynn, R., 1225
Lyons, G. A., 120, 659, 873
Lysaght, E. A., 120a, 874
Lyster, Rev. H. C., 660

MacAmlaoibh, R., 661
Macaomh, An, 121
Madden, R. R., (p. VII)
McBrien, P., 1226

McCartan, P., (p. XXVI), 876–76c
McCarthy, M., 406
McCormick, W., 1226a–28
McCullagh, F., 407
MacCurtain, T., 1049, 1243, 1377, 1381
MacDara, 662
McDermott, F., 233
MacDermott, S. [Seán Mac Diarmuda], 434, 618, 720, 689
MacDonagh, M., 122–23, 877
MacDonagh, S. [J.], 663
MacDonagh, T. (p. VIII), 367, 408, 451a, 550, 663
MacDonald, J. A., 409–10
MacDonald, Rev. W., 1229–31, 1285
MacDonnell, Sir A., (p. XIII), 124–24b
McDonnell, Sir J., 125
McDowell W. W., 1232
Mac Fhionnlaoich, P. T., 663a
Mac Gadhra, S., 451a
McGarrity J., (p. XXVI), 664–65, 1036
MacGarry, M., 126–26a
McGill, A., 1233
McGrath, J., 878, 1234–35
McGuinness, C. J., 1236
Macken, P. See Ó Meacain, P.
McKenna, Rev. L., 127
McKenna, R., 884
McKenzie, F. A., 666
McKnight, W. A., 1238
MacKeogh, M., 411, 1237
McIntyre, J., *Bp.*, 883
McIntyre, P. J., 716
McL., F., 412
MacManus, L., 128
MacManus, S., 129
MacMurchadha, F., 1022
MacNachain, A. O., 667
MacNeill, Eoin [John], (p. XI), (p. XVII), 130, 371, 413–14, 602, 853, 886, 1239, (p. 83). See also Dáil Éireann, *Irish Volunteer*, Irish Volunteers
McNeill, J. G. Swift, 887, 1240
McNeill, R. See Cushendun, Lord
Mac Piarais (Pádraic). See Pearse, P. H.
Macready, Gen. Sir C. F. N., (p. XV), 415–15a, 1241
McSweeney, E. F., 1242
MacSwiney, Mary, 158, 668, 1243
MacSwiney, Muriel, 158, 1244
MacSwiney, P, Marquis, 416, 939
MacSwiney, T. [T. Mac Suibhne], 92, 131, 158, 371, 1245
MacVeagh, J., (p. XIII), 132–32a, 369a, 417–17a
Madrid, 1031a
Magee, W. K., 936
Magennis, Rev. P. E., 888, 1246–51
Magistrates (Return of, 1912–13), 418–19
Magner (Rev. Canon), 1048
Maguire, J. A., 420
Mahaffy, Rev. J. A., 421–22
Mahon, Lt.-Gen. Sir B., 890
Maisonnier, L., 423
Mallin, M. [M. Ó Maolain], 684
Mallow burnings (1920), 1100
Malone, A. E. (ps., i.e. L. P. Byrne, whom see)

INDEX 173

Maloney, W. J. M., (p. XXVI), 132b, 272, 891, 1253
Manchester Courier, 425
Manchester Guardian, 78, 669, 892
Manifestoes of Dungannon clubs, 47–47a
Manifestoes of Irish Volunteers, 372–73
Mannix, D., Archbp., 893–95, 1017, 1071, 1254–57, 1279, 1295, 1331
Mansion House Conference (1918), 896–97
" Manual of emergency legislation " (1914), 427
Marjoribanks, E., 133
Markievicz, C. de, 134, 314a, 636, 670, 724, 898
Marlowe, N. (pseud.), 428–29, 744, 899–900
Marriott, Sir J. A., 430, 901, 1258–59
Martin, H., 1260
Martyn, E., (p. XI), 69
" Martyrer der Irischen Republik " (1916), 645
Mason resolution (U.S. Congress), 1066
Mason, T., 721
Massingham, H. W., 902
Maxwell, Sir H., 135
Maxwell, Sir J., (p. XX), 585
Melchett, Lord, 135a
Mellows, Liam, 135b, 434, 671a, 692
Memoranda on financial provisions (Govt. of Ireland Bill, 1913–14), 332–34
" Memorandum à l'appui des revendications de l'Irlande . . .", 1096
" Memorandum on the censorship," 274
" Memorandum on the official press bureau," 503a
"Memorandum on the pending Anglo-American treaty," 876b
" Memorandum . . . to the . . . United States . . .", 876c
" Men of military age " (1916), 902a
Meredith, J. C., 431
Methodist demonstration committee (1912), 432–33
Meyer, E., 597, 774a
Micks, W. L., 135c
Midleton, Earl of, 136, 672
Military Service Act (1918), (p. XX), 797. See also Conscription
Milligan, A., 606
Milroy, S., 434
Mitchel, S. L., 1321
M. M., 1261
Mohan, Mrs. M., 1261
Moisant, X., 1263–66
Moles, T., 37, 1267
Molony, J. C., 137
Molony, Sir T. F., 138, 538, 716
Mond, Sir A. See Melchett, Lord
Monteagle, 1269
Monteith, R., 673
Montgomery, K. L., 1268
Moore, A. S., 903
Moore, Rev. C., 140
Moore, F. Frankfort, 434a
Moore, Col. Maurice, 455a, 1292
Moore, Myles, 674, 904–05
Moran, D. P., 111a, 141
Morgan, D., 1270
Morgan, J. H., 142–44, 233, 435–37
Morrison, H. S., 145
Morrison-Bell, A. C., 438

Mount street (Easter week, 1916), 621, 707, 722a
Moyne, Lord, 1271
Muldoon, J. A., 438a
Murphy, J. A., 1272
Murphy, T. W., 675
Murphy, W. M., 906
Murray, A., (p. VIII)
Murray, M., 676
Murray, Rev. R. H., 677, 907

Nada [pseud., *i.e.* Moore (Myles) whom see]
Nathan, Sir M., (p. XVIII), 359, 374, 678
Nation (London), 908, 1173–74
National Aid. See Irish National Aid
National Council. See Sinn Fein.
" National land policy," 1090
" National organisations in Ireland," 145a
National Review, 679
National Volunteer, 439
Nationality, 440
" New Home Rule, The," 99
New Ireland, 442
Newman (A.) [pseud., *i.e.* H. M. Pim, whom see]
News Letter . . . Irish National Bureau, 1137
Nicholas, Rev. W., 432
Niven, R., 145b
" No Conscription ! " 897
Northcliffe, Viscount, 910, 1275. See also *Times*
North-Eastern Boundary Bureau, 146
Northern Ireland : Constitution, 1317
Northern Ireland : Parliamentary debates, 1276–77
Northern Ireland. See also Government of Ireland Act (1920), Irish settlement, and Ulster
Norway, Mrs. H., 680
" No surrender " (Grand Orange Lodge), 451
Northumberland, 8th Duke of, 444–45, 1278
Notes from Ireland, (p. XII), 98, 681

O, 146b
O'Brennan, L., 682
Ó Briain, C., 1279
Ó Briain, L., 683–84
Ó Briain, M., 1022
O'Brien, Conor, 446
O'Brien, G., 163
O'Brien, N. Connolly, 685–86a
O'Brien, R. Barry, 148
O'Brien, S., 649
O'Brien, W., 149–50, 449, 897, 911–16, 1280
O'Brien, W. (I.T.G.W.U.), 35, 897
O'Callaghan, D., 1281
O'Callaghan, K., 1282
O'Callaghan, M., 1052, 1282
O'Carroll, K., 687
Ó Cathail, P., 688, 728a
ÓCathasaigh [O'Casey] Seán, 450, 917
Ó Ceallaigh, S. [Sceilg], 160–63. See also *Catholic Bulletin* and Dáil Éireann
Ó Ceallaigh, S. T., 17, 359, 689–90, 1283
O'Connell, D., 1284–85
O'Connell, Sir J., 919–20
O'Connell, J. J., 371, 1287
O'Connor, B., 151
O'Connor, F. J., 921

O'Connor, G., 152
O'Connor, G. B., 922
O'Connor, Sir J., 153
O'Connor, R., 1287
O'Connor, T. P., 56, 153a–53b, 923
O'Connor, W. J., 450a
O'Daly, N., 691
O'Doherty, Rev. P., 924
O Donnabháin Rossa., D., 131, 451–51b
O'Duffy, Eimar, 371
O'Dwyer, E. T., Bp., 925–27, 773a, 820
Ó hEidhin, P., 692
O Faoláin, S., 154–55
O'Farrell, E., 693
" Official correspondence relating to the peace negotiations " (1921), 1084
O'Flaherty, D. C., 1286
O'Flaherty, Liam, 156
O'Flannagan, Rev. M., 928–29, 974
Óglách, An t-, 1287
Ógláigh na hÉireann, (pp. XIV–XXVI), (pp. 74–91), (p. 109), (p. 151). See also Irish Volunteers
O'Hegarty, P. S., (pp. VIII–XI), 18, 92, 157–59, 225, 963, 1288
O'Herlihy, Rev. P., 930
O'Higgins, Brian, 452, 555, 694, 931
Old Ireland, 1291
Oldham, C. H., 164–65, 453, 1115, 1289–90
O'Leary, J. J., 695
Oliver, F. S., 454–5, 1292
O'Loughran, Rev. R., 933
O'Malley, W., 166
Ó Meacain, P., 8, 619
Ó Mórdha, M., 455a, 1292
One of them, 696
O'Neill, B., 696a
O'Neill, Charles, 697
O'Neill, Colmann, 934
O'Neill, E., 166a
O'Neill, Henry, 1293
O'Neill, Hugh, 456, 935
O'Neill, M., 698
Orage, A. R., 936
O'Rahilly, A., 866–67, 1294
O'Rahilly, The, 371, 458
Orange institution, The, 166b, 457
Orchelle, R. L., 937
O'Reilly, M. W., 729
Ó Riain, S., 699
O'Riordan, Rev. M., 167
Ó Roideáin, C., 1022
O'Shannon, C., 8, 35
Ó Síothcháin, S., 167a
Ó Suilleabháin, P., 1296
O'Sullivan, Rev. P. P., 459
Outis, 460–61
" Outrages . . . Return of," 1297–1300
Outsider, An, 462–64
Oxford and Asquith, Earl of, 168, 465–67, 557

Pakenham, F., 1132a, 1300
" Papers relating to the appointment of Maj.-Gen. Sir C. F. N. Macready," 415
Parliamentary and Local Government registration (U.I.L.), 1374

Parliamentary debates (United Kingdom), 168a
Parmiter, G. de C., 169
Parry, M. Sidney, 1301
Paul-Dubois, L., (p. IX), 170–71, 468–70
Peace negotiations (1920–21), (p. 153)
Peace with Ireland Council (1920–21), (p. XXVI), 1303
Pearse, Margaret, 700, 718
Pearse, Mary B., 173a
Pearse, P. H., (p. XI), (pp. XVIII–IX), (p. 27). 8, 17, 39, 113, 121, 126, 173b, 200–02, 371, 451a, 471–78, 661, (p. 86)
Peel, G., 479
Percy, Earl. See Northumberland, Duke of
Philalethes, 480–83
Phillips, J., 484–86
Phillips, W. A., 172–73
Phoenix, The, 938
P. J. F., 939
Pim, F. W., 702, 1305
Pim, H. M., 487–91, 859, 1306–07
Pim, J., 492
Platt, T. Comyn, 493
" Plight of southern Irish loyalists, The," 1119
Plunkett, G. N., Count, (p. XXV), 601, 946, 1083
Plunkett, Grace, 703
Plunkett, Sir H., 1a, 120a, 174, 256, 494, 879, 940, 1308–12
Plunkett, Joseph M., (p. VIII), (p. XIX), (p. 87)
Poe, Sir H., 495
Pokorny, J., 703
Pollard, A. F., 175
Pollard, H. B. C., 176
Pollock, A. W. A., 496
Pollock, Sir F., 177
Pomfret, J. E., (p. VIII)
Ponsonby, Sir F., Lord, 497
Pope-Hennessy, L. H. R., 1313
Porritt, A. G., 498
Posner, S., 499
Prendeville, P. L., (p. VIII)
Prenter, Rev. S., 500–01
Presbyterian Church in Ireland, 500–03
" Presidential statement . . ." (Dáil Éireann), 1111
Press Bureau (Official), (p. XVII), 274, 503a
Price, Major I. H., 440, 704
Primrose, Sir H., 90–91
Proclaimed districts, 942
Proportional representation, 177a, 431, 1016
Pro tanto quid, 1314
Protheroe, Sir G., (p. VIII)
Public finances of Ireland. See Finance (Irish) and Oldham, C. H.
Publicity Department (Dáil Éireann). See Dept. of Publicity

Quarterly Review, 506–08, 943, 1315–16
Quekett, Sir A., 1317–18
Quinn, J., 509
Quinn, M., 944
Quirk, J., 1319
Rashad (I.), 1321
" Reception to the Irish republican delegates " (1921), 1202

"Reception in Paris of the Irish M.P.s" (1915), 510
"Record of the Irish rebellion" (1916), 646
Recruiting (for British army), 511. See also Conscription
Red Hand Magazine, 1322
Reddy, L. G., 946
Redistribution of seats Act (1918), 947
Redmond, John E., (pp. XIV–XVII), 56, 70, 74, 81, 95, 150, 178–85, 231, 361a, 366, 386, 512–21, 740a, 832, 865a, 880, 033, 082. See also Home Rule, Irish Convention, Irish Press Agency, Irish Unionist Alliance, Sinn Féin, Ulster, etc.
Redmond, W. H. K., 187, 984
Redmond-Howard, L. G., 188-89, 521-22, 705, 949
Regan, J. X., 1323
Registration instructions issued by Sinn Fein, 978
Registration (Parliamentary and Local Government), 1374
Reidy, J., 190, 706
Relief of distress (1920–21), (p. 155)
Religious leaflets (Ulster Unionist Council), 569
Repington, C. à C., 523
Representation of the People Act (1918), 950–52
Republic, The, (p. XII), 191
"Republique d'Irlande et la presse francaise," 1118
Resident magistrates : Return (1912), 524
Restoration of Order Act (1920), 1324–26
Revenue and expenditure : returns, 192
"Revolutionary movement in Ireland, The," 1211
Revue de Paris, 1327
Reynolds, J. J., 707–10
Reynolds, M., 711
Richardson, J., 953
Ridgeway, Sir J. W., 526
Rigg, T. G., 527
Ringsend area in 1916, 659
Riordan, E. J., 193, 954–55
"Road to Irish prosperity, The," 997
Robbins, F., 712
Roberts, E. F., 194
Roberts, F. M., Earl, 528
Robinson, Mrs. A. E., 1328
Robinson, Sir H., 195
Robinson, Lennox, 195a
Rolleston, T. W., 955a, 1329–30
Rome (Irish cause in), 1172, 1183
Ronald, 955b
Ronaldshay, Earl of. See Zetland (Marquis of)
Ronayne, Rev. C. F., 1331
Roscommon election (1917), 928
Rosenbaum, S., 529
Ross, Sir J., 196
Ross-of-Bladensburg, Sir J. F., 713
Rossa. See Ó Donnabháin Rossa
Rothenfelder, Dr. F., 530
Round Table, 531–36, 956–57
Royal Commission on . . . landing of arms at Howth, 537

Royal Commission on the arrest . . . of Mr. F. Sheehy Skeffington, Mr. T. Dickson and Mr. P. J. McIntyre, 716
Royal Commission on the rebellion (1916), 714–15
Royal Irish Constabulary, 197–98, (p. 156)
Russell, C., 958
Russell, G. W., 539–40, 959–62, 1334–38
Russell, R., 1332
Ryan, D., 114, 173, 199–201, 717–18
Ryan, Rev. J. A., 1339
Ryan, James. See Ó Riain, S.
Ryan, J. T., 719
Ryan, Mary J., 720
Ryan, Michael J., 1007–09, 1340
Ryan, W. P., (p. XII), 202–02a, 541
Rynne, M., 202b

"Sacred egoism of Sinn Féin, The" (1918), 765
St. Enda's school. See Sgoil Eanna
St. John Ambulance Brigade (1916), 721
Samuel, A. W., 543
Samuel, Sir H., 542
Saoghal Gaedhealach, An, 963
Saorstát na hÉireann Judiciary (1920), 1341
Schiemann, T., 597, 968
Scissors and paste, 545
Scollan, J. J., 722a
Scott, C. P., 78
Scottus [pseud.]. See Hagan, Rev. J.
Secret history of Easter week, 662
Sellar, R., 547
Serena, 1342
Seton-Karr, Sir H., 548
Sexton, J., 549, (p. 157)
Sgoil Eanna, 121, 126, 173a–73b
Shaw, G. B., 203–04, 551, 964
Shaw, T. J., 205
Shaw of Dunfermline, Lord, 538
Shearman, M., 715
Sheehan, D. D., 206
Sheehy-Skeffington, F., 434, 550–51, 617, 716, 980
Sheehy-Skeffington, H., 724, 965, 980
Sheridan, J. C., 966
Sheridan, F. S., 207
Sherwood, I. R., 1343
Shooting outrages : Returns, 552–53
Shorter, D. Sigerson, 967
"Should Irishmen be conscripted ?" 804
Sibbett, R. M., 208
Sichel, W., 968
Simon, Sir J., 1344
Sinclair, T., 554
Sinn Féin, (pp. XI–XXIV), 209–11, 555, 970–78, 1345–48
Sinn Féin. (p. XI), (p. XV), 209
"Sinn Fein and the peace conference," 1349
Sinn Fein : Ard-Fheiseanna (1917–21), 974 977, 1348
"Sinn Fein at work" (1907), 66
Sinn Fein : Corughadh (Constitution), 975
"Sinn Fein leaders of 1916, The," 595a
Sinn Fein leaflets (1917), 970
Sinn Fein movement, The, 226
"Sinn Fein movement" (Documents . . .), 980
Sinn Fein policy, The (1907), 210

"Sinn Fein rebellion handbook," 743
Sinn Fein Schemes of organisation (1917), 972–73
Sinn Fein tracts (1916), 970
Sinn Feiner, The (New York), 1349a
Skinnider, Margaret, 725
"Sli na saoirse," 753
Smith, F. E. See Birkenhead, Earl of
Smith, T. F., 1350
Smith-Gordon, L, 211a, 555a, 1351
Solemn League and Covenant (1912). See Ulster Covenant
"Some arguments against Home Rule," 443
"Some reflections of a soldier," 908
Somerville, H., 1352
Spálpín, 981
Spark, The, (pp. xviii–xix), 555b
Spedding, R., 1355
Spender, H., 982, 1356–57
Spender, J. A., 557
Spindler, Karl, 726–28
Stack, Austin, 163, 213, 728a
Stack, Rev. T. F., 983
Staines, M. J., 729
Stamp, Sir J. C., 1359
Stanuel, C. A., 558
Staples, L. C., 211a
"Statement issued by the . . . Bishops of Ireland," 1027
Statistics (Irish). See 54, 57, 217–18
Statistical tables of the D.M.P. (1916), 626
Steed, H. W., 1360. See also *Times*
Steel-Maitland, Sir A., 559
Steinmayer, C., 730
Stephens, J., 214, 731
Strahan, J. A., 984, 1361–63
"Stranger in Ireland, A," 802b
Street, C. J. S., 1364–5, p. 115
"Struggle of the Irish people, The." See U.S. Congress
Stuart-Stephens, D., 732–33, 985–86
Sullivan, A. M., 215, 987
Suspensory Act (1914), 333
Sweeney, P. E., 734
Sweetman, J., 216–16a, 559a
Sykes, E., 1366
Synnott, N. J., 1208

Talbot, H., 987a
Tangney, J., 1368
"Tentative d'escroquerie, Une," 1097
"Terror in Ireland, The," 1021
Tery, S., 1369
Thompson, Sir B., 735, 1006
Thompson, Sir W., 217–18
"Thoughts and facts for the Irish Convention," 796
Times, The, 219, 1360, 1370
"Times history of the war, The," 736
Toksvig, S., 1371
"Torture and terror," 1023
Tracts for the times (1915–16), (p. xviii), (p. 71)
Trade (Irish), 41, 165. See also Industry
Trade and Commerce. See Department of . . .
Treaty (Anglo-Irish), 1163
Trinity College during the . . . rebellion, 647

Truce, The (July, 1921), 1053
True Irishman, A., 1372
Tudor, Maj.-Gen. Sir H., 1304, 1392
Turner, C., 737–38
Turner, E. R., 220
Two Irishmen, 781
"Two policies . . . The," 1002
"Two years of English atrocities in Ireland," 979
Tynan, K., 561

Ua Fhloinn, R. See Lynd, R.
Ua Rathghaille. See O'Rahilly
Ullswater, Viscount, 563
Ulster, (pp. xiii–xv), (p. 33), (p. 72), (p. 115), (p. 161)
"Ulster business men and Home Rule," 572
Ulster Covenant, The, (p. xiv), 382a
Ulster imperialist, An (pseud., *i.e.* Alec. Wilson, whom see)
"Ulster in 1921," 1367
Ulster Irishman, An, 796
Ulster Liberal Association, 567
Ulster Liberal Unionist Association, 222
"Ulster movement . . . The," 575
Ulster question : Handbook of the, 516
Ulster Unionist Council, The, (pp. xiii–xiv), 37, 223, 567–75, 918, 1046, 1373
Ulster Volunteer Force, The, 25, 37, 77, 479, 1075
"Ulster's opportunity," 852
"Under the terror," 1022
Unificus, 990
Union Defence League, The (p. x)
United Irish League, 224, 738a, 991–93, 1374
United Irish League of Great Britain, 223a. See also 56
United Irish League (Young Ireland branch), 223b, 278, 400
United Irishman, The, (p. xi), 225
U.S.A. (Congress), 994, 1375–76
U.S.A. (Irish organisations), (p. 34), (p. 161)

V.A.D., A, 588
Vane, Sir F., 739
Veteran, A, 740
Vigilant, 996
V M D, 997
"Voice of Ireland, The," 226
Voice of Labour, The, 998

Walker, H. de R., 227, 999
Walsh, A., 1377
Walsh, F. P., 1007–09, 1378
Walsh, J. C., 1379–80
Walsh, L. J., 576, 741, 1380a
Walsh, Rev. P., 228
Walsh, P., 1349a
Walsh, S., 1381
Walsh, W., Archbp., 228
Ward, Lt.-Col. J., 1382
Warren, R. de, 229
Waters, Rev. J., 1000, 1383–84a
Watson, Sir W., 1385
Wedgwood, Rev. G. R., 432
Weekly Irish Times, 743
Weekly Summary, 1385a
Welby, A., Lord, 230

Weldon, Rev. J. E. C., 577
Wells, W. B., 231–32, 744, 1001–02
Western priest, A., 1002a
Westropp, T. J., 745
White, A. C., 1386–87
White, J. R., 578, 1388
Whitla, Sir W., 432
"Who burnt Cork ?" 1194
"Why Ulster objects to Home Rule," 384
Wilkins, W. G., 1389
Wilkinson, E. C., 1390
Williams, B., 233
Wilson, A., 10b, 504, 579a–79c
Wilson, F.-M. Sir H., 262, 1044
Wilson, Woodrow, 843, 876, 896–97, 965, 1248, 1378
Wimborne, Viscount, 511, 714–15

Windle, Sir B., 1003
Wister, O., 1284
Woman of no importance, A, 1392
Women of Easter week, The, 691. See also Cumann na mBan
Woodburn, Rev. J. B., 580
Woods, M., 581–82
Workers' Republic, The, (p. xviii), 582a
Wright, A., 583
Wyndham, G., 584

Young, Ella, 747
Young, T., 748
Young Ireland, 1004

Zetland, Marquess of, 1005

www.ingramcontent.com/pod-product-compliance
Lightning Source LLC
Chambersburg PA
CBHW060515100426
42743CB00009B/1330